THE
COSTA RICA
READER

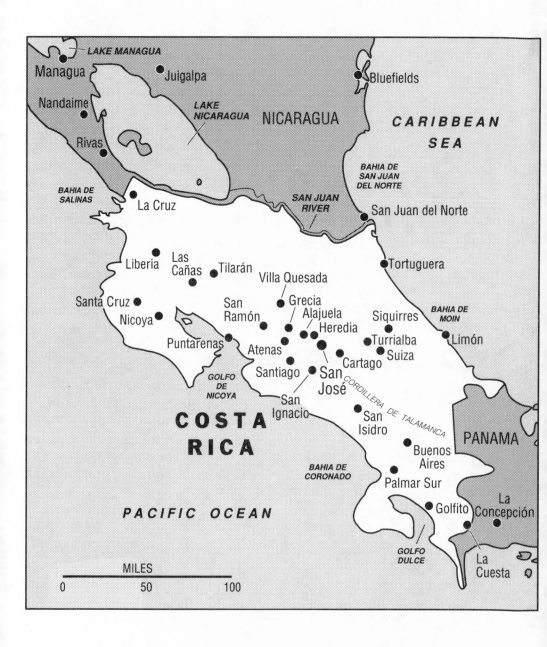

THE
COSTA RICA
READER

EDITED BY
Marc Edelman and
Joanne Kenen

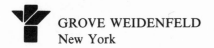

GROVE WEIDENFELD
New York

Published by Grove Weidenfeld
A division of Wheatland Corporation
841 Broadway
New York, NY 10003-4793

Published in Canada by General Publishing Company, Ltd.

Library of Congress Cataloging-in-Publication Data
The Costa Rica reader / edited by Marc Edelman and Joanne Kenen.—
    1st ed.
        p. cm.
    Bibliography: p.
    Includes index.
    ISBN 0-8021-1081-9.—ISBN 0-8021-3124-7 (pbk.)
    1. Costa Rica—Politics and government. 2. Costa Rica—Economic
conditions. 3. Costa Rica—Foreign relations. I. Edelman, Marc. II. Kenen, Joanne.
F1546.C765   1989   88-32681
972.86—dc19   CIP

Manufactured in the United States of America

This book is printed on acid-free paper

Designed by Irving Perkins Associates

First Edition 1989

10 9 8 7 6 5 4 3 2 1

Acknowledgments

We are especially grateful to the Ford Foundation, without which this book could not have been completed. Ford provided funds for translations, the acquisition of reprint rights, and incidental expenses. Many authors whose works appear here made suggestions about materials to include and offered thoughtful criticism of the text. As director of the Documentation Unit at the University of Costa Rica's Institute of Social Research, Rafael Rojas Bolaños sent a constant stream of articles and documents and made many helpful bibliographical suggestions. Jayne Hutchcroft, Solange Muller, Erich Mathias, and John and Sue Trostle sent frequent packets of newspaper clippings that kept us in touch between visits to Costa Rica. Richard and Dery Dyer, and the staff of the *Tico Times,* shared both their files and their many years of experience in Costa Rica. Martha Doggett and other colleagues of Marc Edelman's at the North American Congress on Latin America brought to our attention a number of documents that we might otherwise have missed. The staff of the Department of Anthropology at Yale University, especially Lyz Kyburg and Barbara Mecca, provided cheerful and efficient help in the final stages of this project. We are indebted to Marv Gettleman, who helped us initiate this project and who provided many useful suggestions along the way. Our translators included Deborah Bergman, Rubén Berríos, Ellen Calmus, Amy Dyke, Marjorie Jordan, María Lagos, Rodrigo Muñoz, Suzanne Sangree, Janet Shenk, Débora Soler Munczek, Holly Staver, Jeffrey Stollop, and Mark Vaughan.

At Grove Weidenfeld, our editor Walter Bode gave us welcome advice on compiling and improving this anthology, and we thank him for his patience and thoughtfulness. Finally, we thank family and friends for their encouragement and forbearance.

Costa Rica at a Glance

Area: 51,022 square kilometers (19,652 square miles), slightly smaller than West Virginia

Population (1984): 2,416,809
Annual growth rate (1980–85): 2.7 percent
Infant mortality per 1000 live births (1984): 18.8
Life expectancy at birth (1980–85): 73.0 years
Percentage of literacy of population over ten (1984): 93.1

Gross Domestic Product (1987): $5.61 billion
Per capita gross domestic product (1987): $2,011
GDP growth rate (1987): 3.4 percent
External public debt (1987): $4.52 billion
Per capita external public debt (1987): $1,619
Exports of goods (1987): $1.11 billion
Imports of goods (1987): $1.25 billion
Service balance (1987): − $284.8 million
Inflation (consumer prices, 1987): 16.8 percent
Unemployment (March 1987): 6.1 percent

Sources: Population, literacy from *Censo de población 1984* (San José: Dirección General de Estadística y Censos, 1987); infant mortality, life expectancy, GDP, external public debt, exports, imports, service balance, inflation from Inter-American Development Bank, *Economic and Social Progress in Latin America 1988 Report* (Washington, D.C.: IDB, 1988); unemployment from U.S. Embassy, San José.

Contents

General Introduction

In May 1985, twenty-four U.S. Green Berets arrived in northern Costa Rica to begin training a "rapid reaction" counterinsurgency force of civil guards. Their training ground was Murciélago, a vast estate ten miles from the Nicaraguan border that once belonged to deposed Nicaraguan dictator Anastasio Somoza Debayle. A few months later, just east of Murciélago, U.S. intelligence operatives constructed a secret airstrip, used to supply the Nicaraguan *contra* rebels.

By late 1987, the scene had changed. After a decade of bloodshed, the five nations of Central America were talking peace. Costa Rica's new president, Oscar Arias, won the Nobel Peace Prize for his role in drafting the peace plan that bears his name and shepherding it through tense months of negotiations opposed by the Reagan White House.

The ready explanation for the shift was that the flirtation with militarism and the collusion with the *contras* had been an aberration and that Costa Rica under Arias was reasserting its traditional values: pacifism, democracy, and social reformism. But the ready explanation is not entirely satisfactory. It begs the question of how these values arose and endured, and how, given the mood in the region and in Washington, a small, economically vulnerable nation was able to assert them. It also ignores the extent to which Costa Rican history, so often romanticized or reduced to stereotypes, has been characterized by competing tendencies: democracy versus authoritarianism, pacifism versus militarism, egalitarianism versus elite domination.

The first chapter in this volume explores the roots of Costa Rican exceptionalism from the colonial period through the early decades of independence. It begins with traditional historiography, the story of an isolated "rural democracy" inhabited by independent yeomen farmers, each as poor as his neighbor. This idyllic vision of colonial Costa Rica is often juxtaposed with the despotism, warfare, and exploitation in the rest of Central America, and is used to explain the country's later democratic development. But as several of the readings in this chapter suggest, the traditional view is wanting. Neither land, nor wealth, nor political power were distributed as equitably as was once believed. Nor was the country, which now boasts of its pacifistic past, free of military influence. It went to war against the U.S. freebooters led by William Walker, and witnessed its share of coups and conspiracies into the early twentieth century.

Yet Costa Rica was undeniably different from its Central American neighbors, where conservative groups tied to the Church or the remnants of the colonial bureaucracy were almost constantly at war with pro–laissez-faire and anticlerical liberals. In Costa Rica, where colonial institutions had been relatively weak, liberalism had the upper hand. The country began to export coffee and modernize its economy earlier than nearby nations. This helped lay the groundwork for rudimentary democratic institutions and a less polarized class structure.

In the late nineteenth century, as seen in Chapter II, Costa Rica's liberal governments reached notoriously disadvantageous agreements with foreign investors, at one point surrendering 6 percent of the national territory to U.S. railroad-banana baron Minor C. Keith in return for his promise to pay off the foreign debt. Nor did the liberals adequately address such social problems as poverty and growing landlessness that by the turn of the century could no longer be ignored. Elsewhere in Central America repression became the method of choice for dealing with social tensions; Costa Rica turned toward reform. While not all the remedies proposed for the nation's ills were adopted—indeed, one reformist president was ousted in Costa Rica's sole twentieth-century coup—many would be enacted within two or three decades. More important, reformist ideas became an accepted and significant element of political discourse.

As described in Chapter III, the debate over the shape of reform came to a head in the 1940s. In an odd alliance, Catholics, Communists, and a sector of the elite rallied around President Rafael Angel Calderón Guardia who introduced far-reaching social and labor legislation. But these reforms, targeted primarily at workers and the urban poor, alienated the traditional upper class and did little for the emerging middle class of professionals and small entrepreneurs. These disaffected groups formed their own uneasy coalition against *calderonismo.* The bitterly contested 1948 presidential elections only intensified the polarization as both sides cried fraud. Two months after the vote, civil war erupted.

The antigovernment forces quickly triumphed and a junta took power. Led by José Figueres, the new government abolished the army and enacted sweeping reforms, such as nationalizing the banks. But the junta failed to win legislative support for its draft constitution embodying social democratic ideas. Remarkably, after eighteen months, the junta ceded power to a conservative, a civil war ally who had claimed victory in the 1948 presidential race against Calderón. Figueres and his backers formed the social democratic National Liberation Party (PLN) and he was elected president in 1953. Since then, elections have been held regularly and parties have alternated in power. But the PLN has remained the dominant force in Costa Rica, expanding the state's sphere of action in the economy and social welfare. By the late 1970s, Costa Rica's key indicators—literacy, life expectancy, infant mortality—were among the best in the developing world.

The PLN development strategy brought dramatic improvements, but at a steep price. By the early 1980s, it was clear that Costa Rica could no longer support its bloated state bureaucracy or manage its foreign debt, one of the highest per capita in the world. Chapter V examines the structural causes and the human costs of the economic crisis. By mid-decade, in part because of massive infusions of U.S. aid, the deterioration was arrested, but real recovery had barely begun. Later the aid tapered off, and it was uncertain whether Costa Rica had devised policy alternatives that could assure future economic growth and development.

The economic crisis in many respects paled beside the political one that began with the Nicaraguan revolution and spread across the isthmus. Costa Ricans had long detested the Somoza dynasty and, to an extent not widely recognized today outside the region, threw themselves wholeheartedly behind the Sandinista cause. Chapter VI recounts the origins of Costa Ricans' hatred for the Somoza family, which had long meddled in Costa Rica's affairs and had extensive landholdings in the northern part of the country. It also looks at Costa Rica's deep involvement in the Nicaraguan insurrection, from its diplomatic defense of the Sandinistas to its role as a military staging area and conduit for arms.

But relations with Sandinista Nicaragua quickly soured, a result of the revolution's increasing radicalization, pressures from the new Reagan administration, and the alarm of Costa Rica's own right wing, whose influence was growing as a by-product of the economic crisis. Costa Rica gradually abandoned its neutral stance, and by 1983 was closing its eyes to *contra* activities within its borders and was deeply enmeshed in the Reagan administration's covert crusade to back the rebels. Not since the early days of the United Fruit Company had the nation been so careless with its sovereignty.

Chapter VII, drawing in part on previously unpublished U.S. government documents uncovered during the Iran-*contra* congressional probe, evaluates Costa Rica's involvement in the *contra* war. It also explores how Costa Rica under Arias was able to reverse course, becoming an advocate of peace instead of an accomplice in war.

We have included in this book a wide variety of materials: works by Latin American social scientists previously unavailable in English and by U.S. academic specialists on Costa Rica, some of which compare aspects of the Costa Rican experience to the rest of Central America; primary source materials from nineteenth-century Costa Rica; political analyses and journalistic accounts from the U.S. and Costa Rican media; oral histories, interviews and memoirs about the 1934 banana workers' strike, the 1948 civil war, the Sandinista revolution, and Costa Rican support for the *contras;* memos and cables written by Oliver North's operatives in Costa Rica; and the text of the Central American Peace Plan. By incorporating both classical historical works and more recent critical interpretations of Costa Rican political, socioeconomic, and cultural development, we hope to give the reader a more nuanced view of Costa Rica and insight into its current problems and prospects.

CHAPTER I

The Origins of Costa Rican Exceptionalism—Colonial Period and the Nineteenth Century

Editors' Introduction

When Columbus sailed along the Caribbean coast of Central America on his fourth voyage to the New World in 1502, he stopped at a place he called Cariay, near present-day Limón, Costa Rica. There, he wrote to the king and queen of Spain,

> I gained information respecting the gold mines of which I was in search . . . and two Indians conducted me to Carambaru, where the people (who go naked) wear golden mirrors round their necks, which they will neither sell, give, nor part with for any consideration. They named to me many places on the sea-coast where there were both gold and mines.[1]

Describing "Veragua," just south of "Cariay," he declared, "I saw more signs of gold in the first two days than I saw in Española during four years."[2] But Columbus, who mistakenly believed that "Cariay" was not far from the River Ganges in India, was also misled about the wealth to be had in the region. Subsequent Spanish chroniclers, however, seized on the explorer's description and named "Cariay" Costa Rica—the Rich Coast. The name stuck, but the reality was different. Costa Rica turned out to be one of the poorest of Spain's American colonies.

The area that later became Costa Rica was one of the last to be conquered and settled by the Spanish. In the first decades of the sixteenth century

1

various Spanish conquistadors explored the Atlantic and Pacific coasts of Costa Rica, seizing gold and other booty, converting Indians to Christianity, and feuding among themselves in an effort to gain recognition from the Crown.[3] Bruselas, the first Spanish settlement in what is now Costa Rica, was founded in 1524 near the present-day Pacific port of Puntarenas. It was abandoned after a few years because of Indian attacks and rivalries among the Spaniards, most of whom departed for the more promising region of Nicaragua. Shortly afterward, a permanent Spanish presence was established in Nicoya, on a peninsula north of Puntarenas, where a settled and relatively large Indian population was decimated by European diseases. Many of those who survived were shipped off to Panama and Peru as slave laborers.[4]

Only in 1561, when the indigenous inhabitants of Nicoya were virtually destroyed, did the Spanish press on and settle in the highlands of central Costa Rica, where Cartago, the capital, was founded in 1564. Influenza, plague, and smallpox epidemics had preceded them, however, greatly reducing the already sparse Indian population and thus the sources of tribute labor.[5] The densely forested Talamanca Mountains, just inland from Columbus's "Cariay," became a refuge for many of the remaining Indians, who joined that region's indigenous population in fiercely resisting the Spaniards until the eighteenth century.

The main characteristics of colonial Costa Rica—poverty, few precious metals, a small population, scarce Indian labor, remoteness from the Central American colonial capital in Guatemala—are repeatedly cited in traditional historical literature as giving rise to the democratic institutions and political culture of the postindependence period. How, it is often asked, could political despotism or significant class distinctions arise in a society so poor that even the colonial governor was forced to work the land with his own hands? From this "modest and rustic life," as historian Carlos Monge Alfaro describes it in Reading 1.1, "there emerged the yeoman, with almost no history . . . and the freedom of a man born in the mountains who has lived independent of authorities and social obligations." This yeoman, or smallholding peasant, was, according to Monge Alfaro, "a breed quite different from the *criollo* of Chile, Mexico, Peru, Venezuela or Guatemala." He was, the argument goes, the basis of what eventually would become Costa Rica's "rural democracy," a bearer of a democratic, egalitarian, and pacifist tradition that has persisted to the present day.

This halcyon view of early Costa Rica is widely believed. As readings in this chapter make clear, however, it is also quasi-mythical. Recent empirical research has increasingly called into question the premises of the traditional historiography and the cultural and historical stereotypes it has helped sustain.[6] As Samuel Stone (Reading 1.3) and Lowell Gudmundson (Reading 1.4) indicate, social class differences were greater than previously thought. Landholding patterns, discussed by both Gudmundson and Carlos Meléndez (Reading 1.2), were more complex and less egalitarian than the image of the independent yeoman farmer suggests. Urban commerce was more developed than the "rural poverty" thesis maintains, especially in the early independence period, as Gudmundson makes clear. Finally, after independence Costa Rica suffered the ravages of military rule, as did the other countries in Central America.

As José Luis Vega explains (Reading 1.7), however, the cycles of oligarchic rule and militarism that characterized Costa Rica, though too prolonged and severe to be dismissed as aberrations, were tempered by competing, democratic tendencies. While nineteenth-century Costa Rica had clear class divisions, with large landowners and landless laborers, the dominant groups never reached the levels of wealth and ostentation typical of the upper class in El Salvador, even after the advent of coffee in the mid-nineteenth century. There were military plots and coups, but the officers generally handed power over to their civilian allies. Tomás Guardia, the sole military ruler to become solidly entrenched in the nineteenth century, would also greatly expand the system of public education and pave the way for modern liberal democracy— interrupted only twice in the century since his death. Guardia even abolished capital punishment, hardly a characteristic move for a nineteenth-century despot. Thus, if traditional historians have erred in understating Costa Rica's similarities to the rest of Central America, it would also be inaccurate to contradict too strenuously the traditional emphasis on the nation's exceptionalism, from colonial times to the present. The legacy of "rural democracy" is a curious blend of legend and truth that has taken on a life of its own and become an entrenched political ideology.

Traditional historians correctly note that the colonial institutions of both church and state were less deeply rooted in Costa Rica than in the other provinces of the Kingdom, or Captaincy General, of Guatemala. This was in part a consequence of Costa Rica's sparse Indian population: there was no need for a large military establishment to subdue and control the indigenous peoples nor for a huge clerical presence to convert them. The small size of the Indian labor force in turn implied a lack of economic dynamism. Aside from a minor cacao boom on the Atlantic coast beginning around 1660, based largely on imported slave labor, and a brief expansion of commercial tobacco cultivation and silver mining in the last decades before independence, colonial Costa Rica produced few exports that could stimulate economic growth. The weakness of local institutions and distance from administrative centers meant that it was relatively unaffected by the conflicts that led to Central America's independence from Spain.

Independence movements, unrelated but almost simultaneous, began throughout the Spanish colonies around the start of the nineteenth century. Their roots, however, date back to the beginning of the previous century, with Spain's passage from Hapsburg to Bourbon hands. Under the Hapsburgs, Spain had controlled virtually all trade in and out of its American colonies. The only alternative to trade with Spain was piracy and black-marketeering, often by the British and their allies. Costa Rica's Caribbean coast was one region in which illicit trade was rampant. The Bourbons liberalized trade in the mid-eighteenth century, partly in an effort to suppress contraband commerce. The freer commercial climate contributed to the growth of a merchant class, although the colonies' economies remained overwhelmingly agricultural. The economic reforms had a greater impact on such provinces as Guatemala and El Salvador, which exported cochineal and indigo dyes, than on Costa Rica, which exported little of anything.

In the mid-eighteenth century, Spain's Charles III attempted to improve colonial administration—including tax collection—with a system of regional *intendencias,* which were first established in the Captaincy General of Guatemala in 1786. An unforeseen consequence of the *intendencias* was to fragment the Kingdom of Guatemala by nurturing the provinces' separate identities. Spanish-born *peninsulares,* who served limited terms in the New World as judges and bureaucrats, increasingly came into conflict with American-born *criollos,* who—in spite of their Spanish blood—were excluded from colonial administration and deeply resented the *peninsulares'* privileges (see Reading 1.3). Both groups, however, were united in their desire to keep down the *ladinos,* the growing class of people of mixed Spanish and Indian blood, who usually became wage laborers or small farmers in the countryside.

These conflicts were somewhat less significant in Costa Rica, which was too sparsely populated to merit its own *intendencia* and fell under the jurisdiction of the one in Nicaragua. Moreover, partly because relatively more European women migrated to the colony in its early days, Costa Rica had a smaller *ladino* population than the other provinces.[7]

Under a century of Bourbon rule, the social structure of the colony had grown appreciably more complex. Yet the *criollo*'s antagonism toward the *peninsular* had not yet crystallized into an independence movement. The backdrop for that would be provided by the turmoil—intellectual, economic, and military—caused by the American and French revolutions and the Napoleonic Wars. The two revolutions and Enlightenment philosophy inspired certain intellectual segments of the *criollos.* Spanish military spending was considerable and exacerbated resentment of the *peninsulares,* who administered the Crown's taxes, and colonists, who paid them.

The final revolt against Spain actually began as a rebellion against France. In 1808 Napoleon seized Spain and deposed Ferdinand VII. Appalled, many of the *cabildos* or *ayuntamientos*—*criollo-*dominated local governing boards or councils—swore loyalty to Ferdinand, an act that was tantamount to creating self-government in the colonies. Four years later, the newly created parliament, the Cortés of Cádiz, a bastion of Spanish republicanism and opposition to Napoleon, established a constitutional monarchy and liberal government. The Cortés included representatives from all the Central American provinces; a Costa Rican, Florencio de Castillo, was among its most prominent members. The Cortés's legislation had a significant effect on Costa

Rica: it abolished forced labor by *encomienda* Indians and opened the Caribbean port of Matina, in the cacao area, to foreign commerce, with no taxes to be imposed for a decade.[8]

The liberal opening was short-lived. In 1814 Ferdinand was restored to the throne and, with a stunning display of ingratitude, revoked the constitution and related reforms, fueling proindependence sentiments among colonial liberals. Six years later, Ferdinand was forced to capitulate to the Spanish liberals, but it was too late to regain the loyalty of the colonial liberals. Indeed, events of 1820 only served to push the conservative *criollos*—longing for glorious bygone days of Spain during the conquest—into repudiating this watered-down liberal monarchy. They too opted for independence from the Spanish Crown. Seeing themselves as the representatives in the New World of the old Spain, they were drawn to Mexican independence leader Agustín Iturbide's dream of forming a Mexican empire.

Except for the 1811 uprisings in Guanacaste and small disturbances in Cartago, Costa Rica received its independence without violence. Indeed, it was independent without knowing it for nearly a month. Only when the mail arrived on October 13, 1821, did Costa Rica learn that Guatemala had declared the provinces independent on September 15, 1821. The next day, a *cabildo abierto* or open assembly—including *cabildo* members and other prominent local citizens—met in Cartago and provisionally ratified the Guatemalan declaration.

Spared a bloody divisive conflict over independence, Costa Rica set about determining its form of government. The first problem was whether to join the Mexican empire. Conservatives in Cartago and Heredia favored annexation by Mexico; republicans in San José and Alajuela opposed it, although they muted their opposition as they received reports—highly exaggerated—of an imminent invasion by Iturbide's troops. The conservatives temporarily won out, but in a somewhat halfhearted way. The *cabildos* did declare their adhesion to the empire and were represented in the Mexican Constituent Congress. But the declaration of the *cabildos* also set several conditions for Costa Rica's integration into the empire which were never met. Nor was the formal, legal process of annexation ever completed. As historian Rafael Obregón Loría concluded, "The situation of Costa Rica with respect to its adhesion to the Mexican empire constituted something very complex, obscure, and disputable."[9]

Despite conflict over Mexico, early efforts at self-government were remarkably harmonious, especially compared to the civil wars and bloody rivalries that broke out after independence elsewhere in Central and South America. The Cartago *cabildo abierto* promptly called for the election of a provisional governing body composed of representatives from the main cities and towns. This group—called the *Junta de Legados de los Ayuntamientos*—first met on October 25. A month later it was succeeded by a second junta, which appointed a commission to begin drafting the *Pacto de la Concordia* (or

Concord Pact), the first Costa Rican constitution. Completed on December 1, this agreement would serve as the basis for government for two years. The pact declared absolute independence from Spain and established a legislature, called the *Junta Superior Gobernativa* (Higher Governing Board). But it did not provide for religious liberty.

The dispute over whether to join Iturbide's Mexican empire, however, continued to fester. On March 17, 1823, the republicans asserted their dominance, as an assembly of delegates from the main towns declared Costa Rica independent, while leaving open the option of federation with another American state.[10] The pro-Iturbide "imperialists" then seized the Cartago government, a move that led to what was probably one of the briefest civil wars in history. On April 5, 1823, imperialists and republicans clashed at Ochomogo for three and one-half hours. A total of twenty people were killed, and the republicans were the victors.[11] As usual, news of key political developments had traveled slowly to isolated Costa Rica. The brewing Mexican revolt against Iturbide had triumphed and on March 19, a month before the battle of Ochomogo, the emperor had offered to abdicate and go into exile. His coronation as Agustín I was formally nullified on April 7—two days after the Costa Rican battle.

With the Costa Rican government in disarray, republican leader Gregorio Ramírez, a former member of the 1821 junta who had returned to farming, found himself de facto ruler. Dictatorship held little allure for him, although he was said to have threatened critics with hanging.[12] Ramírez called immediate elections, turned power over to a constituent assembly within eleven days, and went home to his farm.

The capital was moved from conservative Cartago, to liberal-republican San José. In 1824 Juan Mora Fernández was elected the nation's first interim president. A year later, he won the first of two consecutive four-year terms. His nine-year administration was a peaceful period, an "age of consensus," in which aspects of the colonial "rural democracy" were institutionalized. A lawyer, Mora Fernández established a sound judicial system and supreme court. He expanded public education, brought the first printing press to Costa Rica, and founded its first newspaper. The one thing he did not seek to build was a military establishment beyond the existing citizens' militia:

> The public forces—which in other States form a necessary element of government—have often been in them an ominous instrument of tyranny, a dark source of anarchy and disorder, or a plague that has devoured men and their properties. In our State they have not been a necessary agent of the government, which rests instead on the free consent of the people. Our militia is a collection of honest citizens, peaceful laborers, artisans and workers who devote themselves honestly and constantly to their private tasks . . . and who have no aspiration beyond fulfilling their domestic duties and defending the State when the law calls them.[13]

The truth of Mora Fernández's words could be seen all around him in the Central American Federation, which Costa Rica joined under his administration. It was a loose federation, with Guatemala as its seat, and each member maintained its own national government. It was dominated by anticlerical liberals, who were in almost constant conflict with the conservatives, the keepers of the imperialist flame. With the exception of Costa Rica, its members were almost continually fighting civil wars or each other.

During the life of the federation, Costa Ricans took up arms only once. In the mid-1830s, after the Mora administration, tensions once again arose between various urban centers. San José's increasing dominance was the source of resentment. An effort was made to soothe the other cities with the March 15, 1835, *Ley de la Ambulancia,* or Ambulatory Law, an unusually conciliatory document that provided for rotating the capital among four cities: San José, Cartago, Heredia, and Alajuela. Each was to serve as government seat for four years, and with each move, all government offices, furnishings, and archives were to be transferred with what the decree described as "the utmost scrupulousness." The measure proved as ineffective as it was impractical, for on September 26 of that year, the War of the League broke out. San José found itself isolated as the other three cities formed a league, chose a president, and besieged San José. After three battles, however, San José triumphed and has since been both the political and commercial center of the nation.

Although the War of the League marred the age of consensus, it did not end it. That came about in 1838, when a military coup by an anticlerical liberal, Braulio Carrillo, inaugurated Costa Rica's first cycle of militarism (see Reading 1.7). He pulled Costa Rica out of the strife-torn Central American Federation, which soon collapsed. Elsewhere in Central America, the liberals who had dominated the region went into eclipse, and conservatives would prevail for the next thirty years. Carrillo himself was ousted from power in an intraparty dispute that was also one of the Central American liberals' last shows of strength until the late nineteenth century. Francisco Morazán, the liberal leader of the Central American Federation who had been toppled in a bloody reaction against his reforms, returned from his exile and military adventures in South America and in April 1842 invaded Costa Rica. He conspired with Carrillo's foes, brought about his downfall, and had himself elected president of Costa Rica. Whatever popular support he had soon faded when it became evident that he sought to use Costa Rica as a base for an invasion of all of Central America. There was one battle against him, in San José, and his forces were routed. The champion of Central American unity was captured and put to death on September 15, 1842, Central America's twenty-first independence day.[14]

During the next fifteen years or so, Costa Rica was occupied less by politics than by coffee. By the 1830s the "golden bean"—first planted in the late colonial era—had taken root and become the country's principal export.[15] Though coffee was introduced in the other Central American nations, it became more important, faster, in Costa Rica. Coffee cultivation required free rather than servile labor, as well as a market for land. Its introduction in Guatemala, El Salvador, and Nicaragua in the 1870s to 1890s was associated with liberal reforms that divested the Church and Indian communities of properties granted them by the Crown, a process that simultaneously "freed" land for coffee production and created a landless labor force to work the fields. While this led to numerous upheavals in the rest of Central America, in Costa Rica—with its weak colonial institutions and its tiny indigenous population—the liberalization of the economy did not produce either an immediate proletarianization of the peasantry or a strong reaction by conservative forces tied to the remains of the colonial power structure (see Reading 1.6). Moreover, since most of the good coffee land in the central part of the country was held by small farmers, the income from exports was somewhat more evenly distributed than in other coffee-producing countries in the region. Indeed, the Costa Rican upper class, unlike its counterparts elsewhere in Central America, owed its wealth more to involvement in processing and exporting coffee than to direct control of land or production.

In the mid-1850s, trouble loomed, in the form of William Walker, the Tennessean freebooter who managed to have himself elected president of Nicaragua. Walker sought to establish new slave states for the United States in Central America and to take over Cornelius Vanderbilt's Transit Company, which planned to build an interoceanic canal through southern Nicaragua. His designs posed a threat to Costa Rica, whose president, Juan Rafael Mora, encouraged in part by Vanderbilt, declared war. Lambasting Walker's men as "a gang of foreigners, the scum of all the earth, condemned by the justice of the American Union," Mora urged Costa Ricans to join "the loyal sons of Guatemala, El Salvador and Honduras" who were marching on Nicaragua.[16]

Walker was defeated, albeit at a heavy cost (see Reading 1.5). The legacy of the campaign against him was mixed. On the one hand, it contributed to Costa Rica's growing sense of nationalism, fed by yet another infusion of legend mixed with fact. On the other, it created for the first time a military establishment in Costa Rica, one that would exercise power, directly or with the now-powerful coffee oligarchy, until the death of Tomás Guardia in 1882. Guardia, however, would leave a legacy of his own, for his government would open doors to a new age of liberalism that would bring Costa Rica into the twentieth century.

NOTES

1. Christopher Columbus, *Four Voyages to the New World,* ed. and trans. R. H. Major (New York: Corinth Books, 1961), p. 174.

2. Ibid., p. 195.

3. For details, see Ricardo Fernández Guardia, *El descubrimiento y la conquista* (San José: Editorial Costa Rica, 1975 [orig. 1924]).

4. Linda Newson, "The Depopulation of Nicaragua in the Sixteenth Century," *Journal of Latin American Studies* 14, no. 2 (1982): 253–86.

5. Murdo MacLeod, *Spanish Central America* (Berkeley: University of California Press, 1973), pp. 98–100.

6. An interesting analysis of stereotypes of Costa Ricans is Gaetano Cersosimo, *Los estereotipos del costarricense* (San José: Editorial Universidad de Costa Rica, 1978). On colonial landholding patterns, see Elizabeth Fonseca, *Costa Rica colonial: la tierra y el hombre* (San José: EDUCA, 1983).

7. Ralph Lee Woodward, Jr., *Central America: A Nation Divided,* 3d ed. (New York: Oxford University Press, 1985), pp. 57, 79.

8. Theodore S. Creedmore, *Historical Dictionary of Costa Rica* (Metuchen, N.J.: Scarecrow Press, 1977), p. 51.

9. Rafael Obregón Loría, *De Nuestra Historia Patria: Costa Rica en la Federación,* Serie Historia y Geografía, no. 20 (San José: Publicaciones de la Universidad de Costa Rica, 1974), p. 16.

10. Thomas L. Karnes, *The Failure of Union: Central America, 1824–1960* (Chapel Hill: University of North Carolina Press, 1961), pp. 30–31.

11. Casualty figures cited in Creedmore, *Historical Dictionary,* p. 138.

12. Carlos Monge Alfaro, *Historia de Costa Rica,* 16th ed. (San José: Trejos Hermanos, 1980), p. 188.

13. Juan Mora Fernández, "Mensaje del Poder Ejecutivo a la Asamblea, 1828," in *Juan Mora Fernández,* ed. Carmen Lila Gómez (San José: UNED, 1984), p. 115.

14. Karnes, *Failure of Union,* pp. 89–90.

15. Ciro Flamarión Santana Cardoso, "Historia económica del café en Centroamérica (siglo XIX): estudio comparativo," *Estudios Sociales Centroamericanos,* no. 10 (1975): 12.

16. Juan Rafael Mora, "Proclama a los costarricenses sobre el peligro del filibusterismo" and "El Presidente de la República a todos sus habitantes," in *Documentos fundamentales del siglo XIX* ed. Carlos Meléndez (San José: Editorial Costa Rica, 1978), pp. 253–54.

1.1 The Development of the Central Valley*

BY CARLOS MONGE ALFARO

The work of Carlos Monge Alfaro (1909–79) is in many respects typical of traditional Costa Rican historiography. Here he argues that contemporary Costa Rica's democratic institutions and political culture grew directly out of a colonial experience characterized by isolation and extreme poverty, where there were "no despotic officials" and "social classes or castes did not arise." While this vision has been called into question by other historians, Monge Alfaro's thesis that Costa Rica has been a "rural democracy" since at least the late colonial period is still widely believed.

With the opening of the University of Costa Rica in 1940, Chilean-educated Carlos Monge Alfaro became a professor of history and later dean of the Faculty of Philosophy and Letters and secretary general of the university.

*From *Historia de Costa Rica,* 16th ed. (San José: Trejos Hermanos, 1980), pp. 140–45, 156–60.

BY the end of the sixteenth century, the Spanish had founded a number of towns in Costa Rica: Cartago in the central valley and Espíritu Santo de Esparza and Nicoya on the Pacific coast. The Indians were forced to live in *reducciones,* or villages in areas they had inhabited before the arrival of the Spaniards. . . .

The economic and social development of the Central Valley was the work of the descendants of soldiers brought to Costa Rica by Juan de Cavallón, Juan Vázquez de Coronado, Perafán de Ribera, and Diego de Artieda Chirinos. Little by little, this handful of Spaniards populated the valleys. . . . Officers and more soldiers arrived from time to time, reinforcing the core group of Spaniards.

They found lands divided by mountains and sierras, by rolling hills and gentle slopes, with numerous small and narrow valleys irrigated by rivers that crisscrossed the region. Covered with woods and beautiful vegetation, these lands were a temperate paradise in a tropical country. . . .

Land distribution carried out by the first conquistadors and Perafán de Ribera's granting of *encomiendas* were among the most important factors in seventeenth-century colonization.[1] In these ways, soldiers charged with subduing the Indians began to acquire land at the end of the sixteenth century. . . .

The land distribution at the end of the sixteenth and beginning of the seventeenth centuries meant that colonization or settlement began simultaneously, although with varying intensity, in the valleys of Guarco and Aserrí. There were Spaniards in both valleys who owned not only land—in some cases very large properties—but also Indian *encomiendas.* Formed from sparsely populated communities, these *encomiendas* were small from the start. By the middle of the seventeenth century, their size was further diminished, to the point where some barely had three Indians. Mistreated by the *encomenderos,* the Indians often fled to the mountains. . . .

Nevertheless, from the first years of the seventeenth century, the descendants of the conquistadors settled mainly in the central zone of the country. With little hope of growing wealthy by exploiting mines, and with poorly populated *encomiendas,* they aspired to become proprietors. . . .

Large landholdings, however, did not give rise to large-scale agricultural development. The early economy evolved under conditions that did not stimulate or encourage the transition from small, poor farms to the large colonial-style hacienda that arose in the Valley of Mexico, in the altiplano of Peru and Bolivia, and in the central valley of Chile. Furthermore, the *encomiendas* did not produce high profits, or adequate labor, for their owners.

As families grew and the population spread into outlying districts, small farms arose alongside large estates. In this way, the descendants of the Spaniards, as well as *mestizos* and Indians, had no difficulty in acquiring land, and the valleys of Guarco, Aserrí, Barva, and Pacaca were gradually colonized. The settlers took over the land, clearing and tilling primitive plots, just enough for simple subsistence. They lived in isolation, in the mountains, separated from each other by steep ridges and by rivers that were difficult to cross when the rains came. . . .

Isolated from Spain, as well as from Guatemala and the other provinces of the Captaincy General, the brave colonists received no help in trying to transform their farms and ranches into future sources of wealth. Thus began the destitution and sorrow of the sons of our country. Poverty was the sign under which their early labors unfolded. . . .

ECONOMIC AND SOCIAL DEVELOPMENT IN THE BARVA AND ASERRÍ VALLEYS

Rural Landowners

During the eighteenth century, as a consequence of population growth and the need to acquire land, the number of rural landowners increased in the Barva, Aserrí, and Pacaca valleys. Most of the Aserrí Valley was in the hands of big landowners. . . . However, given the lack of commerce, adequate roads, labor, and assistance from the Spanish authorities, they were unable to exploit their land. . . . They were limited to raising cattle and cultivating relatively small plots of sugarcane, corn, wheat, and tobacco. The last of those crops eventually would lead to a new and more significant basis for agricultural development in the colony.

Thus, a considerable amount of good land had been claimed and titled. As the population grew, so did the number of poor families who had never benefited from the labor of *encomienda* Indians and who lived far from Cartago and the Spanish functionaries. The colonists had to turn to the meadows and clearings of the extensive Barva Valley. Slowly, they penetrated the forest, conquering the land for themselves, and the forest yielded to their small cultivated fields. Families lived in humble huts of straw and in primitive shacks of mud, the archetype of the adobe houses that began to appear at the end of the seventeenth century and which by the nineteenth century became a prevalent element of the Central Valley landscape. . . .

The poor settlers spread from Barva to the Río Grande, developing small properties. At the same time, the big landowners provided for apportioning their holdings among their heirs. This created a tendency toward subdivision, which is crucial in understanding the development of small private land ownership in the Central Valley. In other colonies—Chile, Peru, and Mexico among them—large estates often were preserved through primogeniture, under which all property was bequeathed to the oldest son. . . .

Thus, virtually without precedent, the yeoman farmer emerged, an orphan, the son of no one. He was endowed with autonomy and freedom, the freedom of a man born in the mountains who has lived without dependence on authorities and social obligations. His modest and rustic life was dominated by the desperate struggle to subsist, producing in the descendants of the conquistadors a human breed quite different from the *criollo* of Chile, Mexico, Peru, Venezuela, or Guatemala. In the yeoman there germinated the first traces of what would, during the nineteenth century, become the Costa Rican people.

As the central figure of our political, social, economic, and cultural history, the yeoman farmer emerged, and is deeply rooted, in the eighteenth century. But he is not found only within the soul of those who came to settle the valleys, but in the owners of large estates, in the Spanish functionaries who remained in the country, and in the *mestizos.* He was the genuine product of Costa Rica's curious colonial history. Because of the economic conditions in our country, social classes or castes did not arise. There were no despotic officials who arrogantly kept themselves apart from the populace. There were no groups of strong and powerful *criollo* landowners, nor Indians who hated the Spaniards, nor a wretched *mestizo* class which had to endure the landowners' abuse.

We consider the farm laborer a great figure, worthy of reverence and deep love, for he gave Costa Rica the fundamental basis of what would in time become its rural democracy. A great history of democracy lies in his soul. Out of his free and independent spirit, alive yet silent for centuries, came forth the citizen of the nineteenth century. In those early times, he was distant from commerce, society, and politics, attached to his land like a mollusk to his shell. But after the eighteenth century, new institutions arose in which he could participate and he engaged actively in the political process that began in 1812.[2] To understand the special concern for liberty that Costa Ricans have always shown, the respect of the country's leaders for law and for human life, one must know the yeoman who labored upon the land. This is the axis, the backbone of our history, the nucleus of Costa Rican society.

NOTES

1. An *encomienda* was a royal grant that gave the recipient the right to exploit without compensation the labor of particular Indian communities or to receive specified quantities of goods as tribute. Technically, *encomienda* rights did not give the *encomendero* or recipient rights to land, although in practice *encomenderos* often exercised some degree of control over the lands of the communities whose labor they had been granted.—EDS.

2. In 1812, the Spanish Cortés or parliament instituted a series of reforms that had wide-reaching consequences in colonial Central America. These included laws that diminished the power of the Church and ended tribute taxes that Indians were previously forced to pay. Most important, the Cortés provided for the indirect election of local officials and of colonial representatives who sat in the Cortés itself.—EDS.

1.2 Land Tenure in Colonial Costa Rica*

By Carlos Meléndez Chaverri

Discussions of Costa Rica's history frequently focus exclusively on the small Central Valley or Central Plateau, a region encompassing the four largest cities—San José, Cartago, Heredia, and Alajuela—where much of the country's population was concentrated. Indeed, this mentalidad mesetina or "valley-centric" attitude remains characteristic of contemporary analyses of Costa Rica, many of which emphasize the relative prosperity of what is now the central, coffee-growing region of the country. The outlying regions of the country have had different historical experiences which in some respects are closer to those of the rest of Central America.

As Carlos Meléndez Chaverri indicates in this essay, colonial land-tenure patterns were diverse. Not all regions of the country fit the model of "rural poverty" or "rural democracy" described by traditional historians of Costa Rica. Focusing on types of agrarian production units, Meléndez finds that the chacra or peasant family farm of the Costa Rican Central Valley did approximate that traditional model. But in the northwest, where large cattle ranches or haciendas arose and on the Atlantic coast, where cacao plantations were established, the social structure was, he suggests, anything but democratic. The gap between the large estate owners and the laborers on the land was immense and its legacy continues to affect negatively the development of those regions.

Carlos Meléndez Chaverri, the author or editor of more than a dozen books, is a professor of history at the University of Costa Rica.

IN colonial Costa Rica, the structure of land tenure was not homogeneous, as commonly believed. Rather, the small group of Spanish conquerors developed a system of land ownership that reflected diverse factors, many beyond their control, but did not always express their desires or expectations. The existing economy and labor force, as well as natural and geographic factors such as climate and soil, led to the formation in different regions of different kinds of agrarian production units: the hacienda, the plantation, and the small farm. Regional forces thus gave rise to different economic and social structures.

At the end of the colonial period, the settled area was less than five thousand square kilometers, especially if the Partido of Nicoya in the northwest—which was incorporated later—is excluded. This settled region extended from Puerto Limón through the entire Central Valley to Puntarenas, where the settled area extended north to the Salto River. This limited territory encompassed three very distinct regions: the Caribbean and the Valley of Matina; the temperate

*A longer version of this article appeared in *Revista de Historia,* vol. 1, no. 1 (Heredia: Universidad Nacional) 1975, pp. 104–44.

lands in the Central Valley; and the northern Pacific zone that was then called the Esparza Valley.

THE HACIENDA

The hacienda arose in the northern Pacific region. The key determinant of its production structure was the prolonged annual dry season, which seriously hampered livestock production. Because permanent water sources were necessary to breed cattle, arid land had no value. Thus haciendas had to be large enough to include at least some water sources. The landscape of the dry Pacific, a mixture of smooth plains and hills, must have reminded the Spaniards of the distant lands of Andalucía and Castile, where the *latifundio* has persisted until our own times.[1]

The process of land appropriation in what is today the north Pacific province of Guanacaste began near the Indian settlement of Nicoya. The Spaniards could not conceive of working land without servile Indian labor. The *encomienda* was established in this zone in 1523.[2] Initially, the *encomienda* entailed the actual enslavement of the Indian, but the New Laws of 1542 wrought a radical transformation. From a situation where the *encomenderos* (*encomienda* holders) enjoyed almost exclusive control over Indian labor, the new legislation limited the amount of time each year that Indians were obliged to work for the *encomenderos*. At the same time the Indians were forcibly concentrated in settlements called *reducciones,* which largely separated them from the emerging hacienda. The New Laws thus forced the Spaniards to seek alternative sources of labor and led to the colonists' uprisings elsewhere in the New World against the new legislation.

Seemingly overnight, the New Laws deprived the *hacendado* (hacienda owner) of the labor force he needed to exploit his property. As partial consolation, the *hacendado* was able to retain the income provided by Indian tribute, and he used the income in part to obtain a substitute labor force.[3] In this way, the *hacendados* began to acquire black African slaves, who replaced the Indian on the haciendas and became an important part of the labor force of the dry Pacific region during the colonial period.

The New Laws also had important indirect consequences for the land-tenure system. Once Indians ceased to work on the haciendas, the concept of the value of land itself gained in importance. Because Indians could no longer be forced to work on the haciendas, and because black slaves could be sent wherever the master wished, the haciendas did not have to be located in the vicinity of Indian settlements. This led to the appropriation of land in uninhabited areas and to the formation of *latifundios,* such as those in the Tempisque Valley. Initially, then, land without Indians was not appropriated due to lack of capital and alternative sources of labor. The replacement of the labor *encomienda* by tribute suddenly stripped the *hacendado-encomendero* of his labor force. But the new system provided tribute that could be used to replace the Indians with slaves.

By the eighteenth century, the process of miscegenation, especially between blacks and Indians, increased the number of mulattoes and *zambos* (people of mixed black and Indian origin). The Spaniards and *criollos* (people of Spanish origin born in the New World) formed a numerically small group that was nevertheless the most influential and powerful, because it included the *hacendados* and hacienda administrators.

The haciendas of the northern Pacific were *latifundios* dedicated to livestock production. The availability of land and the owners' relatively limited capital resources meant that the hacienda was characterized by extensive land use. Much of the land consisted of grazing savannas with little vegetation. This probably resulted from the Indians' slash-and-burn agriculture. Fires used to clear farmland and even to hunt were not easy to control and they created prairies which the Spanish used for cattle breeding. Although the yield of the natural grasses was good, they grew parched during the dry season, limiting the number of cattle the land could support. Weak market demand, moreover, did not stimulate an increase in the cattle herds.

For these reasons, haciendas used a traditional form of production with limited technical inputs. The animals were slaughtered mainly to remove the skin and tallow. Much of the meat was wasted, except for small portions eaten fresh or made into *tasajo,* a salted and smoked jerked meat that could be preserved. Because there was no market for perishable milk, hard cheese was made in large wooden molds and taken to markets in the dry season. In the rainy season, when the rivers overflowed their banks and overland travel was nearly impossible, the hacienda was completely isolated, and few activities were undertaken.

During the dry season, the landowner resided in the main house on the hacienda. When the rains came, he generally moved to a nearby town. In his long absence, an administrator, often a close relative of the landowner's, managed the hacienda. The laborers slept in barracks on the hacienda and seldom were able to visit their families.

Work tools were simple, even primitive: machetes, staves, different knives like the ones used to castrate the animals, branding irons, large wooden containers for storing grain, and wooden molds for processing cheese. The corrals, made of piled stones, were the principal structures near the houses of the hacienda. Each year cattle were rounded up and placed in the corrals where they were counted, branded, and checked for physical problems. Wild cattle, rounded up with the other animals, were incorporated into the herd.

Social relations between the landowner or *patrón* and his laborers or slaves were patriarchical. The peon, unable to survive solely on his meager wages, was allowed to cultivate maize and beans on land near the hacienda buildings to secure his family's subsistence. From time to time, he could get from the hacienda some low-quality meat for making *tasajo.*

The hacienda generated social isolation and thus had a negative effect on the formation and development of towns in the surrounding area. Landowners often settled in towns in order to be able to attend to their spiritual obligations.

In addition, Hispanic tradition always sought to strengthen these small urban centers as a means of maintaining political and cultural identity. Residence in the countryside could result in the loss of civil rights and in a lower social status. The gentry needed the urban milieu to preserve its position.

The hacienda was the basis of an oligarchical and antidemocratic social order. It has served to maintain a "territorial aristocracy" of *rentier* landlords, which has been able to control power in the northwest region. The landowners have often aligned themselves with the national power structure to ensure their traditional prerogatives. In sum, the structural underdevelopment and the agrarian problems of the northern Pacific region in modern times are direct legacies of the hacienda.

THE PLANTATION

The Costa Rican colonial plantation system grew out of a process of colonization that opened up areas beyond the Central Valley. People from Cartago attempted to extend the economic frontier to the east, toward the rainy plains of Matina on the Atlantic coast. The plantation was an agrosocial unit exploited with slave labor or forcibly recruited Indians. It concentrated on the production of a single product—cacao—and its principal markets were overseas, outside of Central America.

Cacao production in Matina began on a small scale in the mid-seventeenth century. Production increased rapidly. The residents of Cartago who established the first plantations in Matina must have had enough capital to be able to forego immediate returns. First, they had to invest in clearing the jungle. Then, after planting cacao, they had to wait several years until the beans were ready for harvest. In the intervening years, the slave or Indian labor employed in Matina could not be put to use, as there was no other economic activity. Although the labor *encomienda* system had formally disappeared, in practice Indians were conscripted from Talamanca to work the plantations when no blacks could be found. Clearly, establishing a cacao plantation was a costly endeavor, and not just anyone in Cartago could embark on such a venture in a remote place, accessible only by a long and arduous trail.

Land in Matina was so abundant that it was virtually worthless. But the plantation and the crop had value. Documents recording land transactions, whether they refer to inheritance, property transfers, or other business, show not the size of the plantation, but the number and the condition of the cacao plants.

The open shoreline of Matina enabled enemies of the Spanish empire, such as the British-supported Zambo-Miskitu Indians, to land anywhere along the coast. After their first incursion in 1693, the Zambos were a constant threat to Matina. Both the Zambos and the British, who since 1655 had been established in Jamaica, stole cacao from Matina.

The hot, humid Atlantic coastal climate prevented settlement of Matina.

The population never expanded significantly, in part because women were scarce. Even the wives and daughters of the black slaves and Indians were prohibited from living there, to prevent their capture and sale to Jamaica. Thus the plantation was a risky although lucrative enterprise. It made the blacks and Indians the most important actors in the region's development, although the Spaniards in Cartago were its direct beneficiaries.

In 1709, the government of Guatemala authorized the province of Costa Rica, which had little silver, to adopt cacao beans as currency. With this decree, the money economy was downgraded to a system based on the exchange of natural money, although both currencies were in use. Later, in 1777, the value of a silver peso was fixed at two pesos of cacao money.

The Matina cacao plantations were not large enough to be described as *latifundios*. According to historian Carlos Rosés, "This contention is corroborated by the number of trees in each plantation: the largest ones had an average of 3,000 cacao trees, we found only one with 4,000 trees, and the majority had an average of 1,000 trees." Rosés mentions a few families who acquired ownership of several plantations, but this seems to be the exception rather than the rule.

The agrarian structure was simple, with most properties having only two, occasionally three, workers or slaves. Although there was intense exploitation of the plantations, the numerous limitations and risks impeded capital accumulation. This precluded the formation both of cacao *latifundios* and of a very powerful class of cacao producers.

During the eighteenth century, sharecropping became increasingly important in the cacao plantation system. This was probably the result of the owners' lack of interest in the enterprises due to increased incursions by the Zambo-Miskitus. The sharecroppers were Spaniards or *criollos* of low social standing. On a few occasions, mulattoes or blacks, whether slaves or freemen, appear to have been tenant farmers on the plantations; black slaves were able to buy their freedom through such service. In other instances, blacks who were able to accumulate some money, many of them from the black neighborhood of Cartago called Puebla de los Pardos, were able to advance further, both socially and economically.

The plantation's ties with the outside world, established for the commercialization of cacao, made the world view of both landowners and slaves of Matina markedly different from that of the isolated farmers of central Costa Rica. Illegal international trade expanded in the eighteenth century and helped to create a clearer awareness of the damaging effects that Spain's monopolistic trade policies had on the colonies.

Eventually, cacao production in far-off Matina tapered off, abandoned in favor of tobacco, a cash crop that was being grown in the western Central Valley around San José. Tobacco was more profitable than cacao because the state participated directly by purchasing and marketing the crop and eliminating competitors.

THE *CHACRA*

The *chacra,* a word now forgotten but frequently used during the colonial period in Costa Rica, best characterizes the land-tenure system that began to predominate in the eighteenth century in the Central Valley, especially in its western part. The *chacra* can be defined as a small or medium-sized unit of production dedicated to subsistence agriculture and worked by a nuclear family. Only rarely were Indian laborers employed. Sometimes, for instance during the wheat harvest, the family labor force was inadequate, and the land was worked collectively.

Within Spanish America, the conquest of central Costa Rica was relatively late, beginning in 1561 with the arrival of the conquistador Juan de Cavallón. The lateness proved beneficial, because the subjugation of the Indian population, in comparison with what occurred elsewhere, was less exploitative. Indeed, an almost constant complaint of the leading Spanish conquerors was that they came to Costa Rica with limited powers, especially regarding their power to reward or grant land to their subordinates.

Until the Crown provided for the *encomienda* system, the conquistadors could not fulfill their aspirations of becoming a landed aristocracy, as land without Indians to work it had no value. When Spanish colonists had Indians allotted to them, they began to appropriate land. However, *encomienda* Indians, unaccustomed to intensive forced labor, were mostly reluctant and unproductive workers. In addition, the number of Indians at each *encomendero*'s disposal was very limited, because the Indian population was sparse, except in the eastern part of the Central Valley. The Spaniards' dreams of accumulating great wealth through the *encomienda* system thus rapidly dissipated. But they retained their right to legally appropriate land.

The transformation of labor *encomiendas* into tribute *encomiendas,* which began under the New Laws, must have represented a severe blow to more than one *encomendero* who was stripped of his labor force. As has been noted, the landlords who had accumulated capital through the labor *encomienda* system or from tribute purchased slave labor. But the landowners who arrived later, after all the Indians had been distributed to *encomenderos,* often lacked the resources to purchase slaves, and were unable to become members of the landed gentry.

Bereft of their seignorial illusions, many colonists had no choice but to take tools in hand, face the sun, and plant what they needed to survive. Although this had a leveling effect on colonial society, daily life was nonetheless based on status differences defined in accordance with Spanish tradition. The original colonists and their descendants behaved as a landed gentry, albeit a poor one. Social differentiation persisted but, in practice, each colonist lived on what he produced. Pressed by agrarian poverty, the colonists became more democratic.

During the seventeenth century, property in the Central Valley was increasingly fragmented. Primogeniture was not the rule in the region and all family members inherited the property. In addition, water resources were abundant, which allowed people to settle where they chose.

Families, lacking resources to hire workers, continued tilling their own land. There was not a sizable work force in any case; with land still available on the periphery of the settled areas, population growth could be absorbed without giving rise to a surplus labor force. Thus by the eighteenth century the *chacra,* typically large enough only to sustain a single family, had emerged as the predominant unit of production in the valleys of central Costa Rica.

The remarkable growth of agricultural production in the Central Valley in the eighteenth century was caused partly by external stimuli, and partly by local population growth and land fragmentation. From mid-century, the process of land fragmentation coincided with the settlement of previously unoccupied areas, especially west of Alajuela.

It should not be forgotten, however, that state policies intended to benefit Costa Rica, such as the effort to stimulate tobacco production, also brought about a greater level of agricultural specialization. This in turn increased the value of land in some zones and sparked a new exodus into unsettled areas. Yet the magnitude and importance of these trends cannot be compared to what occurred during the nineteenth-century coffee boom.

For the Costa Rican peasants in the dispersed settlements in the Central Valley, life undoubtedly improved during the eighteenth century. Abundant land was still available on the valley's edges. To some extent these improved conditions contributed to the peasants' personal independence. The experiences of the eighteenth-century peasants helped to form the character of present-day Costa Rica, whose roots lie in an underdeveloped agrarian economy.

NOTES

1. *Latifundium* or *latifundio:* a very large, usually underutilized landed estate.—EDS.

2. *Encomienda:* a Crown grant to Spanish settlers of rights to exploit labor or receive tribute from specific Indian settlements or regions. *Encomienda* rights did not imply ownership of land.—EDS.

3. Tribute payments generally consisted of agricultural goods, cloth or other products that the Indians were obliged to give "their" *encomendero.* —EDS.

1.3 Aspects of Power Distribution in Costa Rica*

BY SAMUEL Z. STONE

In contrast to those authors who maintain that Costa Rica has long had an egalitarian social structure, Samuel Stone concentrates on the study of the elites descended from the original Spanish conquistadors. Using a wealth of genealogical data, he demonstrates that a remarkable number of Costa Rica's leaders can trace their lineage to a handful of sixteenth-century colonists. Stone has sometimes been criticized for tautological reasoning for referring to all of the conquistadors' current-day descendants as members of a powerful "political class." By no means are all descendants of the original conquerors economically or politically powerful, nor are all of the powerful in Costa Rica able to trace their roots back so far. Moreover, membership in the "dynasty of the conquistadors" does not provide any guide to political behavior; the group includes not only representatives of the monied classes, but labor leaders and Communists. Nevertheless, Stone's analysis of the Costa Rican elite sheds important light on the way in which a few families are able to exercise substantial control in a small society.

Samuel Stone, a professor of political science at the University of Costa Rica, holds a doctorat d'état *degree from the University of Paris.*

THE most important factor in the economic development of Costa Rica has been coffee cultivation. This activity was first undertaken on a large scale by a small group of planters shortly after independence from Spain in 1821. By mid-century their entrepreneurial ability had stimulated progress to a degree where the country emerged from having been the most miserable economic quagmire on the continent to a position of prosperity far surpassing the other nations of the Central American isthmus. . . .

Tracing the ancestries of the first members of this planter group to the beginning of the Spanish Conquest makes it evident that they were descended from a colonial political and economic elite; following their lines of descent into the twentieth century reveals a significant portion of those who have occupied political posts even to this day. In fact the ascending and descending lines of consanguinity and affinity among the planters from the beginning of the colonial period to the present reveal a political class whose

*Excerpted from Samuel Z. Stone, "Aspects of Power Distribution in Costa Rica," in *Contemporary Cultures and Societies of Latin America,* ed. Dwight B. Heath (New York: Random House, 1974), pp. 403–21.

members have exercised the functions of government in the executive, legislative, and judicial branches to a far greater extent than any other group in Costa Rican society. . . .

THE SPANISH CROWN AND THE BIRTH OF THE POLITICAL CLASS

During the sixteenth and seventeenth centuries Spain created a pattern of power distribution that still continues to determine the nature of Costa Rican politics. It reserved access to political posts to conquistadors and *hidalgos* (nobles), thus giving control of the province to a small group of families by virtue of their descent. This monopoly of power, enhanced in many instances by wealth, enabled the elite also to monopolize cacao cultivation, the most profitable activity of the colonial period. The group stood in contrast with the rest of the population, which subsisted on a primitive type of agriculture.

Two factors account for the organization of an almost exclusively agricultural economy. At the same time, they help explain the presence of a population consisting primarily of small farmers under the political tutelage of a landed gentry instead of ambitious and avaricious fortune-seekers such as existed in many other parts of Latin America. One of these factors was the absence of sufficient Indians to constitute an important labor force. This consideration alone seriously limited the scale of any type of activity and practically restricted the choice to agriculture. As a result, a majority of the settlers, who had been attracted (principally from the working classes of Andalucía) by the idea of becoming landowners under special incentives offered by the Crown during the seventeenth century, had arrived with the intention of working their newly acquired lands by themselves. The other factor was the scarcity of gold, which not only ruled out mining but also had the effect of attracting farmers of both noble and plebeian stock instead of ambitious adventurers. Even before undertaking the journey to Costa Rica, all the settlers had known that the province of their choice offered neither glory nor riches. . . .

The elite continued as a small group of closely related families during the colonial period, inheriting power from generation to generation. Its predominance was greatly facilitated by the small size of the society and by the isolation of the territory. Approximately three months were required to travel by horse from Costa Rica to Guatemala, the seat of its colonial government. The effect of such isolation on the population can be appreciated by considering that the bishop in charge of the province, who resided in Nicaragua, was able to pay only eleven visits to the unfortunate territory between 1607 and 1815, the intervals between visits ranging up to thirty-three years. Such seclusion kept the inhabitants unaware of social and political trends that in other parts of the isthmus defined the positions of ruling classes.

By the eighteenth century the policies of the Crown and Guatemala had resulted in complete economic stagnation to the point where even cacao had to be abandoned. The Church and piracy are also to be blamed. The *hidalguía,* or elite, while retaining its political power, was forced to lower its standard of living, thus leading to a discrepancy between its modest manner of life and its high social and political rank. Even governors had to work their own land. By independence, this economic leveling had favored an approaching of the social categories to a point where society presented a notably equalitarian aspect. The elite was there, however, and thanks to its political power would soon become the motor of economic expansion, finding its fuel in coffee. . . .

EMERGENCE OF THE ENTREPRENEURIAL PLANTER GROUP

In 1821, with independence, the colonial political class inherited the leadership of the new nation and began to concentrate on finding an activity that would allow its members to raise their standard of living to a level in keeping with their political and social positions. Among the many agricultural products tried was coffee. This had been cultivated since the first half of the eighteenth century but, as with other crops, the absence of an accessible market had limited production to an almost insignificant scale. An opportunity came in 1833 when a German immigrant was able to effect a small shipment to Chile, thus allowing many to foresee the possibility of further exports. Land was taken by assault and many members of the class took advantage of their positions of power to acquire the best areas of the fertile Central Plateau. Costa Rica, however, was on no important trade route, nor was it a regular port of call, and for these reasons exports could not be relied upon. Furthermore, coffee was processed in Chile and shipped to Europe, where it was sold as Chilean coffee at prices that appeared exorbitantly high to the Costa Rican planters. The disillusionment brought on by their not having direct access to European markets was aggravated by being obliged to work through inter- mediaries. The group therefore began to neglect cultivation until, quite by chance, a British shipowner gave them direct access to the English market in 1845.

From this time on, national society began to undergo a transformation. The first exports had been financed by the wealthier planter families; but, as the volume of business increased following the opening of the London market, these sought credit in England on future crops. This accentuated the division of labor between modest coffee farmers from the lower social category and the growing export planters from the political class. The latter, by negotiating the sale of their own crops as well as coffee purchased from the former, soon came to control the situation. A new social category arose when partnerships of export planters began offering credit to small producers. When these could not meet their obligations, their lands went to their creditors, thus giving birth to the large plantation as well as to the social class of peons, or former landed peasants who had lost their holdings. The small property disappeared only in terms relative to the colonial agrarian structure, however, for the great majority of landowners continued to be humble farmers. The large plantation in Costa Rica was (and still is) quite small by comparison with large properties in other parts of Latin America. It never developed beyond certain limits because of the markedly limited supply of capital and labor.

The coffee complex that developed in this way around the elite export planter consisted of a small independent farmer and a laboring class of peons, with a strong interdependence between them. On the one hand, the success of the enterprise was subject to the productivity of the peon, and this to the paternalistic rapport the planter could maintain with his scanty labor force. If the peon depended on the planter for his salary and home, the planter depended on the peon for good production, which was the basis of both his wealth and his prestige within his own class. The relationships that developed between the two as a result of this mutual dependence reflected the society's equalitarian values that remained from the colonial experience. All the events around which contact between them took place were of a social nature and revealed a reciprocal respect that could not have developed between similar counterparts in societies with feudal traditions. . . .

DIVISIONS OF THE PLANTER ELITE

As coffee production furnished growing prosperity, the first planter families increased their investments. This led to rivalries among them, and the group began to divide into factions belonging to the same families but vying for political power. The twentieth century marked the arrival of several new forces for change, not the least of which was the United Fruit Company, whose effort to attract manpower to the coastal banana zones severely depleted the already inadequate coffee labor force. Many of the coffee peons, however, were unable to tolerate either the hot climate or the new relatively impersonal type of labor-management relationship with the foreign company, and they soon returned to the coffee plantations, despite the inferior salary; this wage differential became a source of resentment, nevertheless. The peons obtained a certain degree of political autonomy with the introduction of the secret ballot; in 1929 came the depression and with it the Communist Party. . . .

During the process of subdivision of the coffee elite, which began toward the middle of the nineteenth century and continues today, its factions have tended to diversify their economic activities. Coffee is still important, but its preponderant position in the national economy has made it particularly vulnerable to taxation designed to finance [postdepression social programs]. In addition, with the exception of the 1970 increase in demand and price boom resulting from Brazil's temporary decrease in production, the world market has been steadily deteriorating. Planters, then, have tended to lose their dominant role in the economy. Furthermore, all groups in the political class have tended to lose power, due in part to the social legislation that has been in the process of creating a powerful government bureaucracy not effectively under the control of any single group.

The foregoing is a sketch of the evolution of the political class that has played a dominant role in the development of Costa Rica. The changes it has undergone are clear: during the colonial period its members were united and engaged in cacao cultivation; during the nineteenth century many of them became coffee planters but prosperity led to divisions; today they have diversified into fields including cattle, law, medicine, and the like, and are extremely divided. The power of the class, the effects of the decentralization of its influence, and the present-day significance of the class within the context of modern national society can best be appreciated, however, by tracing and analyzing the lines of descent of several important families who settled in Costa Rica during the early part of the colonial period.

FAMILIES OF THE PLANTER CLASS

Speaking in general terms, the first conquistador and *hidalgo* families constituted the political class. Some were more influential than others, and money was undoubtedly a factor that contributed to enhancing status within the class. An example of an opulent *hidalgo* who settled in Costa Rica in 1659 and whose descendants have played a most important role in the political life of the country is don Antonio de Acosta Arévalo. The presidents and the equivalent chiefs of state in his lineage are listed in Table 1. Nine of these presidents have held office during the twentieth century, the most recent being Mario Echandi Jiménez, president between 1958 and 1962 and candidate in 1970 [and 1982]. A few other important families, but by no means all of them, were those of Nicolás de González y Oviedo, Juan Vázquez de Coronado, Jorge de Alvarado Contreras (brother of Pedro de Alvarado, conquistador of Guatemala), Juan Solano, and Antonio Alvarez Pereira, often called Antonio Pereira. In their lines of descent are to be found many people who have occupied the presidency or the equivalent. In those of Acosta Arévalo, González y Oviedo, and Vázquez de Coronado, for example, there are thirty-three of the forty-four presidents in the history of the republic, with twenty-five descended from Acosta Arévalo alone. . . .

The political class can also be seen at the level of the Legislative Assembly, where fully 220 of the 1,300 deputies the republic has had since independence are descended from Juan Vázquez de Coronado, 150 from Antonio de Acosta Arévalo, 140 from Jorge de Alvarado, and 40 from Nicolás de González y Oviedo, to mention only a few. . . .

CLASS ENDOGAMY

An interesting aspect of the political class is that, in the lineages of almost any combination of an equal number of the aforementioned families, there can be

Table 1   PRESIDENTS DESCENDED FROM DON ANTONIO DE ACOSTA ARÉVALO*

Generation	Name	Generation	Name
4th	Manuel Fernández Chacón		Federico Tinoco Granados
	Juan Mora Fernández		Vicente Herrera Zeledón
	Joaquín Mora Fernández		José J. Rodríguez Zeledón
			Juan Rafael Mora Porras
5th	José María Castro Madriz		Julio Acosta García
	Próspero Fernández Oreamuno		Aniceto Esquivel Sáenz
	J. M. Montealegre Fernández	7th	Rafael Yglesias Castro
	Bruno Carranza Ramírez		Mario Echandi Jiménez
	Braulio Carrillo Colina		Rafael Calderón Muñoz
	Manuel Aguilar Chacón		Teodoro Picado Michalski
	José R. Gallegos Alvarado		León Cortés Castro
			Juan B. Quirós Segura
6th	Demetrio Yglesias Llorente	8th	Rafael A. Calderón Guardia
	Bernardo Soto Alfaro		

*Presidents, chiefs of state, and vice-presidents or the equivalent who actually exercised the highest post of the executive branch.

found roughly the same number of presidents and deputies—who are, moreover, generally the same people. This is an indication of a high degree of class endogamy. The list of the first 100 planter families reveals an extraordinary number of marriages between members of the class, and in many instances between cousins. . . .

THE DECENTRALIZATION OF POWER

Shortly after the beginning of the twentieth century, an event occurred that changed the relationship between the national political class and the other groups that had previously participated in political life. This was the campaign of Ricardo Jiménez Oreamuno, elected president in 1910. A member of the national political class, don Ricardo was considered by some of his contemporaries to have espoused leftist views while others regarded him as excessively aristocratic. In order to obtain the electoral support necessary to defeat his opponent he turned to rural zones and sought the backing of groups that until then had not participated in the political process. This he accomplished through rural community leaders *(gamonales)* of the *Meseta Central* (the Central Plateau, where roughly three-quarters of the population are concentrated). His strategy, which appears in his party's platform, was to encourage the establishment of a strong municipal governmental system, independent of the executive branch. It was through the municipal structure, then, that members of families prominent in small communities throughout the country began to get access to the Legislative Assembly after 1910. In this respect, don

Ricardo's advent to power appears to have marked the beginning of the decline of his own class. Since his campaign, there has been a greater participation in the Legislative Assembly of groups not connected with the families we have analyzed.

THE POLITICAL CLASS AND MODERN NATIONAL SOCIETY

National society is often characterized by an arbitrary division of the population into an upper, a middle, and a lower class. This generalized pattern is applicable to the situation in Costa Rica. If we were to identify at any moment in history all the living descendants, either direct or by marriage, of the first conquistadors and *hidalgos,* we could see that this group holds a majority of the important political offices. In any subsequent change of government resulting from elections or even revolution we would see those in power replaced with other people from the same group. The people in power at any given time constitute the political elite of the moment, but the point is that the elite, regardless of party affiliation, are always recruited principally from the same group. This group is the national political class and, with a few notable exceptions, is also the upper economic class. Within it there exists a certain horizontal and vertical mobility, but a person born into it will continue to form part of it regardless of economic or other adversities. Changes of position within the class are due to political changes (which are always temporary), to changes in the economic status of the individual, and to marriages contracted with members of other social strata. Generally speaking, the class is inaccessible, except by marriage, to those not born into it.

Several characteristics distinguish the middle class from the political upper class. While education and occupations are similar at both levels, members of the middle class generally occupy secondary positions, especially in government and commerce. In professions such as law or engineering, they often look toward government or autonomous institutions for employment. By contrast, members of the political upper class tend to establish their own firms or join existing firms belonging to others of that class. In medicine, the only difference between the two would be the clientele: middle-class doctors would seldom have access to upper-class patients. In agriculture and particularly in coffee, middle-class farmers have smaller holdings and tend to live on their farms more frequently than upper-class farmers, who often reside part of the week in the capital area and manage their lands through an administrator. The outstanding characteristic differentiating the middle class from the upper, however, is the former's virtual lack of kin ties with the six named families. In rare cases where such ties do exist, they are indirect and remote, and they have little or no instrumental value to the individual concerned.

Members of the lower class are also employed in government, commerce, and agriculture, but their lower levels of education relegate them to menial administrative positions or manual labor. They occasionally find an opportunity through the national educational system to study professions such as law and medicine, which are their principal means of mobility toward the middle class. Most members of the lower class have very scanty economic means. . . .

A word should be mentioned about values. These do not differ significantly from the values found in other Latin American societies, except in what concerns the tensions between "elitism," as manifested by the presence of the political class, and the equalitarianism resulting from the colonial experience. The general orientation of values is particularistic, diffuse, and ascriptive, but the equalitarian tendency gives rise to a concern with personal security closely associated with the welfare ideology that has made itself increasingly patent in national politics. In this sense the colonial period, which endowed the society with its equalitarian aspects, also gave it a propensity to welfarism. . . .

FINAL CONSIDERATIONS ON THE POLITICAL CLASS

In considering the retention of power by the political class, the small size of Costa Rican society must not be overlooked; the present population is slightly over a million and a half.* This is not so small, however, as to preclude the existence of a pluralistic society or the emergence of rival groups to defy the position of the dominant class.

Another factor that helps explain how the elite class has been able to maintain its preponderance is the role of the capital city in the life of the country, for it is the only important economic, political, and social center. This has prevented the emergence of rival groups in other zones and from other lineages. Marriage has also been important in the retention of power by the class. . . .

An important question arises concerning the extent to which it is still meaningful, in mid-twentieth century, to talk of the political dominance of this small class. An examination of its influence at the level of the executive branch during the four campaigns between 1958 and 1970 shows that of the ten presidential candidates representing the major parties, seven were descended from Juan Vázquez de Coronado alone. . . . In the Legislative Assembly, however, there would appear to have been a decline in the power of the class. . . .

A hypothesis could be advanced to explain the situation: Until the twentieth century, when other groups came to participate in the political process, most administrative levels of government were dominated directly by the class. Since 1910 the participation of new groups in congress has been stimulated by rival factions within the class, and this sharing of power has lessened its direct control over this and many other branches of government. What appears to have happened is that the new arrivals, representing diverse interests from

*It is now almost 3 million.—EDS.

widely scattered geographical regions, have come under the domination of the national political class from the capital area. The class, then, appears to have changed from "owner" of power during the last century to "leader" of power during the present. However, it must be remembered that these new groups have given their support to the contending factions of the national political class in exchange for a participation which will undoubtedly acquire greater proportions in the future. . . .

Within these processes of power the greatest unknown in terms of power is the relatively new and rapidly proliferating state bureaucracy. Its growth may soon pose new problems to the traditional political class and effect significant changes in the distribution of power in Costa Rica.

1.4 Costa Rica Before Coffee: The Village Economy of the Late 1840s*

BY LOWELL GUDMUNDSON

Using previously unanalyzed census materials, Lowell Gudmundson tests the traditional historians' thesis of a pristine Costa Rica dominated by a self-sufficient, smallholding peasantry and finds it sorely wanting. Instead, he suggests, nineteenth-century Costa Rica, before the introduction of coffee, was characterized by a developed urban artisan class, significant division of labor, inequality in landholding, and considerable commercial activity. An elite did exist before coffee, he stresses, but it derived power and wealth from a variety of activities, not merely landownership.

Gudmundson, a social historian, holds a doctorate from the University of Minnesota. He is the author of several books on Costa Rica, including Costa Rica Before Coffee *(1986). He has taught at Costa Rica's National University in Heredia and at Florida International University and is currently on the faculty of the University of Oklahoma.*

IN the early nineteenth century, the Costa Rican village economy was characterized by complex and unequal land tenure and a social division of labor that affected all but the most isolated peasants. Tangible differences existed between the "elite" and the peasant masses, as well as within the peasantry and among a surprisingly well-developed urban artisan group and the agricultural sector.

By the mid-1840s the Central Valley region had approximately 60,000 to 70,000 inhabitants (61,714 were listed in the 1843–44 census manuscripts used throughout this study). They were distributed in the four major villages or

*Excerpted from the *Journal of Latin American Studies* 15 (1983). Edited with permission of the author.

"cities" of San José (5,068), Cartago (5,630), Heredia (2,478), and Alajuela (1,834), and their surrounding suburbs or parishes. Generally, they inhabited either the neighborhoods or *barrios* that formed older and large settlements close to the "city" or the newer, more isolated villages on the fringes of settlement, generally with less than 500 inhabitants. The size and age of the settlement, municipal land policy, and proximity to the virgin-lands frontier helped determine the division of labor and landed inequality that clearly existed within the cities and suburbs. In a sense, only in outlying hamlets was there a literal basis for the rural egalitarian and homogenous peasant image of Costa Rican society [see Reading 1.1].

In San José, Cartago, and Heredia we find a surprising number of artisan callings, in addition to the primary distinction between agriculturalist or farmer and laborer (in descending order of land wealth). Older suburban villages perhaps had fewer artisans but similar differences in status within agriculture. This generated weak migratory movements toward newer and smaller villages or *barrios* close by. Socioeconomic inequality between the land-rich and the land-poor, or between smallholders and "laborers," was quite real in the precapitalist village economy. It extended to major suburban villages whose communal land claims both conflicted with privatization of land by poorer village dwellers and limited the viability of migration as an easy escape from inferior status. Even so, this pattern of inequality and poverty in the midst of plentiful land (in the abstract) was qualitatively different from, and surely less severe than, that of later society which fully privatized land and created true proletarians.

Only at the city level were traditional handicraft and artisan activities well developed as independent occupations. In smaller villages such activities, if not avoidable through exchange in the nearest city market, were usually carried out within the agricultural household. However, even in villages some heads of household declared either artisan or handicraft callings (carpentry, weaving, spinning, hatmaking, basketweaving, etc.), especially in former Indian *reducciones*. The three major cities also developed limited specialization, such as metal- and powderworks (La Puebla de Cartago), cigar rolling (Heredia and later San José), and cloth spinning (first Cartago and later San José), in addition to the ever-present callings of silversmithing, carpentry, weaving, and tailoring-seamstressing.

These diminutive cities functioned as specialized centers of production and distribution for their surrounding villages. With approximately one-quarter of their households declaring artisan callings, and another quarter to one-half of households listed as laborers, transformational enterprise was well represented prior to coffee or agrarian capitalism. Pre-coffee Costa Rica was no self-sufficient household economy, however much its agricultural frontier may have continually approximated this image. Coffee would change this reality. But initially the change was toward ruralization and agroexport specialization, and away from artisan development.

The major impulse for trade in Costa Rica during the late colony was tobacco (1770–1840) and, later, silver mining (1810–40). The influx of Panamanian and Spanish merchants, the increasing prosperity of local traders, the growth of consumer markets for cloth, and the increased use of locally mined silver are well-documented processes. Petty commerce was well developed in all areas of the Central Valley.

International trade involved the local construction of small ships for the Pacific coast trade with Panama, Guayaquil, and Callao. Even more important were the frequent visits of Pacific merchantmen after independence in 1821. Moreover, the designation of merchant appears to have been the ultimate in local prestige, however small the fortune involved. Indeed, merchants as a group, and foreigners in particular, were the wealthiest members of society. They characteristically diversified their economic activities toward agriculture and mining, typically after marriage to a well-placed creole damsel.

Foreign trade was limited to a relative handful of the wealthiest merchants. Surviving lists of exporters and importers from the Pacific port of Puntarenas in the period 1836–46 give some idea of the scale. A single exporter, Francisco Giralt, a Catalan merchant married locally, accounted for a near majority of the legal export shipping trade by value in 1839. This oligopolistic trade pattern was quite typical until major coffee exporters wrested control from other merchants. Overland exports, mainly of tobacco to Nicaragua and Panama, were also important, but as they were technically a state monopoly they were not listed with other foreign trade. Contraband exports of tobacco to both Nicaragua and Panama were important in bringing in additional imports before the 1840s. There is also some evidence of a large-scale contraband trade in silver, in exchange for English goods by way of Jamaica and Panama after about 1820. In any event, by both legal and illegal means, more merchants participated in the import trade, mostly of textiles, than in legal exports.

Local market-day trade in both foodstuffs and handicrafts was well developed in all four cities. Nearly all the travelers' reports of early to mid-nineteenth century highlight both the size of local markets and the merchant activities of the most prestigious citizens.

Pre-coffee Costa Rica, with its general isolation, backwardness, and low productivity presents something of an extreme case in terms of wealth. Here, having servants or monetary income in themselves often qualified one for membership in "society." The general pattern, increasingly found to be the norm throughout Latin America, was key merchant dominance over the local lords of the land. This commercial preeminence was almost always intertwined with bureaucratic, ecclesiastical, and landed interests through familial or political alliances when not in one and the same entrepreneur [see Reading 1.3]. Political and religious office went hand in hand with the generation and preservation of wealth, just as in other, more dynamic Spanish colonial societies. Land ownership was not the surest or quickest road to enrichment in this society, however much it may have been a form of security and a requirement for acquiring elite status and acceptance.

While poverty was widely distributed in pre-coffee Costa Rica, what wealth that existed was relatively concentrated. At the bottom of the scale were the *jornaleros* (day laborers), few of whom had any property to report. Farmers and artisans ranged from the propertyless to the wealthy. *Agricultores* (agriculturalists) were markedly richer than other tillers of the soil, although the wealthiest among them were miners, merchants, and cattlemen as well.

Whatever might be said about the Costa Rican elite and its commercial-agricultural complexity, there can be no doubt that land ownership itself was neither its defining characteristic nor its basis of power. Wilhelm Marr commented caustically upon this uninhibited commercialism of the local elite at mid-century:

> On marketday the President of the Republic does not disdain to cut some yards of gingham for a peasant; the Treasury Minister becomes hoarse in his efforts to prove to the purchaser that he ought to buy a miserable glass. Behind the improvised counters there are Officials, Captains, and Majors selling nails, feather cutters and scissors; Magistrates of the Supreme Court sell cotton socks; lawyers find buyers for underwear: physicians give out soda water in their pharmacies. What's more: ecclesiastics occupy the office of Lord of the measuring stick on an interim basis while the proprietor dines. . . . This mercantile spirit is a sad phenomenon in a country agricultural by nature. . . . The so-called Jewish Exchange in Hamburg is a drawing room compared to the baseness of small business practiced here. All of the refinement of commerce oscillates in miniature. . . .[1]

Commerce, then, was the necessary and expected complement of any even marginally successful *agricultor.* Very few merchants, in fact, were without landed interest as well.

Studying the economic and political activities of the elite and examining its sources of income reveal two essential features of wealth and the transition to coffee: (1) the pre-coffee elite existed as a clearly superior group, nearly all of whom would eventually become coffee growers and from whose ranks many of the first planters would logically come; and (2) even after coffee came to dominate, the elite continued to hold interests in all major wealth-generating and -preserving activities, especially trade and politico-religious officeholding. In other words, a narrowly coffee-based and landed oligarchy it was not, nor did it ever really become one over the course of the nineteenth century.

The late colonial elite in Costa Rica had been merchant-landlords, just as the later coffee barons would be, but their economic horizons were extremely limited and their productive system far more primitive than the coffee growers'. The precapitalist elite had presided over a social system based on both significant division of labor and marked inequality. The consideration of the major outlines of pre-coffee society and its dominant class should lead to a reconsideration not only of that earlier society's dynamics, but also of the initial impact of coffee. Far from being socially regressive, a fall from grace that led to the "demise of the peasantry," the rise of cities, and the first social division of labor, coffee essentially revolutionized a colonial order much more complex and solidified, however much in miniature, than the existing literature would suggest. It is a tribute to coffee's productive revolution that even the historiographical memory of the village economy has been largely erased.

NOTE

1. Quoted in *Costa Rica en el siglo XIX*, ed. Ricardo Fernández Guardia (San José: EDUCA, 1970), pp. 178–79.

1.5 Report of President Don Juan Rafael Mora on the Battle of Rivas of April 11, 1856

The battle of Rivas, in southern Nicaragua, was a decisive though costly victory for the Costa Rican forces against William Walker and his filibusters. These North American adventurers had invaded Central America to annex territory for new slave states for the United States. They also hoped to take over Cornelius Vanderbilt's isthmian transport business which, in the pre–Transcontinental Railroad era, shipped fortune-seekers from the eastern United States across Nicaragua and to the newly discovered California gold fields. Within a year of the Rivas battle, Walker would be forced out of Central America. But he returned twice before being vanquished by the Central American armies and executed by the Hondurans in 1860.

Curiously, President Mora's battle report does not mention drummer boy Juan Santamaría, to this day a national folk hero of Costa Rica, who died while torching an enemy command post. Santamaría remains a symbol of resistance to foreign intervention.

General Headquarters, Rivas   April 15, 1856
Señor Minister of War:

I have already sent a report of the glorious day of the eleventh and I repeat it now in more detail, although it would never be possible to justly summarize the heroic actions of my valiant troops.

At seven in the morning, in response to the cunning maneuvers of the Filibuster Chief W. Walker, I sent a column of four hundred men under the command of Major Clodomiro Escalante in the direction of the little town of Potosí, where we had detected the enemy's presence.

The city of Rivas is open and surrounded by thick banana groves and peanut fields. Hardly a quarter of an hour had passed since the column left when Walker, doubtless hidden beforehand on the outskirts, invaded the city like a torrent from the side opposite to that taken by Major Escalante's men. Walker seized the plaza and came very close to the house occupied by my General Staff and the gunpowder depot across from it, which are both only two blocks from the plaza.

The first minutes were terrible. Our people and positions were outflanked, nearly encircled in a ring of fire and bullets. All of us gripped our weapons and went to the defense. Colonel Lorenzo Salazar backed up the General Staff with a handful of people and held off the enemy, giving the column that had left the city time to return and to occupy advantageous positions, until we could almost change the defense into an attack, forcing the enemy soldiers to hide in the houses.

We had stationed a small cannon with only four artillerymen near the plaza and the filibusters took it in their first charge. In an ill-considered effort to retake it, we lost some people. Three times our soldiers left the corner where our headquarters is located (the house of don José María Hurtado) and went running toward the cannon, two blocks away. And three times they suffered the murderous fire discharged by the enemy in the plaza, in the Town Hall and military building (where Walker was with his best people), in the church, in its belltower and the house of Señora Abarca, which our men called Doctor Cole's house.[1]

At eleven o'clock the filibusters occupied the plaza and all the avenues around the church.

From the street in back of the war building, the city was ours toward the N.E.; we had the roads to La Virgen and San Juan.

The situation had improved, but we still had not won.

Strict, simultaneous orders went out from this headquarters: it was my wish to unite certain units that were fighting in isolation. First, to organize, and then to surround the enemy, dislodge him, and throw him out of Rivas. A squad of dragoons was stationed in the door of the headquarters with the single purpose of passing written orders, and all officers were told to provide me with reports on the situation. I ordered that the ammunition stored in the other house be brought here, and I advised all officers to come and outfit themselves abundantly with munitions.

At nine o'clock I had requested reinforcements of one hundred men from La Virgen. Right away I sent orders for the troops stationed there and in San Juan to concentrate themselves in Rivas.

From this moment there began to be a progressive, decisive change in our favor.

Our men had set fire to one side of the war building and our fire was outflanking or closing in the enemy.

In mid-afternoon Commanders don Juan Alfaro Ruíz and don Daniel Escalante arrived with the people from La Virgen: these troops occupied part of the war building, to the right of the church, and continued closing in the enemy until, in the night, they were able to seize Doctor Cole's house, the last one on this side of the plaza.

At night Colonel don Salvador Mora arrived with the people from San Juan del Sur.

Although the filibusters already had been surrounded, this force completed the security of our positions.

The firing had nearly ceased: the only things heard were occasional rounds from time to time which our people fired at the enemy troops who were fleeing and the joyous "vivas!" which our men yelled for the republic and its leaders.

Don Juan Alfaro Ruíz had surrounded the church and prepared to assault it at daybreak, at which time our soldiers invaded the plaza from all sides. Not finding any enemy troops other than those in the church, they entered and finished them off with bayonets.

Immediately I sent out pickets in all directions to pursue the fugitives.

This triumph has been great, due to the well-conceived surprise attack on the filibusters. Nevertheless, so much glory has been mixed with painful cries and sad mourning. We have lost the valiant officers General don José Manuel Quirós, Major don Juan Francisco Corral, Captains don Carlos Alvarado and don Miguel Granados, Lieutenants don Florencio Quirós, don Pedro Dengo and don Juan Ureña, Second Lieutenants don Pablo Valverde and don Ramón Portugués, and Sergeant don Jerónimo Jiménez. The valiant Captain don Vicente Valverde also perished.

We counted 260 wounded, among them various notable leaders.

My first concern was to prepare the hospital, to bury the dead, and to organize the army again.

Walker's defeat is greater than I had thought. We have seized a large number of rifles, swords, pistols, more than fifty saddled horses, and many other things. It is not known what else the inhabitants may have hidden on the outskirts of the city.

Each moment prisoners arrive, both healthy and wounded. As of today we have shot seventeen.

In summary: our losses, counting the wounded who may die, will not exceed 110 men, including officers.[2] The enemy's losses are not below 200, counting those we have executed. As at the battle of Santa Rosa [in northern Costa Rica on March 20], their wounded wander through the fields and many will die for lack of rest and care.

Among the multitude of reports and dispatches I have received, the most certain is that Walker entered Granada the night before last with three hundred men, of whom twenty-five or thirty are wounded.

All the officers and soldiers of the army have distinguished themselves, especially General don José María Cañas, Colonels don Lorenzo Salazar and don Manuel Argüello, Lieutenant don Juan Alfaro Ruíz, Captains don Santiago Millet and don Román Rivas.

According to careful examination of the various reports I have received, Walker attacked with a force of between 1,200 and 1,300 men.[3] I on this occasion, weakened by the dispersal of my people in the outposts at La Virgen, San Juan del Sur and elsewhere, had an equal or perhaps lesser number of soldiers.

I would have pursued the enemy without allowing him to rest, but we had all passed thirty hours without food and fourteen hours of massacre and fatigue.

It was my first duty to attend to the wounded, and now I am preparing to continue the campaign, flattering myself with the hope of being able to say to you very soon that *filibusterismo* no longer exists.

May God keep you,
JUAN R. MORA

NOTES

1. Byron Cole was a wealthy New Englander who owned the Honduran Mining and Trading Company and the conservative San Francisco newspaper, *The Commercial Advertiser,* which he invited Walker to edit. Cole was responsible for financing Walker's first expedition to Nicaragua, which he saw as a means of protecting and expanding his interests in the Central American area. He was killed in September 1856 while leading a filibuster unit at the battle of San Jacinto.—EDS.

2. This figure is incorrect. Costa Rican losses in the battle of Rivas were actually around five hundred.—EDS.

3. Walker claimed to have 550 men and an additional 200 Nicaraguans in a separate unit.—EDS.

1.6 Reckoning with the Central American Past: Economic Growth and Political Regimes*

BY HÉCTOR PÉREZ BRIGNOLI

In this essay, historian Héctor Pérez Brignoli outlines a framework for rethinking the last century of Central American history. While there is a consensus that the region's current crisis is deeply rooted in history, he believes that historical analyses, in both the United States and in Central America, often lack depth and emphasize national studies at the expense of comparative regional analysis. Here, Pérez Brignoli compares the nineteenth-century coffee booms in Costa Rica, Guatemala, and El Salvador. He finds that Costa Rica, with its more egalitarian land-tenure patterns, developed a class structure and state that were unique by regional standards. Examining the ways economic conditions molded the ascendant liberal state, Pérez finds once again that Costa Rica was exceptional. While other liberal states became efficient guarantors of repression, the Costa Rican state rested upon implicit collaboration, agreements, and conciliation between the different social classes.

Pérez Brignoli has written extensively on demographic, economic, and social history. He holds a doctorate from the University of Paris and is professor of history at the University of Costa Rica.

*A longer version of this article appeared as Working Paper No. 160 of the Latin America Program of the Smithsonian Institution's Wilson Center, which supported the research. The statements and views expressed in it are those of the author and not necessarily those of the Wilson Center.

IT seems indispensable to go beyond the two types of approaches currently in vogue: (1) Manichean views that, although derived from different ideological perspectives, reach similarly gross simplifications, and (2) the type of "structural history" proposed by the "sociology of dependency."

In the first case, we have interpretations, mostly implicit, derived from the "Roosevelt Corollary to the Monroe Doctrine": that the successive crises, the continuing political instability and social protest are the products of backwardness and the "lack of civilization" of those tropical regions, the "Banana Republics." A second set of Manichean views can be called "conspiracy theories": all misfortunes are seen as products of an elaborate scheme involving the multinational corporations, local oligarchies, and imperialism. Or, from another perspective, the supposed conspiracy is seen as the result of a satanic conspiracy controlled from Moscow or Havana. In each of these "catechisms" there are elements of truth conveniently placed so as to form a convincing tale of "Good" versus "Evil."

The second focus has a solid academic status. But the "structural history" proposed by the "sociology of dependence"[1] lacks (a) a sufficient comparative perspective, (b) an adequate consideration of the interrelationship between economics and politics, and (c) an adequate consideration of international political factors, as well as of other historical circumstances often judged as merely fortuitous or circumstantial.

Looking at the scenario of the crisis of the last ten years, what catches one's attention is the sharp contrast between the political stability and validity of the representative democracy in Costa Rica and the military coups, social upheaval, and popular insurrection that have afflicted the rest of Central America. The contrast is more surprising if one considers that Costa Rica and its four neighbors—Guatemala, El Salvador, Honduras, and Nicaragua—have many common traits: similar export economies, an industrialization process under the Central American Common Market, and a history that is, to a certain degree, shared.

During the nineteenth century, the export of tropical products assumed the role of "engine of growth" and, with minor changes, this continues to be the case today. Central American industrialization is not only a recent phenomenon, but one that took place during a period of prosperity based on traditional exports. The open character of the Central American economies, typical of small countries, is a constant in the history of the last hundred years.

[Pérez next discusses the Central American countries' relative success in integration into the world economy through their basic exports—coffee, bananas, cotton, and minerals. He notes that "the concept of integration with the world market is used in its economic and political dimensions: that is, the development of an export economy and the consolidation of the national state." He finds that Costa Rica and Guatemala were successful with coffee and bananas, and El Salvador with coffee. Nicaragua experienced "frustrated" integration with coffee, cotton, and minerals, while Honduras experienced "belated" integration with bananas and minerals.]

By "successful" integration, we mean a continual process; that is, once the possibilities of exports to the world market open up, there is a gradual overcoming of obstacles (such as the cost of transportation). The process can be considered fully developed by the eve of World War I. "Frustrated" integration is a frequently interrupted process with diverse obstacles that follows an uneven path with retrocessions and diversions. Its "belated" character means that on the eve of World War I the process was not completed. The affected countries thus lost the "relative advantages" of the 1870–1913 world economic upswing, which was favorable for international trade and investment. Success depended, obviously, on the internal ability to mobilize production resources. Political stability was as much a requisite as a result of successful world market integration.

Coffee clearly predominates in the economies of Costa Rica, Guatemala, and El Salvador. In Costa Rica, it prevailed early, in the 1840s. In Guatemala and El Salvador it competed first with cochineal and indigo dyes, exports inherited from the colonial period. However, the coffee industry "takeoff" was consolidated in Guatemala in the 1870s and in El Salvador in the 1880s.

In Costa Rica and Guatemala the need for coffee transportation helped give rise to the banana industry, when railroads were constructed to transport the coffee from the central highlands to the Atlantic ports and bananas were planted along the routes [see Reading 2.3]. Additional railroad and land-grant concessions and banana operations combined to form a new and particularly profitable business from which the huge banana companies expanded. The structure of coffee production, however, was little affected by this new sector. The banana plantations developed in areas recently opened for colonization, in the Atlantic lowlands, and did not compete for land with highland coffee. The competition for the labor force was more intensive but not decisive. The working conditions and the climate in the plantations favored Jamaican immigration to the Atlantic coast of Central America. Regarding power relations, the banana companies faced a hierarchy created and dominated by the coffee interests. In spite of the economic impact of the new product, Guatemala and Costa Rica continued to develop as "coffee republics."

The incorporation of land for production depends on transportation and labor availability. The first can be considered an "induced" variable; the opening of new roads, railroads, and ports was an internal response to the advance of settlement and colonization. The second, the mobilization of labor, then becomes a particularly significant variable.

The labor supply and work systems depended on two basic factors: population densities (or in economic terms, the land/labor ratios), and the nature and action of the state. The first factor is structural, modifiable only in the short- and medium-term by a policy of massive immigration (or emigration). The second involves the state's role as a "promoter of exports," and in this particular case, the formation of a legal and institutional framework for the provision of labor. It also involves sociocultural aspects, such as the capacity, qualifications, and discipline of the work force and the types of relations that exist between *patrones* [employers] and workers.

[Pérez writes that Costa Rican population density was much lower and land/labor ratios much higher than in coffee-producing El Salvador and Guatemala. In other words, there was more available land per worker—11.4 hectares in Costa Rica in 1880, as opposed to 2.35 hectares in Guatemala and 2.34 in El Salvador (one hectare = 2.47 acres). Also, a much larger proportion of the area in coffee was in small farms of just a few hectares in Costa Rica than in El Salvador and Guatemala. Relatively small farms thus dominated rural Costa Rica, while large coffee farms were the norm in Guatemala and El Salvador.]

The different countries' labor systems in the late nineteenth century also showed notable contrasts. The coffee harvest, from November to January, signified a sharp peak in labor demand [for a commercial crop that was heavily labor-intensive, and which could not be mechanized]. In El Salvador, an abundant supply of wage labor was available. In Costa Rica, the same wage system was used, but complaints abounded about the scarcity of labor. In Guatemala, compulsory systems were used to force the Indians down from their highland communities to the coffee zone.

A correlation seems obvious between the low population densities of Costa Rica, the predominance of relatively small farms, and the extended use of family labor; in brief, the existence of what we might call a "rural middle class."

To understand the development of a forced labor system, as in Guatemala, or the fairly clear predominance of wage labor, as in El Salvador, one must consider an additional factor, that is, the role and nature of the state.

In the 1870s, the so-called liberal reforms brought about certain internal structural changes that facilitated the "takeoff" of coffee production. In El Salvador, lands were expropriated from the Indian and *ladino* communities that still occupied lands useful for coffee. In Guatemala, the same occurred with Church land, and labor legislation reintroduced compulsory work systems from the colonial period to guarantee the supply of labor from highland Indian communities. In both cases, the rise of liberalism was a response to declines in exports that had predominated in the colonial era [such as cochineal and indigo dyes]. The reforms redefined key group and institutional relationships, notably the status and rights of the Church and Indian communities. The result was the advance of secular power, but at the same time it was a definitive rejection of more radical social change. Relationships between the ruling class and the peasant masses continued in the same patterns, perhaps with less paternalism than during the conservative period, but based—as before—on oppression and violence. The main new feature of liberalism was the guarantee of more efficient repression by the respective states.

The case of Costa Rica differs notably again. Coffee production was increased in the 1840s, and it permitted a new type of development. There was nothing like the liberal reforms of Guatemala and El Salvador. The construction of the national state was a gradual process, parallel to the expansion of coffee cultivation. The colonial heritage was limited to an economy based on isolated subsistence activities by a society of peasants and landowning farmhands. Although large differences in personal wealth existed, cultural homogeneity and a strong individualist tradition seem to have been the most significant characteristics of the rural petty bourgeoisie.

[In El Salvador and Guatemala, the best option for the coffee entrepreneur was the appropriation/accumulation of land and the exploitation of cheap or colonial-style forced labor.] No spontaneous force in the market brought about changes in the distribution of income. Peasants could only better their position if they succeeded in acquiring a plot of land of their own or if they obtained through labor organization the right to collectively negotiate for wages. Both possibilities, typical of any real reform program, signified truly revolutionary changes in the context of the socioeconomic structures of Guatemala and El Salvador.

[Costa Rica followed a second route in the expansion of coffee production:] the development of small and medium properties worked by family labor. This resulted from the nature of the state and the characteristics of the colonial heritage. The entrepreneurs who initially arranged for more capital or who had particular success in the coffee business fashioned a powerful but open ruling class that based its wealth on a monopoly of the coffee processing plants and the management of commercial capital (credit, marketing the production, and export). Although these entrepreneurs in general also possessed the larger agricultural properties, their role in production was relatively insignificant. The coffee industry expanded as the result of a slow and gradual colonization process, with new families settling in the frontier zones; the agrarian structure was thus based primarily on small and medium-sized landowners subject to the domination of commercial capital. On the other hand, with the passage of time, the subdivision of properties (by inheritance) and the end—around 1930—of the agricultural frontier (in terms of finding suitable new lands for coffee growing) formed the bases for the emergence of an agricultural semi-proletariat. In a structure of this type, the relationship between the "coffee entrepreneurs" (commercial capital and processors) and small and medium-sized producers constituted a key axis of social relationships. Most important, all enjoyed the profits from exports, although in unequal measure. The strategies developed by both sectors were of a typically reformist nature; each sought to better its relative position in the market of goods and services. The institutionalization of these conflicts constituted a powerful element of legitimation for the Costa Rican state. That it could occur in a gradual, unfettered way was because of the nature of the colonial heritage and the fact that, by way of its geographical situation, Costa Rica remained fairly isolated and detached from civil conflicts during the Central American Federation period (1824–39). Collaboration and agreements between different social classes were essential factors in the gradual, slow process of constructing the national state in Costa Rica.

NOTE

1. For example, Edelberto Torres-Rivas, *Interpretación del desarrollo social centroamericano* (San José: EDUCA, 1971).

1.7 The Dynamics of Early Militarism*

BY JOSÉ LUIS VEGA CARBALLO

In this excerpt, José Luis Vega examines the disruption of the early postindependence "age of consensus" by mid-nineteenth-century militarism and political instability. He identifies two militaristic cycles, one that grew out of the needs of an ascendant new upper class and the other that led to the establishment of an "oligarchic-patriarchal state." Yet, he argues, the "liberal criollo" ideology and traditional pacifistic, democratic tendencies remained alive and tempered the militaristic impulse. After the coups, the generals usually returned to the barracks, and power remained in the hands of civilians who typically sought a legitimate popular base. Ironically, it was Tomás Guardia, a general who did not return to the barracks but ruled dictatorially for over a decade, who put an end to militarism and paved the way for the liberal reforms that were the fulfillment of the criollo dream.

José Luis Vega is a sociologist educated at the University of Costa Rica, Brandeis, and Princeton. The author of three books and numerous articles, he is currently on the faculty of the University of Costa Rica.

THE DYNAMICS OF EARLY MILITARISM

During the first years of independence, at least until Braulio Carrillo's 1838 coup, the Costa Rican state apparatus was created "from below," with considerable support from the general population. These local sectors were organized within a rudimentary but important system of suffrage that was exceptional at that time.[1] European and North American liberal ideology also influenced the relatively isolated and autonomous southern colonists of the Captaincy General of Guatemala. From here arose the ideological base for the country's future republican institutions, inspiring the concept of a centralized state organized on the principle that political succession be mandated via popular consent and not imposed by force. . . .

*Excerpted from José Luis Vega Carballo, *Orden y Progreso: La Formación del Estado Nacional en Costa Rica* (San José: Instituto Centroamericano de Administración Pública, 1981), pp. 242–63.

Nonetheless, it would be a mistake to assume that the process of slow democratization and control of the authoritarianism initiated at the dawn of national life followed a direct, uninterrupted line through a rose-colored nineteenth century. The two administrations of Juan Mora Fernández (1824–29, 1829–33) were characterized by a "patriarchal" style, patronizing yet respectful of the demands of all strata of the population while not giving primacy to any particular group. This period, as compared to what would follow, can be called the "era of consensus," a time when balancing different interests was the principal goal.[2]

In those early years, efforts centered on the simple search for subsistence, and for successful alternatives to the restrictions and archaic production methods of the colonial regime. Also, it was during Mora Fernández's progressive governments that the meticulous legal structure, which today remains an integral part of Costa Rican political culture, was carefully developed. And, according to an 1824 report by [the influential liberal politician] José María Peralta, the military played an insignificant role, which would not change for more than a decade. Peralta wrote:

> The civilian militia, endowed with neither armaments nor officers to direct or discipline it, is insignificant for a military operation, with few militiamen even possessing guns. The other disciplined militia, because it is new, is composed mostly of recruits and has no chiefs or officers, with only one low-ranking veteran officer. There are few rifles, and many are not serviceable. The Artillery Company lacks leadership and even though there are some light pieces ready for placement, it has very few shells. Military supply is bad; there are no war supplies nor gun shot, and only a few boxes of powder and lead. The militia of this State, which for its robustness, sobriety, obedience and subordination to the inhabitants could be superior to any other State, is today very insignificant due to a lack of direction, discipline and supply of arms.[3]

Such was the situation, favorable to pacificism, that prevailed at the time that other forces, which were to bring about the establishment of an oligarchic state, got under way. Though maintaining a vision of liberalism, this oligarchic state carried within it the germ of the authoritarianism that would plague the country throughout the nineteenth and into the first years of the twentieth century. . . .

In May 1838, with support from the San José military barracks and in particular from then-Captain José Manuel Quirós, Braulio Carrillo inaugurated the era of political change through armed force—he himself would be deposed and exiled in 1842.[4] Carrillo's rise coincided with a fundamental change in Costa Rica's social structure. Increasing coffee exports to the United States and Europe led the government to provide land and offer incentives for coffee cultivation. The so-called coffee oligarchy was constituted rapidly, and in order to advance its business goals it needed not only state support but also control of the principal centers of political and military power. In this manner, it could firmly navigate the population's passage through the drastic adjustments demanded by the cultivation and harvesting of coffee and could keep the machinery of a dynamic export economy on track. Thus, within the bosom of a society previously characterized by relative equality, a social class arose with sufficient financial weight and force to become the principal protagonist in the process of historical development. . . .

The first military cycle began with Carrillo and ended when President Juan Rafael Mora Porras forced the Quirós family, Máximo Blanco and his cronies into exile.[5] According to contemporary sources, that group was responsible for the wave of mutinies and coups that destroyed the presidency of José Rafael de Gallegos on June 7, 1846 (actions in which both Captain Lorenzo Salazar and Second Lieutenant Blanco participated).[6] During the [José María] Castro Madriz government, military groups took part in eleven revolts; Castro Madriz fell victim [in 1849] to a military plot led by then-General Quirós and partly promoted by the future president Juan Rafael Mora; the following year Mora expelled Quirós and his followers from the country. Militarism had apparently suffered a rude blow. Mora Porras was the first president [1849–53, 1853–59] clearly of the coffee class and, even though the differences that were bound to arise within that class had yet to be settled, the oligarchy had never before functioned with such security. Commerce was going well, there was room for all, and the dangers of violent reaction from below were nonexistent. The people toiled quietly in the fields, attended markets where they bought European goods paid for with the "golden bean," and used their own carts to participate in the lucrative transport of coffee to [the port of] Puntarenas. In short, the workers mixed right into the feverish mercantile activity. The oligarchy and government had little to fear. . . .

But something happened to alter this Phoenician commerce with its reigning sense of brotherhood. In 1856 the war against the North American filibusters, a group of plundering freebooters [led by William Walker], got under way.[7] At about the same time Juan Rafael Mora's relationship with oligarchic families began to sour. Acting in his own interest, Mora moved to establish a national bank—which was going to undermine the lucrative, widespread usury of wealthier *cafetaleros,* who gave credit to small and medium-sized farmers. This was a key reason that Generals Blanco and Salazar engineered the 1859 coup against Mora, resulting in his downfall and [after a failed bid to recapture power] in his execution the following year. These events heralded the second cycle of militarism in Costa Rica, which opened amid a series of disagreements that split the dominant class into rival bands.

If the first cycle of militarism was directly related to the rise and consolidation of the dominant class in the government, and its utilization of the state as an apparatus through which it could keep various local factions in line, the second cycle must be seen in the context of internal class divisions. The various factions used military power to determine which members of the oligarchy could keep the powerful posts, and thus be able to mete out the shares in the state enterprise among family members and allies. As is characteristic of a patrimonial oligarchic state, there were no rules of the game or widely accepted norms for how to divide up the riches or how to transfer political power from one sector of the dominant class to another faction on the rise. Hence the recourse to army uprisings or to "buying" military units to resolve the problem of government succession. The military did not, however, intend to gain and hold onto power. Rather, it was used as a tool to install whomever had been chosen to govern under the direction of a clique of close advisers who were to protect the interests of the people who truly controlled the country.

It is important to remember that there was virtually no genuine popular participation in the political-electoral process; the trend in this direction had suffered serious setbacks decades earlier. According to historian Cleto González Víquez [who later became president himself], elections were organized and executed "within closets, with the door closed, decided in conversations whispered from ear to ear. And when the decision was reached, the word was passed down through the authorities to the citizens, who for the most part did not react spontaneously, but instead acquiesced to the desires of the high political and military officials."[8]

The war of 1856 is interesting in this respect because it was partly responsible for reestablishing army bases, a military budget, and the buying and selling of officers and generals. Heroic or not, the military men took credit for the exploits of the war and returned from the battlefield swollen with prestige and the desire for dominance. The army had protected the country from the grave menace of the North American freebooters; it symbolized defense and national unity. Better armed and better trained, it possessed an aura of legitimacy. When the military deposed Mora Porras and brought José María Montealegre to power, it was evident that the new president needed army support to carry out his objectives. Despite the conditions that had been imposed—a call for the army to return to its barracks and for a transition to a civilian government that could easily be manipulated by the oligarchy, without the backing of the military chiefs—it was clear that the dominant classes could no longer control the presidency, whether by election or by coup. Democracy trailed in the dust, and the presidents did little but pave the way for military control, making the sword far mightier than the vote.

Nonetheless, it is important to observe how the leaders incessantly searched for a legal or constitutional political formula to legitimize power acquired by force. Sometimes this led them to install civilian leaders, who then had to seek such a legitimizing formula on their own behalf. Thus began the military struggles that strengthened the liberal tradition and moderated the praetorianism of the times. One early example of this was seen during the ephemeral dictatorship of Gregorio José Ramírez in 1823 [who led the republicans to victory over the imperialists at Ochomogo and held on to power just long enough—eleven days—to call elections and yield to a constituent assembly].[9] On the other hand, as historian Carlos Meléndez noted of Blanco and Salazar, the famous coup-making generals of the 1860s, "Presidents were either made or broken by virtue of their relations with these generals. However, it is important to emphasize that they [the generals] always engaged in these activities without any intention of becoming themselves president of the republic. This case is undoubtedly unique in Latin America."[10] In other cases, such as the overthrow of President Juan Rafael Mora, military intervention had strong public support.

Thus, in several cases there was a certain legitimization of the coups, from popular forces or from strong currents of public opinion, meaning that such military actions in Costa Rica were different in several respects from similar events elsewhere. In these cases, the coup was not simply the result of barracks politics, in that it was not merely following the interests of a military caste enthroned in power. Nor was it carried out in the service of an oligarchy that did not dare to involve itself directly in government, or which as a class did not have the capacity to dominate a civilian government. Instead, in Costa Rica, military intervention evolved toward a status of constitutional legitimacy, a posteriori, which prevented an extended illegal stay in power by those responsible for the action. Moreover, the outcome was often previously sanctioned by a climate of general support from the population (especially in the principal towns), which gave the coups a certain legitimacy from below.

There was one other political phenomenon that provided an antimilitary and prodemocratic coloration. This was the curious tendency, which recurred historically, of the military hierarchy moving against itself. . . . One case in point, interesting because it also ended the dominance of Blanco and Salazar, took place on November 1, 1869. A military conspiracy organized with the consent of the two generals did away with the progressive government of Castro Madriz, who was deposed for the second time (he had also been forced out in 1849). There was general alarm because Castro had named his own successor, the lawyer Julián Volio. For the first time, a president stimulated popular interest and involvement in the electoral process from above, something unprecedented which provoked discussion among the public and in the press. The moneylenders were particularly worried about Volio's plan to strengthen the *Banco Nacional,* which would have greatly affected their profits. Many people were also alarmed by what appeared to be a growing distance between Blanco and Salazar, who had joined antagonistic electoral advisory groups. The situation appeared to be disintegrating into chaos; when military intervention finally came, to the relief if not with the support of the populace, it was seen as a savior. As historian González Víquez observed, "The spirit of the urban population was inflamed, their passions excited; everyone feared a catastrophic ending, everyone thought the electoral battle, developing as it had with such life and ardor, would have to resolve itself in the streets and with bullets. In this situation, the coup smothered the flames like a cold shower, and as if by magic, everything grew quiet."[11]

On the other hand, once the coup had taken place, a series of measures were taken to limit the government's power and influence, and it was agreed to call for the rapid election of a new assembly. Within twelve days of the coup, a return to legality had taken place and a new political formula, advantageous to the dominant interests, had been introduced. On February 18, the assembly issued a new constitution that for the first time included provisions for social reform. Public primary education was declared free and obligatory, and a civil guard was established as a "moderate" alternative to the military's role of domestic peacekeeper. However, it was not only in these ways that this new government—born of a coup—distanced itself from praetorianism in spirit and practice. It is important to point out the role of Eusebio Figueroa, a lawyer and an astute and respected civil libertarian, who as the minister of war took charge of the armed forces. It was Figueroa, pistol in hand, who forced General Salazar to resign; later, he restrained Blanco and the other officers. He thus effectively disrupted the conspiratorial command center and initiated the subjugation of the officers and men to the president or executive power.

But Figueroa was not responsible for the final submission of the military. It was General Tomás Guardia who brought this about, the same General Guardia who deposed President [Jesús] Jiménez [Zamora] in the famous coup of April 27, 1870. It was Guardia who appeared as the aggressive organizer of military coups, who strengthened the country's war machine and military budget during the 1870s until it reached a level of nearly twenty thousand men, and who captured the absolute loyalty and admiration of the commanders and officers through the heroism he had cultivated since the war of '56. On the one hand, Guardia's strong and centralized government was the epitome of militarism; it enthroned a military leader who ruled with absolute power. But in his more than a decade in power, Guardia suffocated numerous conspiracies and rebellions by other officers, leading political families, and disaffected oligarchic interests. The outcome was the destruction of the *criollo* militarist model.

In effect, by debilitating or exiling political figures and by destroying the conspiratorial structures that could have sustained militarism once he had gone, Guardia also provided the foundation for a democratic resurgence and for the great anti-oligarchic reaction embodied in the so-called *Generación del Olimpo* [the term for the group of young liberals that emerged from the campaign of 1889], which opened the way for an expanded process of popular participation inspired by a liberal and republican creed. . . .

In conclusion, two important points must be mentioned that contributed to the liquidation of Costa Rica's military establishment during the 1860s, and which to a degree also influenced events during the Guardia period of 1870–82. These were (1) the problem of military costs versus the importance of public education, and (2) the transformation of *criollo* capitalism that demanded a different political and ideological climate and a more stable method of making the transition from government to government.

THE DEATH OF MILITARISM AND OTHER CHANGES

The upheavals and military coups between 1838 and 1870 resulted in prodigious losses, not only in lives but in public finances and materials. The very capitalists who utilized the military to introduce changes in government, be they winners or losers, protested that it was indispensable to reduce the cost of these intraclass feuds, which increased the public debt in involuntary and unforeseeable ways. The war against the freebooters in 1856 further complicated matters when it became necessary to take out loans domestically and abroad (from Peru) to make damage payments and to provide for veterans and widows. Together with the instability provoked by *morismo,* which became acute after the killing of the "supreme leader," ex-president Mora, in 1860, this put succeeding governments in a tight spot. . . .

The idea soon took hold that it was indispensable to rationalize public spending for the sake of the stability of the private finances of the dominant class, which were jeopardized by the arbitrary taxes levied by the militarists. Moreover, this taxation was often shaped by vengeance emanating from the triumphant party. Often, the result was not only the confiscation of properties of the vanquished but also of his entire extended family. Since the state was little more than a patrimonial court, the governing factions could reserve for themselves privileges they denied to those who had not been involved in the conspiracy that brought them to power. With the personal wealth—both familial and mercantile—of large sectors of the dominant class constantly threatened, stability thus soon came to be seen as a requisite to general prosperity.

Mandatory military service also had a curious effect on the agricultural labor supply, which was scarce in central Costa Rica. To avoid conscription, many young men migrated to the prosperous farming frontiers or into isolated jungle areas where they could find uncultivated land and favorable conditions for small-scale, subsistence farming. After the 1856 cholera epidemic decimated the population by nearly 10 percent, the need for farmhands was even more pressing. Any attempt by the military at that time to enforce mandatory service would have stirred the marked national pacifist tradition that formed a part of the liberal creed which, from the outset, had been proclaimed in the press and among the most influential and educated circles of the population. . . .

In 1859 the traveler Anthony Trollope observed the poverty of the barracks and the sad state of the militia. "There are no uniforms," he noted, "and you can only recognize the soldiers, when they are on duty, by the very rusty rifles." Although the full complement of the militia should have been nine thousand, the force seldom exceeded six thousand, and "of this number only five hundred are actually quartered in barracks, being rotated for others after a month's duty."[12] Such was the attraction of this poor militia for an industrious population whose well-rewarded hands were greatly needed to cultivate for the export sector as well as the domestic market. . . .

Military status, such as it was, held little attraction, except in the hands of a liberal politician using it as a decorative tool at ceremonies. During the heyday of the oligarchic-patrimonial state, provincial commanders and their squalid militia did acquire importance by participating in the revolts and coups that determined presidential succession. But once their intervention had ended they fell into their habitual prostration and calm, under the iron control of the oligarchs. . . .

This does not negate the importance of the military, which did play a vital role within the dominant oligarchic-patrimonial system. But it does signal factors that worked as countertendencies in the military's social-historical development and were initiated by several transcendental changes that began once Guardia had disappeared from the political scene in 1882. Perhaps the most crucial of these was the sustained growth of the national education system. In state hands and with a secular, liberal orientation, the education system became an effective substitute for the harsh and repressive methods of controlling the population and resolving conflict within the political system. It was a true system of indirect domination. . . .

By the 1860s, the advantages of popular access to knowledge and even compulsory education were fully appreciated in Costa Rica. Education implied improvements in labor productivity and contributed to the formation of a collective mentality that made it possible for society to be self-administered without resorting to state repression. Opposition to the establishment and expansion of public education are much more evident where income distribution is greatly skewed—for example in an export economy based on the plantation system and on coercive and extra-economic methods of manipulating the work force—than in more open and flexible social structures. Where benefits are more equally distributed, investment in human capital is seen in a better light by the political and economic elite whose own socioeconomic power is less pervasive. In an open society, the elite not only comes to realize the positive effects that the acquisition of knowledge has on social mobility and on the labor force, but also to appreciate the importance of education in the political-ideological formation of the citizenry and thus in the transition from the rule of the sword to the rule of the vote.

Under such structural and sociocultural conditions, Costa Rica was able to increase public spending on education. As early as 1833, when the coffee growers were barely producing enough to export, there were forty-one schools in the country; five years later (when the Carrillo coup ended the "age of consensus") there were fifty-eight schools. In 1843 a university was established at the old Casa de Enseñanza de Santo Tomás; the next year the new constitution guaranteed education as "a sacred right of the Costa Ricans" and in 1858 education was declared mandatory. Finally, in 1869 a new constitutional clause made "primary education for both sexes obligatory, free, and at the cost of the Nation." In 1883, after twelve years of Guardia's "illustrious" dictatorship, the country had 234 schools. A great transformation had taken place, one that would have profound consequences.

Without a doubt, under this new system it became more and more difficult to define the population as "ignorant plebeians" requiring a hard despot to control them, to prevent them from dissolving into anarchy, from shredding the fabric of state and society. The view of the working class as a dangerous entity lost its validity; through education, it had been transformed into a sort of modeling clay that did not need the weight of the military to control it and could, without undue difficulty, aspire to be included within the framework of the emerging citizenry. This represented the fulfillment of the liberal *criollo* dream.

Thus by the end of the century, the ability of the oligarchic-patrimonial state to politically exclude vast sections of the population was greatly diminished. Indeed the oligarchic-patrimonial state had been transformed into what has been called the "educator" or "pedagogue" state. . . .

It is important not to overestimate the limited gains of the liberal-democratic reforms. Reversing the tide of civic exclusion and ignorance of the working class would take years. Nevertheless, the foundation of a popular regime had already been firmly established when Guardia assumed power. Rather than disrupting the liberalization process, his dictatorship opened the doors to change. But this would not have been possible if the productive forces of the country, the material base of Costa Rican capitalist society, were not also undergoing profound transformations. The economic surplus increased and the standard of living rose, permitting a gradual democratization of the country's political life and pulling it out of the grasp of the military and the strict lineage of traditional oligarchy.

NOTES

1. The 1821 *Pacto de la Concordia* and the 1824 Federal Constitution established suffrage based on the indirect votes of successive territorial representatives. Male citizens of eighteen years or more who met certain property and educational criteria were able to vote for local representatives who in turn voted for regional and national representatives. This system and the age, educational, and property criteria for exercising the vote changed numerous times in the nineteenth century. Only in 1913 was direct voting for candidates established and only in 1928 was the secret ballot written into law.—EDS.

2. Mora Fernández, for example, granted pardons to all participants in the brief 1823 civil war.—EDS.

3. National Archives of Costa Rica, *Serie Provincial Independiente,* no. 1184, 1824.

4. Braulio Carrillo, president during 1835–37 and 1838–42, was known for abolishing ecclesiastical taxes and Church holidays. During his second term, he was declared president for life shortly before being deposed by Francisco Morazán. He fled to El Salvador, where he was murdered in a dispute that apparently had nothing to do with his political activities.—EDS.

5. Juan Rafael Mora Porras, president for two terms during 1849–59, was best known for rallying Costa Ricans against the 1856 invasion of the North American filibusters (see Reading 1.5). During his first term (1849–53), he also built the state-owned liquor factory and helped found the University of Santo Tomás. Overthrown in 1859, he raised an armed band of supporters the following year in a futile attempt to regain power. He was captured and executed in Puntarenas.

General José Manuel Quirós led an unsuccessful 1852 revolt against President Juan Rafael Mora. General Máximo Blanco, a leader of the campaign against William Walker, collaborated with General Lorenzo Salazar to topple Mora in 1859.—EDS.

6. José Rafael Gallegos was head of state, in 1835–36 and 1845–46, when he was deposed in a coup. José María Castro Madriz, a lawyer and founder of the University of Santo Tomás, served in numerous political posts, including head of state during 1847–49 and 1866–68. Though removed from office by the military during his second term, he was able to expand the educational system and establish the first telegraph system in the country. On Lorenzo Salazar, see note 5.—Eps.

7. William Walker was a Tennessean freebooter who invaded Central America three times between 1855–60 in hopes of annexing new slave states to the United States and of seizing Cornelius Vanderbilt's isthmian transit company. Walker was defeated by united forces from the different Central American republics and ultimately executed by a firing squad in the Honduran port of Trujillo. The campaign against Walker remains a symbol of nationalism and resistance to foreign intervention throughout Central America.—Eps.

8. Cited in Ricardo Fernández, ed., *Costa Rica en el siglo XIX, Antología de viajeros* (San José: EDUCA, 1970), p. 179.

9. Gregorio Ramírez was briefly interim head of state in 1823, before he turned power over to an elected assembly (see Editors' Introduction to this chapter).—Eps.

10. Carlos Meléndez, *Dr. José María Montealegre* (San José: Academia de Geografía e Historia, 1968), p. 165.

11. Cleto González Víquez, *Obras históricas* (San José: Publicaciones de la Universidad de Costa Rica, 1973), p. 289.

12. *Revista de Costa Rica en el Siglo XIX,* p. 377.

CHAPTER II

Liberalism and Early Costa Rican Reformism—Late Nineteenth and Early Twentieth Centuries

Editors' Introduction

Costa Rica was the first Central American country where classic liberal ideology took hold. The country's history as Spain's poorest New World possession left few conservative forces linked to the Church or to the export of colonial-era products, such as the indigo and cochineal dyes that were so important in El Salvador and Guatemala. The near destruction of the indigenous population, never large in the first place, meant that village or communal landholdings were relatively unimportant. In part because of this weak "colonial heritage," fewer obstacles existed to liberalizing Costa Rica's economy and institutions.[1] The country was the first in the region to engage in coffee production for export, an activity that required access to land, "free" labor, and an agile credit system unhindered by anachronistic restrictions.[2]

Already in the 1830s, under President Braulio Carrillo, the Costa Rican elite had taken steps to end ecclesiastical taxes and limit Church and communal landholding. The influence of liberal conceptions of laissez-faire and anticlericalism grew stronger later in the nineteenth century. The roots of this process were diverse and included the spread of European liberal ideas, the example of the Mexican reforms of 1856, the coffee-induced modernization of the Costa Rican economy, and the 1873 accession to power of liberal strongman Justo Rufino Barrios in Guatemala. Liberalism appealed to the Costa Rican elite as a program for institutionalizing its hold on the country's economic and political life and wresting control from the military. In the economic sphere, it stood for free trade, encouragement for foreign investors, and the privatization of Church and communal or village landholdings. Politically, liberalism sought to limit ecclesiastical influence and to establish a system of formal democracy with periodic elections, secular education for the citizenry, and greater press freedom.

By the 1880s, Costa Rican militarism was in decline, with the upper class increasingly cognizant that the instability and concentration of power inherent in army rule was damaging to its interests. As Readings 2.1 and 2.2 indicate, General Tomás Guardia, the country's last nineteenth-century military dictator (who ruled from 1870 to 1882), played a key role in encouraging this transition from the chaotic militarism that had reigned since the mid-nineteenth century. Whether governing on his own or through civilian figureheads, Guardia brought the armed forces under control and, through a significant program of public works which included construction of the first rail lines, helped set in motion economic forces that ultimately became bulwarks of liberal ideology and the modern state.

Following Guardia's death in 1882, most sectors of the upper class embraced liberalism, but as Rodrigo Facio argues in Reading 2.1, in the Costa Rican context this meant little beyond the restructuring of a civil state and commitment to an "exaggerated individualism" that was largely unconcerned with popular political participation or broader questions of social welfare. One of the characteristics that distinguished Costa Rican liberalism from that in other Central American countries was that its leaders did not form what Facio terms "a permanent ideological party." Instead, liberal politics in the late nineteenth and early twentieth centuries were largely dominated by members of the so-called Generation of '89 or *Olimpo,* a group of liberal leaders who, in the 1889 presidential race (generally believed to be Costa Rica's first genuinely free election), united around the unsuccessful candidacy of Ascención Esquivel.[3]

Yet the lack of a strong ideological party organization, which Facio saw as a failure of the liberals, may have been a blessing in certain respects. During the late nineteenth and early twentieth centuries, when liberals and conservatives in the other Central American countries struggled for supremacy in a nearly continuous series of bloody regional and civil conflicts, Costa Rica was, for the most part, at peace. Efforts related to the implementation of the liberal program, such as the 1884 expulsion of the Jesuits and the 1885 law on secular public education, met with relatively little resistance, even when proclerical regimes, such as that of José Joaquín Rodríguez (1890–94), returned to power.

Other criticisms by the liberals' contemporaries were more telling. The opening to foreign capital, a key plank of the liberal platform, was epitomized in the Soto-Keith Contract of 1884 (Reading 2.3). This agreement traded a rescheduling of Costa Rica's foreign debt by the U.S. railroad magnate Minor

Keith for long-term rail concessions and an outright grant of 800,000 acres of land, nearly 7 percent of the national territory. Much of this land soon became plantations of the United Fruit Company and came to symbolize foreign domination and control. Although some liberal politicians later campaigned against the worst abuses of foreign capital, on the whole they welcomed outside investment and took pains to downplay what many others saw as severe social and political costs of foreign economic penetration: increased exploitation, decreased sovereignty, and only limited new income for the national treasury.[4]

Costa Rica's peaceful reputation in this period also had regional repercussions. In 1908, after a Mexican- and U.S.-sponsored Central American peace conference in Washington, the country became headquarters for the Central American Court of Justice, the first international mediation body of its kind, with one justice from each of the five Central American republics. After successfully mediating several regional disputes, the court was called upon to examine the Chamorro-Bryan Treaty, in which Nicaragua granted the United States perpetual rights to build an interoceanic canal along Costa Rica's northern border using the San Juan River and Lake Nicaragua. Costa Rica protested that the U.S.-Nicaraguan agreement infringed on its navigation rights and sovereignty and in 1916 the court found in its favor.[5] But in 1918 Nicaragua, angered at the ruling, blocked efforts to extend the court's original ten-year mandate, and a potentially fruitful mechanism for peacefully resolving regional conflicts was allowed to expire.

Costa Rica was not, however, entirely immune to the violence that plagued its neighbors in the early twentieth century. The first significant effort to reform the system that the liberals had put in place came from Alfredo González Flores, who was president from 1914 until 1917, when he was overthrown in a military coup. As Jorge Mario Salazar indicates in Reading 2.4, the fall of González Flores was due primarily to his advocacy of tax reforms that affected the rich and his opposition to concessions to a U.S. oil company. It is also important that González Flores had to govern during a severe economic crisis, with greatly reduced export earnings and tax revenues, when World War I had cut Costa Rica off from its main coffee market in Europe. González Flores came to power with the slogan: Either we change course or we go under. But the efforts of Costa Rica's first reformist president were blocked by the upper class and he was replaced with Federico Tinoco's military dictatorship.

The thirty-month Tinoco dictatorship, which Hugo Murillo describes in Reading 2.5, brought repression, militarization, and the creation of an efficient network of government informers. Although the coup was at first widely welcomed, little time elapsed before resistance movements formed. The pressure they, and Washington, brought to bear eventually brought down the regime. The experience of dictatorship was, for Costa Ricans at the time, a frightening reminder of still recent nineteenth-century military rule and of the fragility of the country's institutions. It is probable that the legacy of this episode included a strengthened commitment to democratic processes on the part of broad sectors of the population. Opponents of the dictatorship, such as General Jorge Volio, also built political careers on their actions during 1917–19 and used their newfound prominence to call for fundamental changes in Costa Rican society.

The continuing failure of liberal administrations to seriously address the needs of the Costa Rican poor or to defend the country's wealth and sovereignty against the inroads of foreign capital, brought calls for more radical reform and for a more active state role in the economy. Jorge Volio, a flamboyant, iconoclastic general and priest steeped in European social Christian doctrine, became the main exponent of change in the 1920s and the leading figure of the first major reformist political party. Reading 2.6 provides background on Volio's Reformist Party, a group which, despite its seemingly radical program and its considerable (although short-lived) success at the polls, remained in the mold of the personalistic parties then dominant in Costa Rica.

The 1930s depression only exacerbated the problems that had concerned earlier reformers such as González Flores and Volio. The economic crisis provided a fertile milieu for the Communist Party, founded in 1931 (Reading 2.7). The party had some support from urban intellectuals and artisans but its main base was among the workers of the Atlantic-coast banana plantations. Its influence in Costa Rica's nascent labor movement expanded significantly after 1934, when a dramatic Communist-led strike against the United Fruit Company brought gains in the areas of salaries, housing, and working conditions (Reading 2.8).

The depression also highlighted the inadequacies of the liberal approach to economic progress, based on laissez faire, a free rein for foreign capital, and export-led development. As in the United States, where New Deal programs put the unemployed to work and attempted to stimulate economic growth, increasing calls were heard in Costa Rica for more interventionist economic policies. Only in the 1940s—when social Christians and Communists, and later social democrats, were in the government—were basic reforms, many of them similar to those sought by González Flores and Volio, enacted. This period, which marks the final demise of the liberal state and the rise of reformism, is discussed in Chapter III.

The question remains why the reformist impulse was so pronounced in Costa Rica, even in the late nineteenth century. In other Central American countries there were few, if any, equivalents of a González Flores or a Volio, upper-class politicians who expressed strong reformist views. While the brutal Tinoco dictatorship was an exceptional episode in twentieth-century Costa Rica, elsewhere in the region institutionalized violence and repression were the preferred means of dealing with contradictions between the dominant groups and the poor majorities. Indeed, even in our times, the suspicion with which the Guatemalan and Salvadoran oligarchies look upon even the most mild social reforms is notorious. In contrast, the Costa Rican upper class has historically been more "enlightened" and inclined to compromise and share at least some of society's wealth.

A number of elements must be considered in explaining this Costa Rican penchant for reform, most of them best if somewhat nebulously described as "political culture." Even in the interprovincial conflicts that took place at the time of independence (see the introduction to Chapter I), strong tendencies existed that favored compromise and dialogue over armed solutions. The absence of a strong "conservative reaction" in Costa Rica, like that which existed in Guatemala, El Salvador, and Nicaragua, made it possible to modernize economic and political institutions with a minimum of violence. The presence of a large agricultural frontier and the relative freedom of movement of the rural population (which was limited in late nineteenth- and early twentieth-century Nicaragua, in spite of that country's large agricultural frontier) provided a safety valve for tensions caused by inequitable agrarian structures. The limited presence of subordinate ethnic groups, such as Guatemala's Indians or the *mestizo* majorities in El Salvador, Honduras, and Nicaragua, meant that racism could only rarely be employed as a rationalization for denying the poor their basic human rights. In this context of a more fluid social order, assumptions about the bounds of appropriate political action, social justice, and the duties and rights associated with membership in civil society tended to be broader and more democratic. Thus, the visions of a González Flores or Volio might be seen as premature or even extreme and both brought forth strong responses from powerful reactionary forces. But they were not so far beyond the pale that they were unable to reach positions of influence and power or were denied a voice.

NOTES

1. Stanley J. Stein and Barbara H. Stein, *The Colonial Heritage of Latin America* (Princeton: Princeton University Press, 1970).

2. Ciro F. S. Cardoso, "Historia económica del café en Centroamérica (siglo XIX): estudio comparativo," *Estudios Sociales Centroamericanos* 10 (1975): 9–55.

3. The *Olimpo* group, so named because its "olympian" members were considered above reproach, included Ascensión Esquivel (president 1902–1906), Cleto González Víquez (president 1906–10 and 1928–32), and Ricardo Jiménez Oreamuno (president 1910–14, 1924–28, and 1932–36). Although the 1889 election was the first in which there was widespread political participation, the franchise was limited to males, and voters chose an electoral college (as in U.S. presidential elections) rather than voting directly for candidates. The first election in which there was direct voting was in 1914, when the new system resulted in a deadlock and a political deal that brought Alfredo González to the presidency. Women did not receive the franchise until after the 1948 civil war.

4. The first presidential campaign of Ricardo Jiménez in 1909 was based on his having waged, while still a congressional deputy, a battle against tax exemptions that had been granted to the United Fruit Company. See Eugenio Rodríguez Vega, *Los días de don Ricardo* (San José: Editorial Costa Rica, 1971), pp. 36–37.

5. El Salvador also protested the Chamorro-Bryan Treaty's granting the United States a naval base in the Gulf of Fonseca. Ironically, in the early 1980s, El Salvador allowed the United States to establish a radar facility on an island it controlled in the gulf. On the history of the court, see Carlos José Gutiérrez, *La Corte de Justicia Centroamericana* (San José: Ediciones Juricentro, 1978).

2.1 The Expansion of the Private Sector and Liberal Economic Policy*

BY RODRIGO FACIO

This selection by Rodrigo Facio briefly outlines the rise in Costa Rica of classic nineteenth-century liberalism, with its laissez-faire economic orientation, anticlericalism, and exaltation of individualism. Facio lauds the liberals for vanquishing militarism and breaking the nineteenth-century oligarchy's control over the country. But he faults liberal leaders for establishing political parties based on personalities and cliques, rather than on a coherent ideology. Liberalism, he argues, degenerated into an "abstract formula" unable to adapt to the nation's changing needs.

A scholar and lawyer, with expertise in economic affairs, Rodrigo Facio was one of the most influential social democratic thinkers of his generation. He played a key role in the Centro para el Estudio de los Problemas Nacionales *in the 1940s, and many of his ideas were incorporated in the 1949 Constitution and the fledgling National Liberation Party. He was instrumental in establishing the modern University of Costa Rica, and was its rector from 1952–61. The university campus was later named in his honor.*

IN the political arena, the aristocracy, supported by military forces from the San José garrisons, established itself as an oligarchy with dictatorial control over the country from 1858 to 1868. Its role in the fall from power and subsequent execution [in 1859–60, see Reading 1.7] of Juanito Mora is the best example of the direct and violent character of its activities in this early period. But under the dictatorship of General Tomás Guardia, which, in social terms, signified a democratic opening, the aristocracy was forced to modify its attitude. Pressured by Guardia's strict but progressive government, the oligarchs began to comprehend that the establishment of a liberal, orderly, and stable regime was in fact more advantageous for their business interests and foreign credit ratings than the perpetual instability of coups d'etat and military interference in the affairs of state. The change in attitude also affected their economic views, as they came to favor free competition over their traditional monopolistic control.

By the time of Guardia's death in 1882, this new attitude was firmly en-

*Excerpted from *Obras de Rodrigo Facio. Estudio sobre economía costarricense* (San José: Editorial Costa Rica, 1972), pp. 65–68.

trenched. From then on, it was a matter of imprinting it on the country's institutions. That was the essence of the liberal reforms of 1884 and 1888: the restructuring of a civil state, free from clerical or other forms of religious interference, capable of serving without obstruction the interests of the aristocracy. It should be noted that these interests coincided almost entirely with those of the country, inasmuch as they sought to assure steady economic growth and to promote development. Hence, these reforms must be considered part of an economically and politically progressive phase of our national history.

The Law of Universal Education, inspired by the intellectuals of the epoch, served to perfect and train the country's human capital. The Civil Code liberated private transactions from rules that were alien to the interests of the concerned parties. The principal example of this was the freedom to fix interest rates on loans, which had previously been regulated by law.

In practice, laissez-faire philosophy manifested an almost absolute lack of interest in the collective concerns of the country. In political terms, since our liberal leaders failed to organize public opinion and form permanent parties to educate the populace, it led to an utter absence of democratic, public control over the developing private businesses and the problems that they engendered.

These businesses began to expand dramatically: both agromercantile and strictly mercantile enterprises, established during the boom in international trade, gradually became larger and more stable. The country began to live in an atmosphere of continuous prosperity; even this very concentration of property had not yet reached a point where it would lead to serious social consequences. The countryside could still provide many opportunities for earning a living, even for workers and small landholders; in the city, large- and small-scale commerce, crafts, industries, and the professions provided ample and remunerative opportunities. The state had more or less sufficient income to underwrite its expenditures and undertake a vigorous public works program. In a word, the rapidly developing capitalist interests had not yet come into conflict with the country's general interests; rather, in the majority of cases, they largely coincided.

This expansion and development of economic activity was the logical consequence of the laissez-faire policies promulgated after 1870 by various administrations—including those produced by the clerical reaction against classical liberalism. Regrettably, however, the political representatives of liberalism, the men often called the "Generation of '89"—Mauro Fernández, Ascensión Esquivel, Cleto González Víquez, Ricardo Jiménez, etc.—with their olympian and mistaken individualism, did not concern themselves with civic education. They did nothing to popularize, organize, or provide a rational and emotional basis for the liberal thought that prevailed, albeit in diffuse form, in the country. Such a [political] base, embodied in the leadership of a permanent ideological party, would have served to ensure that the problems being generated under the shelter of this new doctrine would be studied, controlled, and eventually perhaps rectified within a more advanced conception of liberalism.

Politically, this was the great failure of Costa Rican liberalism, or rather, of its major representatives—this lack of a popular connection that could have conserved the vitality of liberalism as an instrument of civic action, improving it and adjusting it to the general needs of the country. Instead, liberalism in Costa Rica became an abstract formula, divorced from national realities. . . .

Liberalism stood for economic freedom, free competition, free trade, the end of monopoly and legal privilege. As a result, it put an end to nascent militarism and oligarchic control over the private sector; it made commerce independent of traditional formulas and ecclesiastic influence. . . .

It was not a question of the state doing nothing, but rather of the state allowing economically competent actors to operate. This negative sense of freedom is, in effect, the essential characteristic of Manchesterian liberalism or laissez faire.

2.2 Law on Individual Rights, 1877

BY PRESIDENT TOMÁS GUARDIA

Tomás Guardia, the strongest military leader to rule Costa Rica in the nineteenth century, was in many respects a transitional figure. He seized power in 1870 and, although there were a few brief spells of nominal civilian rule, held onto it until his death in 1882. As discussed in Reading 1.7, he managed to maintain himself in power in part by quashing rival military groups and thwarting several plots against his government. His dictatorship also had a benevolent side, or at least a progressive element. Public education was vastly expanded, and, in an extraordinary move for the nineteenth century, capital punishment was abolished in 1882 and has never been reinstated.

Under Guardia, work on the Atlantic railroad was begun, and the first bananas were exported from the port of Limón. He paved the way for both late nineteenth-century economic growth and for the liberal reforms that would begin two years after his death. Many of the seminal ideas of classical liberalism were codified by this decree, which Guardia issued in 1877.

THE LAW OF INDIVIDUAL RIGHTS

Tomás Guardia
General in Chief of the Army and Provisional President of the Republic of Costa Rica

Whereas the Grand National Council of the Republic of Costa Rica has issued the following decree:

The Grand National Council of the Republic of Costa Rica. While the Constitution of this Republic is being written the government has taken the initiative to establish individual rights in law.

DECREE:

ARTICLE 1: The lives of the inhabitants of Costa Rica are inviolable, as is property, except in cases of expropriation, which is only permitted when legally proven to be in the public interest and when preceded by indemnification based on a just appraisal of the losses determined by experts appointed by both parties. This is to include not only the value of the expropriated property but damages that will be incurred as a consequence of the expropriation. In the event of war or domestic upheaval, prior indemnification is not required for objects which are essential for the public good.

ARTICLE 2: Laws can have only future, not retroactive, effect.

ARTICLE 3: Freedom of religion exists, and this decree consecrates it in law.

ARTICLE 4: The homes of the inhabitants of the Republic may not be entered and searched without due process of law.

ARTICLE 5: All inhabitants of Costa Rica are free to travel in and out of the Republic, to travel within the interior of the country, and to live wherever they please.

ARTICLE 6: The confidentiality of telegraphic and written correspondence is inviolable; evidence obtained through violation of this confidentiality will not be admissible.

ARTICLE 7: The right to petition may be exercised in writing either collectively or individually.

ARTICLE 8: No one shall be harassed or persecuted for holding political opinions unless a person commits or conspires to commit criminal acts.

ARTICLE 9: No one shall be judged or punished by magistrates or special tribunals, other than those which have legal jurisdiction, except in those cases where the law establishes a special trial.

2.3 The Soto-Keith Contract on Foreign Debt and the Railroad, 1883*

During Costa Rica's first several decades as a coffee exporter, the country's coffee could only reach its principal markets in Europe through an expensive, roundabout route. Coffee was carted to the Pacific port of Puntarenas and then shipped around Cape Horn,

*Excerpted from "Aprobación del contrato Soto-Keith sobre deuda exterior y ferrocarril," in *Documentos fundamentales del siglo XIX,* ed. Carlos Meléndez (San José: Editorial Costa Rica, 1978), pp. 321–30.

the southern tip of South America. The nearly impenetrable jungles on Costa Rica's Atlantic coast prevented more direct links with the European market. In the early 1870s, the Costa Rican government, hoping to construct a railroad from the central, coffee-producing region to the Atlantic coast, contracted a series of obligations with London banking houses. The British bankers, taking advantage of the unsophisticated and trusting Central Americans, retained much of the money as commissions and only a fraction of the loans actually reached Costa Rica.

Unable to either meet its payments or finance the railroad, the government arranged in 1883 for a renegotiation of the debt that would also assure the completion of the desperately needed outlet to the Atlantic. Minor Cooper Keith, a U.S. citizen, had come to Costa Rica in 1871 to supervise construction of the first segment of the Atlantic railroad being built by his uncle. Within a short time he accumulated a sizeable fortune from exporting bananas grown along the railroad tracks. In the contract excerpted here, Keith and Costa Rican secretary of state Bernardo Soto agree on a number of measures that were to have far-reaching consequences. In return for renegotiating the British loans, that were to be guaranteed with customs revenues, the Costa Rican government granted Keith 800,000 acres of land, nearly 7 percent of the national territory. Keith was required to cultivate the land and was to mortgage it in order to raise capital for building the Atlantic railroad, that would then become his own private property.

Although much of the 800,000 acres was eventually returned to the government because of Keith's failure to cultivate it, this massive handout became the basis of the United Fruit Company's operations in Costa Rica. In addition to having interests in United Fruit (in Honduras, as well as in Costa Rica), Keith became an important presence in virtually every sector of the Costa Rican economy, including mining, livestock, banking, and retail trade. The Soto-Keith contract illustrates the ease with which U.S. capital was able to enter Costa Rica under one of the first liberal administrations, the difficulties underdeveloped countries often experience in building modern infrastructure, and the continuing dependence of the government on a foreign company for such basic needs as transport and telegraph communications.

XI

. . . The company will build a railroad that, beginning near the Reventazón River on the Atlantic railroad line, will cross the river's valley, and will end in the city of Cartago. The gradients of this railroad will not exceed 3 percent on the tangents, nor will the curves exceed twenty degrees, and the materials to be used will be as good as the best ones used in the construction of the railroad between Limón and the town of Carrillo (formerly called Río Sucio). . . .

XIX

. . . the Executive Power is authorized to grant special faculties and powers to Mr. Keith, within the limits of the present agreement, for the settlement of the Republic's debt in Europe, to negotiate new conditions with holders of presently existing bonds, as well as for the conversion of such bonds and the issuance of new bonds to be guaranteed by revenues generated by the National

Customs. . . . And considering that the aforementioned Mr. Keith has agreed
to return to Europe with these objectives, we agree for the present that the
period established for beginning negotiations for the construction of the railroad will start from the date of the final agreement and conversion of the debt.
That is to say, the construction will start six months after the debt's conversion, and will be concluded in a period of three years. If at the end of the
three-year period, beginning on the date of approval of the present contract,
the company has not obtained a settlement of the debt and capital for the
construction of the railroad, this contract will be null and void without requiring anything of the parties.

To further guarantee that the railroad will be completed, it is agreed that
if it is not finished within three years, the concessionary or the company
created for this purpose will be subject to penalties mentioned in . . . this
contract [a later clause specifies fines running from five thousand to twenty
thousand pesos per month]. It is understood that the government in no instance will contribute to expenses incurred by Mr. Minor Cooper Keith,
whatever they may be, because they will be paid out of his own resources. . . .

XXI

The government of Costa Rica cedes to the company, in full possession for
ninety-nine years, the railroads built between Limón and Carrillo, between
Cartago and Alajuela, and the one to be built between Cartago and the existing
Reventazón bridge on the Atlantic railroad line. This includes telegraph lines,
buildings and their land, as well as all the other rights and objects considered
in the service of the railroad, or those built in the future for this purpose. From
the moment the company begins work on the section it is required to build,
the constructed lines and their facilities will be handed over to it. The ninety-
nine years referred to in this clause will take effect when the railroad between
Reventazón and Cartago is completed and put in service.

XXII

The government concedes to the company 800,000 acres of uncultivated state
lands, along the railroad or at any other place in the national territory of the
company's choice, including all natural resources within, in addition to the
land necessary for the construction of the railroad and required buildings, as
well as all kinds of materials needed for the construction work found inside
the public lands all through the extension of the line, and two lots of the public
land that was measured today in Limón harbor, to build docks, warehouses,
and stations, all without any cost. The surveys and all the preliminary work
for the division and distribution of the 800,000 acres of land will be the
company's responsibility, since the government's only responsibility is to extend free property titles when needed. The government will not be able to

establish taxes on that land for twenty years from the beginning of the period of the present concession, it being understood that, after the end of the twenty years, lands that had not been cultivated or otherwise utilized will revert to the government's possession without compensation of any kind. . . .

2.4 The Reformism of Alfredo González Flores*

BY JORGE MARIO SALAZAR

Jorge Mario Salazar describes the first twentieth-century reform movement. Alfredo González Flores, appointed to the presidency by Congress after the 1913 presidential race ended in a stalemate, proposed a number of significant economic and tax reforms intended to modernize the economy, improve government administration, and make the economic system more equitable. Some of these measures were broadly similar to the early progressive reforms in the United States. The initiatives of the young president—he was in his late thirties—were not viewed with sympathy by the upper classes and foreign companies. In 1917 his one-time benefactor and minister of war, Federico Tinoco Granados, overthrew him. It was the first successful coup since 1870 and the only one in the twentieth century.

Jorge Mario Salazar was educated at the University of Costa Rica and Tulane University, where he received his doctorate. He is a professor of history at the University of Costa Rica.

THE first twentieth-century attempt at reforming the liberal state came from President Alfredo González Flores (1914–17) who proposed several measures, not all of which were enacted, to solve the economic crisis. His concern with the inequities and inadequacies of the tax system marked the first serious effort to adapt the nation's juridical institutions to new economic and social realities.

González Flores presented himself as a statesman with new ideas on the role of government. He also showed himself to be a leader with a degree of sensitivity; he tried to improve the precarious economic status of the lower classes, which he regarded as a consequence of the prevailing liberalism. Adopting a stance that ran counter to contemporary views, he regarded Costa Rican political parties not as truly democratic but as little more than groups of friends revolving around *caudillo*-like personalism. His reform efforts, nevertheless, were not essentially of a political nature; rather, they were a product

*Excerpted from Jorge Mario Salazar, *Política y reforma en Costa Rica 1914–1958* (San José: Editorial Porvenir, 1981).

of the need to find a way of financing the state itself and of controlling bank lending, which was still in oligarchic hands.

González Flores's reforms were designed to create a broad and secure base for the government's finances and to benefit the country in general. He hoped to establish a rational relationship between government revenue and spending. But though primarily fiscal in character, his reforms sought to bring about justice, to put the democratic system on a solid footing, to defend the autonomy threatened by large foreign economic obligations, and to secure the independence of public administration.

Costa Rica's tax system was based on an unjust mechanism: the state collected the greatest proportion of its taxes from poor and marginal sectors of the population, to the obvious advantage of the dominant class. Conceiving of the state as an entity called on to perform a social role greater than that of individuals, González Flores called for state intervention that would alleviate national economic problems. Indeed, without such intervention, he believed, an economically powerful group would constitute a monopoly that would certainly harm the weakest sectors and pose a danger for the entire community.

The president contended that his proposed reforms were essential in order to modernize the national tax system. He argued that the state must participate in solving socioeconomic problems. He claimed, too, that the middle classes and the economic elite were not experiencing economic hardship, given that they owned the means of production and had not been greatly affected by the world war. Exports had been at or above prewar levels, and national production for local consumption had been unaffected by the war.[1] He said the nation enjoyed adequate overall prosperity, and decided to introduce a bill that would establish a system of direct, progressive taxation, so that nationals and foreign guests paid taxes, following the principle that the rich would pay as rich and the poor as poor.

But during 1914–17, Costa Rica experienced a serious fiscal crisis, as the European war interrupted commerce. The crisis became more acute because the government's principal source of income—import duties and tariffs collected by customs—declined significantly. At the same time, social malaise and protest intensified in the working class, giving rise to strikes in workshops of shoemakers and tailors, in bakeries and stores, and even in the banana company. . . .

The fiscal crisis had three basic elements: the drop in public revenue because of the war's effect on commerce, rapidly increasing state spending in new areas, which made sharp budget cuts impossible, and the heavy debt burden. The main reason for the González Flores administration's deficit were the foreign (French and English) and domestic debts it had inherited, a reflection of the extent of the nation's economic dependency.

There were three possible solutions. The administration could save by reducing public sector salaries. It could seek more domestic and foreign credit. Or it could create new taxes—the solution that González Flores chose. Aiming to place the financial life of the state on fairer and firmer ground, González Flores in 1915 introduced five major bills. One would establish a Cadastral Survey or Land Census and Registry, an administrative innovation that was a prerequisite to some of the other measures contemplated in the four tax bills he introduced: the Direct Tax Bill; the Land Tax Bill; the Income Tax Bill; and the Public Works of Special and Local Interest Bill, which required that the beneficiaries of certain public works bear a part of their cost. . . .

The government did succeed in enacting several important measures. It created agricultural credit boards, under the aegis of the [state-owned] *Banco Internacional,* to grant credit to peasants to better their situation and to diversify production. It established a mortgage section, which permitted long-term repayments. It created an Office of the National Paymaster to prevent irregularities in the payment of public-sector salaries, including police and army personnel. And it imposed a tax on beer.

Unfortunately for Costa Rica, the president's program was only partly applied, not because of its shortcomings, but because of the reaction of the dominant class. The economic and political elite did not accept the attempts at reform—and decreed the fall of González Flores.

An additional factor in his downfall was his veto of the Pinto-Greulich contract. This agreement would have conceded oil export rights to a foreign company, and the liberal oligarchy had vested interests in the contract.[2]

On January 27, 1917, Federico Tinoco Granados, González Flores's confidant and minister of war [who had been crucial in bringing González Flores to the presidency in 1914] led a coup d'etat against González Flores, who fled to the United States. His overthrow left no doubt that the elite was not ready to surrender any of its privileges, and that it unquestionably retained economic and political power in the country. González Flores's attempt to bring about change failed in large part because the agroexport bourgeoisie and the mercantile-import bourgeoisie united against him—a process that implied the coalition of national and foreign capitalists who feared economic reform. He also failed because he lacked any organized power base that could sustain him in power.

Obscuring the real reasons for the coup and his own political ambitions, Tinoco declared to his countrymen that the coup had been carried out to prevent the reelection of González Flores and thus restore legitimacy to the presidency, referring to González Flores's election by Congress rather than by popular vote.[3] Nevertheless, the United States deemed the new government illegitimate and withheld recognition [Reading 2.5].

Thus, this first attempt at change was frustrated both by its eminently reformist character and because the dominant class was not prepared to accept it. Nevertheless, González Flores presaged changes that were to come; most of his ideas would be enacted into law during the 1940s.

NOTES

1. Exports remained fairly stable but, imports dropped by half from 1913–15, seriously affecting government customs revenues and urban retail trade.—EDS.

2. In fact, Costa Rica's oil resources turned out to be negligible.—EDS.

3. González Flores was in effect put into office by outgoing President Ricardo Jiménez, after none of the three candidates in the 1913 presidential elections emerged as a winner, and various pacts and bargains struck between them ended in impasses. González Flores was not a candidate, but after other deals failed, his name was suggested as a compromise solution. Congress was to appoint him as "first designate" and call on him to exercise the presidency. Before Congress acted, Jiménez, who detested all three of the candidates, handed over to González Flores command of the police and armed forces. As expected, Congress soon appointed him to the presidency. See Rafael Obregón Loría, *De nuestra historia patria. Hechos militares y políticos* (Alajuela: Museo Histórico Cultural Juan Santamaría, 1981), pp. 259–62.—EDS.

2.5 Tinoco, Wilson, and the U.S. Policy of Nonrecognition*

BY HUGO MURILLO JIMÉNEZ

Historian Hugo Murillo Jiménez discusses President Woodrow Wilson's refusal to recognize the government of Federico Tinoco, who seized power in a 1917 coup against his former protégé, President Alfredo González Flores. Tinoco initially had the support of the Costa Rican elite, notably the coffee growers hostile to González Flores's reforms (Reading 2.4). The United Fruit Company and other U.S. business interests also backed the new government. But Wilson himself regarded Tinoco's government as illegitimate. He invoked the Non-Recognition Policy, which was introduced by the United States in 1909 in an effort to promote peace and stability in the Caribbean basin and which was later employed as a warning to Mexican revolutionaries.

Murillo questions the wisdom and the sincerity of Wilson's decision. He argues that there were legitimate doubts about the constitutionality of González Flores's ascension to the presidency and that the United States, suspecting the toppled leader of pro-German sympathies, never intended to try to restore him to power.

Nonrecognition, Murillo contends, turned out to promote not peace and stability but rebellion, repression, and upheaval. The economic isolation encouraged by the United States harmed an economy already shaken by World War I, and the resultant hardship undercut support for Tinoco. Two armed groups arose against him, one based in Panama and counting Jorge Volio among its leaders (Reading 2.6). The second, led by Julio Acosta, inflicted more damage although its campaign was not decisive.

The United States, which had rejected requests from González Flores's supporters that it dispatch marines on his behalf, kept its distance from the armed resistance and urged leaders of neighboring nations, particularly Nicaragua, to follow suit. The uprisings never directly threatened Tinoco's regime, but he responded harshly to them, turning a repressive government into an outright military dictatorship and thus undermining his own

*Hugo Murillo Jiménez, *Tinoco y los Estados Unidos: Génesis y Caída de un Régimen* (San José: Editorial Universidad Estatal a Distancia, 1981), pp. 42–43, 51–52, 135–48.

remaining bases of support. In the final months of his rule, Costa Rica saw internal strife and political assassination, and was brought to the brink of international conflict.

Tinoco survived the U.S. pressure for thirty months. Although the United States did not intervene in Costa Rica, it was the threat of direct intervention—the specter of U.S. warships off the coast—that ultimately forced Tinoco to step down in August 1919. The United States also withheld recognition of Tinoco's chosen successor, and insisted that power be handed over to the man who under the previous constitution had been in line to succeed González Flores. He led an interim government, and oversaw clean elections that brought rebel leader Acosta—acceptable to the United States—to power. Nonrecognition, Murillo concludes, thus became a form of intervention in Costa Rica's internal affairs.

Murillo, a historian, received his doctorate from the University of California at San Diego. He teaches at the University of Costa Rica.

PRESIDENT Wilson had closely followed events in Costa Rica. Apparently he was in no mood to wait and countenance Tinoco's flagrant violation of the standards of conduct that the U.S. administration had been endeavoring to impose in the Caribbean. He ordered the State Department to prepare a memorandum on the subject. The task fell to Herbert Stabler of the Division of Latin American Affairs, who submitted it to the president on February 7. Its recommendations closely followed the ideas expressed by Wilson in 1913 with regard to revolutionary movements in Mexico. Stabler viewed Tinoco's coup d'etat as a family affair, pointing out the family connections between Tinoco and some of the people slated for cabinet positions. One case in point was Carlos Lara, the proposed minister of foreign affairs, who was apparently related to United Fruit Company vice-president Minor Keith. Stabler also pointed out that Tinoco had appointed his brother Joaquín, "who has been charged with several crimes," as minister of war. Stabler concluded: "Aside from the illegality of his action there is no question that he is absolutely unsuited to be given any recognition by this government as he is an unscrupulous character." Paradoxically, Stabler did not favor the restitution of González Flores either, noting that the González administration had been friendly with the German colony in Costa Rica. Stabler also feared the coup's effects on the rest of Central America. It might, he thought, be connected with a general conspiracy against the Emiliano Chamorro government of Nicaragua, prepared by "professional revolutionaries" in Nicaragua and Honduras. He noted that the coup had deeply disturbed the presidents of El Salvador and Nicaragua.

But Stabler's suspicions over who organized the coup centered on the United Fruit Company. Its obvious desire to inform the State Department immediately of the coup d'etat, its insistence that the United States should not intervene, its refusal to cooperate with the American minister in Costa Rica, as well as the family connections between Keith and Tinoco convinced Stabler that the United Fruit Company must at least have known beforehand of Tinoco's plot.

Noting Costa Rica's proximity to the Panama Canal, Stabler stressed that it was essential to have a friendly government. Fearing that Tinoco's example could have a far-reaching effect on revolutionary parties elsewhere in Central America, he recommended that the United States pursue a strong policy. He felt that the Latin American policy enunciated by Wilson in 1913 "should again be brought clearly to the notice of the governments of Central America and particularly to the people of Costa Rica." He further recommended that Tinoco be advised that the United States "will not give recognition to him or to any government which he may form, since he came to power through a revolutionary, illegal and unconstitutional act" and that recognition would only be granted to a government that was constitutionally formed. Both Secretary of State Robert Lansing and Wilson concurred with and approved Stabler's recommendations. . . .

The policy of nonrecognition of Tinoco, as outlined by Lansing in a February 9, 1917, telegram, seemed final and irrevocable. But new circumstances forced the State Department to reevaluate its policy and conclude that Tinoco should be recognized, both as a matter of expediency and because there was no alternative to him. Any illusions that nonrecognition by the United States would cause Tinoco to crumble immediately faded as, convinced he had support within his country, he remained in power and refused to yield to American pressure.

Tinoco also adopted a pro-Allied, pro-American foreign policy and his agent in Washington conducted a forceful and intelligent lobbying campaign for recognition. The elections in April 1917 would, Tinoco hoped, give his regime the appearance of constitutionality and further his chances of recognition.[1]

Another factor in the policy review was the U.S. effort to forge a united diplomatic front in Latin America that would support its war against Germany and its postwar efforts. This, plus Lansing's personal doubts about the efficacy of the nonrecognition policy, brought the secretary of state to the conclusion that Tinoco should be recognized. Nevertheless, and notwithstanding the recommendation of Lansing himself—backed by the views of John Foster Dulles, senior U.S. envoy to Costa Rica Edward Hale, and the commanding officer of the Panama Canal Zone—Wilson was adamant. His administration initiated a concerted effort to diplomatically isolate the Tinoco regime, pressuring European and Latin American countries, as well as Costa Rica's immediate neighbors, into following Washington's line. . . .

The recall of U.S. envoy Stewart Johnson in November 1918 did not end the quarrel between Tinoco and American representatives in Costa Rica. The San José consul, Benjamin Chase, was now the senior U.S. diplomat. Like his predecessor, he soon clashed openly with the Tinoco regime. The conflict brought American gunboats to ports in Costa Rica and nearby Nicaragua, and with them the specter of American intervention. For Tinoco, hard pressed by Acosta's rebels in Guanacaste, by the possibility of open conflict with Nicaragua, by domestic disorder, and by economic problems, the prospect of intervention constituted the last straw. . . .

Chase's problems, like Johnson's before him, stemmed from his constant involvement in Costa Rica's internal affairs. The American consul made no secret of his intense dislike for the Tinoco regime or of his strong desire to see another man assume power in Costa Rica. According to one report, Chase's attitude reflected the desire of some Americans in Costa Rica, who, hoping to improve business and stabilize the currency to benefit their own interests, openly condemned Tinoco's government and sympathized with and protected the revolutionaries. Chase continued Johnson's practice of keeping in close contact with the government's enemies and his public statements and repeated reports, which attributed to Tinoco aggressive intentions against Nicaragua, infuriated Tinoco's government. . . . Conditions did not improve with Chase's constant advocacy of American intervention in Costa Rica.

Not surprisingly, relations between the Costa Rican government and the American consul soon reached the point of confrontation. On March 4, 1919, Tinoco's agent in Washington sent a note to Frank L. Polk, acting secretary of state, accusing Chase of collaborating with Tinoco's enemies. . . . Chase in turn attributed the worst intentions to Tinoco and did not hide his fears of assassination at the hands of Tinoco's soldiers. Minister of War Joaquín Tinoco had uttered menacing statements, Chase said, and had "under his direction as reckless a lot of criminals as are in existence." There was, he said, a great possibility of a grave "accident" befalling him. Buttressing his call for direct American intervention, he wrote: "People outside of Costa Rica seem to look upon this condition . . . as nothing more than a pimple on the body politic which can be healed by a little salve, but those who are here realize that it is a cancerous sore and that nothing but the most drastic surgical operation without delay will bring a cure."

In early May, the Costa Rican exiles in Nicaragua began military operations in northern Costa Rica. Chase's nervousness neared paranoia. He cabled the State Department on May 10 requesting that "prompt and adequate measures be immediately taken for the protection of American lives and property in Costa Rica." He informed the State Department through the U.S. legation in Nicaragua that he was "cut off from all communications" and "menaced by Tinoco with assassination" and repeated his request for "the presence of war vessels at both ports and if possible soldiers in San José during the present situation."

His open skepticism notwithstanding, Polk asked the navy to keep warships near Costa Rican waters. He explained that the situation was somewhat uncertain and that "the necessity may arise for the sending of warships to Costa Rican ports in order to protect American lives and property." He asked that vessels be stationed in the Atlantic port of Bluefields, Nicaragua, and in the Pacific port of Amapala, Honduras, from where, if the occasion arose, "they could reach Costa Rican ports in a short time."

Chase considered Polk's measures insufficient for his own security and continued to send inexact reports. . . . According to him, "the almost universal cry is for the United States to step in and prevent the complete destruction of the country and the slaughter of innocent people." The American ships stationed in Bluefields and Amapala, he said, "are too distant for timely aid. The danger is real here." . . .

In a personal message Polk sought to allay Chase's fears . . . but again ruled out dispatching warships to Costa Rican ports as action that could be interpreted as interference in Costa Rica's internal affairs. Sending marines to San José, he said, would be "out of the question unless some actual danger threatens you or the American colony." Polk said American businessmen in Costa Rica had assured him that they were satisfied with the situation and that American interests were afforded adequate protection. . . .

Early in June 1919, the opposition to Tinoco began to manifest itself openly in San José. This time, the vanguard of the opposition was formed by schoolteachers and high school students, who had previously shown their dissatisfaction with the Tinoco regime and their sympathy with the Acosta rebels. . . . Demonstrations continued until June 12, when a crowd dressed in green and bearing pictures of Acosta tried to hold a meeting in San José's Central Park. Police closed the park, alleging that such protests were forbidden there. The leaders then spread the word that the American consul had ceded the consulate for the meeting and the crowd proceeded there. A large crowd gathered, waving flags and shouting "*vivas*" to Acosta, Wilson, and Costa Rica. From the consulate balcony, the protest leaders delivered speeches fiercely attacking the Tinoco brothers as "bandits." The crowd cheered and begged Chase to make a speech. He complied, thanking them in Spanish and saying that "the world would sympathize with them if it knew what had happened to them." That was enough for the police, who began to disperse the crowd by striking them with leather thongs or their clubs. Everyone who could scrambled into the consulate. Someone among the protesters began to shoot at the police from the consulate balcony. The police returned fire, presumably in the air, as no one was struck, except one policeman who was shot in the foot. During the turmoil, Chase stood exposed on the balcony, some say holding an American flag. . . .

[Riots and protests continued, and several people were killed. Chase continued seeking U.S. military protection, Polk continued to deny it, although the State Department again warned Tinoco and ordered four warships to ports in nearby nations. Chase later sent messages to two of those ships, asking for assistance. One did sail to the Pacific port of Limón, but the captain, upon finding no disorder or threat to Americans, did not land his men.]

The arrival of the American war vessel in Limón undoubtedly complicated Tinoco's political situation, since most people, including Tinoco, thought that intervention was imminent. Its presence also reinforced the position of Tinoco's enemies and raised their hopes for his early withdrawal. . . . Already pressed by the growing unrest in San José, the military activity of Acosta, and the ever-present threat of intervention from Nicaragua, the arrival of the

U.S.S. *Castine* may have been the last straw for Tinoco. Three days later, he began to signal his intentions of withdrawing from power. . . . One condition for his departure, Chase reported, was Tinoco's insistence on dictating his own successor.

Finally, on June 25, the Chilean ambassador in Washington called at the State Department to transmit Tinoco's conditions: first, that the American consul in San José "be put in jail"; second, that the American vessel in Limón be withdrawn immediately; third, that Juan Bautista Quirós be appointed provisional president; and fourth, that the United States recognize Quirós. Upon acceptance of this plan, the Tinocos would leave Costa Rica. . . .

By the end of July, events were unfolding rapidly. On July 30, Tinoco called an extraordinary session of Congress for August 1. A day later, Minister of War Joaquín Tinoco told soldiers and policemen that the Tinocos had decided to abandon power in order to prevent "the United States from intervening in Costa Rica." That afternoon, Federico Tinoco delivered a bitter speech in Congress attacking the United States. At the same time he requested permission to go to Europe, alleging that ill health required him to leave the country for the present. . . .

The details seemed to have been worked out by August 9. That evening, Joaquín Tinoco delivered a rambling speech in Congress accusing the United States of intervention in the internal affairs of Costa Rica and of collusion with Nicaragua in helping Acosta's movement. He then submitted his resignation as next in line for the presidency. The Congress immediately accepted it and appointed Quirós as his substitute, thus designating him as Federico Tinoco's successor. Immediately afterward, Congress authorized President Tinoco to leave "for the period of time that according to the circumstances would be necessary to recuperate his health." Unfortunately for Joaquín Tinoco, he would not leave with his brother. Two days after his resignation, on the evening of August 11, he was assassinated by an unknown person, who shot him in the right temple as he walked a few blocks from his home.

Joaquín Tinoco's death evidently hastened the departure of his brother. In a brief, simple ceremony at 6 A.M., August 12, 1919, Federico Tinoco handed over power to Quirós. At the same time he signed his resignation, which was kept secret until presented and approved by Congress on August 20. An hour later, a train left the San José station, taking Tinoco and his party to Limón where he embarked, England his destination, never to return to his country.

NOTE

1. Although Murillo argues that Tinoco probably could have won a fair vote at that time, he blatantly resorted to fraud, further antagonizing his critics in Washington.—EDS.

2.6 The Reformism of Jorge Volio*

BY JORGE MARIO SALAZAR

Jorge Volio (1882–1955) was an extraordinary figure: priest and soldier, politician and intellectual. He was educated and ordained in Europe, where he was deeply influenced by social Christian thought. Upon returning home, he founded a progressive Catholic publication, and then went to Nicaragua in 1912–13 to fight the U.S. occupation. He came back to Costa Rica a general—and was suspended from his parish. During Tinoco's rule, he went into voluntary exile and later joined the fight against the dictator. His brother led, and was killed in, the abortive Sapoá revolution against Tinoco. After the dictator fell, Volio won a seat in the National Assembly and in 1923 he formed the Reformist Party, the first party to advocate a broad program of social reform. In the next elections, it performed sufficiently well that Volio was selected as second vice-president in 1924. His political movement left its mark, but his personal influence waned after he was involved in a provincial uprising in 1926, and he was later defrocked. He reentered politics later and also was a professor of philosophy and university administrator.

Jorge Mario Salazar (also the author of Reading 2.4) holds a doctorate from Tulane University and is a professor of history at the University of Costa Rica.

DURING the 1920s and after the unsuccessful reformist attempt of 1914–17, a petty bourgeois reformist movement emerged, reflecting the philosophical and ideological orientation as well as the activism of its leader, General Jorge Volio Jiménez. An ex-priest, ex-guerrilla, and ex-soldier, Volio was a leader who aspired to reform his country.

The *Partido Reformista* [Reformist Party] was founded on January 25, 1923, after the *Confederación General de Trabajadores* [General Confederation of Workers] proclaimed Volio's candidacy for the 1924–28 presidential term. Trade unionists found in Volio, already an Assembly deputy, an enlightened man, a leader, and a friend. General Volio wanted to create an ideologically based, enduring party with popular support, a party that would not be subject to the traditional control of political bosses. . . . He wanted Costa Rica to achieve a social revolution through peaceful means, within the strictest adherence to the law.

In the context of Costa Rica in 1920, Volio's ideological principles and objectives seemed "radical" or "revolutionary." Some even characterized it as a "socialist party"—incorrectly, because in fact its goal was only to

*Excerpted from Jorge Mario Salazar, *Política y reforma en Costa Rica 1914–1958* (San José: Editorial Porvenir, 1981).

substantially reform the prevailing liberal capitalist system. In the socioeconomic sphere, the Reformist Party attempted to achieve the following:
agrarian reform, decent housing, job security and protection for workers, the
formation of cooperatives, creation of a social security fund, nutritional programs, recovery by the government of idle land, prison reform, sanitation
programs, and construction of sewer systems.

Politically and ideologically, the party's goals were to eliminate personality
cults in politics; to promulgate a new constitution; to achieve municipal autonomy, administrative control, and decentralization, equitable distribution of
national wealth in order to reduce regional disparities; and to integrate foreigners into the affairs of the country, settle Panamanian border disputes, and
stabilize the currency through a sound monetary policy.

In the area of education, the Reformist Party proposed to eradicate illiter-
acy; establish a university, agrarian schools, technical institutes, trade and arts
schools, and special education centers; incorporate the educational system into
the workplace; encourage cultural development in the countryside through
agricultural centers; respect freedom of religious conviction; and provide free
education and adequate funding for the educational system.

The reformist character of Volio's party was also evident in its efforts to
replace idols with ideals, and personal disputes with the fruitful struggle
between political values, a struggle that should engage all those who have a
political understanding of the need for sociopolitical development. . . .

The Reformist Party accepted the idea of private property, but as limited
by the common good. In other words, it viewed property in a social sense, in
which the state may intervene in disputes between capital and labor on behalf
of the poor and the weak who would otherwise be exploited.

Jorge Volio's religious and philosophical studies in Europe led him to look
closely at social Christian doctrine, which permanently influenced his thinking, goals, and works. Ideologically, his political movement represented a
union of social democracy with Christian democracy, in that its leader combined the influence of his Catholic and Christian background with a strict
adherence to the ideas of liberty and democracy. Volio himself stated that his
desire was that "the postulates of authentic Christianity" be realized in Costa
Rica. By the same token, he manifested his reformist position by attacking the
abuses of capitalism and proposing a number of solutions. But he also made
clear his anti-Communist position, calling communism "a cheap demagogy
that destroys society and the family," and the "negation of the human personality."

Volio's religious training strongly influenced his ideas, although his understanding of the role of the Church and clergy was nontraditional. He believed
that the priest "brings to the people the Christian doctrines of charity, good-
ness, [and] social justice" and that he "opens the minds of peasants, politicians,
economists, and sociologists, so that they may become aware of the problems
that oppress the contemporary world."

The reformism of Jorge Volio emerged at the beginning of the twentieth century, when Latin America was confronted with the need to incorporate into society both the middle class and the emerging working class. This was reflected in a number of reformist and "revolutionary" movements, such as the Mexican revolution in 1910, the political movement of José Batlle y Ordóñez in Uruguay, the Córdoba student movement in 1918, the political ideas of APRA in Peru, etc.[1] In essence, Jorge Volio was influenced not only by his European experience, but by the ideas and political movements in Latin America. His movement in Costa Rica should not be viewed as an isolated one.

His movement was popularly received both because of its objectives and because neither Socialist nor Communist parties existed in Costa Rica during the 1920s to attract the proletarian class, as would occur in the following decade. Nevertheless, the conservative elements of society—the ruling class and the Church hierarchy—opposed his reformism, and he was [later] attacked by the Communist Party, which accused him of having sold out to the capitalists and of not being sufficiently radical in doctrine or in practice. In fact he was opposed by the capitalists, the ecclesiastical hierarchy and the professional politicians. . . .

The importance of Volio's political movement is that it represents one of the first great attempts on the part of a small sector of the working class to accelerate the *Olimpo* [liberal elite] reforms, contrary to the desires of the coffee growers. His reformism was closely related to the natural evolution the country had been experiencing. That is, he was not attacking the fundamental traditions, the system itself, intending to replace it with another one. The Reformist Party program received the support of the masses because it addressed a number of democratic, nationalist, and anti-imperialist concerns. But as a reformist movement it did not intend to put the people, much less the working class, in power, nor did it aspire to abolish the state or social classes.

The reformism of Jorge Volio is considered a forerunner of the reforms enacted at the beginning of the 1940s. Most of the issues he raised were institutionalized by the middle of the century when his social Christian views were reflected in the government of Rafael Calderón Guardia and his *calderonista* Republican Party, whose activists included former leaders of the Reformist Party.

NOTE

1. APRA [*Alianza Popular Revolucionaria Americana* or American Popular Revolutionary Alliance] was a political party founded in 1924 by Peruvian Víctor Raúl Haya de la Torre. Originally Haya conceived of APRA as a continental movement seeking justice for Latin America's Indians and *mestizos.* APRA's impact was limited outside of Peru. With a somewhat changed ideology, it remains Peru's largest political party today.—EDs.

2.7 Minimum Program of the Communist Party of Costa Rica, 1932*

Various small leftist movements and labor organizations existed before the 1930s depression, but the Partido Comunista or Communist Party, was not formally established until June 16, 1931. Its first secretary general, Manuel Mora Valverde, would remain among the party's most prominent members for over fifty years. Although the party would go through various phases over the decades, it recognized from the start that revolution was not at hand, and often concentrated on promoting more pragmatic reforms. As Chapter III makes clear, the Communists would become a particularly influential force for social change during the 1940s. The Communist Party's first program, reproduced here, outlined a series of concrete social, political, and economic reforms. Written during the pre-1935 ultraleft period of the international Communist movement, it also voiced a commitment to continue struggling for "the formation of a great socialist soviet republic on the American continent."

COSTA RICA is a country with a dependent or semicolonial economy, inasmuch as its industry, commerce, and agriculture are influenced by the imperialism of the great capitalist countries (United States, England, etc.). Due to this fundamental fact, the complete Communist program (abolition of private property, socialization of the means of production, etc.) will not be implanted in the country without social revolution already having materialized in the metropolis upon which we depend economically, or without the concurrence of extraordinary special factors, which would permit the organization of the economy and social life of the country on totally communitarian bases without provoking imperialist interventions. As long as neither of these objective conditions have been met—a social revolution in the great capitalist countries or a conjunction of events so favorable as to allow us to achieve wholly the Communist program without provoking imperialist interventions—the COMMUNIST PARTY OF COSTA RICA will struggle via the conquest of power for the establishment of the following minimum program.

Political Goal

1. All political power for the working class. Creation of worker and peasant councils.

*This document originally appeared in the newspaper *Trabajo* on March 13, 1932.

Social Security and Insurance Policy

2. Establishment of social security, as the responsibility of the state, for unemployment, work-related accidents, illness, old age, maternity, etc.
3. Abolition of work for children under age fifteen. Regulation of labor for those fifteen and older, and for women, based on the principle of equal pay for equal work, with the fundamental purpose of protecting the weakness of those components of society.
4. Mandatory work for all consumers over eighteen years of age, according to their physical and intellectual capabilities.
5. Eight-hour workday for workers in general and a six-hour work day for those employed in especially strenuous industries (mining, etc.).
6. A minimum wage law, to be administered by a Council of Workers and Peasants, which will have the authority to set this salary in line with the cost of living.
7. Labor union organization laws. Explicit consecration of the "right to strike."
8. Provision of hygienic dwellings for urban and rural workers.
9. Hygienization of the country. State creation and maintenance of medical centers for infirm children; of modern dispensaries, hospitals, and maternity homes; of rest homes in the countryside for workers. Education campaign among the masses on the need for rational nutrition. War against social diseases (venereal disease, tuberculosis, drug addiction, etc.).
10. Suppression of the [state-owned] National Liquor Factory.
11. Political-juridical emancipation of women.

Economic Policy

12. Revision of the treaties and conventions celebrated by the state with national and foreign capitalism. Repudiation of treaty articles onerous to the country.
13. Agrarian legislation eliminating *latifundismo* and authorizing expropriation of uncultivated lands for the public good. Socialized exploitation of all lands belonging to the state.
14. Development of infrastructure in all regions of the country (new roads, railways into the interior, etc.). Nationalization of the transport system.
15. State expansion of agriculture and industry, based on rational social planning.
16. Nationalization of the subsoil.
17. State control of industries that by their character constitute monopolies of public services (electrical industry, energy, etc.).
18. Complete revision of the tariff and tax system of the country.
19. Creation of a National Economic Technical Council.

Public Administration

20. Reduction to a minimum of the bureaucratic apparatus.
21. Civil Service Law.
22. Establishment of the principle that no salary of a public employee can be greater than the maximum salary of a worker.

Education Policy

23. Complete reform of education laws, in accord with the following basic principles: a) preference given to preschool education (foundling homes, schools for children aged two to four years, kindergarten, schools for mothers); b) work as the axis around which primary and secondary schools will revolve (special attention to manual and agricultural labor); c) free education at all levels and mandatory education in the levels required to produce free and conscientious citizens.
24. Constant and resolute cooperation in the labors to be carried out for the formation of a great socialist soviet republic on the American continent.

2.8 The Great Atlantic Banana Plantation Strike of 1934*

BY CARLOS LUIS FALLAS

Carlos Luis Fallas (1909–66) began to work for the United Fruit Company at age sixteen. Several years later he returned to his native city of Alajuela and became involved in the labor movement and the Communist Party. In 1933 he was sentenced for his organizing activities to a year of internal exile in Costa Rica's remote Atlantic region. It was there that he became one of the leaders of the 1934 banana workers' strike, vividly described in this speech delivered twenty-one years later to an audience of striking union members. The 1934 walkout was a pivotal event in Costa Rican history, with some 10,000 workers on strike in a country whose total population at the time was barely 500,000. It was also one of the largest strikes ever in Latin America against a North American company.

"Calufa," as he is affectionately known in Costa Rica, wrote several books considered Costa Rican literary classics, among them Mamita Yunai, *which is about life on the Atlantic plantations of the United Fruit Company.*

COMPAÑEROS:

. . . I want us to remember tonight some of the past struggles, so you'll know that the workers of the banana companies of Costa Rica always knew what

*Based on the stenographic version of a speech given on September 18, 1955, and reprinted as an appendix to *Mamita Yunai* (San José: Librería Lehmann, 1980).

it was to fight. Before 1934 life in the United Fruit Company banana plantations was hell. . . . I was a very young boy when I arrived in the banana zone.
. . . We had a hard and humiliating life, working in the banana zone of the
Atlantic. . . . At that time, in the immense banana plantations of the Atlantic,
there was not a single dispensary, nor were there medical services of any type,
with the exception of the Limón Hospital. . . . The commissaries, through
which the United exercised a total monopoly of commerce in the banana
region, sold articles of whatever quality they pleased and at the most scandalous prices, even though through the tolerance of our government, the company
did not pay taxes of any type for importing these articles. . . .

The United has always known how to defend very well its great interests
in Costa Rica. . . . At that time, production in the Atlantic was organized in
a very particular way. Its policy was to create private planters and national
farm owners. It rented land and advanced the money to them; and if they
already owned land, it simply gave them the money they needed to start the
banana plantation. But in every case obligating them to sign one-sided contracts, written up by the company's own lawyers, according to which those
private farmers were committed to sell their bananas exclusively to the United
Fruit Company at the meanest price indicated per bunch received (note well:
per bunch received), less a percentage that was subtracted from each bunch as
a payment on the debt contracted. . . .

The United Fruit Company, which has always monopolized the United
States' banana market, could operate in that market at the expense of the
private [Costa Rican] farmer, because sometimes when the price tended to go
down in the Yankee market it was more convenient for the United to throw
away the bananas here, since the bananas that were discarded were not its loss
but the national farmers' loss. Everything was organized with the intention of
facilitating these infamous operations. . . .

And when a Costa Rican firm began to purchase all those discarded bananas
from the farmers at a magnificent price to sell within the country and also
abroad, the United forced the farmers to chop up the bananas that they threw
away, so they wouldn't be able to sell them. That's how far the United Fruit
Company went.

The rulers would humble themselves before the powerful foreign companies
in order to obtain onerous loans from them. . . . Our bourgeois press servilely
buttered up the United in order to obtain expensive advertisements. The
national farmers worried about assuring themselves a small profit despite the
rejected fruit, sacrificing the workers. In other words, they defended themselves at the price of their workers' hunger.

The labors of the "cut" or harvest were obligatory for all the plantation
workers. On harvesting days all those required by the boss had to work as
cutters, *concheros* [workers who catch the bunches of bananas after the cutter
cuts them], *muleros* [those who carry the bananas on mules to the carts], and
carreros [who receive the fruit from the *muleros,* put it in carts, and carry it
to the main train line]. And since the United's ships "couldn't wait at port,"

the jobs had to be done at any time and under any circumstances. Sometimes sick men had to do the cutting in furious storms. Sometimes they had to finish hauling the bananas at night under the rain, using gas lamps for light, struggling with frisky mules, running on badly constructed rails, crossing improvised and dangerous bridges. And that's why the same accidents occurred time and again. And all these labors of the "cut" were paid by the farmers at so many cents per bunch received (note well, *compañeros, per bunch received*). This means that workers on a small plantation who had sweated and toiled all night to put 1,500 bunches of bananas on the platform only saw payment on that occasion for the 225 bunches received by the United. The harvesting and hauling of the other 1,275 was for those workers a futile effort, work and sweat thrown away.

The company, to be safe from possible rebellions, would stir up the hatred of the whites against the blacks and of the blacks against the whites. And it was successful. More than once, when the black workers there in Limón were exasperated and tried to rebel, the white workers willingly offered themselves to help abort that effort. Of course, the black workers responded in the same way when the whites tried to protest. The company tranquilly exploited each group equally [see Reading 4.10].

The United's representatives never thought a serious strike was possible on the Atlantic plantations. Blinded by their stupid arrogance, deaf to the clamor of the peons, they could not understand that the workers were human beings, with the right to life and the spirit to fight for it. Nor could they apprehend the profound discontent that agitated the workers. But there on the plantations the workers, fed up with mistreatment, exploitation, and misery, remembering the violent rebellion that had occurred years earlier on the plantations of the north coast of Honduras (a rebellion that was brutally smashed), spoke more frequently of demanding improvements with the machete and the shotgun, of having a shootout with the gringos, of razing the plantations with machetes. It was precisely to avoid disorderly explosions of violence, which could bring no good to the workers, that we began to organize the plantations, to orient the workers toward an organized struggle capable of taking on the powerful imperialist enterprise.

Compañeros, it was a hard task, requiring great patience. We covered every inch of the Atlantic zone by foot, through the jungle and plantations, in the rain and often in darkness. Frequently we held meetings late at night at distant camps, so government agents and the company wouldn't catch on. I called them "meetings in underwear." In spite of these precautions we had to hold the Congress of Workers of the Atlantic, convoked to discuss and approve the list of demands that would be presented to the United, in the middle of the jungle in the glow of the gas lamps and among clouds of mosquitoes, because small squads of police were already roaming the plantations looking for the Communist agitators. . . .

The list included demands for the national farmers, such as an end to the unjustified rejection of fruit, better prices for their bananas, etc. But the farmers nevertheless all pronounced themselves against the strike from the outset. . . . It was fear of the powerful imperialist enterprise!

The demands were sent to the management as a basis for negotiation and a copy was also sent to the president of the republic, Ricardo Jiménez. During that time Mr. Chittenden was the United manager in Costa Rica, a true exponent of the Yankee imperialist policy, an insolent and rude gringo who considered Central Americans an inferior race and was not about to concede the workers the right to converse with him. Three days before the strike broke out, we sent a new copy of the demands to Limón with three *compañeros* charged with depositing it in the very hands of Mr. Chittenden. He refused to see them and had the port police arrest and jail them. We were told that on the day before the strike, Mr. Chittenden phoned the gringo bosses of all the United banana plantations and all of them assured him proudly that work continued as usual on their plantations. The next day, more than 90 percent of the banana plantations were paralyzed, and two or three days later all the Atlantic laborers had joined the strike! Ten thousand strikers in the province of Limón! . . .

Days passed. A violent storm broke out in the entire Atlantic region. But even more violent was the defamation campaign the bourgeois newspapers let loose against the strikers. . . . According to those newspapers and those newspaper writers, the strike had no reason for being, the workers on the plantations earned well, lived well, they were very happy and the majority opposed the strike. According to those newspapers and writers, the strike had been provoked artificially by an audacious group of Communists, professional agitators; the Communists, on a direct order from Moscow, kept the strike going by frightening the workers; the Communists were interested in provoking disorders and, above all, in harming the great American enterprises that operated in our country! It was necessary for the government to proceed energetically to put an end once and for all to the murky and criminal actions of the national Communists. That intense and dirty press campaign disoriented large sectors of Costa Rican public opinion, which applauded the dispatch to the plantations of the first hundreds of armed police under the command of Colonel Gallegos, who has since become sadly celebrated. And what about the outstanding Costa Rican intellectuals? With one or two exceptions they kept a comfortable silence, some because they couldn't descend from their olympian heights to intervene in an affair so plebeian as a vulgar banana strike; others because they didn't want to appear as blind instruments of the Communists. . . . Only the organized workers, especially those in the capital, gave their enthusiastic support. They collected money, they sent food, although the police confiscated almost everything they sent. And in the meantime thousands and thousands of workers, their wives and children went hungry on the somber plantations of the Atlantic.

We had bananas. And the strike brigades were organized and went to the faraway coast to gather turtle eggs and meat, to hunt in the jungle, to collect the *yuca* and *ñamé* roots that the poor farmers of the region, black and white, gave to the movement. But all of that was not enough, for there were many people on the plantations. . . . It rained day and night, the entire region was an immense sea of mud, and the most active strikers, who constantly came and went in groups to keep watch on the more distant plantations, had their shoes destroyed, ripped to pieces, and they walked barefoot.

And each day the number of those prostrated by fever increased. Nonetheless, the workers, their wives, and their children remained firm and disciplined, without committing a single act of violence, prepared to win the strike with their prolonged sacrifices. . . .

Police, trained beforehand, tried to provoke the strikers. When they saw a group go by they would yell, "Nicas! Faggots! Why don't you stand up like men?" (because according to the bourgeois press the strikers were all Nicaraguans). And the people would arrive at the camp at Twenty-Six Miles where the Strike Committee was, crying with rage and saying, "*Compañero* Fallas, let us show those pricks that we're real men! Let us go give them a surprise tonight!"

We had to hold an assembly to teach the strikers against responding to these provocations and we sent *compañeros* all over sounding the voice of alarm. The United Fruit Company, trying to take advantage of the workers' hunger and misery, also planned base provocations. One rainy evening a group of strikers, all of them hungry, tired, almost naked, with their shoes falling apart, were returning along the railroad tracks. When the employees of the Matina Commissary saw them go by, they called them over in a flattering tone, "Come here, boys, we're with the strike! Where are you coming from?"

"From guarding Damasco and Diamantes [plantations]."

"And you haven't eaten anything?"

"No, and we've been up since four in the morning."

"Poor things!" the employees of the commissary said and gave each of the strikers a beer, a loaf of bread, a piece of cheese, and a Camel cigarette. And afterward they said, "It's a shame that you're suffering hunger and are needy, when we have piles of clothes, shoes, and foodstuffs here. We would give you all of this gladly. But if we do it, we will be punished. Come in a group of at least fifty and take everything that's here and in that way we'll tell the gringos it was due to circumstances beyond our control and there was nothing we could do."

As soon as they arrived at Twenty-Six Miles, those *compañeros* told me what had happened and added very happily, "*Compañero* Fallas, we and the women and the little ones are undergoing hardships because we're stupid. The boys at the commissary are very good, they're with us, they want to help us. Let's go bring all the food that's there!"

How naïve! The employees would give us that food so afterward the United and the press at the company's service would accuse us of assault and robbery. Which would be an excuse for the authorities to brutally attack the workers! We had to hold another assembly to alert the workers against these new provocative maneuvers. So then the United, with the help of Colonel Gallegos, staged the plundering of a few commissaries, among them the one at Bananito.

But the simulation was so coarse that they were not able to obtain the order from President Jiménez for the massacre they had planned.

Local growers and plantation owners also maneuvered against the strikers. With government help, they tried to recruit scabs from Puntarenas and Guanacaste. Some of them took strong contingents of armed police to their plantations to scare the workers. . . . But in spite of it all, days went by and more days went by and the strike continued in the entire region. . . .

Jiménez's administration sent its minister of government, Santos León Herrera, to the Atlantic to solve the conflict "directly with the workers." Don Santos traveled throughout the region in a United train with his secretaries and surrounded by journalists. They would arrive at a town and gather the neighbors together (the vast majority women, because the more combative strikers remained in the mountains) and they would tell them more or less the following: "Here is the minister with extensive powers to favorably resolve the complaints and demands of the workers. The government wishes to resolve your situation in the best possible way, but by talking to you directly, you who really work and sweat. Because the government, the company and the national farmers want nothing to do with the Communist agitators, who have never worked and who are now fooling the workers. Come on, what do you want?"

And the people would answer, "What we want is for you to go to Twenty-Six Miles and discuss the solution with our Strike Committee. You have nothing to solve with us!"

Everywhere the minister received the same response. And *compañeros,* do you know what the journalists concluded to explain that surprising unanimity of opinions? Well, that we, the Communists, were probably using who knows what extraordinary means of communication (a Soviet invention, possibly) that allowed us to scare and train the residents of each town moments before the minister arrived to visit them. Blind and deaf, they do not know the workers' soul nor do they understand their language.

In the end, don Santos, his secretaries, and the journalists finally arrived at Twenty-Six Miles in search of the Strike Committee. The minister's propositions were unacceptable. But since hundreds of workers were concentrated there and since the press had declared that a few Communists from Twenty-Six Miles imposed their will on the workers, we took advantage of the occasion to show the journalists the falsity of such a declaration. Don Santos offered us, in the name of the local growers, an increase of a few centavos per cubic meter of ditches dug. We would then yell, "Ditchdiggers, come find out the increase the minister is offering you!"

And a hundred or more men, half-dressed, skinny, yellowish, eaten up by malaria, would come closer upon hearing the proposed increase and would yell furiously, "Go sweat up your armpits and eat mud for a little while, so you can find out what it takes to make a cubic meter of ditch."

The same thing happened with the *hacheros* [workers who fell trees after the bananas are planted on a field for the first time] and with the rest of the workers. The solution roundly failed. . . .

In spite of all the lies and the provocations, the discipline of the workers never wavered. And four long weeks of a hard struggle had gone by . . . when President Jiménez, after many conversations with the United's agents and the national farmers' representatives, resolved to call the strikers' delegates to San José to discuss a formal solution that brought an end to the strike. We came to the capital and negotiated for many hours and at last a solution pretty favorable to the workers was signed, that the government promised would be respected.

The newspaper sirens were sounded announcing the end of the strike. And we went to the Atlantic zone to give the order to work. That was a great day of celebration on the banana plantations of the Atlantic! After that everyone returned to work. The strikers concentrated at Twenty-Six Miles returned to their respective places of work. The vigilance brigades disbanded, as did those that took care of our communications service, and the Strike Committee was dissolved.

By pure chance, I was ill and decided to remain at camp Twenty-Six Miles a few more days with some of the boys who wanted to stay with me. What luck! The first day of work at all the United plantations, the gringo bosses arrived early in the morning with their foremen and police escorts to tell the workers that there wasn't any kind of deal and that they would continue working under the same conditions as before. Because, they said, I, Carlos Luis Fallas, who was already on a boat headed toward the United States, had sold myself to the company for thirty thousand dollars. Something like the thirty coins of Judas! Taken by surprise, the workers hurled thousands of curses upon me and, furious, declared themselves on strike again. Very soon they realized they had been tricked, that it was all a vile provocative maneuver organized by the United's agents, with the complicity of the Costa Rican military that operated in the region. But it was too late!

Colonel Gallegos, under the pretext that the workers had broken the agreement, came down brutally on the workers. Rifles and machine guns crackled on the gloomy Atlantic plantations. Hundreds of men were mistreated and imprisoned. Hundreds of Nicaraguan workers were thrown out of the country with only the rags on their backs, and hundreds of women and children were left without support. And then, yes, the workers did respond to violence with violence, razing banana plantations with machetes, destroying train tracks and bridges. And Colonel Gallegos answered in turn by burning camps and straw huts, threatening the neutral population with terrible reprisals if they helped the strikers. . . .

They were two black weeks of violence and terror on the plantations of the Atlantic! Two weeks that forged forever the indomitable, combative spirit of the workers of the banana plantations, which has since been proven so many times. *Compañeros,* that great strike of 1934, so violent in its last stage, so important to the later development of the Costa Rican revolutionary and anti-imperialist movement, made the United Fruit Company back down.

CHAPTER III

The Crisis of the 1940s and the 1948 Civil War

Editors' Introduction

The 1940s were a decade in which Costa Rica, as sociologist José Luis Vega has noted, was unable to go forward and unable to go back.[1] The result would be civil war.

The decade began unspectacularly. Rafael Angel Calderón Guardia, an upper-class, European-educated physician, was elected president with strong support from fellow members of his class. He soon surprised and antagonized them by advocating a broad range of social reforms that included a social security program for the ill, disabled, poor, and elderly (see Reading 3.1). He initiated a progressive labor code and the Social Guarantees, a series of constitutional amendments codifying workers' rights. After 1942, in a move widely viewed as an attack on private property, the government seized large coffee and sugar holdings from people of German and Italian descent and forced many to wait out the war in internment camps.

Calderón did not consider himself a radical or even a populist. Rather, the implementation of his program was essentially elitist, with changes imposed from above in the paternalistic manner typical of enlightened upper-class reformers elsewhere. Calderón did little to alter the nation's economic and class structures, despite the need for major changes after the dislocations of the depression and World War II. He offered no real challenge to the social and economic dominance of the coffee oligarchy, the bankers, or the urban commercial interests. Yet because of his reforms and social vision, they viewed him as an enemy and a traitor to his class.

Politically, Calderón paid a steep price for his reforms. Abandoned by his erstwhile backers from the upper class, he was forced to seek new allies. Viewing his reform program as a natural outgrowth of his social Christian training and beliefs, he turned to the Church hierarchy for political support and granted Catholicism an influence in public life it had not enjoyed since its eclipse during the anticlerical liberal period of the late nineteenth century.[2] The new archbishop, Víctor Sanabria, eagerly supported Calderón in order to heighten Church influence, to further reformist goals that he genuinely shared, and to undercut the Communists, whose own drive for political change was gaining force.

Calderón's attempt to broaden his political base also led him directly to an unlikely alliance with the Communist Party (see Reading 3.2). The Communists at this time were seeking evolution rather than revolution, reflecting their wartime policy of building alliances against fascism and a realistic assessment of what was possible in Costa Rica. The main base of the Popular Vanguard Party—as the Communist Party was known after 1943—remained in the banana zones, where it played a key role in labor organizing (see Reading 2.8). In the more populous central Costa Rica, the Communists' appeal was limited and their support restricted to a few intellectuals and some sectors within the small urban working class.

Social reforms, however, were only one of several changes Costa Rica required. With the closing of European coffee markets at the outbreak of World War II, economic growth slowed and expanded public spending on the new social programs fueled inflation. The country's extreme dependence on coffee and banana exports could only be modified with economic diversification and industrialization, both of which became key planks in the platform of the anti-*calderonista* Social Democrats (see Reading 3.3). And, as John Patrick Bell has pointed out, Calderón neglected three other controversial areas: the need for sweeping electoral reform, especially important after the abuses committed under Calderón's predecessor León Cortés; the issue of the Communists' strength—which would come to deeply disturb Washington; and fiscal corruption and mismanagement.[3] Calderón would later admit that administration was not his forte and integrity not always a characteristic of his associates.[4] By focusing almost exclusively on social reforms, Calderón let his opponents seize, and ultimately monopolize, the other issues.

The opposition encompassed a disparate array of political forces that initially had little in common. It included members of the old elite, who felt betrayed by Calderón, as well as professionals and small-business people, a rising social group that sought to radically change the socioeconomic structure in order to create a more secure place for itself. While threatened as employers by Calderón's labor code, small-business owners also resented the coffee elite's near total control of the nation's banks and thus sought to democratize the economy. As Jacobo Schifter points out, in an unflattering but provocative description (Reading 3.4), this group sought to transform anachronistic and restrictive economic, social, and political structures to further its own aspirations.

The young and ambitious men who formed the leadership of this new social group gravitated to two main opposition organizations, *Acción Demócrata* (Democratic Action) and the *Centro para el Estudio de los Problemas Nacionales* (Center for the Study of National Problems).

A youthful and progressive wing of Cortés's Democratic Party, *Acción Demócrata* had a social democratic outlook and emphasized administrative, fiscal, and electoral reform. Among its key leaders was José "Pepe" Figueres, who received national attention in July 1942 after a German submarine torpedoed a United Fruit Company ship in Limón harbor (see Reading 3.2). A little-known farmer and the son of Spanish immigrants, Figueres delivered a fiery radio speech lambasting Calderón's government and its handling of the riots that followed the ship's sinking. Arrested in mid-sentence while on the air, Figueres was briefly jailed and then sent to Mexico, where he remained for two years, the first government critic exiled since the Tinoco dictatorship. Figueres would work with more conciliatory opposition figures over the next six years, but began preparing for an armed uprising almost as soon as he was forced abroad. He also formed alliances with other Central American and Caribbean opposition movements and helped to create the so-called Caribbean Legion, a military force of exiles from throughout the region who hoped to topple such dictators as Nicaragua's Anastasio Somoza García and the Dominican Republic's Rafael Trujillo (see Reading 6.1).

The other main opposition organization, usually known simply as *El Centro,* was somewhat further to the left than *Acción Demócrata* and was, initially at least, a study group composed of young intellectuals concerned with theoretical and philosophical questions. But as Costa Rica became more polarized toward the close of Calderón's administration, the *Centro* took on a more overtly political role. Led by Rodrigo Facio, a prominent intellectual, the *Centro*'s theoretical bent complemented the more pragmatic *Acción Demócrata,* which had greater political experience from its days as a faction within Cortés's party. In March 1945, the *Centro* and *Acción Demócrata* merged and became the Social Democratic Party (Reading 3.3). The Social Democrats pledged to build a political movement based on principles instead of personalities and vowed to struggle for the "Second Republic" of Costa Rica.

The various opposition groups did not coalesce in time to prevent a *calderonista* candidate from winning the 1944 elections. Backed by the "Victory Bloc" of the *calderonistas,* the Church and the Communists, Teodoro Picado defeated León Cortés for the presidency in elections marred by violence and, said the opposition, by fraud. Picado solidified Calderón's reforms, but took only limited steps to extend them. His emphasis on reform within well-defined boundaries led some Cortés partisans, upper-class supporters of the opposition, to make overtures to the administration. They were motivated by dread of further reforms that would damage their interests and by alarm over growing Communist influence in the government. This anti-Communist sentiment intensified after World War II, when the Popular Front era ended and the cold war began.[5] Attempts to unite the *calderonista* and anti-*calderonista* factions of the oligarchy collapsed with the unexpected death of Cortés in March 1946. The conservative opposition splintered, with one faction following Fernando Castro Cervantes, who would try to overthrow Picado in an abortive 1946 coup, and another following the powerful and wealthy newspaper publisher Otilio Ulate.

Picado lacked the ability to heal the country or repair its economy, still suffering from the effects of the depression and World War II. The faltering economy, the imposition of higher taxes on the wealthy, the Communist presence, widespread official corruption, and the questionable election practices of the ruling party provided an ample basis for discontent. The various opposition groups formed what seemed to many an unnatural alliance, with the conservative oligarchs and the firebrand social democrats joining in 1947–48 to fight the candidacy of Calderón, who was still backed by the Church and the Communists in his second presidential bid.[6] During the campaign, alliances were formed not out of shared beliefs, but from a desire to defeat common foes. In many ways, the most radical group was not the Communists, who had secured themselves a niche in the power structure from which they were able to engineer some significant reforms, but the young social democrats, who wanted to completely reshape society and the economy in a basically capitalist yet modern and progressive framework.

After great efforts to forge unity, the opposition in 1947 rallied around the conservative Ulate as a candidate in the presidential elections due the following year. Tensions throughout that year were high and sometimes led to violence. This provoked a general strike by small businesses in support of the opposition, known as *la huelga de los brazos caídos,* literally, the strike of the fallen arms. Settlement terms included an agreement on electoral freedoms and a measure to grant the Election Tribunal power over the police in matters pertaining to the campaign or the balloting.

Tensions did not diminish, and they spilled over during the elections in February 1948. Ulate won, but the government and the Communists cried fraud (see Reading 3.4). The *calderonistas,* however, had won control of the unicameral legislature, which had to ratify the election results. Some ballots were destroyed by a mysterious fire while in storage at a girls' high school. Congress, controlled by the *calderonistas,* refused to declare Ulate president and annulled the elections on March 1. Twelve days later, the civil war began with simultaneous uprisings near Figueres's farm in the south and in San Ramón in the north.[7]

By early April, the insurgents had control of much of southern Costa Rica and several key cities. But *Vanguardia Popular* maintained control of the capital. Anastasio Somoza García, fearing that a victorious Figueres would allow his Caribbean Legion collaborators to use Costa Rica as a base to attack Nicaragua, offered to help "pacify" Costa Rica—but on his own terms. The Communists, ironically, threatened to join forces with the insurgents to fight a *somocista* invasion. Picado, who had little stomach for a foreign invasion and even less for civil war, managed to get negotiations under way, with the help of foreign diplomats, around April 13. Over the next few days, the situation worsened. Rebel forces under Figueres were poised in Cartago, some twelve miles from the capital, where a militia of Communist banana workers commanded by Manuel Mora was preparing to resist. Mora's militiamen, disparagingly known as *mariachis* because they wore Mexican-style ponchos to ward off the highland chill, moved hundreds of their prisoners to top floors of buildings where they would bear the brunt of any artillery or air attack. Meanwhile, the Nicaraguan National Guard occupied the northern town of Villa Quesada and rumors of a U.S. invasion to rout the Communists abounded. By April 17, Costa Rica confronted the strong possibility of "an unprecedented holocaust."[8] Negotiations appeared to be the only alternative.

On April 19, the two sides signed a pact at the Mexican Embassy. It named Santos León Herrera, a senior official in the Picado administration, interim president, promised protection against reprisals by both sides, and guaranteed a general amnesty. Although Mora won a clause guaranteeing protection and expansion of workers' rights, in the war's aftermath, the Communist Party was outlawed and six of its members executed while in government custody.[9] When Figueres marched into the capital on April 24, some 2,000 people had died—in a nation of 750,000. Most of the fatalities were government supporters or civilians. Only about 100 were insurgent combatants.

In May, Figueres and Ulate signed their own pact, recognizing Ulate's victory in the presidential election, but making Figueres the head of a junta that governed the country by decree for eighteen months. Figueres did not achieve all his goals during those months, but did bring about significant economic reforms, such as nationalization of banking (discussed in Chapter IV). On December 1, 1948, he also announced that Costa Rica would dissolve its army—which since the end of the Guardia era in the 1880s had been a relatively small and weak institution—and the new constitution in 1949 permanently abolished the army.

Figueres's champions regard that move—replete with such dramatic symbols as taking a hammer to the tower of San José's main fort—as a visionary, definitive blow to militarism. His foes regard abolition of the military as an astute maneuver, reflecting awareness that he had not solidified his power base and that lacking the certain loyalty of the army, he would do better to disband it. The truth is probably a blend of both views. Figueres, as his own actions in the 1940s attest, was not a pacifist. Neither was he militarily helpless. He controlled the victorious National Liberation Movement forces, who would be loyal to him if armed conflict broke out within the insurgent alliance, splintering now that its members no longer had a common enemy. But he also recognized the benefits—economic, political, and moral—of getting rid of the army and the expediency of turning power over to Ulate. The civil war after all had ostensibly been fought to defend Ulate's victory in the 1948 election. Figueres, by dissolving the junta and fulfilling commitments made to Ulate's conservative backers, enhanced his own legitimacy. He would use the years of Ulate's presidency to build his own electoral base and create the National Liberation Party, which has dominated Costa Rica ever since.

Electoral honesty, communism, government corruption—these were the themes that the first generation of post–civil war scholars stressed in their interpretations of 1948. More recent analyses, some of which are included in this chapter, probe beneath the quasi-official version of history, which has tended to acquire the same semimythical status as accounts of the bucolic democracy inherited from the colonial period.[10] The traditional versions retain some validity; those explanations are part of the story. But recently scholars have stressed that the 1948 civil war was fought as a three-way struggle within the bourgeoisie, which was undergoing a process of modernization and transformation. *Calderonismo,* one of these three forces, was a form of populism. It championed the poor and struggled to win their support. But it was tainted by corruption and chose allies—the Communists—that made it an easy target of antigovernment propaganda and earned it widespread distrust, particularly among the peasantry and the urban middle class.

The two other bourgeois groups were the traditional agroexporting class and the new class of young professionals. The agroexporters wanted to roll back reforms that threatened their traditional prerogatives. The professionals, entrepreneurs, and budding manufacturers were eager to transform the economy and the state, instituting a new form of state capitalism that would guarantee them power, enable them to expand economically beyond the parameters of the traditional coffee economy, and lay the groundwork for industrialization.

In many ways, the most significant battle would be fought not between the winners and losers of the war of 1948 but by the two victorious groups, the conservative *ulatistas* and the social democratic *figueristas.* Schifter (Reading 3.4) is, to a degree, correct to argue that modern Costa Rican democracy was an inadvertent side effect of the civil war, a form of "class neutralization" that was an outgrowth of the impasse reached by the two victorious factions. But ultimately, the conservatives, while they remained economically powerful, were not "neutralized" but overpowered at the polls. For nearly forty years, Figueres and his followers have dominated but not monopolized Costa Rican politics. Whatever their initial intentions, under their rule the wounds of the 1940s have largely healed and a more genuine, albeit imperfect, democracy has taken root.

NOTES

1. José Luis Vega Carballo, *Hacia una interpretación del desarrollo costarricense: ensayo sociológico* (San José: Editorial Porvenir, 1980), p. 204.

2. Calderón allowed the Jesuits to return to the country for the first time since their expulsion under President Próspero Fernández in the 1880s.

3. For the best general work in English on the 1948 civil war, see John Patrick Bell, *Crisis in Costa Rica: The Revolution of 1948* (Austin: University of Texas Press, 1971).

4. Ibid., p. 63. Indeed, even though Calderón's salary was only $68 a week, he became quite wealthy during his four years as president, acquiring several large properties and building luxurious homes for himself and members of his family. "It was," writes journalist William Krehm, "too bewildering a success story for the liking of the *Ticos,* who had always taken pride in the poverty of their retiring presidents." See *Democracies and Tyrannies of the Caribbean* (Westport, Conn.: Lawrence Hill, 1984), p. 134.

5. By the beginning of the 1947 election campaign, even Calderón felt it prudent to declare himself an anti-Communist. Picado asserted that his government was not and had never been Communist and that Costa Rica was totally identified with U.S. foreign policy and the democratic doctrine of the West. See Manuel Rojas Bolaños, *Lucha social y guerra civil en Costa Rica* (San José: Editorial Porvenir, 1979), p. 136.

6. Costa Rican presidents are allowed only one term. In the past, however, they were permitted multiple terms, as long as they were not served consecutively. Many Latin American countries have similar rules.

7. A useful summary of the military campaigns in the civil war is in Oscar Aguilar Bulgarelli, *Costa Rica y sus hechos políticos de 1948* (San José: Editorial Costa Rica, 1969), pp. 320–50. According to Vega Carballo, *Interpretación* (p. 208), the government army "had no real officer corps and regular soldiers numbered no more than 300, reinforced by some poorly trained volunteers." Ironically, this force owed much of its modest fighting potential to a small shipment of U.S. lend-lease armament sent to Costa Rica during Calderón's presidency. See Krehm, *Democracies,* p. 136.

8. Bell, *Crisis in Costa Rica,* p. 150. Bell writes that Picado was informed that day that the United States had organized a force in the Canal Zone. It was to be ready to move as a "police force" to intervene in San José against the capital's Communist defenders. Other accounts say that the United States and Great Britain actually had ships off Costa Rican coasts. See Tord Hoivik and Solveig Aas, "Demilitarization in Costa Rica: A Farewell to Arms?" *Journal of Peace Research* 18, no. 4 (1981): 336. Whether the United States would have intervened militarily if the conflict continued remains in dispute.

9. Jacobo Schifter, *La fase oculta de la guerra civil en Costa Rica* (San José: EDUCA, 1979), p. 114.

10. For an excellent concise discussion of the main tenets of the new scholarship, see Lowell Gudmundson, "Costa Rica and the 1948 Revolution: Rethinking the Social Democratic Paradigm," *Latin American Research Review* 19, no. 1 (1984): 235–42.

3.1 Social Reform in Costa Rica: Social Security and the Presidency of Rafael Angel Calderón Guardia*

BY MARK ROSENBERG

Rafael Angel Calderón, in the eyes of Mark Rosenberg, was a populist without knowing it. A physician and devout Catholic, he came to power as a representative of the upper class, but with a more finely honed social conscience than was typical of that class. Once in office, he immediately promulgated a series of reforms that antagonized many of his initial supporters. Although his reforms were farsighted and ultimately greatly beneficial to the poor and to the hitherto weak organized labor movement, they were also reforms imposed by an elite, and characterized by the traditional paternalism of the upper class. In Rosenberg's view, Calderón revolutionized Costa Rican politics by demonstrating the reformist potential of this state, without ever comprehending that power himself.

Rosenberg is a political scientist and director of the Latin American and Caribbean Center at Florida International University in Miami.

BY 1940, most South American countries had undertaken state-sponsored programs to meet basic problems arising from urbanization and the economic depression of the 1930s. . . . The social reform orientation in the southern continent contrasted with explicit antireformism in the Central American republics. In the early 1940s, however, Costa Rica attempted to break the traditional pattern and although José Figueres and his Social Democratic followers are generally credited with being Costa Rica's most important social reformers, it was in fact Dr. Rafael Angel Calderón Guardia, and not Figueres, who established the modern reformist basis of the Costa Rican state. Calderón introduced three measures fundamental to social reform: social security, social guarantees, and labor regulation. While Figueres was able to use reformist rhetoric with a few select public policies in the early 1950s to earn his reputation as a populist, it was Calderón who reoriented the state as an instrument of the working and middle groups during the 1940s. This reorientation is remarkable if viewed in the general Central American context: Calderón's presidency (1940–44) coincided with the personalist, antireformist dictatorships of Anastasio Somoza in Nicaragua, Tiburcio Carías in Honduras, Maximiliano Hernández Martínez in El Salvador, and Jorge Ubico in Guatemala.

*Excerpted from *Hispanic American Historical Review*, 61, no. 2 (1981): 278–96.

. . . Under his presidential sponsorship, social protection in fact became a public right, mandated by the state.

Social security would provide a means by which to protect laborers against risks that made it impossible to work and earn an income. It might also forestall future class struggle in Costa Rica. Thus, social security was seen as the "only formula to harmonize the conflicting interests of capital and labor." Calderón's Catholic, paternalistic definition of the problem helped to clarify social reality. To him, class differences should not exist, "for the only differences were between men who suffered and men whose duty it was to alleviate that suffering."

Studies on the subject have treated the Calderón reforms as though they were rationally and logically conceived as a means by which Calderón could establish a political constituency within the growing ranks of organized labor at a time when his traditional base of support among the coffee oligarchy was being eroded. In fact . . . his social security program, introduced in 1941, was not presented in a larger reformist package, nor was it the result of an articulate or well-defined working-class or other interest-group pressure. It was an elitist reform, paternalistically sponsored by the state. Coupled with Calderón's poor political and administrative management of the Costa Rican state and his close association with the Catholic Church, this reform cost him heavily in conservative circles, a situation that Calderón did not realize until mid-1942. It was then that he consciously sought an alternative following. State-sponsored social reform through "social guarantees" and the "labor code" was used explicitly to generate that support. . . .

THE SOCIAL REFORM ISSUE

Before 1940 Costa Rica had made but little progress at the public level toward mass social welfare. A limited workmen's compensation program was established in 1925 under President Ricardo Jiménez. . . . Limited old-age pension programs were provided ad hoc for the country's teachers and communications workers. . . . Throughout the critical 1930s, the social question was systematically neglected for a number of reasons: (a) the lack of competitive political parties that might employ social welfare as a political device; (b) the absence of a populist movement that might use social programs as a means to mobilize the masses; (c) the rural orientation of the small, well-organized Communist Party; and (d) the continued political domination of Costa Rican politics by the traditional coffee oligarchy.

The Costa Rican presidential race of 1940 resembled most other Costa Rican electoral campaigns during the twentieth century. The oligarchy's candidate was Dr. Rafael Angel Calderón, whose political career was undistinguished except for his leadership of Congress and his widespread popularity. Calderón's only opponent was the Communist leader Manuel Mora Valverde, of the *Bloque de Obreros y Campesinos,* which favored a Moscow-oriented foreign policy but a reformist domestic policy milder than Calderón's. . . . Even while Calderón enjoyed the support of the country's oligarchy, however, he differed from his predecessors in his approach to social problems. He openly acknowledged his profound belief in the logic of Catholic social reform doctrine, a view learned during the late 1920s under the guidance of one of Europe's leading Catholic social reformers, Désiré Joseph Cardinal Mercier, in Louvain, Belgium. Calderón's father, whose daily medical contact with poor Costa Ricans convinced him that social reform in his country, following the papal encyclicals of Leo XIII and Pius XI, would work, had been recognized as a leading Catholic reformist layman as early as the 1920s. Catholic social reformism was seen as an appropriate Christian alternative to the growing influence of Marxism in Costa Rica.

While the younger Calderón was careful to avoid concrete issues of social reform and mass-based mobilization during the electoral campaign, the night before his election he openly mixed politics with social reformism [when] he modestly suggested that social policy under his administration would break with past precedent, implying that he envisaged a new state role following the interventionist view outlined in the encyclicals *Rerum Novarum* and *Quadragesimo Anno*. Calderón further stated that his fundamental preoccupation would be with the poor. . . . But Calderón viewed himself neither as a social reform candidate nor as a populist. His patriarchal style was more akin to that of his oligarchic predecessors, and it was this style that had earned him the presidential candidacy and, ultimately, the presidency.

SOCIAL REFORM AND THE CHURCH

Calderón's election coincided with the seating of Monseñor Víctor Sanabria as the Costa Rican Catholic Church's new archbishop. . . . Monseñor Sanabria was actively committed to social reform through Catholic social action and state intervention. . . . The Church provided a major base of support for Calderón's reformism. Sanabria's first pastoral letter . . . called attention to the social role of the Church and the need for it to be involved in public-welfare issues. The alternative, according to the archbishop, was disorder, injustice, and violence. . . . Thus, by mid-1940, two important Costa Rican leaders had recognized the need to use public power to attack the social problems of the country.

THE SOCIAL PROBLEM DEFINED

Upon taking office in May 1940, Calderón surrounded himself with a group of progressive Catholic reformists who had previous experience in unsuccessful social reform movements. These included Jorge Volio, a former priest and leader of the short-lived Reformist Party of the early 1920s, and Carlos María Jiménez, unsuccessful presidential candidate in 1928 on a reformist platform.

. . . They apparently had only limited impact during the first twelve months of Calderón's term. . . . The president's definition of the social question and available policy alternatives was still quite narrow. . . . Calderón had decided by late 1940 that a social security program should be established. . . . No evidence suggests that Calderón directly consulted with, or was pressured by, any labor groups, including the Communists, during the early stages. . . .

Calderón sought to establish an open alliance with the Church, and support from Sanabria was ample. In June and July of 1941, two important documents were issued. The first sought to legitimize the expanding role of the state by calling for direct state intervention in the social problems of its citizens. The second declared that the axis of the social question was the "salary, an infallible index of social justice," and that the state possessed definite duties and obligations, especially with respect to workers' salaries. Indeed, social security was seen as a reasonable state response to the social problems that Costa Rica confronted. Sanabria obviously intended the Church's nascent support for Calderón as a means to gain greater access to government decision making. This access was especially critical to the archbishop, who had become alarmed at the growing influence of both Marxism and Protestantism in Costa Rica. . . .

The social security project was presented to Congress in July 1941. For the first time since 1924 . . . the Costa Rican Congress was confronted with an executive-initiated program of social reform. Much to Calderón's displeasure, the project was not immediately given the force of law, and several modifications were suggested. . . . A number of compromises affected the coverage stipulations. Congress set a *salario tope* (salary limit) of three hundred *colones* per month for all categories of workers. This change is important because it revealed the mentality of the times toward the new social welfare program: it was not to be a matter of redistributing income across classes, a purpose often mistakenly associated with social security programs; and it was an onerous new tax to be avoided if possible by the more privileged groups who could afford to purchase health care in the private market. Thus, in effect, the 1941 social security law established a parallel health-care market in Costa Rica. Those workers who could least afford social protection were obligated by law to contribute a fixed monthly portion of their incomes, while those who could most afford to finance a public health-care program were given the option of not contributing at all. . . . In November 1941, Congress finally approved the modified social security law.

The introduction of a state-sponsored social-welfare program could obviously have a decided impact on definable interests in Costa Rican society. While the Communists did not claim credit for the project, they did take credit for creating the "propitious" moment for the introduction of social security by proclaiming: "We ourselves have fertilized the ground so that the seed can now be sown." In essence, the Communists were conceding that this social reform had been paternalistically granted by the state.

THE CONTEXT

While the passage of the social security law was not a subject of great political scrutiny by the country's oligarchical interests, the implementation of the program and the struggle to make it successful were. This struggle was a result of a complex of events that translated into growing dissatisfaction with Calderón and the policies associated with him.

One of the most important concerns . . . was the war in Europe. Germany was one of Costa Rica's leading coffee importers, and many of Costa Rica's most prominent residents and landholders were of German descent. When Pearl Harbor was attacked, Calderón committed Costa Rica to the Allied powers. He suspended all constitutional guarantees, and, as had his neighbor Anastasio Somoza in Nicaragua, confiscated all German property. Germans were sent to "relocation" camps. Calderón's response came as both a surprise and an outrage to the Costa Rican oligarchy.

Shortages followed the outbreak of international hostilities in late 1941. . . . Calderón's government proved incapable of developing a coherent policy to deal with the shortages. A steady inflationary trend also set in, with 60 percent price increases between 1939 and 1942.

These problems were compounded by gross administrative mismanagement, a legacy inherited from Calderón's predecessor, León Cortés. The national debt increased and the same government budget was submitted for two successive years (1942–43) because of economists' inability to meet new demands. These problems were the subject of severe criticism by the Center for the Study of National Problems, a newly formed group of young reformist intellectuals who had been excluded from government circles.

The Soviet Union's alliance with the Allied powers also had a deep political impact on Costa Rica. For the first time, the local Communist Party could claim to be legitimate, using the larger United States–Soviet alliance as its legitimizing instrument. The party called for national unity and patriotism against the "fascist menace." And it was the only organization speaking for and trying further to educate and organize Costa Rica's urban working class.

Against this background of growing uncertainty, the true meaning of social security was finally understood. While few members of the oligarchy openly disagreed with the need for some form of obligatory social security, employers' potential tax burdens seemed onerous in a time of economic hardship and inflation. This new form of state intervention was dimly viewed, given the growing perception of Calderón's poor managerial skills and the implications of an expanded state bureaucracy to serve the interests of the poor. Growing apprehension was further exacerbated by the emerging split between Calderón and his predecessor, León Cortés, and the latter's serious effort in early 1942 to mobilize a broad-based coalition of conservatives and reformist Social Democrats against the incumbent and his administration. . . .

The 1941 law called for the establishment of old-age and maternity insurance, but the social security administration did not follow that mandate. Instead, a decision was made to initiate a vast program of health-care coverage, much to the chagrin of the country's medical profession. . . . Thus, despite Calderón's broad definition of the social problem in Costa Rica, the initial application of his remedy, social security, was very limited, with those in urban centers favored over those in rural areas.

One of the major problems encountered . . . in attempting to implement the new social policy was that of public apathy to and ignorance of the new social security programs. . . . The apathy was partly a result of the intentionally secretive manner of the drafting of the program. . . .

The biggest boost for the social security program came in the spring of 1942. President Calderón finally realized that he must actively seek worker-based political support if he was to maintain himself in office. He proposed a series of constitutional amendments, the Social Guarantees, which were to function as a Bill of Rights. These guarantees gave workers the legal right to form unions and to strike. A minimum wage was established, and the principle of state protection of workers was formalized.

This reform became a catalyst for worker unionization and mobilization. The Communist labor movement in particular became active in urban labor-union organization. And Monseñor Sanabria began to give serious thought to a parallel labor movement sponsored by the Catholic Church.

Because the Social Guarantees and the social security program were linked together in the new presidential reform project, the Communists took both issues and presented them to the public as worthy of popular support. The organizational success of the Communists proved useful as a means of disseminating information about the social security program. . . .

Costa Rica's 1941 program of obligatory social security was seen by President Rafael Calderón as a comprehensive way to deal with a variety of problems related to the social question, including access to health care and income-maintenance programs. Despite the fact that the intended programs were mass based, Calderón sought very little participation from the masses in the design and implementation of the program. . . . By design, the program was quite limited during the first two years of operation. The program's bureaucracy was concerned that too much activity would arouse concerted opposition.

In Costa Rica, then, one of the most critical social reforms of the twentieth century was brought about by an elite committed to the social welfare and well-being of the citizenry. This elite was remarkably naïve about the political implications of such a reform. Costa Rica's coffee elite and the reformist middle class soon realized, however, that the state apparatus could be used consciously as an instrument of social reform. The ensuing political struggle, which began after social security was implemented in 1942 and culminated in the civil war of 1948, can be understood as a struggle to control the reform potential of the state. Calderón and his advisers did not understand the reform potential, and were overwhelmed by it. Others, like José Figueres, were later able to capture the state as their own political apparatus, but only after major social reforms had been implemented. Figueres's success can ultimately be explained by the fact that he was able to wrap the reformist program (initiated under Calderón with social security) in respectable reformist rhetoric.

3.2 Origins of the Calderonista-*Communist-Catholic Alliance**

BY MANUEL ROJAS BOLAÑOS

In this selection, Manuel Rojas Bolaños reviews the genesis of the strange alliance between the Calderón Guardia administration, the Catholic Church, and the Communist Party. Calderón was seeking support for his radical social welfare reforms. The Church, meanwhile, was promoting reform, partly to counteract the growing influence of the Communists. And the Communists, during this era of the Popular Front against fascism, were advocating limited reform, not social revolution. For a time, the goals and needs of the three groups dovetailed, and they were able to maintain their alliance in the face of a growing but still divided opposition.

Rojas Bolaños is a sociologist who holds a doctorate from the National Autonomous University of Mexico (UNAM). He teaches at the University of Costa Rica.

THE midterm elections of February 1942 made clear the government had lost support among all social classes. The administration had tried unsuccessfully to assume a mediating role, placing itself above the different social groups. As rumors circulated of a coup d'etat, the government urgently needed to broaden its popular base. It had not lost all bourgeois support, because the Calderón Guardia administration had benefited many of them. However, the opposition front was better organized every day, winning the backing of dissatisfied capitalists, the urban petty bourgeoisie, and the rural masses. The government had only two alternatives: to shift to the right and regain the confidence of the bourgeoisie, or to insist on its role as mediator, winning mass support by pursuing social reform.

The government opted for the second route. The decision, however, depended less on the wishes or preferences of Calderón Guardia and his group than on the balance of power between social classes. The 1942 election results showed the direction in which the urban masses—industrial workers and part of the petty bourgeoisie—were moving and also indicated that an alliance with the Communist Party was conceivable.

*Excerpted from Manuel Rojas Bolaños, *Lucha social y guerra civil en Costa Rica* (San José: Editorial Porvenir, 1979), pp. 77–93.

The Communist Party after 1936 had been moving toward those government sectors that regarded continuation of reformist policies as essential. The
Communists had obviously abandoned for the moment the goal of revolutionary social transformation. Yet it would be an oversimplification to say that
they had become reformist, for socialist revolution remained at the heart of the
Communists' proposals. This objective, however, was to be achieved only after
the bourgeois revolution, which had still to occur in Costa Rica.

The backdrop for these developments was the fight against fascism that was
taking place around the world, which brought the Soviet Union and the
capitalist powers into an alliance. Within Costa Rica, this facilitated a partner-
ship between the government and the Communists. At the beginning of 1942,
both domestic and foreign conditions encouraged a closer relationship between
the two. . . .

On May 1, 1942, in his annual message to Congress, Calderón Guardia
announced a bill to reform the constitution to include a chapter on social
guarantees. . . . Later that day, he took part in a May Day parade with
Communist leader Manuel Mora. On May 12, an executive decree created an
ad honorem commission to draft a proposal for a labor code. Four days later,
the government sent Congress its proposal on Social Guarantees, a group of
articles that defined workers' rights. . . .

Foreseeing criticism, the government tried to justify its bill by citing papal
encyclicals. At the same time, Archbishop Víctor Sanabria publicly backed the
Social Guarantees. . . . Sanabria already had shown interest in making the
Church a leader in the popular struggle—partly to counteract the growing
Communist influence, but also because he was genuinely troubled by the
difficult living conditions of most Costa Ricans.

The reformist policies of the government, which identified with social
Christian ideology, made it easier for Sanabria to achieve his goals. The
administration viewed the Church favorably, reinstating religious education
in public schools and recognizing diplomas conferred by parochial schools.
The archbishop could not forego such opportunities, even at the risk of attracting criticism from conservative sectors of the bourgeoisie and petty
bourgeoisie.

To counteract opposition propaganda directed at the masses, Calderón
Guardia toured the country soliciting support for his reforms. Communist
leader Manuel Mora often accompanied him. . . . During 1942, government
reform efforts picked up momentum, as the Communists brought popular
support.

Around the same time, political maneuvering began in advance of the 1944
elections. . . . The opposition began rallying around the candidacy of former
president León Cortés, while Teodoro Picado's position as contender for the
ruling party's nomination grew stronger. The government's political mistakes
made the opposition's task much easier. In late March and early April 1942,
rumors circulated that Calderón Guardia hoped to amend the constitution to
prolong his term by two years, creating a political uproar. . . .

In July 1942, a ship called the *San Pablo,* carrying a cargo of bananas, was sunk in the port of Limón, apparently torpedoed by a German submarine. The Communists immediately organized a demonstration, at which Mora and Calderón Guardia delivered speeches. The protest turned violent, and shops owned by Germans, Italians, and pro-Franco Spaniards were looted. The authorities did not intervene to pacify the enraged crowd. This provoked a wave of attacks on the government, with critics accusing it of being in the hands of Communist vandals eager to destroy lives and property. Even Church authorities felt obliged to condemn the government for its inaction.

Several days later, on July 8, a farmer and small industrialist, previously unknown in political circles, made a radio speech castigating the government's economic and fiscal policies. He denounced the administration for having played into the hands of the Communists and blamed it for the sinking of the *San Pablo.* José Figueres could not finish his speech. He was interrupted by the police, thrown into jail and, a few days later, exiled. . . .

The Figueres incident generated new attacks on the government, but it was the controversy over the Electoral Code that outraged and mobilized the urban petty bourgeoisie. The government had introduced a proposal in Congress to amend the code, transferring responsibility for vote counting from electoral boards to the government itself. The risk of wide-scale fraud was obvious. Students and the urban petty bourgeoisie mobilized immediately, taking to the streets to demand withdrawal of the proposal. Among the protest leaders were members of the Center for the Study of National Problems. Founded in 1940 by intellectuals and petty bourgeois students, the center, which previously played an insignificant political role, now became an important actor within the opposition. . . .

The opposition's ability to mobilize a large part of the urban petty bourgeoisie and *campesinos* was not just due to its propaganda, however effective. Objective economic and political conditions made these social classes receptive to the opposition's arguments. The cost of living was still rising, basic consumer goods were scarce, the government's administrative disorder and corruption were common knowledge, and the benefits of social reform had not yet reached the masses, especially the impoverished *campesinos.* . . .

The *campesinos* were more inclined to follow León Cortés, whom they knew as the powerful leader of an orderly administration [1936–40]. He had opened roads into remote parts of the country, built bridges and schools in rural areas, and established a credit agency for small farmers. Cortés's 1944 campaign propaganda depicted the Communists as enemies of public order, religion, and private property. In the imagination of the *campesinos,* Cortés seemed to be the only man who could save the country from chaos.

It was not only the peasantry that backed the former president. In March 1943, after publishing his platform, Cortés received the support of important coffee growers, businessmen, and bankers. . . .

By May the ruling party and its candidate Picado were forced to formalize their alliance with the Communists. This was not entirely unexpected, given the sympathy that existed for the Soviet Union's fight against the Nazis. The new alliance, nevertheless, had to neutralize the effect that the opposition's intense anti-Communist campaign was having on the masses of *campesinos* and the urban petty bourgeoisie. Its only hope was to win the Church hierarchy's support.

Though Archbishop Sanabria and many priests indisputably sympathized with the Calderón Guardia government and its reforms, the Communists were another story. Sanabria had been fighting them since he was named archbishop three years earlier. Now the situation had changed. Mora and Sanabria began discussions on an accord that would treat equally the interests of the ruling party, the Church, and the Communists. This was facilitated when the Communist International in Moscow was dissolved in the spring of 1943, leaving the Costa Rican Communists without international affiliation. On June 13 the National Conference of the Communist Party of Costa Rica officially dissolved the party, creating in its place the *Partido Vanguardia Popular* [Popular Vanguard Party]. . . .

Congress approved the Social Guarantees on June 23; on August 23 it approved the Labor Code . . . enacted on September 15, 1943. The occasion was marked as "the second national independence day."[1] As crowds cheered, Calderón Guardia, Sanabria, Mora, and Picado drove through the streets in an open car. Seven days later, the agreement between the *calderonista* National Republican Party and the Popular Vanguard Party was signed. Both agreed to campaign for Picado and the Popular Vanguard Party's platform. In exchange for its support for the National Republican Party, *Vanguardia* did not require political posts in the future government nor favors for its members. It simply reserved the right to demand the fulfillment of the accord. . . .

A violent political campaign developed, with armed confrontations between members of the ruling party and the opposition. On February 6, 1944, a few days before the elections, a huge San José rally organized by Cortés's Democratic Party ended in an uproar. Attacks on the government were renewed, along with accusations that it would not respect the election results.

In the February 13 elections, the incumbent National Republican Party obtained 90,403 votes and the Democratic Party received 46,403.[2] The Democrats immediately denounced the elections as fraudulent. On February 24 their representatives presented Congress with a petition to nullify the elections and hold new ones. The request, of course, was turned down.

NOTES

1. Central American Independence Day is September 15.—EDS.

2. Rojas Bolaños writes that however questionable the election results, they did reflect a weakening of support for the so-called Victory Bloc—of the National Republican and Popular Vanguard parties—when compared with the 1940 and 1942 elections. In 1940 the coalition had obtained about 95 percent of the votes cast; in 1942, about 80 percent. In 1944 it received only

66 percent. The coalition lost votes in most districts from 1940 to 1944, and there was a notable change in electoral behavior. The coalition gained support in the most important cities, except for Heredia and Alajuela. It lost ground in rural areas, especially in the coffee-growing region, even in districts with a high number of salaried farm workers and a concentration of small properties. In other rural areas with a high number of wage laborers but a low proportion of family farms— that is, in districts where there was a rural proletariat—the ruling coalition obtained the majority.—EDS.

3.3 Declaration of the Social Democratic Party, 1945*

In the fall of 1943, two groups—the Center for the Study of National Problems, an organization of progressive young intellectuals and professionals, and the left-leaning Democratic Action faction of the Democratic Party—agreed to merge. The result was the Social Democratic Party. In March 1945 the following manifesto was published in the journal Acción Demócrata. *These were the stated goals that led the Social Democrats to fight in the 1948 civil war. In the early 1950s, the Social Democrats reconstituted themselves as the National Liberation Party, which for over thirty years has been the dominant political party in Costa Rica.*

To Costa Ricans from the Social Democratic Party:

Declaration to the people of Costa Rica by the first National Executive Committee of our party:

FELLOW CITIZENS:

The first permanent and doctrinal party of genuinely national character was just founded in Costa Rica. It was baptized Social Democratic because those who attended the national convention of March 11, 1945, knew that the fundamental problems of our country at this moment (of history) are social problems [*la cuestión social*] and the issue of democracy.

From 1890 to 1940 (for half a century) the predominant characteristics of this small republic were an atmosphere of freedom, respect for the citizen, respect for Public Finance, [and] a system of elections based on universal and direct suffrage honorably guarded by the public authorities.

Until 1940 our governments were the expression of what Costa Rica was, with its qualities and defects. In that year an unhealthy period began. In a few years respect ended completely for [state] institutions and the national treasury [Public Finance]. In 1944 there was a fraudulent coup [carried out] for the

*This manifesto appeared in the Social Democratic Party publication, *Acción Demócrata,* on March 17, 1945.

satrapy's continuation in power, with impunity for the crimes they perpetrated.

Thus ended the first Republic of Costa Rica.

Today we find ourselves under a de facto government.

We believe in suffrage (universal, direct, secret, democratic).

In 1940 came the disaster: *social legislation was put to use as a demagogic weapon.*

We understand that judicious legislation must march a little ahead of the life of the country, so that the nation follows it. But it [the social legislation of Calderón Guardia] should not get so far ahead that customs cannot assimilate it. This legislation should never divorce itself from the national life and become a dead letter, discrediting the movement (in favor of social justice).

We (the SDP) understand social progress to be effective progress.

We do not want to confuse economic realities with the philosophical abstractions of any system.

In the so-called relations between capital and labor, we have been preaching and living the evangelism of cooperation and oppose the theory of class struggle. Collaboration between labor and capital can be a more effective means to end poverty.

The current bosses of Costa Rica, who have had in their hands the course of the country, have not done all they could for the well-being of the workers, the great part of the population. But the current bosses of Costa Rica are of flesh and blood, and they feel noble sentiments.

Businessmen and workers have a mutual need for each other; they are true associates in the business of national production. They can produce more wealth together if they reject the idea of the destructive [class] struggle, and if they adopt an intelligent attitude of good-willed collaboration.

We remember the martyrs of Llano Grande[1] and Sabanilla; it is the memory of the popular will trampled and of political rights ruined.

Costa Ricans:

From our lacerated flesh must come the material to build the Second Republic.

Today the SDP assumes the initiative in this grand national crusade.

The color of the SDP is purple—that of the *guaria morada,* the national flower.

NOTE

1. Llano Grande de Cartago is a small village north of Cartago, where several people were killed during electoral disturbances in February 1944.—EDS.

3.4 Democracy in Costa Rica as the Product of Class Neutralization*

BY JACOBO SCHIFTER

Historian Jacobo Schifter offers an unorthodox interpretation of the 1940s, focusing on the conflict between "populists" and "transformists." The populists, whom he admits championed a uniquely Costa Rican breed of populism, were led by President Rafael Angel Calderón Guardia. Their supporters included the urban poor, the Communists, and the Church, and their goal was to enact social reform but not to fundamentally alter the economic system of the country. The transformists, however, sought literally to transform the economy. Their ranks were filled by intellectuals, the expanding class of professionals, and the new industrial and commercial bourgeoisie, all with much to gain from a new, more modern economic order. The oligarchy, though not sharing transformist aims, nonetheless joined the opposition, out of distrust of Calderón and his successor Teodoro Picado, and distaste for their Communist allies and social reforms.

Schifter, though critical of the calderonistas, *is wholly cynical about the opposition. As is clear throughout this excerpt, he has a particularly harsh view of José Figueres, whom he views as a potential tyrant who chose democracy not as an end but as his means to retain power. The contemporary democratic state, he argues, is not the result of an egalitarian colonial legacy, nor of Costa Rica's peaceful political evolution (see Reading 1.1). Rather, he argues, it was the result of a stalemate between the various sectors who won the 1948 civil war. Unable to agree on how to share power among themselves, the contending social classes and interest groups "neutralized" each other politically and turned to liberal democracy rather than cede power to their respective competitors.*

Schifter, who holds a doctorate in history from Columbia University, is the author of several books on twentieth-century Costa Rican history, including one extensive analysis of the U.S. government's view of the 1948 events.

OUR thesis on democracy in Costa Rica is based on the theory of class neutralization which began with the civil war of 1948. This neutralization was the fruit of ideological polarization between the nontransformist populism of the *calderonistas* and the nonpopulist transformism of José Figueres and his supporters. The *calderonista* regime and the *figuerista* authoritarian corporativist movement neutralized each other to such an extent that the democratic solution became the lesser evil for ending a political impasse, the first and most desirable solution for each side being the retention of power.

*Excerpted from Jacobo Schifter, "La democracia en Costa Rica como producto de la neutralización de clases," in ¿*Democracia en Costa Rica? Cinco opiniones polémicas,* ed. Chester Zelaya (San José: Editorial Universidad Estatal a Distancia, 1978), pp. 175, 177, 182–86, 189–210.

That neutralization of class conflict is responsible for present-day democracy in Costa Rica. Democratic government is perpetuated due to an implicit pact between the victorious sectors of 1948—the middle class and the oligarchy who, thanks to such repressive measures as the suppression of trade unions and economic blackmail, distribute the wealth in a manner detrimental to the lower classes. . . .

It is crucial for our thesis to clearly differentiate between a transformist or nationalist-developmentalist ideology and a populist movement. . . . Transformist ideology may be defined as a non-Marxist current of thought oriented toward social, political, and economic change. Its main aim is to restructure dependence to facilitate a more autonomous process of economic development. Transformist ideology calls for (a) reducing the oligarchy's power, (b) restructuring foreign trade, and (c) economic intervention to modify the export-oriented model and promote economic diversification.

A populist movement, in contrast, seeks to incorporate the popular classes into the political system under elite direction, in alliance with other social classes. Populism, in our view, amounts to a mechanism for manipulating and controlling low-income populations, providing a means of integrating migrants into urban life. Such movements generally have limited interest in changing the economic structure. . . .

The 1948 revolutionary movement should not be interpreted as the fortunate onset of a middle-class democratic system, but as a transformist attempt to impose an authoritarian corporativist development model. Authoritarian corporativism means, among other things, a system of representation the state imposes, through its ability to concentrate resources created by development, with the aim of dominating and manipulating the process of representation of autonomous sectoral, regional, or class associations.

Although such a system of representation does not necessarily accompany a transformist ideology, it becomes an ideal weapon for political movements that attempt to put an end to underdevelopment and dependency. . . .

Costa Rican populism was a particular type within Latin America. Although linked from the start to economic considerations, Costa Rican populism was ideologically oriented more toward problems of urbanization than of industrialization. Nor was Costa Rican populism a movement uniting the industrial bourgeoisie, middle class, and workers. On the contrary, populism's most striking characteristic in Costa Rica was the absence of the middle class and industrialists in its alliance and, therefore, the absence of developmentalist and transformist ideologies. Populism in Costa Rica became a political movement organized within the status quo, with distributive goals. . . .

The country's transition from a distinctly agricultural to an urban society broke the workers' links to the countryside. Once in the urban areas, these workers lacked access to political participation and thus constituted masses at the disposal of any political movement that might incorporate them. And although in the 1940s Costa Rica provided for the direct election of its rulers, the great working masses were effectively manipulated and controlled by the liberal bourgeois regime. Before the 1940s, the regime had systematically repressed popular participation. It had repeatedly altered election results through fraud with the help of an anachronistic electoral system. It stifled the free association of interest groups, as there was no real protection for public employees, rural workers, or urban laborers to organize into class associations. Authoritarian paternalism was the pattern of social relationships at all levels, from the president of the republic to the most progressive landowner. The difficult circumstances under which the masses were educated and sustained helped increase their apathy and mistrust of a regime that was clearly not representing their interests.

The Costa Rican bourgeois political system operated on behalf of the national elite. They were the direct beneficiaries of the regime's corruption, thanks to the lack of control over public bidding, the absence of direct taxation, and the administrative anarchy and lack of planning that allowed the regime to satisfy the political *caciques* (chiefs) with highways, infrastructure that served their landholdings, or with high-ranking bureaucratic positions. The democratic mask of liberal Costa Rica was highly questionable, but it was not ready to turn to dictatorship to maintain the coffee oligarchy in power. . . .

The principal populist leader was Dr. Rafael Angel Calderón Guardia, who was president from 1940–44. Calderón Guardia came to power as the representative of the oligarchy via the National Republican Party. He had the backing of the authoritarian administration of outgoing president León Cortés, and won a landslide victory, with 86 percent of the vote. Everything seemed to indicate that Costa Rican politics would remain dominated by oligarchic paternalism. But Calderón Guardia came to power with a social vision, as yet unknown to many. And the international situation, a world at war, would transform what seemed to be the logical pattern of development. . . .

Unexpectedly, Calderón's administration promulgated social legislation, the Social Guarantees, and founded an agency that would in 1942 become the *Caja Costarricense de Seguro Social* (Social Security Institute). . . . This social legislation transcended the country's level of economic development, surpassing even that of Argentina—and Costa Rica did not have a labor movement strong enough to demand such reforms. Calderón Guardia continued and consolidated González Flores's failed attempts to provide basic legislation for the Costa Rican worker in 1914–17 [see Reading 2.4]. The president's personal participation in securing passage of these social laws was decisive. When these measures were enacted, he lacked worker support, partly because of the antigovernment stance of the Communist Party, which had viewed the privatization of the electricity industry as scandalous. It is precisely because of this disjunction—the gap in time between passage of Calderón Guardia's social legislation and the time the Communist Party began to support him—that this social reform came to be identified with the leader and gave birth to a movement, *calderonismo.* During the last thirty years [now forty], *calderonismo* has been a political, electoral, and social reality, the preeminent popular movement in Costa Rica. . . .

Calderonismo was more a distributive than a developmentalist movement. Reflecting a mentality more liberal than transformist, Calderón Guardia himself put an end to the state monopoly on electricity because he wished to create more incentives for private enterprise. It was not *calderonismo's* intent to initiate industrialization. On the contrary, coffee was exempted from export taxes during World War II. And earnings from high coffee prices were plowed right back into expanding the coffee crop, not into industrialization. Nor did the *calderonista* government intend to broaden the domestic market through agrarian reform or expanding the state. *Calderonismo* was concerned with securing the dignity of the Costa Rican worker, which, in fact, became its greatest achievement. In this sense, *calderonismo* was not far wrong: Costa Rican industrialization during the 1960s did not adequately improve the conditions of the working class. The defeat of *calderonismo* in 1948 was a defeat for the entire working class.

Costa Rican populism, based on the support of the better organized unions led by the CTCR (Confederation of Costa Rica Workers), and of other intellectual and petty bourgeois sectors, forged a social alliance that shaped the nature of Costa Rican society. The alliance's lack of support from certain sectors of the so-called middle class was of paramount importance in determining the political outcome of 1948. For particular reasons, these middle sectors— imbued with transformist ideology—did not reach an accord with *calderonismo.* And it was these groups that became the principal architects of contemporary Costa Rica.

Costa Rican historians have sought an explanation for the country's democracy in the particular circumstances of its colonial past. . . . But although these historians have tried to explain the Costa Rican democratic system as an inalienable inheritance from the colonial period, they have suffered from a compulsion to "democratize" the entire history of the country in order to continue rationalizing the democratic colonial legacy. In other words, they have ignored the study of authoritarian tendencies throughout the country's history [see Reading 1.7]. . . .

Colonial Costa Rica may well have been characterized by lack of social stratification, caused and intensified by the scarcity of precious metals, the relative distance from the administrative center in Guatemala, and the absence of exploitable indigenous labor. It is not at all certain, however, that its "democratic" inheritance was a legacy of all these factors. Nor is the romantic myth of a homogenous and relatively egalitarian "agrarian democracy" completely valid. Both myths, nevertheless, have gathered strength and become rooted in Costa Rican historical tradition, which systematically ignores all evidence of authoritarianism, and which, when it does address authoritarian periods, interprets them as exceptions, deviations, or aberrations. But such "deviations" have been considerable, and have wrought social changes that would have been difficult to promote by democratic means.

Democratic stability was only one of many tendencies that existed in the political system. During the 1940s, a spectrum of tendencies existed, autocratic as well as democratic. During that decade the most extreme social polarization occurred. On one side was the consolidated, quasi-hegemonic coffee oligarchy, with well-established repressive tendencies. On the other, an ideology was developing that was transformist, not democratic, a product of middle-class economic and social frustration. Ironically, the "transformist" coalition was consolidated when both groups, the oligarchy and the middle classes, united against *calderonista* populism.

By the 1940s Costa Rica had ceased to be an "agrarian democracy" of small producers. . . . Data for 1940 from the *Instituto del Café* [Coffee Institute] indicate increasing land concentration. . . . The 5 percent of coffee producers who in 1940 owned more than ten thousand trees controlled more than half the coffee trees in the entire country. With 54.7 percent of the work force employed in agriculture, the economic and political power of that 5 percent was significant.

By the 1940s Costa Rica had also ceased to be a country of self-employed workers. Wage laborers accounted for 66.4 percent of the economically active population, 10.1 percent were employers, and just 10.9 percent were self-employed. A decline in the proportion of agricultural workers in the labor force stemmed from the growth of the *latifundios* [underutilized large properties] and consequent expulsion of *campesinos* from the land, as well as from growth of the country's nascent industry and commerce. . . .

The coffee oligarchy maintained important links with other economic sectors and its political power was thus possibly greater than its participation in the export of coffee. That power represented a constant threat to any attempt at social reform. If in the nineteenth century the *cafetaleros* intervened with dictatorial powers in order to weaken the Church, in later eras they sponsored coups d'etat to check any attempts at redistribution such as that by González Flores [see Reading 2.4]. This class tolerated constitutional governments—as long as the governments did not act against its interests. Thus, the coffee oligarchy and its commercial and financial offshoots were prepared to overthrow Costa Rican populism starting in 1942 because of ethnic repression and the *calderonistas'* social legislation.[1] But the oligarchy, facing the populist coalition and worker mobilization of that year, sought new tactics.

The oligarchy's new approach was to try to defeat the government at the polls, using any trick at its disposal, while also seeking allies among the opposition. The Social Democratic Party [*Partido Social Demócrata*] seemed to be the ideal choice for an alliance [see Reading 3.3]. But the Costa Rican oligarchs would pay dearly for help from the transformist middle sectors. Ultimately, they would have to yield to the political and economic demands of those who controlled the arms.

The origin of the developmentalist movement in Costa Rica was closely associated with the creation of the *Centro para el Estudio de los Problemas Nacionales* [Center for the Study of National Problems], which included a new group of professionals who came to be known as the "Generation of '48." The center began as an institute for planning and assessment, and its objective was to report on and devise alternative solutions for the nation's most pressing problems. Although officially "apolitical," the fact that it set up offices throughout the country and required of its members ideological conformity is evidence that it was politicized from the start. More obvious was its transformist ideological posture in proposing policies against the interests of certain social groups, an indication that the attitudes of the center's members were not very "scientific" or "objective."

The center was a product of middle-class frustration over the nation's slow economic transformation. Its ideological position was sharply anti-imperialist, as can be seen in this quotation from its magazine, *Surco:* "The country is a victim of foreign capital represented by the United Fruit Company, the electric companies, and Standard Oil Company, which divide much of their sizeable profits among their foreign shareholders."[2]

The same issue stresses that the state's worst problem was its manipulation by foreign and domestic capital. The center held an anticapitalistic position without accepting Marxist theory and was also anti-oligarchic. . . . Its opposition to the oligarchy, to imperialism, to the status quo, combined with the absence of a class analysis, are hallmarks of a transformist ideology.

Another force behind the emergence of Costa Rican developmentalist nationalism was the *Acción Demócrata* [Democratic Action] faction, the "left wing" within the *cortesista* or Democratic Party. Its main leader, José Figueres, shared many aspects of the center's ideology. Like the center, Figueres was anticapitalist, anti-oligarchic, and anti-imperialist, but did not identify with Marxist philosophy:

I have no arguments with which to oppose Marxist philosophy, not even of a spiritual order . . . but I do not commit the blunders [Communist leader] Manuel Mora makes in reference to fighting the Yankee and capitalism in direct combat. I will achieve more radical economic reforms than Mora and his whole party, and in a short time I will win more battles against Yankee imperialism than they have won in twenty years, simply because it is a question of tactics. . . . I will befriend the capitalists and the Yankee State Department in order to fight and win the battle from within. I do not care what label I have to do it under to gain their trust. Once they trust me, I will know what to do.[3]

Finally, like the center, Figueres wanted to concentrate in state hands the economic resources generated by development, a sign of an authoritarian corporativist outlook. . . .

The center joined with Democratic Action in March 1945, to become the Social Democratic Party [see Reading 3.3] and, upon doing so, demonstrated its democratic "ideals" by declaring the death of the first Costa Rican republic, long before the electoral pantomime of 1948. . . .

The Social Democratic Party, in its eagerness to take control of the Costa Rican state, found in 1945 that its choice of political allies was severely limited. Under the administration of Teodoro Picado, the populist forces managed by Calderón Guardia had been consolidated. Picado had introduced an income tax which, added to the social legislation enacted earlier, provoked the oligarchic classes led by Otilio Ulate to withdraw their support. . . . By 1945 the upper class, led by the influential newspaper publisher Ulate—who had characterized the Social Guarantees as "the opium of the people"—was in clear opposition to the government.

The leaders of the Social Democrats, representing the professional middle classes who amounted at most to 3.8 percent of the economically active population, and who in December 1948 would obtain no more than 6,500 votes in the legislative elections, realized that their chance of attaining power depended neither on the elections nor on compromising with *calderonismo*. Therefore, they decided in 1946 to forge an agreement with their most bitter enemy, the oligarchy, represented by the *cortesista* party.

Although Social Democratic ideology was obviously closer to the lower classes than to the aristocrats—who cared little for the transformists—the Social Democratic Party's only worker support came from the few Christian unions, taken in by the divisive tricks of the Rerum Novarum Costa Rican Workers Confederation [*Confederación Costarricense de Trabajadores Rerum Novarum*].[4] The Social Democrats were opposed by the entire organized working class. But the transformists, as they had stated in 1945, aspired to a Second Republic that did not necessarily include *ulatistas* or *calderonistas* at the helm. Costa Rican politics from 1946 on came to be characterized by opposition to populism on the part of the middle classes and the oligarchy. In other words, it was the populist *calderonista* movement versus the transformist *figuerista* movement allied with Ulate and the oligarchs. . . .

Although the *cortesista*-Democratic coalition achieved some gains in the 1946 legislative elections, its chances for a triumph in the 1948 presidential race began to fade. The transformists thus began to exert pressure, through the "slowdowns" and strikes of 1947. Their goal was to obtain favorable appointments on the newly created Electoral Tribunal and Electoral Register. The very president of the tribunal, Benjamín Odio, would demonstrate his political partisanship by fleeing on February 9, 1948 [one day after the elections], to join the revolutionaries.

The acceptance of the conditions the coalition had imposed by the famous *huelga de los brazos caídos*—literally, the strike of the fallen arms—in 1947 was a mortal blow to the Costa Rican populists. The agreement that ended the strike gave the *ulatistas* control over the Electoral Register, and thus their opportunity to defeat *calderonismo* in the elections. This also gave the transformists an excuse to launch their "revolution."

The Social Democrats had been preparing for revolution since 1942, with deals between Figueres and other Central American mercenaries in the Caribbean Legion. The 1948 elections became a convenient excuse to begin the legion's "democratic crusade" in Costa Rica. But to execute the operation it was necessary to force the government to disavow the elections won by Ulate. Thus, the electoral "irregularities" had to be as flagrant as possible.

With respect to the electoral fraud of 1948, it is important to remember the "abstention" of almost 75,000 registered voters, and the sharp decrease in turnout in *calderonista* provinces: Puntarenas (20.7 percent more abstention in 1948 than in 1944), Limón (20.4 percent more), Guanacaste (9.18 percent more), and San José (3.6 percent more). "Abstention" was minimal in opposition provinces: Cartago (2 percent more than in 1944), Alajuela (0.97 percent more), and Heredia (no increase at all). . . . The Electoral Register apparently became more "efficient" in issuing identity cards, electoral lists, and voter registrations in opposition areas. It may be supposed that had there instead been greater "efficiency" in *calderonista* areas, the election's outcome might have been different.

The *calderonistas'* distrust was not aroused simply by Ulate's victory. The tribunal counted votes based on telegrams from polling places instead of the actual ballots themselves, one of its three members was reluctant to sign the statement certifying Ulate's victory, and it engaged in a premeditated delay in issuing the results. Finally, a fire in the *Colegio Superior de Señoritas* [Girls' High School—where the ballots were stored] helped guarantee that the results would be submitted to a tense Congress which could not ignore the blatant irregularities and would be reluctant to accept the opposition victory.

On March 2, 1948, Congress annulled the elections, and despite settlement attempts between *calderonistas* and *ulatistas, figuerismo* had its pretext to begin the revolution. The Electoral Tribunal had eliminated Calderón Guardia; Congress had eliminated Ulate. Figueres and his party counted on the civil war to carry them to power. . . .

The civil war was the pivotal historical event that consolidated the class polarization in Costa Rica. The middle classes, in a fragile alliance with sectors of the oligarchy, took up arms against a populist movement that rested on the shoulders of Costa Rican trade unions. The victory of the opposition coalition and its repressive authoritarian policies further deepened these schisms. The transformist revolutionaries wanted to enter San José triumphantly and deny recognition to the candidate elected in 1948, Otilio Ulate. "They are wrong," said Figueres, "if they believe that I am going to give the presidency to Otilio Ulate, or to any corrupt politician. I am here to transform the country."

And Figueres, with the help of the junta, unleashed a wave of repression and manipulation of all the groups and classes of the country. Obviously, the *Central de Trabajadores Costarricenses,* the Costa Rican Workers Central, its leaders and members, were the first to be repressed, punished and even assassinated. . . . The unions and their leaders, the supporters of the *calderonista* government and Communist Party members were not the only ones who suffered. All those workers, public employees, teachers, and intellectuals who favored social legislation, trade unionism, and income redistribution during the *calderonista* period suffered as well.

Martial law was declared, properties were expropriated, interventionist policies were enacted against elite sectors linked to *calderonismo.* Political parties, newspapers, and radio stations were banned, and forced nationalizations took place. The junta's de facto government acted as it wished against its wartime adversaries. Yet it exceeded the limits defined by its base of support, and turned against its comrade-in-arms, the Costa Rican oligarchy, with decrees that nationalized banks and imposed a 10 percent tax on capital of more than 50,000 *colones* [approximately $9,000 at the time]. These decrees revealed the junta's true repressive intentions against the powerful classes of Costa Rica, and its desire to withhold power from their representative, Otilio Ulate.

The junta's plans for a new constitution reflected its desire to centralize in the state the principal powers to intervene directly in the economy and in society. Added to the political powers the state enjoyed under the junta, this was indicative of an authoritarian corporativist model of development, intended to concentrate economic resources in the hands of the state, controlled by the junta. This was the perception, too, of those groups that had, until then, supported the junta, its former comrades-in-arms. . . .

When the junta called elections for a new constituent assembly, Ulate's party began to manipulate public opinion in order to attain an overwhelming majority in Congress, thus defeating the junta's transformist program and impeding its consolidation of power. It was at this point that the final impetus toward social polarization in Costa Rica occurred, when the oligarchic sectors withdrew political support from the Social Democratic Party and revoked a draft constitution that would have permitted the junta to transform the country.

The junta paid a high price for its tactical error: a lack of popular backing. *Ulatismo,* which was not precisely a political force dedicated to changing the status quo, *calderonismo,* and communism were all now fervent enemies of the junta. Both *ulatismo,* which had popular backing but not arms, and *figuerismo,* which controlled the arms but had no popular support, were prevented from seizing power by force, as each may have wished. . . . Thus, they had to come to terms with one another.

This process is what we have called the "neutralization of classes" in Costa Rica. By 1948 both populism and authoritarian transformism showed definite autocratic tendencies. Either would have resorted to dictatorship to retain power. *Calderonismo,* had it triumphed, would have been obliged to do so to counter the military *figuerista* movement against the constitutional regime; and *figuerismo* could have done so by exploiting the military victory that enabled it to control the state for several months.

But the victorious coalition contained internal class contradictions that would neutralize it. Neither side could overpower or outmaneuver the other; both had to seek an alternative. Although neither side had sought democracy, it emerged as the next best solution, the lesser of the evils. The *figuerista* junta decided to make a pact with *ulatismo* on two conditions. The first was the abolition of the army—an instrument the *ulatistas* might use to keep power. The second was that the social legislation not be repealed, a move that would prevent the junta from losing all future worker support and allow it to proclaim that it had struggled for democracy through a political party, the one that would come to be known as *Liberación Nacional* [National Liberation].

NOTES

1. This refers to the World War II–era expropriations of property belonging to German and Italian nationals and their descendants. Some members of these groups were also interned for the duration of the war.—EDS.

2. *Surco,* no. 23 (1940): 1.

3. Oscar Aguilar Bulgarelli, *Los hechos políticos de 1948* (San José: Imprenta Lehmann, 1969), p. 265.

4. The *Confederación Costarricense de Trabajadores Rerum Novarum* was a Church-dominated union federation organized in the early 1940s as a counterpart to the Communist-dominated *Confederación de Trabajadores de Costa Rica* (Costa Rican Workers Confederation). It was named after an 1891 encyclical by Pope Leo XIII, still a cornerstone of social Christian doctrine, which held that the state should protect labor from undue exploitation and that unions or other workers' associations could be formed for this purpose. After 1946, the Rerum Novarum federation moved ever closer to the Social Democratic opposition, in spite of its initial sponsorship by the Church, which was allied with the government.—EDS.

3.5 Central Intelligence Agency and State Department Memoranda, 1948*

The United States initially reacted calmly to the Communists' role in Costa Rican politics in the 1940s. It was, after all, the era of the Popular Front against fascism, the United States was allied with the Soviet Union, and Communists were tolerated at home as well. But by the time the issue came to the fore in Costa Rica, the cold war was in full flower. The complex social changes and class rivalries that Costa Rica was experiencing were thus ignored, and the problem, in Washington's view, became predominantly one of the Red Menace, not that Washington's view was necessarily lucid. The following CIA report, top secret before declassification in 1975, was entitled: "Disturbances in Central America and Antarctica." A State Department report a few weeks later likened the situation in Costa Rica to Eastern Europe.

*CIA declassified document.

MEMORANDUM TO THE DIRECTOR, CENTRAL INTELLIGENCE
SUBJECT: DISTURBANCES IN CENTRAL AMERICA AND
ANTARCTICA

A. H. McCollum, Capt. USN
Deputy Assistant Director
Reports and Estimates

Summary: CIA estimates that the most serious Central American revolutionary situation at present exists in Costa Rica, where a civil disobedience strike as a result of the present political impasse is likely. There are no new developments since special memorandum of 27 February on the revolutionary situation in Guatemala, Honduras, and Nicaragua. . . .

Chances of Revolution in Costa Rica: The 1 March vote by the Costa Rican Congress voiding the recent presidential elections has created a revolutionary situation. The Electoral Tribunal by a two-to-one vote had previously declared the opposition candidate Ulate the winner. Unless a last minute compromise can be effected, a civil disobedience strike—which will force all banks and many business establishments to close their doors and which will impair the functioning of the country's major public utilities—is to be expected.

MEMORANDUM BY MR. WILLIAM TAPLEY BENNETT, JR., OF
THE DIVISION OF CENTRAL AMERICA AND PANAMA
AFFAIRS**

Secret   [WASHINGTON] March 26, 1948

The attached dispatch from the Embassy at San José [not printed] provides an excellent appraisal of the extent of Communist participation in the present Costa Rican political crisis. A summary of the dispatch is submitted as of particular interest in connection with the forthcoming conference at Bogotá and possible informal approaches there by other governments with respect to the Costa Rican situation.

Communism in Costa Rica, operating under the name of *Vanguardia Popular* since the 1943 Comintern dissolution, today occupies a position of importance far out of proportion to its numerical strength. With an estimated seven thousand militant members, representing less than 1 percent of the total population of the country, *Vanguardia* was successful during the recent political campaign in increasing its representation in Costa Rica's unicameral Congress to at least six and possibly eight seats out of a total of fifty-four. Since the other two parties are evenly matched with about twenty-three seats each, the Com-

**Foreign Relations of the United States 1948,* The Western Hemisphere, vol. 9, DOS Publication 8626, Historical Office, Bureau of Public Affairs (Washington, D.C.: U.S. Government Printing Office, 1972).

munists have thus been successful in obtaining an effective balance of power in the Congress.

Vanguardia's influence on the National Republican (administration) Party is paramount. It constitutes the bulk of the government's support today. The embassy describes *Vanguardia* as being both directly and indirectly responsible for the present state of chaos and uncertainty in Costa Rica. The *Vanguardia* leader, Manuel Mora, who is on intimate terms with the candidate Calderón, appears to have been primarily responsible for stiffening the will of the latter (who had conceded defeat on the night of the election) to resist a compromise solution, and *Vanguardia* propaganda has steadily endeavored to sabotage negotiations to that end.

Aside from its congressional position, the infiltration of *Vanguardia Popular* into the machinery of government is summarized as follows:

Armed Forces: With the addition of hundreds of irregular troops *(mariachis)* in the present crisis, Communist elements now constitute some 70 percent of the police and army. Recent events have shown beyond a doubt that the primary allegiance of these irregulars is to their Communist leadership rather than to the government. The *mariachis* replaced the regular police on missions where brazen disregard of the law was a prerequisite. Acting under orders which have apparently emanated from the Calderón and/or *Vanguardia* headquarters rather than from the government, they have spread a reign of terror unparalleled in Costa Rican history.

Social Security Administration: Except for a few top positions, the great majority of posts in the administration is held either by *Vanguardia* members or individuals approved by *Vanguardia.* Dr. Rudolf Pomeranz and his wife, both international Communists of Polish nationality, spent two years in the administration indoctrinating their fellow Communists before returning to Poland last year.

Transport: The Department of Public Works contains several hundred *Vanguardia* members. In the government-owned Pacific Railway there is a not unduly large but important number of *Vanguardistas,* especially in the San José shops.

Communications: Between 20 and 25 percent of the personnel in the general telegraph office at San José and approximately 15 percent of the employees in the general post office in San José are controlled by *Vanguardia.*

The embassy concludes that one of *Vanguardia*'s greatest achievements has been the replacement of members of the Costa Rican middle class in government positions by *Vanguardia* members. Nongovernment facilities owned by *Vanguardia* include a radio station, a newspaper, a sound truck, and other expensive activities.

The Embassy states that the situation of uncertainty and insecurity which now exists in Costa Rica is in many respects similar to that prevailing today in Eastern Europe. While this estimate may be a bit overdrawn it is perhaps worthwhile to recall that [Víctor Raúl] Haya de la Torre of Peru, in a recent statement to the United Press, described Costa Rica as "the Czechoslovakia of the Western Hemisphere."

3.6 Pages from a Diary*

BY EUGENIO RODRÍGUEZ VEGA

In 1948 Eugenio Rodríguez was a young partisan of José Figueres with a flair for propaganda. He was on the staff of a key opposition newspaper, and worked for various antigovernment radio programs. He later served in the rebel forces—with a unit that, try as it might, never saw action. These excerpts from his diary recount his experiences.

Rodríguez is a historian at the University of Costa Rica. Except where indicated by brackets, the ellipses indicate Rodríguez's own omissions.

THIS week, we could not work, study, nor even read. We could not do anything. Everyone is thinking about this Sunday. . . . Just a week ago I was sure that there would be no elections. . . . I was absolutely certain. Today although nothing has happened to make me change my mind, I am no longer so sure. Anything can happen. . . . We live in a dangerous calm . . . (February 3, 1948).

The level of political [tension] which yesterday seemed normal, today has risen precipitously and threatens to explode. . . . There are crowds in the streets, and at any moment the spark may flare. Perhaps even as I write this, it has already been ignited. . . . We all wait . . . (February 5, 1948).

I am writing with great emotion, joy and enthusiasm . . . I shall simply say that the Opposition has risen to power. . . . Later, calmly, I will write an extensive commentary . . . (February 9, 1948).

I am waiting for something to happen. . . . Last night and today, extraordinary grave events have transpired. . . . We are left with only one path: Resistance. And their only path is dictatorship. There is no middle ground. No shades of gray. The die has been cast (February 10, 1948).

Rumors are swirling around us. We live on the edge and tensely wait. The National Election Tribunal still has not decreed the outcome, but its most

*Excerpted from *De Calderón a Figueres* (San José: Editorial Universidad Estatal a Distancia, 1980), pp. 188–200.

recent report indicated that [opposition candidate Otilio] Ulate was ahead by 10,000 votes. . . . It was a marvelous election, with authentic popular participation. There was no plan that had to be rigidly adhered to, the pre-election work had not been organized, there was no established hierarchy of functionaries to give the party a unified orientation. The National Opposition must be strong to triumph under such adverse circumstances. . . . Don Otilio is firm, with a firmness that inspires admiration in us all. I am sure that all the nation's citizens will rise up with one voice . . . (February 13, 1948).

Possibly, by the end of this week the Tribunal will announce its judgment. And then, twenty-four hours later, the barracks should be turned over to Ulate. If the transfer does not occur, it would amount to a coup d'etat and would spark a civil war. The same thing would happen if the Congress calls for another election. . . . Civil war is an agonizing route. Therefore it would only be our final recourse. But God knows what faces us if circumstances make war necessary (February 15, 1948).

I am director of *El Social Demócrata,* the strongest and most combative opposition paper. Also, I am one of the people in charge of *"Onda Libre"* [Free Wave], a political radio program that always provokes controversy. In addition, I contribute to the political broadcast *"El Alma Tica"* [The Costa Rican Soul] which, with other stations, forms "The Voice of the National Opposition." I am there several hours a day. At eleven or twelve at night, I come from the station to my house, crossing the whole city. During this tumultuous campaign, I have had tremendous luck. A few of my friends from the party, in fact, almost all of them have suffered jail, assaults, and threats. Yet I have experienced no harm at all . . . the thing is not play; the threat of civil war hangs ominously over the country. It is a certain threat, present before us all, with all its possibilities of horror, devastation and misery (February 16, 1948).

We are on the verge of a civil war . . . The Electoral Tribunal gave us the victory, but it is possible that Congress, in tomorrow's session, will engineer a coup (February 29, 1948).

Yesterday, three friends and I barely escaped death when Dr. [Carlos Luis] Valverde's house was mercilessly machine-gunned. Two minutes after we left, a group of about fifty, this most respectable citizen's home was riddled by machine-gun fire . . . Carlos Luis is almost in death throes . . . I am working in the Opposition's radio network. . . . Yesterday and today I have been at the typewriter, writing page upon page. . . . We have continued the radio program on our own initiative, saying how things seem to us, in the tone we believe is right. We are trying to sustain the Opposition's enthusiasm, which is difficult given don Otilio[Ulate]'s silence. We say that orders for everything will soon come, without really knowing if this is certain given the circumstances in which we are living. . . . The entire nation is hanging on our broadcasts . . . we speak and we speak, waiting until they come to silence us (March 2, 1948).

Don Otilio was in the area that was cordoned off. Last night at ten he turned himself in to the police and at this moment is prisoner in the Penitentiary.

. . . We are sleeping at the radio station, infused with our self-importance because the eyes of the entire country are on us—hanging on our every word, on each movement (March 3, 1948).

On March 3, in the morning, we were informed that don Carlos [Valverde] was dying. We decided to prepare the announcement that we would have to make to the country. I wrote a funeral oration at ten in the morning . . . Carlos died at three-fifteen that afternoon. . . . On the eve of his burial, shooting erupted, more ferocious than ever before. From eleven at night, until two in the morning, San José was subject to intense machine-gun fire . . . three straight hours of relentless shooting. Shots were fired toward San Juan de Dios Hospital to terrorize the Costa Ricans who were going to see, for the last time, the face of Carlos Valverde. . . . Those of us working in "The Voice of the Opposition" have, of our own accord, been totally separate from the party's directors. Especially, this last week, it has made us feel . . . (March 7, 1948).

It is unchanged, after the week's truce. No "accord" has been reached, and it will all end in the most absolute failure. . . . We have had in our charge the radio campaign in the most difficult moments. . . . These are marvelous countrymen who intuitively create solutions. . . . During the strike of 1947, each group acted for its own part. . . . Each Costa Rican did his part and did it well. . . . So it will happen now. . . . The cease-fire ends tomorrow at midnight. . . . There will be no resolution. There will be none, because there cannot be one. . . . The Archbishop . . . has already withdrawn, reluctantly, from the negotiations. Talks continue only at the insistence of the bankers . . . we all know that it will end in nothing . . . (March 12, 1948).

The conflict has been ignited. There was a gunfight in the southern region, dominated by Figueres. Armed struggle has begun (March 12, 1948, at night).

I return to this notebook after a month of not seeing it . . . I am going to copy the notes jotted on a pad that I got in Río Cuarto, that sketch palely some of our actions (April 25, 1948).

Today we leave San José and head for Río Cuarto. . . . From the beginning I have assisted in dangerous missions: especially in drawing up and printing these clandestine leaflets . . . but we all want to go to the front, and for this we seek a way out. . . . We go to Grecia by car and continue to Río Cuarto on foot. In Grecia, two *compañeros* await us. We proceeded with two guides (April 3, 1948).

Today we arrived filthy and exhausted at Colonia de Toro Amarillo. We are at the front. (There are no notes for the next days. They were long days, with bad sleep and worse food. Days with a seven-hour watch, under sun or rain. None of us brought a blanket, and we were cold in the chilly early mornings. We go under direct orders—to open a second front. At the Río Cuarto camp, planes with arms are due to arrive. I summarize here, because I have no time. We are leaving Colonia de Toro Amarillo to go to Venecia de San Carlos. We hope to meet with other rebel groups in the region. The people of Venecia have made an indelible impression on me. Both rich and poor arrived with grain and cheese for us. We remained in Venecia for two days, until a message came

. . . ordering us to return because the arms . . . were to be unloaded at Río Cuarto. Well, we returned to Colonia. A day later, we had a rendezvous with a dozen others from San José . . . accompanied by the military commander to organize the second front. (I forgot to mention that whenever possible we confiscated weapons which provided the few arms we carried. A military excursion was made to trap the rear guard in Río Cuarto as they retreated to the mountains. The mission was a success; we seized a few guns . . .) (April 4, 1948)

We returned to Río Cuarto and as always set out in search of weapons that were to come one day. A few men have become impatient and begun to doubt that we will ever be supplied. . . . We have wasted two weeks hiking along trails and winding through the mountains between sun and rain, looking for rifles and machine guns. . . . We will stay here until we receive further orders. . . . Doña Delia, an admirable woman, at least fifty years old, came from Venecia to help us; because of her obesity, it is a struggle for her along these paths of God. We respect and appreciate her. . . . Last night it was terribly cold (April 16, 1948).

At noon, two planes passed overhead—we assumed they were the government's. They flew at a low altitude, just above the camp. We rapidly took cover in nearby trenches, fearing a bombardment. But nothing happened. Several people shouted enthusiastically, hoping that our arms shipment had finally arrived. Here we all, including our friends from San José who are accustomed to the comfortable life, are willing to tolerate rustic conditions. They sleep on the ground without covers, are weak from cold and fatigue, and patrol the trails to safeguard the peaceful dreams of their countrymen (April 17, 1948).

It is difficult to wait. [. . .] Here we are in Río Cuarto, virtually unarmed, yet willing to defend . . . the landing strip. People come and go. Old faces wander the paths in futile search for adventure that leads them nowhere; and, daily, boys flock in from all over the country. Most are city boys: students, workers, professionals, employees in commerce. They have traveled on foot for days to reach the front. . . . Some become impatient because the weapons never come, others set off through the jungle toward Cartago where there is fighting. . . . The gesture is noble but undisciplined. . . . Those of us from San José will go as a group wherever we are sent. They ordered us to stay and defend the landing strip. . . . I thought that our pacifist tradition would hinder the outbreak of a violent battle, but the Costa Rican has proven to be a valiant, daring soldier. . . . Not only those who fight, but also each and everyone who helps the combatants is doing his duty. It has been touching to find in Toro Amarillo, Río Cuarto, and Venecia unexpected gestures of understanding and support; there was a poor woman who did not want to charge us for coffee . . . another who made us detour by giving us delicious fresh cheese; the good people, everywhere, take us in lovingly, giving us food and clothing. There is no doubt that this is proof that we will come through this purified (April 19, 1948).

Last night we left Río Cuarto for a strategic site on the banks of the Toro

Amarillo. It is a half an hour from Río Cuarto and from here we have full control of the bridge that enemy troops will have to force their way across. We have fifty men, four women, and are ridiculously armed. But here we are beneath the trees, behind the embankments that guard the bridge over the Toro Amarillo River. Some people have rifles, though bad ones, there are a couple of Mausers and those who do not have guns hold bombs or grenades. The bridge is below us, it won't take much to wreak havoc with a small bomb. Coming from Villa Quesada, enemy troops have no alternative but to cross the river here. I doubt that they will march this way. In Río Cuarto we were relatively comfortable in ————————'s house. . . . Here we constantly stay in the jungle, always vigilant. A few of us try to sleep while others keep watch, I slept until about 8:00 P.M. when I was disturbed by a ruckus. . . . A sergeant arrived announcing the surrender of the government. . . . We went to the hut where doña Delia prayed and ecstatically said her rosary (April 20, 1948).

At daybreak we went to San José. We left Río Cuarto at eight-thirty in the morning, following the old Cinchona road, and arrived there at three in the afternoon. (It is a beautiful route, though rugged. . . .) We ate something in Sarapiquí. Upon arrival in Carrizal, a pleasant surprise awaited us; we were detained by a patrol . . . which accompanied us to Heredia, where they had some doubts about our identities. For quite a while, we were hostage to their scowls . . . until, finally, some acquaintances arrived and escorted us to San José (April 21, 1948).

I returned home with my green shirt and Capuchin beard. I bathed, shaved, and went out to breathe the new air. It is a marvelous morning. The city awakens and fills with flags (April 22, 1948).

Tonight Figueres is going to deliver an explosive speech. . . . Costa Ricans haven't the remotest idea of what he will say. But he will shake them violently (April 19, 1948).

[For the next few months, Rodríguez writes of Dostoevski, Gide, and other literary and philosophical musings. He returns to politics the following October.]

Next week, the month-long campaign to elect the deputies for the Constituent National Assembly begins. We have been campaigning for months; weekly, we transmit four half-hour radio programs written almost entirely by me. It is a slow process, but we can see results (October 24, 1948).

We Costa Ricans have not yet realized the extreme importance of our civil war . . . least of all those who were proud and fortunate enough to go in search of danger. . . . Only with the passage of years, when all our deeds are mere memories, will the true judge come—he who never heard the revolver's shots nor lived through these decisive days will put the events in perspective. . . . Today, I spoke with two brothers . . . they were in Terrazú at the outset of the war. They were cooks and nurses . . . they are poor boys, and live on the outskirts of town. Now, with their worthy humility, they speak of yesterday with simplicity and good-naturedly . . . they will continue to work as always. . . . Others, who did nothing . . . now raise their voices (October 31, 1948).

Today, I am almost dizzy with memories. How ready to look on it all with tenderness. How with a heart clean of prejudice and hate, ready to pardon and to pity all. There are days in which thoughts combat. On others, we dedicate ourselves to thinking systematically. On others, we feel filled with joy, but joy that makes room, that moves, that pushes. Today no. The joy that I have is a tranquil joy of the church bells [. . .] (October 31, 1948).

The election was the day before yesterday. It was a resounding victory for Ulate's party, the National Union. A marvelous triumph for the *Junta del Gobierno* which assured electoral freedom, more perfect than there had ever been. Our Social Democrats had limited success, winning only four seats in the Assembly. . . . We are struggling under difficult circumstances. The National Union took full advantage of the fact that its leader is the president-elect; while the Constitutional Party hoisted Calderón's fallen banner. . . . We . . . struggle against communism, against *calderonismo,* and against Ulate . . . but it does not matter. Time will speak for us . . . (December 10, 1948).

3.7 Letters to a Citizen*

BY PRESIDENT JOSÉ FIGUERES

José Figueres, known universally in Costa Rica as "don Pepe," was a leader of the 1948 insurgents and president of the Founding Junta of the Second Republic from May 8, 1948, to November 8, 1949, during which the army was disbanded and the banks nationalized. He helped found the social democratic National Liberation Party, and served two terms as Costa Rica's elected president, 1953–58 and 1970–74. Born in 1906, he is at this writing still playing the role of elder statesman and has supported cordial relations between Costa Rica and the Sandinista government of Nicaragua.

This letter is one of a series he wrote in the mid-1950s in an effort to popularize the ideology of the National Liberation Party.

ON SOCIAL REFORM

Dear Citizen:

In this letter I will address another of the definitions, or choices, that form a part of the ideology of our movement and that serve as guides to the current government.

One transcendental definition that a permanent political party must make in our time is whether or not it believes in twentieth-century social reform; whether it recognizes that modern science makes possible the production of sufficient goods and services for all members of the community, through the coordinated work of all; whether it believes that the poor and uneducated

*Cartas a un ciudadano (San José: Editorial Universidad Estatal a Distancia, 1983).

majorities that characterize underdeveloped countries should disappear; whether for these reasons it is or is not willing to study the social and economic sciences, to undertake plans for development, and to take measures for justice, and in general to promote a transformation of the country that would convert it into a society where all members enjoy at least a reasonable minimum of the material commodities and the facilities of health and culture that our epoch allows.

There is no need to state that our movement has defined itself perfectly on this dilemma. We are for social transformation and we accept its implications. On the other hand, we respect the opinion of a certain sector of public opinion that does not believe in reform, or has not studied it, or simply does not want to go through the trouble that accompanies change in the society in which one lives.

Many people do not notice (or did not notice until very recently) that we live in an antiquated society, which is disappearing. A society divided between "the governing class" and "the people," which inhabit two different stages of civilization. This phenomenon is more acute in other Latin American countries, but it is also present in Costa Rica.

Those who constitute the governing class, with "European" culture and life-styles, were raised within view of barefoot people, ragged children, and shacks with dirt floors. They have become as accustomed to that human spectacle as to the countryside that surrounds them. They don't see it.

Perhaps when they return from a trip to more advanced countries abroad, they find the sight of our people's wretchedness conspicuous and shameful. But routine quickly imposes itself and, again, they stop seeing it.

In general these people go through life carelessly believing that their country consists of themselves, the few who are privileged with fortune or education. The rest of the human beings who constitute our fellow citizens in political life and our collaborators in economic activity are seen unconsciously as simple necessary things: peons who were born to do the work on the coffee plantations, domestic servants who free us from disagreeable household chores, laborers who build our houses and operate our machines, keepers of the owners' account books. In other words, instruments for the comfort of the few.

For their part the poor, having been raised in poverty, have not yet conceived of another, better kind of life.

This routine manner of seeing the society in which we live is owed in part to the selfishness of some and the conformity of others, but mostly to custom, to habits of thought. How the governing class can reconcile its attitude toward the majority of its neighbors and fellow countrymen with its Christian faith and democratic feeling is a mystery. It is at least a topic of study that goes beyond the modest range of these letters.

But what is certain is that many people still see our society, thus divided, living simultaneously through various stages of civilization, as if it were as natural as night and day. For them this is a normal situation, nothing to think about.

When a member of a distinguished club says: "Everyone thinks that . . . " he is actually only expressing the opinion of the components of his social group. For him that group constitutes "everyone," and thus he is convinced that "everyone" in Central America drinks whiskey instead of French wines, that "everyone" wears wool coats in Quito and prefers English cashmere, that "everyone" buys an American rather than a European car.

"Everyone . . . !" What frivolity and what irony for those of us who know the peoples of America! How much closer to the statistical truth it would be to say that "everyone" goes barefoot! It is clear that this way of speaking is no more than a form of expression. But without doubt it is also an unconscious reflection of a spiritual attitude.

That attitude is what is changing, with twentieth-century social reform. Reform is already advanced in the richer and more educated countries, and it is gathering force now in the underdeveloped countries. Within a few generations, the poor and undereducated human masses are going to disappear. They will be incorporated into the life of their countries, until "everyone" really means everyone.

That old social scheme which is still seen in many countries cannot be justified in our time. Perhaps it had a justification, or at least an explanation, in previous eras without machines or scientific methods of production. Man was the only machine. Perhaps this was the painful price humanity paid for the birth of the arts and sciences, cultivated almost exclusively by the few.

But those conditions of low productivity, of low work yield, are changing with the advance of technology. As a consequence, people's mental habits must also change. What yesterday could be seen as normal, or as a sad necessity, must today be considered unacceptable.

At least that is how the National Liberation Movement defines its position on the social dilemma of our time.

I believe that this choice coincides with the desires of the majority of the citizens of Costa Rica (and of all America, at least), although some cannot formulate that wish in precise terms.

My feeling for the peasant comes in part from my admiration for the direct, fundamental, naked way in which he expresses equally a natural phenomenon (the banana trees "give birth to" bunches of bananas) or a current of universal thought. At a town meeting in Santa Ana, a man who looked old at age thirty gave me his stiff hand, saying to me in an almost trembling voice: "Don Pepe: I don't want my children to be coffee pickers!"

Here I will end my second letter on the ideology of the National Liberation Movement, according to which this country is being governed. As you see, Citizen, the subject becomes easier, at least for now.

Respectfully,
JOSÉ FIGUERES FERRER

CHAPTER IV

The Modern State and Society

Editors' Introduction

Contemporary Costa Rican society has been shaped by the political system
and class alignments that emerged in the aftermath of the 1948 civil war. The
social democratic insurgents had fought the war in large part to transform
the country's antiquated, coffee- and banana-based export economy and to
break the agroexporters' monopoly of political power. Simply put, they
hoped to create conditions for the rise of a middle class consisting of bureaucrats, professionals, and small entrepreneurs. They also sought to modernize
and industrialize Costa Rica and, particularly after the formation of the
Central American Common Market in the early 1960s (see Reading 4.5),
welcomed multinational companies and other foreign investors.

In many respects, their efforts were successful. The middle class expanded,
acquiring greater economic as well as political power. Though the social
democrats discouraged working-class organization per se (see Readings 4.2
and 4.7), the institutionalization of a welfare state and labor policies that
ensured constant increases in real wages contributed significantly to improved standards of living. Building on the reforms of the *calderonista* era,
successive Costa Rican governments in the post–civil war period created an
impressive array of health, education, and social welfare programs. This shift
toward a more active, "interventionist" role for the state required a massive
expansion of the government bureaucracy.

In the immediate postwar years, not all those on the winning side shared
the social democrats' radical reformist ideas. As noted in the previous

chapter (Introduction and Reading 3.4), the victors were divided into two main camps, the social democrats grouped around José Figueres and the conservative followers of Otilio Ulate. Immediately after the war, Figueres and Ulate signed a pact on who would govern.

The pact enabled Figueres to rule by decree as head of a junta for eighteen months, with a possible six-month extension. In return, Ulate—whose victory in the 1948 presidential election had been annulled by the *calderonista* Congress—was to take power at the end of the Figueres junta's term. Figueres and Ulate also agreed to hold elections in December 1948 for a constituent assembly that would write a new constitution for what Figueres termed Costa Rica's "Second Republic."

This arrangement essentially gave Figueres eighteen months to make his mark. His first move came within weeks. In a startling radio address, he announced the nationalization of banking (see Reading 4.1). This measure radically diminished the power of his erstwhile upper-class allies and paved the way for the economic and political ascendance of middle-class elements linked either to new sectors of business or to the expanding state bureaucracy.

Six months later, on December 1, 1948, the Figueres junta dissolved the army. At a ceremony held at San José's Bella Vista fort, Figueres declared that through abolishing the military "we want to uphold the idea of a new world" in the Americas. The junta's public-security minister turned the fortress keys over to the minister of education and Figueres, in a characteristically dramatic gesture, pounded the stone wall with a sledge hammer, symbolically beginning the renovation that would turn the barracks into the National Museum.

Less frequently recalled is the junta's treatment of its vanquished foes. The Mexican Embassy Pact that ended the civil war contained guarantees against reprisals (see Reading 3.4). But within weeks, Figueres abrogated the agreement and unleashed a wave of repression. Many Communists and *calderonistas* were dismissed from their jobs and had their property confiscated by special tribunals that operated outside the regular judicial system, and some went into exile.[1] The Communist Popular Vanguard Party was declared illegal and remained so until 1970. In December 1948, at the time of a brief abortive invasion by *calderonistas* based in Nicaragua, several imprisoned Communist leaders were taken under mysterious circumstances from a railroad car on the Atlantic line and executed at an isolated curve in the track called *Codo del Diablo* (Devil's Elbow).[2]

Though it limited the power and political activities of organized labor, the junta was clearly committed to a deepening process of social reform and the strengthening of democratic institutions. Women were, for the first time, given the right to vote in the 1949 Constitution. The junta repealed the harsh laws that had restricted blacks of West Indian descent—most of them Costa Rican-born—to the Atlantic region. It established a commission to provide blacks with documents they needed to function as full citizens.[3] The junta oversaw clean elections for a constituent assembly in 1948 and accepted the poor showing of Figueres's supporters, who captured only four out of forty-five seats. After eighteen months in power, Figueres did not exercise the option of prolonging the junta's rule by six months, quelling the fears of those who had never expected him to surrender his extraordinary powers. The Constituent Assembly had completed a new constitution and Figueres stepped down as promised, enabling the conservative Ulate to begin his four-year presidential term (see Reading 4.1).

Yet in the junta's brief tenure, the social democrats laid the foundations for steadily expanding state intervention in the economy. In broad terms, this intervention passed through three stages that corresponded roughly to the post–civil war decades: in the 1950s government policies emphasized the use of macroeconomic policies, especially subsidized credit from the nationalized banking system, for stimulating new kinds of development; in the 1960s, with the creation of the Central American Common Market, industrialists—including many multinationals—benefited from tax breaks and protectionism; in the 1970s, with slowing economic growth and two successive National Liberation Party (PLN) administrations, the state became increasingly involved in directing its own diverse industrial and service enterprises, grouped under the Costa Rican Development Corporation (CODESA). Over these three decades, the state assumed broader responsibilities for social welfare, setting up numerous agencies and "autonomous institutions" to deal with such issues as low-income housing, land reform, health care, and community development. As state intervention grew deeper and more complex, the bureaucracy expanded dramatically (see Readings 4.3 and 4.4). Its members eventually constituted a bulwark of political support for the PLN. By the beginning of the 1980s, Costa Rica experienced an economic crisis (discussed in Chapter V) that led to more changes in the state's role.

This state expansion also had a dark side, inasmuch as government agencies were often used to exert control over grass-roots efforts for change. As Diego Palma argues in Reading 4.2, the state and the dominant National Liberation Party have become expert at opening channels of "apparent resolution" that co-opt popular movements and do not always provide real solutions to social problems. "Whenever conflict threatens," he writes, "the Costa Rican state does not unleash repression, but simply creates another autonomous institution with which to provide a little space."

The National Liberation Party (PLN) became the principal advocate of state-sponsored development and reform, leaving its mark on Costa Rican society even in periods when its opponents controlled the presidency. The PLN was founded in 1951 by Figueres and his allies, who sought broader electoral appeal than their Social Democratic Party could provide. By naming the new party for the 1948 insurgents' National Liberation Movement, they soft-pedalled their ideology and won supporters among the anti-*calderonistas,* including some who were not sympathetic to social democratic ideology. The party took credit for the restoration of democracy and for the achievements of the junta, and the Social Democrats—now calling themselves *liberacionistas*—greatly increased their political strength. In the 1953 presidential elections, Figueres defeated wealthy landowner Fernando Castro Cervantes by an almost two-to-one margin.

As the state assumed wider responsibilities, the Church—which had played a pivotal role in securing the reforms of 1940–48—largely ceased its involvement in politics, although a handful of individual priests worked with the Figueres forces. Closely identified with the defeated *calderonista* movement, the Church had made significant political advances during 1940–48, particularly the institutionalization of Catholic religious education in public schools and the repeal of the anticlerical liberal laws of 1884. The Figueres junta and subsequent elected governments never challenged these Church gains. The Church was thus able to distance itself from the political fray. After the death in 1952 of the visionary Archbishop Víctor Sanabria, a champion of the *calderonista* reforms (see Readings 3.1 and 3.2), the hierarchy's interest in social concerns diminished and its political activism waned.[4]

In other Central American countries, where government-assistance programs were inadequate or nonexistent, Catholic organizations attempted to address pressing social problems, later playing an important role in bringing lay religious into close contact with the poor. In Costa Rica, with its expanding welfare state, such Church efforts were often superfluous. Yet some members of the Costa Rican clergy were adherents of liberation theology and called for debate over the Church's role in society.[5] They centered their activity in slum communities unreached by state-assistance programs. Reading 4.9 describes how, in one poor neighborhood near the Pacific port of Puntarenas, priests have been instrumental in building community organizations that work to improve living conditions.

In the countryside, peasants have also struggled to improve their lot, although less militantly than in neighboring countries. Land invasions and squatting have long been common in several regions of Costa Rica.[6] Yet here too the state has responded with reformist solutions that effectively neutralize calls for more radical change. Costa Rica's first major land reform agency— the Lands and Colonization Institute (ITCO)—was established as an outgrowth of the U.S.-sponsored Alliance for Progress. This massive hemispheric aid program was intended to undercut leftist movements inspired by the Cuban revolution. By urging Latin American governments to carry out agrarian reforms and institute other social programs, the alliance hoped to both generate pro-U.S. sentiment and ameliorate conditions that might fuel political upheavals. However, as Mitchell Seligson suggests in Reading 4.11, much of the agrarian reform's early activity did not involve land redistribution. Instead, it promoted settlement of unused lands and granted squatters legal title to lands in their de facto possession. Despite the state's efforts at agrarian reform and Costa Rica's image as a land of yeomen (see Chapter I), the landholding pattern remains remarkably unequal.

While the middle classes, industrialists, and agroexporters have benefited from the post-1948 Costa Rican political system, not all sectors of the Costa Rican population have been so fortunate. As noted above (see also Readings 4.2 and 4.7), the urban working class has faced major obstacles in union organizing and in defending its interests. The peasantry has, for the most part, been more sympathetic to the National Liberation Party but has also endured the often difficult conditions in the countryside. In Reading 4.13, A. Douglas Kincaid examines the relative quiescence of the Costa Rican peasantry in comparison with its counterparts elsewhere in Central America. Kincaid is critical of Palma's thesis on the state's ability to co-opt grass-roots movements (Reading 4.2), but he concludes that even though the peasantry's lot is not always an enviable one, the reach of government social programs has often been sufficient to defuse otherwise explosive situations in the rural areas.

Costa Rican blacks, the country's largest minority, were for many years targets of racist immigration and residence laws that restricted them to the Atlantic coast province of Limón, where they were isolated from national society and culture. In Reading 4.10, Philippe Bourgois analyzes antiblack discrimination and notes that blacks, though not fully assimilated, have often been quite upwardly mobile. Attributing black economic success to their abandonment of plantation employment for more lucrative cacao farming, Bourgois describes how in recent years many young blacks have entered the professions and migrated to the central part of the country.

Thirty years after the civil war, Costa Rican society had been thoroughly transformed. The basic principles of the social welfare state were almost universally accepted. In an era of economic growth, the state could afford its ever-expanding responsibilities, particularly as it spent so little on arms. Much of the population enjoyed rising standards of living and, with greater access to education, was able to take advantage of new opportunities in the industrial and public sectors. As could be expected, in the immediate aftermath of the civil war, intense rancor divided victors and vanquished. What was remarkable, however, was the speed with which the wounds healed. Some of this could be attributed to Costa Ricans' long experience with and commitment to constitutional government and civil society. But the state also contributed by absorbing real and potential social conflict and conciliating opposing interests. Critics such as Palma and Rojas note that such state intervention has often masked co-optation and efforts to mute independent organized efforts for change. Yet the advantages of this state role were obvious in the country's political stability, social peace and—until recent years—its relatively widespread prosperity.

NOTES

1. Oscar Aguilar Bulgarelli, *Costa Rica y sus hechos políticos de 1948* (San José: Editorial Costa Rica, 1978), pp. 439–41.

2. Jorge Mario Salazar, *Política y reforma en Costa Rica, 1914–1958* (San José: Editorial

Porvenir, 1981), pp. 155–56; Francisco Gamboa, *Costa Rica: ensayo histórico,* 4th ed. (San José: Librería Internacional, 1974), p. 144.

3. Carlos Meléndez and Quince Duncan, *El negro en Costa Rica,* 6th ed. (San José: Editorial Costa Rica, 1979), pp. 91–92, 134–36.

4. Pablo Richard and Guillermo Meléndez, *La iglesia de los pobres en Centroamérica: un análisis socio-político y teológico de la iglesia centroamericana (1960–1982)* (San José: DEI, 1982), pp. 251–300.

5. On the debate within the Costa Rican Church, see Ibid., pp. 251–300; and Javier Solís, *La herencia de Sanabria: análisis político de la iglesia costarricense* (San José: DEI, 1983).

6. Peasant land invasions and squatting are analyzed in Beatriz Villarreal, *El precarismo rural en Costa Rica, 1960–1980: orígenes y evolución* (San José: Editorial Papiro, 1983).

4.1 The Social Democrats and the 1948–1949 Junta*

BY JORGE ROVIRA MAS

Under the pact reached with the conservatives in 1948, José Figueres and the government junta were to have eighteen months in power. That gave them eighteen months to try to create a more interventionist state and an economy more oriented toward industrial development. In the short term, as Jorge Rovira Mas explains here, the junta achieved mixed results. In a truly radical move for the day, Figueres nationalized the banks, a measure tantamount to granting the state power to reshape the economy and the class structure. Many other economic moves, such as a revamped national Coffee Office, the establishment of a publicly owned utilities company, and the creation of autonomous social welfare institutions, also contributed to reorienting the economy and creating a framework for a more interventionist state. Yet on the political front, specifically in legislative elections and the drafting of a new constitution, the junta and its followers experienced setbacks at the hands of conservatives.

Rovira Mas holds a doctorate in sociology from the National Autonomous University of Mexico (UNAM). He teaches sociology at the University of Costa Rica, where he was also director of the Institute for Social Research.

THE spring of 1948 was a milestone in Costa Rican history, but the significance of the civil war and its aftermath varied for different social groups. The working class, for instance, had in 1948 reached its most advanced level in terms of political organization and participation in the struggle to redirect Costa Rica's destiny for its own benefit. Yet in the next years the working class would be subject to considerable repression [see Reading 4.7].

*Excerpted from Jorge Rovira Mas, *Estado y política económica en Costa Rica: 1948–1970* (San José: Editorial Porvenir, 1982), pp. 39–40, 47–56, 62.

For the elite, 1948 brought important changes. The dominant bloc was reconstituted, and other social groups, with new political and economic goals, rose to political power. For the principal sector of the dominant class, rooted in the agroexport system dating from the previous century, this change meant a loss of supremacy and the unmistakable beginning of its disappearance as the primordial force in Costa Rican society.

The apparent impulse for the 1948 insurrection was the struggle for liberty and honest elections. . . . But the middle classes had deeper motives. They sought to redirect the state's power in accordance with their own interests, increasing its involvement in the economic and social life of the country.

In May 1948, the government junta led by José Figueres came to power. It ruled for eighteen months, and then yielded to Otilio Ulate Blanco, the victor in the February elections. The junta began a series of economic reforms that aimed at sustaining a deeper type of capitalist development and encouraging the formation of new strata within the Costa Rican bourgeoisie. . . .

It must be stressed that the junta did not question the progressive measures of the two previous administrations, such as the Labor Code, Social Guarantees, and Social Security laws. Naturally, the *calderonista* reforms were not preserved at the behest of the large capitalists. On June 19, 1948, Figueres stunned the nation and disclosed the true direction of the junta. In an unexpected radio broadcast, he announced that the junta had conducted a detailed review of all ministries, was imposing a 10 percent tax on capital, and had nationalized the banks.[1]

From our contemporary perspective, it is difficult to appreciate the magnitude and significance of the bank nationalization in Costa Rica in 1948. The capitalists screamed to high heaven. They had reason to do so. In one swift stroke, nationalization of banking liquidated the political and economic power base of a major capitalist sector: finance capital. The government junta's action, possible only because of its extraordinary power, with one blow banished the bankers—one of the most reactionary groups in the bourgeoisie—from the economic scene.

There were other repercussions. Nationalization lessened the economic power of other groups among the large capitalists, particularly the commercial-importer sector, heavily reliant on bank credit. From then on, loans were granted according to diverse new criteria, principally to the various sectors and economic activities the government hoped to stimulate.

The daily newspaper *La Nación,* the clear and loyal voice of the old dominant bloc, stood closely allied with the traditional agroexporters. . . . Fully aware of how the availability of credit could make or break a capitalist, the editors saw which way the wind was blowing. . . .

The conscious intent of nationalization was to weaken, at its economic roots, the principal segments of the dominant class. Moreover, and more importantly, it was a tool to promote the emergence and formation of new bourgeois groups. These emerging nuclei of political power for the most part lacked capital, although they had a wealth of bourgeois aspirations. In time, the state-run banks became their most loyal allies. . . .

In the radio address, Figueres also outlined other endeavors that the junta intended to carry out: (1) installation of electric generators; (2) studies of the country's petroleum resources; (3) construction of a cement factory; (4) establishment of a national dairy to make condensed and powdered milk; (5) a broad five-to-six-year public works program; and (6) construction of low-cost housing. He also announced raises for some public employees and a 10 percent increase in the minimum wage for coffee and sugarcane laborers.

In its eighteen months in power, the junta acted on a broad front to modify existing institutions. For instance, the Institute of Protection for Coffee, founded during the depression, became the Coffee Office. By fixing the price to be paid to small producers, it allowed the state to assume a key role in regulating Costa Rica's most important export. The immediate aim was not to destroy the agroexport bourgeoisie, but to promote a more equal relationship between large businessmen and small growers.

Regarding the U.S.-controlled banana industry, the other important agroexport, the government began negotiations to curtail the near monopoly of the United Fruit Company. It imposed a 15 percent tax on company profits, as well as a special package of related taxes.

The National Production Council (CNP), a commodities agency, became a publicly owned, semi-autonomous institution in 1948, charged with creating incentives for producers serving the domestic market. It made loans to small farmers and stimulated output of basic foodstuffs by establishing price supports. The CNP also opened *expendios* or sales outlets that directly benefited consumers by offering staples at low cost, especially in rural areas where prices tended to be high.

The Costa Rican Electricity Institute (ICE) was founded in 1949, a cornerstone for the long-range political and economic ascent of new social groups. Establishing a large, secure energy source, it fulfilled a basic requirement for industrialization and capitalist development. Little by little, ICE absorbed foreign-owned utilities and telephone and telegraph services.

Finally, the junta reintroduced the New Industry Law—promulgated in Rafael Calderón Guardia's administration but limited under Teodoro Picado—designed to encourage imports of industrial equipment. The main stipulation was that the machinery had to be employed in factories that used at least 75 percent Costa Rican raw materials.

We must now examine the junta's efforts to redefine and expand the powers of the state. The Figueres-Ulate pact of May 1, 1948, was simply an accord between the victorious political sectors. It made possible a quick return to political and social normalcy by establishing certain prerogatives for each of the triumphant groups. The pact allowed the junta, with Figueres at its head, to govern for eighteen months, with a possible six-month extension. For the Social Democrats, this was the principal fruit of their participation in the civil war. The pact further recognized Ulate's victory in the February polls, and guaranteed him the presidency. The problem of control of Congress was addressed by a decision to hold elections on December 8, 1948, to select a National Constituent Assembly to work on a new constitution. Meanwhile, the junta appointed a commission to draft a constitution that could serve as a starting point for Assembly discussions.

Naturally, each political group had its own vision for the constitution. Parties controlled by the large capitalists wanted only minor modifications of the 1871 Constitution, which stressed liberalism, individualism, and a strong executive. The junta and the Social Democrats saw in the Assembly an extraordinary opportunity to modify the state's legal foundations and institutions, with the goal of creating conditions for broader supervision of, and deeper intervention in, the economy. . . .

The nine-member commission responsible for drafting the constitution included four Social Democrats, among them the eminent Rodrigo Facio Brenes [see Reading 2.1]. . . . The commission presented its draft to the junta, which made some changes and submitted it to the Assembly for discussion and ratification. . . . Meanwhile, the December 1948 elections were held, and the results were disheartening to the Social Democrats; they won only four of forty-five seats. . . . Ulate's National Union garnered the majority, and control of the Assembly. The conservatives' resurgence made ratification of a progressive constitution unlikely.

As drafted, the constitution would have profoundly altered the role of the state and dramatically shifted the traditional balance of power, as key articles make clear:

ARTICLE 59: The state will regulate the economy to the benefit of the collective. The production and distribution of basic goods are within the public domain.

ARTICLE 60: The state must protect the small landowner. It shall minimize the disenfranchisement of laborers and support private enterprise that operates in the social interest.

[Other articles set progressive land settlement and distribution policies; authorized the state "to regulate the economy scientifically for optimal productivity"; and established an array of autonomous institutions of the state, ranging from banking to public health to the sugar regulatory agency.[2]]

This draft of the constitution, with its clear Social Democratic imprint, was soundly rejected by the Assembly in April 1949. The overwhelming majority of the legislators belonged to the old conservative oligarchy; they were not willing to approve a new role for the state that facilitated and required intervention in the economy. The deputies did agree to modifications that would modernize the state in ways that the experiences of the last decade had clearly shown were desirable, but they did not admit clauses that would spur excessive state growth. The Assembly ended up approving the Constitution of 1871, adopting it as a starting point for debate and eventual reforms. . . .

Despite setbacks, a new constitution was approved on November 7, 1949. It was no longer identical to the Constitution of 1871, but the most radical components were eliminated. Several key points were incorporated that dealt with the Election Tribunal, the Comptroller General of the Nation, and the Civil Service system. A section was added granting municipalities greater autonomy. Included too in the ratified version was a momentous passage that established the autonomous institutions, a long-term goal of the Social Democrats [see Readings 4.3 and 4.4]. . . .

Although the Assembly initially rejected the constitution proposed by the junta, the version it did adopt established the legal foundation for a new modernized state with an unmistakable interventionist orientation. This state has continued to develop in the thirty years following the passage of the constitution.

NOTES

1. The 10 percent tax on capital was applied to amounts over 50,000 *colones* (then approximately $9,000), provoking alarm and opposition within the upper classes.—EDS.

2. Autonomous institutions are public-sector entities, outside direct control of the executive or central ministries, charged with specific tasks. Examples include the Social Aid Institute (*Instituto Mixto de Ayuda Social*—IMAS), charged with ameliorating poverty, and the National Housing and Planning Institute (*Instituto Nacional de Vivienda y Urbanismo*—INVU) responsible for building low-cost housing.—EDS.

4.2 The State and Social Co-optation in Costa Rica*

BY DIEGO PALMA

One distinguishing feature of the Costa Rican state is its capacity to absorb class conflict and channel demands of the poor through a series of institutions that partially ameliorate pressing problems while at the same time limiting popular participation. Unlike Guatemala and El Salvador (or the Somozas' Nicaragua), where the dominant groups have frequently resorted to violent repression to quell protest, the Costa Rican state and upper class have preferred to develop programs to co-opt or "demobilize" the citizenry. This essay by Diego Palma analyzes some legal, political, and ideological mechanisms employed in this process and describes shortcomings of Costa Rican democracy.

A Chilean sociologist, Palma has been a research associate of the Central American University Confederation (CSUCA) and a professor at the universities of Honduras and Costa Rica.

*Excerpted from "El Estado y la desmovilización social en Costa Rica," *Estudios Sociales Centroamericanos* 27 (1980): 183–206.

THE key to Costa Rica is the political ability of its dominant class to impose a system that corresponds to that group's own interests, and to have society as a whole accept this system as legitimate. The architects of this model have sought to distract and appease the popular sectors with respect to their own class goals and to incorporate or co-opt them as a supporting force for the goals of the dominant group.

Italian Marxist Antonio Gramsci elaborated the dual concept of hegemony-coercion as a tool for analyzing domination.[1] A dominant social group exercises hegemony over subordinate groups that accept its control, while it exercises coercion toward antagonistic groups that reject this control. In the hegemonic relationship, the interests of the dominant-class bloc prevail and direct the social whole, while the interests that correspond to secondary groups are selected, reformulated, and prioritized according to their compatibility with the goals of the hegemonic group. To exercise political hegemony requires some compromise.

As far as this article is concerned, hegemony dilutes the identity of subordinate groups. In contrast, coercion underlines the differences between government goals and those of the subordinates. Reinforcing the subordinates' aims, it creates the objective conditions necessary to develop class consciousness.

In general terms, Costa Rica is undergoing the same process as the rest of Central America, yet traits particular to its earlier history influence its later development:

a. In Costa Rica, coffee has been socially and economically dominant, in contrast to countries where foreign-owned banana farming predominated (such as Honduras and Panama). This situation allows the hegemonic class in Costa Rica to maintain some degree of control over economic resources and political power.

b. As the population historically has been rather small, relations of production have been based on a permanent scarcity of labor. This explains why such precapitalist relationships as *colonato* [lending plots of land or homes to coffee workers] and *aparcería* [sharecropping] had limited development in El Salvador and Guatemala, and why in Costa Rica wages have been relatively high. Costa Rica's ruling group has manifested fewer oligarchical tendencies than others in the region.

c. These demographics created a wide and highly mobile agricultural frontier. In periods of economic contraction, excess, unemployed population could be displaced toward the self-sufficient economy on the edges of the frontier. This process of spontaneous colonization served as an "escape valve" to relieve social pressures that the system of domination could not contain.

The opposition groups that compete every four years in elections do not represent significantly different social sectors or political programs. Rotation

of power is an interesting device. Elections with a choice of alternatives offer
the possibility of rejecting the dominant group—which does occur—but to
vote against the dominant group is, ultimately, to support the same continuing
political program. . . .

If for decades the principal mechanism of social stability had been to maintain an "escape valve" that would eliminate critical pressure directed against
the status quo, the bourgeois domination that established itself after 1948
intentionally and intelligently created its own "escape valve" mechanisms that
demobilize the sectors over which it exercises hegemony.

Autonomous institutions [see Readings 4.3 and 4.4] are such hegemonic
tools. Wherever conflict threatens, the Costa Rican state does not unleash
repression, but simply creates another autonomous institution which provides
a little space. The state thus opens a channel of apparent resolution, and
institutionalizes the conflict in order to relieve pressure.

In fact, our assertion is incomplete; the Costa Rican bourgeoisie simultaneously uses hegemonic and coercive policies. Hegemony is directed toward
the urban middle class, the rural petty bourgeoisie, and the *campesinos,* sectors
seeking support from the dominant group. Targets of coercion are the urban
and rural proletariats, sectors with which the bourgeoisie cannot compromise
without risking its own fundamental interests.

The tremendous effort invested in the educational system [see Reading 4.6]
and its role in preparing personnel for the large public bureaucracy [see Reading 4.3] have created a small vehicle of upward mobility for that part of the
urban middle class with no links to the private sector. Even now, this channel
is essential to the system's continued existence.

The bureaucracy, because of its technical character, is the sector that is
usually considered in the initiatives and programs of the bourgeois bloc. The
initiatives in which there is symbolic participation—a fundamental principle
of the dominant ideology—are much more refined when they relate to other
social sectors. Studying these situations clearly reveals that it is not a question
of alliances as such, but of small concessions made by the ruling groups to the
pseudoparticipation of the dominated sectors. This is how hegemony works.
It eliminates criticism by getting other groups to identify themselves with the
program of the ruling class, but fails to produce the benefits of incorporation
it purports to offer.

The petty bourgeoisie has been dealt with by various initiatives that, in
different ways and to varying degrees, bring together proposals for "community development." Institutions that reach rural centers generally try to carry
out programs with some community-based support. Such is the case of the
Ministry of Health in promoting rural health programs; the Ministry of Education promoting community-school relations; the Ministry of Agriculture organizing clubs for young people and housewives; and the National Housing and
Planning Institute in its programs of rural housing. The Ministry of Transport
forms committees that contribute to the construction of roads, schools, and

community centers. Even the national water and sewer utility has a Community Education Department to encourage grass-roots participation. This general philosophy crystalized in 1963 with the creation of the National Directorate of Community Development (*Dirección Nacional de Desarrollo de la Comunidad*—DINADECO).

The resources channeled through this initiative have been noteworthy. For example, between 1971 and 1974, DINADECO trained 18,663 community leaders and established 270 community associations. But data provided by DINADECO reflect the co-optive or "demobilizing" nature of this hegemonic initiative:

- 35.7 percent of the community associations, with 28.7 percent of the members, have functioned in a restricted manner, that is, only the directorate actually meets, while the members just pay dues or donate labor or materials.
- Only 41.6 percent of association funds were spent on local infrastructure works that directly address the most pressing problems cited by community leaders who were surveyed.
- 63.5 percent of associations have no collaborative relationship with similar organizations, and 66.9 percent have never joined another group on a project. This concentration on local concerns distorts political perspective.

These findings are confirmed by a survey of leaders' interests and concerns: only 1 percent cited the importance of "social problems," and just 1.4 percent selected "popular participation."

Hegemonic and coercive policies are not necessarily mutually exclusive. Coercive policies can in fact complement hegemonic ones, particularly when applied to sectors—such as the rural *precaristas*[2] [squatters] and the industrial proletariat—whose initiatives arise outside of and in opposition to the rules of the game imposed by the bourgeois program or directly challenge fundamental aspects of capitalist accumulation. . . .

The entire process known as "agrarian reform" [see Reading 4.11] should be understood as the ruling class's attempt to open an "escape valve" to release, and handle in an institutionalized manner, pressure from the landless. In 1960 the agricultural frontier in Costa Rica was considered exhausted or closed. Actually, this was a question of an act of law, since there were no more untitled lands, but much of the land remained uncultivated. The law left open the possibility that the state could purchase land and provide it to members of the excess population, that is, those who were landless and unemployed.

The law is based on an explicit and unalterable "respect for private property"—precisely what created the problem in the first place. The law's conditions ensure that it remains an initiative intended to ease, but not solve, the problem. Without addressing the roots of the problem, the law demobilizes the *campesinos* through an offer of an institutional channel of apparent resolution that does not bring them into conflict with the status quo.

Peasant land seizures occur outside this established institutional channel. Although part of this conflict lends itself to an institutional solution, a larger part does not; the escape valve is, and should remain, narrow to avoid attracting too much attention, which might cause too many people to resort to it. In the name of order, the [Rural] Guard burns farms and jails *precaristas,* who then generally remain available as a source of cheap seasonal labor.

This institutionalized foresight, neatly undermining attempts at mobilization that might prove to offer alternatives to the bourgeois program, is also evident in the treatment of potential organization by the proletariat. It is difficult to assert that in Costa Rica there exists "repression of trade unions." Yet, the conditions that are legally imposed on the right to engage in union activity have resulted in so little union development as to render "repression" unnecessary. [For a discussion of labor, see Reading 4.7.]

Although hegemony and coercion can coexist, in Costa Rica hegemony is key to the domination process. It is basically this manipulation of the political and ideological superstructure that makes Costa Rica seem distinct from other Central American societies where coercion prevails, and veils the similarities that impose a common neocolonial condition.

The Costa Rican model is "expensive," as the state's responsibilities and responses multiply, filling gaps that elsewhere would not be in its purview. The development of the state apparatus reflects this, but it is only the tip of the iceberg regarding the extent of the plans and programs that the state will shoulder to make the system work [see Reading 4.3].

The effectiveness of the model depends on a certain accommodation between the parties that join in this relationship. The system's ability to respond is challenged by the quantity and quality of the demands made on it by the popular sectors. . . . After 1948, the class parties (basically the Communist Party, called *Vanguardia Popular*) were more interested in creating and improving their party organizing than in attempting to attack the heart of the system. Thus, the popular movement has been guided fundamentally by a desire to enhance its position within the system—and the system can, up to a point, absorb it. The Costa Rican Left has not in recent years proved to be an attractive alternative to ongoing domination [see Reading 7.7].

Amid the economic crisis, the "expensive" model of domination could not function as it had. Throughout 1979, budget cuts were made in almost all "nonproductive" programs, resulting in stagnation in state social welfare institutions. The limits within which the state can operate hegemonically are narrowing. This general situation accentuates the importance of fine political management by the governing team. The National Liberation Party, with a codified doctrine and a political presence even when it is not in power, has always shown a greater and better ability to maneuver than the various coalitions that have challenged it.

In summary, an open period began in 1948, characterized by an efficient, optimistic political program, conceived and supported mainly by the National Liberation Party. Changes have occurred and will continue to occur in the context within which authority is exercised, which could result in a loss of its legitimacy. Nevertheless, we believe that if, as expected, there is continuity in the political process and even if individual and collective consumption levels decline, Costa Rican democracy will still continue to function for a long time.

NOTES

1. Antonio Gramsci, *Oeuvres Choisies* (Paris: Ed. Sociales, 1959).

2. The term *precarista* derives from *ocupación precaria,* used to refer to occupations of property that are de facto or of precarious legal status.—EDS.

4.3 The Bureaucratization of the Costa Rican State*

BY LUIS GARITA

This essay analyzes qualitative and quantitative changes in the state apparatus since the 1948 civil war, and explores how the administrative structure reflects widely held beliefs about political and economic priorities, particularly as embodied in the National Liberation Party (PLN) model. It examines how Costa Rica has tended to substitute bureaucratic growth for genuine problem solving, and notes the way that the bureaucracy itself becomes a self-perpetuating, self-protecting institution.

Luis Garita holds a doctorate in public administration from the University of Paris. He is rector of the University of Costa Rica, where he is also a professor of public administration.

THE world economic crisis of the 1930s encouraged a significant reorientation and reorganization of the Costa Rican state apparatus, especially during the 1940s. New classes and political parties came to power, and changes in the structure of government became necessary to realize their aims. A model of economic growth was chosen that relied heavily on state intervention. . . . Let us list some changes in the state between 1940 and 1949:

First, the merging of independent academic faculties to create the University of Costa Rica (UCR). The founding of the UCR had great cultural repercussions, but more important, it was an effort to bolster the economy by supplying

*Excerpted from "El proceso de burocratización del Estado costarricense," *Ciencias Económicas* 1, no. 1 (1981): 105–15.

the state with the technically skilled personnel it lacked. . . . The whole process of bureaucratization required technical backing, capable of breaking the public sector's traditional paternalism and simultaneously ensuring rational behavior by personnel. . . .

Second, the establishment of the social security system and the Social Guarantees, part of the 1943 constitutional reforms [see Reading 3.1]. These set out general principles for the state concerning public health, the protection of the family and children, regulation of labor-management relations, and even the formation of cooperative production units. . . .

Third, the National Production Council was set up to foster agricultural development through price intervention. Similarly, an entity was created to begin the construction of low-income housing. Both were part of an emerging welfare state.

Fourth, approval of the Labor Code was a further move in this direction. Besides creating new tribunals and government bodies, it signified the first step toward breaking the spoils system of political appointments and instituting more rational public-sector personnel practices. . . .

The 1949 Constitution, based largely on the model sought by the National Liberation Party, provided a framework to make the expanding state bureaucracy more efficient. The constitution helped to advance plans for increased government intervention in the economy, technological advance, and social reform [see Reading 4.1]. . . . It established new institutions and supported older ones as they grew and consolidated. Among the changes were strengthening the judicial system, abolishing the army, establishing the General Comptrollership of the Republic and setting rules for the national budget, setting up autonomous institutions, appointing a Supreme Electoral Tribunal, and instituting a civil service.

At the start of the 1950s, conditions thus favored quantitative and qualitative bureaucratic growth linked to the political model endorsed by the National Liberation Party. Many qualitative changes stemmed from the civil service system created in 1953, which guaranteed a greater level of rationality in public administration. The new system hired bureaucrats on merit, followed strict hierarchical job classifications for filling positions and promotions, provided job stability, advancement, and retirement benefits. . . .

Support for the Civil Service in the 1949 Constitution grew out of reformist attitudes held by the youth within the Social Democratic Party. It was not the result of a change in the attitude of the general public, but of an idea that was just beginning to take hold. . . . The spoils system was formally and explicitly maintained until 1953, the end of President Otilio Ulate's term, when the civil service statute was approved. Thus, the first effect of the enactment of a civil service system was the formal modification of preexisting practices and norms. Its second effect was to secure the positions of followers of the party in power. Instead of erasing the past and making a fresh start, the system was used to consolidate an existing situation. The statute also helped to consolidate a new social group: the Costa Rican bureaucracy.

From that moment, the role of this new class or group in national life would steadily grow. With the new formal protection and security conferred by the Civil Service, and with the politicians' sway steadily diminishing, the bureaucrats slowly but surely began forming their own groups, their own means of guaranteeing themselves an important and relatively comfortable position in society. Organized in unions, they defended their interests with a very strong group consciousness. . . .

A concommitant process was the simple quantitative growth of the bureaucracy, which was linked to changes in the economy and to qualitative changes in the administrative structure. The reformist, developmentalist orientation of the National Liberation Party favored and required state growth. Simply put, this implied big government. But because the state also had to be efficient and effective, bureaucratic forms were adopted to channel its growth. . . .

As an illustration of the magnitude of the growth of the Costa Rican state, three points should be highlighted: (1) the budget, (2) the number of institutions, and (3) the number of public-sector employees. This table depicts the growth of the state budget:

EXPENDITURES

Year	Colones (in thousands)	US$ (in thousands)
1900	6,699	3,156
1916	7,530	2,955
1937	32,834	5,853
1950	220,000 (approx.)	36,567
1970	1,070,000 (approx.)	162,121
1973	2,028,975	307,420
1977	4,700,000	545,512

Source: Table elaborated by the author based on data from the Central Bank (1969–77) and the national archives for 1900, 1916, and 1937. Dollar amounts calculated by the editors.

The number of public-sector institutions varied enormously after 1950, because according to the National Liberation Party, every time the state took on a new function, a new institution was needed to perform it [see Reading 4.2]. Thus, in 1955 there were 10 ministries and 8 autonomous institutions; in 1975, 12 ministries and 28 important autonomous institutions. By 1979, the number of autonomous institutions was over 180.

This growth nevertheless occurred during periods of acute economic crisis and rising political tension. The political model that had been adopted was unable to respond fully to public demands, and the creation of government institutions appeared to be a temporary solution to a crisis that, in any event, was reaching its limits.

The creation of IMAS [*Instituto Mixto de Ayuda Social*—Social Aid Institute], for instance, illustrates this point. A structural problem—poverty—had to be solved. However, this had to be done by offering palliatives, not by confronting the causes. Besides, IMAS duplicated the administrative work of other institutions such as INVU [*Instituto Nacional de Vivienda y Urbanismo*—National Housing and Planning Institute], OFIPLAN [*Oficina de Planificación Nacional*—National Planning Office], the *Patronato Nacional de la Infancia* [National Child Welfare Organization], etc.

The growth of the budget and the multiplication of government institutions indicate that the public sector absorbed a significant share of available labor. In 1950 the state employed 6 percent of the working population; by 1958, 10 percent; by 1974, 12 percent. Taking into account only the economically active population—those with jobs—the state employed about 15 percent of the work force in 1974. . . .

Indeed, the state has had to compensate for the deficiencies of a model that was not based on national industrial growth. The Costa Rican model of industrialization is similar to that of industrialized countries inasmuch as the technology employed tends to generate little employment. Agricultural modernization, moreover, contributes to both growing unemployment and a tendency for the state to absorb excess workers. Not only did the state now assist economic development, offering better and more sophisticated services, but it also had to absorb labor.

These quantitative changes in the bureaucracy modify the very nature and functions of the administrative structure. This in turn poses new administrative problems. In this respect, criticisms of the state's enormous growth in personnel are naïve or ill-intentioned. This situation is simply the result of a political model that has been followed for thirty years with the approval and consent of successive governments and the population.

4.4 CODESA, Autonomous Institutions, and the Growth of the Public Sector*

By Mylena Vega

In the previous reading, Luis Garita outlined the bureaucratic expansion that accompanied state intervention in diverse areas of social and economic life, a process that naturally corresponded to changes in the National Liberation Party's model for a mixed economy. Here, Mylena Vega discusses the two major phases of that model, prior to the recent economic crisis. From the 1948 civil war through the late 1960s, Costa Rica had

*Excerpted from *El Estado costarricense de 1974 a 1978: CODESA y la fracción industrial* (San José: Editorial Hoy, 1982), pp. 35–46, 56–63. The excerpts have been condensed in translation, and minor omissions have not been indicated. The order of several paragraphs has been rearranged.

what she terms an Estado-Gestor—*a state that actively encouraged development but had limited direct participation in the economy. The state also dispersed the concentrated power of the executive branch and assigned some of its tasks to new entities called autonomous institutions. The second phase began around 1970, when the state became not only a stimulator of economic development, but a participant in it, primarily through the Costa Rican Development Corporation, known as CODESA. In this period, the independence of autonomous institutions was curtailed, and power was again concentrated in the executive branch.*

Vega studied at the Johann Gutenberg University in West Germany, and received a licenciatura *degree in sociology from the University of Costa Rica, where she has worked in the Institute of Economic Research and the School of Anthropology and Sociology.*

FOR some twenty years after the civil war, the Costa Rican state was an *Estado-Gestor* that sought to stimulate economic development. Its function was to build infrastructure, develop social welfare programs and services, establish financial and regulatory institutions, and promote protectionist measures for industrial development. The same dynamic of development required the state to participate in the reproduction of capital, for example, in improving the work force and health care. The state, in essence, created better conditions for development in a period characterized by import substitution within the context of the Central American Common Market [see Reading 4.5].

The development of the *Estado-Gestor* was in the interest of various ascending social groups—primarily the industrial sector—that the state itself had promoted. By 1949 a parallel process of executive decentralization was occurring through the founding of "autonomous institutions." Politically, their creation may also have helped break the domination, centered in the executive, of the traditional agricultural-exporting sectors.

In this sense, as Ana Sojo has noted, the creation of the autonomous institutions was intended to "avoid the concentration of many duties in a few hands. This act was a blow to the executive, which, during the era of domination by bourgeois agricultural export interests, had decided the state's duties more directly and delegated important functions to institutions which enjoyed a certain amount of independence."[1] That independence is relative; the executive appointed the boards of directors of these institutions (later naming four while the opposition appointed three), although their autonomy was stipulated. . . .

Meanwhile, the industrial sector was broadening and consolidating; the middle class was growing; personnel with new political and technical skills were forming in the National Liberation Party (PLN). The growth of representatives of the new industrial and agricultural sectors, with interests closely linked to the economic diversification carried out by the PLN, strengthened the bloc in power. . . .

Around 1969, state orientation began changing under PLN influence. The tendency was toward centralization of executive functions, and state intervention in the economy assumed different traits from those of the earlier *Estado-Gestor*.

No longer was state intervention limited to regulation, services, and infrastructure development. Increasingly, it extended into the productive cycle and the reproduction of capital. This was achieved fundamentally by creating new public or state-owned enterprises and by institutionalizing greater public-sector participation in the reproduction of capital, for example, in improving the work force, health care, and transport.

As the state changed and expanded its economic role, its structure tended to again centralize functions in the executive. . . .

A number of measures advanced by the PLN were adopted, amounting to an attempt to affirm executive dominance and consolidate certain groups' powers. Several reforms affected the autonomous institutions. For instance, a Coordination Commission on Autonomous Institutions was created within the Planning Ministry, and a 1974 law enabled the executive branch to appoint a president for each institution, responsible directly to the president of the republic. These changes tended to strengthen the executive's political control over the autonomous bodies, while leaving them administrative independence.

Among the other reforms contributing to centralization of power was a campaign-financing law. Called the "political debt" [*la deuda política*], it benefited established parties, particularly the National Liberation Party.

The dominant feature of state intervention during the 1970s was the systematic initiation of state capitalism, that is, state acquisition of the means of production. The state created enterprises formally constituted as corporations, with the same legal status as private businesses.

Most state enterprises of this type were created by the Costa Rican Development Corporation, known as CODESA [*Corporación Costarricense de Desarrollo Sociedad Anónima*].

Some other corporations, including the oil refinery, were also nationalized. The Costa Rican Petroleum Refinery (RECOPE) was created in 1963, with 15 percent state ownership. By 1973 the state controlled more than 65 percent of the shares; in 1974 it owned 80 percent, and by October of that year, it acquired the remaining shares. . . .

In later years, RECOPE's activities also encompassed financing other state enterprises [such as some public transport]. Together with CODESA, it is thus closely linked to other parts of the public sector and constitutes an integral part of the state capitalist system. But RECOPE, though controversial, never provoked serious conflict with industrial capitalist sectors. Perhaps the nationalization of RECOPE, occurring amid the energy crisis in the early 1970s, was easier to accept, since the state appeared best suited to take charge of this activity that involved the interests of capital as a whole.

CODESA was a different story. Created in 1972, CODESA grew rapidly between 1975 and 1978 to become the country's principal and most representative institution of state capitalism. The corporation financed various private projects and also set up its own businesses in areas previously controlled exclusively by private capital. . . . In addition to embodying the new state orientation, CODESA became the most controversial public-sector institution and a principal source of conflict with the industrial sector.

CODESA was conceived, according to one of its own brochures, as "a system of operations different from commercial banks, that will lend support to the work of the entrepreneur and which, under certain circumstances, will act as an investor by assuming the risks inherent in the early stages of enterprise development, with the intention of transferring the enterprise to the private sector once those risks have diminished and the enterprise is well rooted in the marketplace."[2] The state was assuming a necessary economic function, one that complemented the activities of the private sector.

By law, CODESA would be a joint venture, 67 percent state owned and 33 percent privately owned. Its authorized capital would consist of 100 million *colones*, 67 million *colones* to be generated by the sale of government bonds and 33 million *colones* from public sale of shares. The law did not state whether the government shares or state participation would be permanent or transitory.

CODESA was a *sociedad anónima*, a type of corporation. It was thus governed by the Commercial Code and was not subject to supervision by the Comptroller General. Neither CODESA nor its subsidiaries had to submit purchases of materials or equipment to public bidding. . . .

The industrial sectors and the Chamber of Industries supported CODESA's creation, regarding it as necessary to complement the process of domestic capital accumulation, which had long been inadequate because of weak capitalist development. Later, the industrialists questioned the support they had given.

The influential Costa Rican industrialist Richard Beck commented on the controversy in an April 31, 1978, interview, just days before he took up his post as CODESA's executive president. CODESA had, he noted, invested in areas that the private sector had been reluctant to enter, because of the size of investment and the degree of risk involved. Yet, he said, in other areas CODESA had entered into direct competition with the private sector. This "incursion" into private territory is at the heart of the dispute. . . .

CODESA's legal mandate was to promote Costa Rican development by strengthening private enterprise within the framework of a mixed economy. Among other things, it had to modernize, expand, and improve the efficiency of existing activities; develop new activities; advance import substitution; diversify exports; integrate the various economic sectors; create new businesses; provide administrative and technical assistance to old and new firms; extend loans and credits; and develop national capital markets. This range of functions, designed to stimulate development, explains the diversity of CODESA's investments and tasks.

CODESA has guaranteed businesses in bankruptcy, financed or endorsed private enterprises, created joint ventures, and assumed responsibility for diverse projects that failed [in private hands] in their initial stages. It has also formed its own enterprises, constituted as corporate subsidiaries. CODESA's actions clearly complemented private capital. In the case of its subsidiaries, where the property belongs entirely to CODESA, there may be possible areas of competition with the private sector.

NOTES

1. Ana Sojo, *Estado empresario y lucha política en Costa Rica* (San José: Editorial Universitaria Centroamericana, 1984).—EDS.

2. In fact, no CODESA enterprises were transferred to the private sector until the mid-1980s, when international lending institutions began to pressure for "privatization" of the Costa Rican public sector.—EDS.

4.5 Costa Rica and the Central American Common Market*

BY EDUARDO LIZANO

Ever since independence, Central Americans—at least sporadically—have dreamed of unity. But efforts to form a union failed, or ended in the bloody turmoil that characterized the Central American Union in the 1820s and 1830s. Over the decades, as thoughts of a political federation were discarded, the idea of a regional economic union took root. In the early 1960s, the Central American Common Market came into being and, though it has not always thrived, it has continued to function ever since.

Costa Rican representatives attended the initial sessions of the United Nations Economic Commission for Latin America (ECLA) in 1951 when the resolution on economic integration was approved, and the country joined the Central American Common Market two years after its formation in 1960. For Costa Rica, economist Eduardo Lizano concludes, the Common Market accelerated industrialization by broadening and protecting markets. It has also led the Central American nations to greater interdependence, altered the type of foreign investment in the region, and increased Costa Rica's dependence on foreign technology, financing, and culture.

Dr. Eduardo Lizano is a leading Costa Rican economist and president of the Central Bank. In this 1979 essay, he examines the Common Market's impact and addresses problems inherent in the model of industrialization it encouraged. He also raises questions about the patterns of industrialization it fostered and their effect on Costa Rica's social structure.

*Excerpted from Eduardo Lizano, "Costa Rica y la integración económica centroamericana," in *Costa Rica contemporánea*, vol. 1, ed. Chester Zelaya (San José: Editorial Costa Rica, 1979), pp. 279–83, 290–98.

BEFORE examining the Costa Rican debate on integration, it is worth establishing a historical perspective on the impetus for such cooperation after World War II. . . .

The arguments in favor of integration stemmed from diverse schools of economic thought and varying ideologies:

a. The ideas that gained ascendancy through ECLA in the 1950s were critical. ECLA viewed the world depression of the 1930s as evidence that the prevalent model of development, with its emphasis on exports, had been exhausted. Instead, it turned its attention toward the domestic market, specifically by trying to stimulate industrialization by import substitution. . . . In Central America, however, this practice faced nearly insurmountable obstacles, because the domestic markets were so small. . . . Consolidation of the five small markets—integration—appeared essential. . . .

b. Businessmen knew that to compete internationally, particularly by exporting manufactured goods, they must first secure a base in national markets. This would require them to develop entrepreneurial experience, train personnel, and accumulate capital in order to later try to export. Again, the problem of narrow national markets emerged as an obstacle, and integration seemed the desirable solution. . . . In this case, integration was not viewed as a new development model, but as a means of bringing export-oriented growth to a more advanced stage, where exports would be diversified to encompass manufactured goods as well as traditional agricultural products.

c. Social groups responsible for the agroexport growth model (emphasizing agricultural exports and industrial imports) considered their sociopolitical position in jeopardy, as they were subject to fluctuations in international markets over which they had little control. They thought it opportune to enter other productive activities, so that they would be less dependent on factors beyond their control. On the contrary, they would be under the protective umbrella of tariffs, special duty exemptions, and fiscal abatements. These socially and politically influential groups viewed Central American integration as a means of broadening their investments while lessening their risks.

d. Integration was viewed as a path toward rebuilding the Central American Union. The *Patria Grande* would not be achieved via despotic generals, or political cabals, or idealistic dreams. It would be constructed on the carefully laid plans of businessmen and investors who would gradually build a system based on the reciprocal interests of the business community, consumers, workers, and government officials. Regional interests would slowly transcend national interests. . . .

e. Finally, critics viewed Central American economic integration as just a new form of dependency generated by the international capitalist system.

The capitalist objective would be unchanged: subjugation of the less-developed countries, like those of Central America. Integration would, it was argued, establish diverse new bonds of dependence, such as multinational businesses' control of a vast part of the production units in the area, financing from foreign sources, and implantation of foreign standards of consumption and technology. All this would allow developed countries to export capital, technology, and norms of consumption to nations on the periphery, thus deriving the benefits of a regional, and virtually captive, market. . . .

[When the Central American Common Market came into being], intraregional trade expanded greatly, as regional trade barriers were lifted and, simultaneously, tariffs were enacted to protect the fledgling alliance from international competition. Consequently, the flow of foreign commerce changed appreciably. . . . Prior to integration, all exports were sold in international markets; currently, a fifth of foreign trade is intraregional. . . . Traditional agroexports, furthermore, account for a smaller share of Costa Rica's foreign commerce.

With the expansion of intraregional commerce came a marked increase in the payments among the member nations. To simplify these transactions, the integration program established a Central American Chamber of Compensation. . . . The countries agreed to settle accounts every six months, which allowed them to appreciably expand foreign trade without having to make available more hard currency, which was chronically in short supply.

In the initial multilateral phase of the integration program, import taxes comprised more than half of total governmental revenues. Integration addressed the problem in a sensible manner. Goods that were once imported from outside the Central American Common Market were now imported from members, without duties. And the government granted extensive customs exemptions as part of its policy of fiscal incentives to encourage the establishment of as many industries as possible. The drop in import-tax income required substantial modifications in Costa Rica's tax system, and the introduction of consumer and sales taxes. . . .

The *raison d'être* of integration was the need to promote industrialization and find solutions to the problems arising from the old export-oriented growth model. The expanded markets and protectionist tariffs that accompanied economic integration proved to be the key to the industrialization of the isthmus. Industrialization was based on import substitution, particularly in the production of consumer goods for regional markets. But little emphasis was given to agroindustry or the production of goods for export beyond Central America.

In Costa Rica the industrial component of the gross national product grew steadily, rising from 12 percent in 1952 to the current 21 percent. Other economic indicators, such as number of jobs, salary levels, exports, and electricity consumption, also showed marked increases.

Yet despite the healthy impact on industrialization, a number of problems have risen for Costa Rica. Protectionism has created inefficient industries incapable of exporting outside Central America. . . . It could be argued that protectionism must be temporary, and must be gradually lessened if the industrial sector is to become competitive. However, industrialization has created sectors with strong interests, who oppose phasing out protectionism. The social costs of industrialization are extremely high, not only with respect to prices and employment, but also because of methods of financing. Costa Rica took the path of offering financial incentives to industrial enterprises. The result was adjustments to the tax system that, in effect, made all taxpayers pay the industrialists' taxes. . . .

An increase in foreign investment has been one of the most significant aspects of integration. Investors have been lured for two reasons. They hoped to continue exporting to Central America, but the high tariffs imposed on goods imported from beyond the Common Market posed a barrier. Thus, they installed plants within the Common Market to "leap over" the protectionist barriers. Second, the five nations adopted a policy of liberal tax breaks to entice foreign investors. The result was a virtual incentive war. Competing for investment, the countries failed to develop a unified regional investment policy.

These vast new investment opportunities brought "de-Central Americanization," an influx of foreign capital, and a simultaneous increase in foreign ownership of Central American property. In Costa Rica, foreign investment rose approximately $100 million between 1959 and 1969, $36 million of which was channeled into industry. . . . Foreign investment in industry serving the regional market (and banking and advertising) can be considered a new stage in the economic development of the isthmus. The first phase was exploitation of natural resources (mineral and agricultural). Then came foreign investment in such public services as energy, transport, and communications. Finally, through integration, a third stage—industrialization—is being reached.

For some analysts, the extent of foreign investment in the region is indicative of a new form of dependency. Other components of the dependency include industry's reliance on imported raw materials, parts, and technology; a tremendous public and private foreign debt; and pervasive penetration of foreign consumption patterns in Central American societies. . . .

Economic integration has had social repercussions as well, a consequence of industrialization. . . . First, an incipient industrial proletariat has been created, though without yet assuming the role it has played in other countries. Second, artisans and cottage industries have been weakened and displaced by manufacturing. . . . Third, establishment of new manufacturing enterprises has required the services of a broad range of middle- and high-level managerial, administrative, and technical personnel. . . . This group, primarily professionals, has expanded and strengthened the growing middle class, along with high government bureaucrats and professionals. Fourth, the ranks of the captains of industry have swollen. Understanding this group's importance is critical to comprehending the evolution of the Costa Rican power structure.

The remaining question, as yet to be studied, is whether the new industrialist class is different from the traditional oligarchy of agroexporters and commercial importers, or whether the same old groups are engaging in new activities. If it is a new group, then it is important to examine why traditional groups, with political and economic power, permitted the formation of a new group that would challenge their long-standing economic influence. If, however, the new industrialists are the old elite, why have they put their money into manufacturing?

4.6 Costa Rican Education: Making Democracy Work

BY LOUIS F. MIRÓN

In the 1890s age of liberalism, Costa Rica's leaders recognized the role of an educated citizenry in a democracy. In the 1940s and 1950s, as several authors in this chapter have noted, education became a tool for providing the modern state with much-needed trained personnel as it assumed broader and more complex social functions, and for providing the growing industrial sector with the technical and managerial staff it required. After 1948, as the traditional elite was forced to yield to a more fluid social structure, higher education became a crucial path of upward social mobility, an entrée into the growing middle or professional classes. The high literacy rate, and the unmistakable if not easily quantifiable value the nation places on education, have also permeated Costa Rica's culture and helped define its national identity.

In this reading, Louis Mirón briefly surveys the Costa Rican education system. He stresses the way the system has been modified in recent years to give students with varied needs and prospects a variety of options, in academic or vocational programs. He also describes efforts made to improve rural education, and the vast and inexpensive opportunities that exist for university education and professional training.

Mirón, a native of Guatemala, received a doctorate in Latin American Studies and Public Policy from Tulane University, where his dissertation was on the Costa Rican educational system. He is currently on the faculty of Loyola University in New Orleans.

IT is often taken for granted that the Costa Rican educational system is related to the country's democratic tradition and stability. Indeed, a widely held cliché, often found in tourist advertisements, boasts that Costa Rica has more teachers than soldiers. There is some truth to both of these statements. Since 1948, when the military was disbanded, the country embarked upon a series of educational reforms that were part of the development of the welfare state in Costa Rica. Unlike other countries in Central America, when faced with socioeconomic problems brought on by inequities in the export-based economy, Costa Rica's leaders, particularly after the 1948 civil war, chose to respond in nonauthoritarian ways that sought to reduce social inequalities. Of course, there were political, as well as humanitarian, motivations for the Costa Rican "response" to crisis. But in general, the country's advances in social security, health care, and education were aimed at attacking the broad social questions of inequality and injustice.

This article provides an overview of the national system of education, primary through university, and attempts to demonstrate how the system helps reduce inequality, thus containing class conflict and reinforcing the democratic tradition.

The Costa Rican education system has its roots in the 1949 Constitution and embraces the following principles:[1]

1. Public schooling is a continuous process of lifelong learning from preschool to university.
2. From grades one through twelve, education is free, and it is compulsory from age six through fourteen.
3. The Higher Board of Education is the government body in charge of public elementary, secondary, and higher education.
4. The institutional autonomy of the universities is guaranteed.[2]
5. Private education is overseen by the state.

In 1954 the Fundamental Law of Education established the objectives of Costa Rican education; and in 1965 the Organic Law of the Ministry of Education reorganized the ministry and spelled out how it would administer the national system of education. The educational reforms following the 1948 social revolution were consolidated under Uladislao Gámez, a confidant of José Figueres and the only person to serve three times as minister of education.

Under Gámez, the ministry pushed through the National Plan for Educational Development, which was approved in 1973 by both Figueres and Gámez as an executive decree. It outlined a program for restructuring the school system and for qualitative changes in the four "educational cycles" (see below). The plan sought to further national development by mandating free and compulsory education through ninth grade ("basic" education), instituting a parallel system of informal education to serve those with special needs, and expanding the country's universities to serve an increasing student population.

The National Plan for Educational Development restructured the school system, scrapping the traditional "primary" and "secondary" divisions and establishing the four new cycles, each lasting three years. The first three cycles—through ninth grade—cover basic education and are compulsory. The first two cycles include study of the basic subjects (language, social studies, math, and science); aesthetics (art, music, dance, drama); and religion. Schools also offer a variety of electives—including one called "democratic participation."

One shortcoming of the primary school system was the number of one-teacher schools in rural areas. A 1973 Ministry of Education study found 943 one-teacher schools, many staffed by *aspirantes,* who had not completed their training and lacked official state certification. The study found many teachers did not have adequate teaching materials and were, as they themselves admitted, deficient in administration, methodology, and evaluation. In response, the ministry initiated a "nuclearization" program. It started in two rural regions in 1975, where schools were grouped around one "nuclear" school to share materials and support services. Plans were later made to extend the program during the 1980s.

In the third cycle, students have more options. They can follow the traditional academic route, or they can opt for a program that includes both basic academic instruction and vocational training. In 1980, according to the Ministry of Education, about 14 percent of the students were enrolled in technical schools. Vocational students continue studying basic academic subjects, as well as English, French, religion, and industrial arts or family education.

As part of the educational reform plan, Costa Rica also abolished the traditional grading system in the lower cycles, replacing it with a system of continuous evaluation, focusing on identifying and working on deficiencies. It also abolished national comprehensive examinations at the secondary level. After satisfactorily completing the third cycle, students in both the academic and vocational programs have the option of entering the fourth and final phase—called the "diversified" cycle—or of entering the job market. Ministry of Education figures in 1977 estimated a combined dropout rate of 5.8 percent for the third and fourth cycles, indicating that a strikingly high percentage of students reach the fourth cycle.

The diversified cycle blends a common curriculum with a degree of specialization that is not typical of U.S. secondary schools. The cycle lasts two or three years, depending on the student's field of concentration. The academic program, stressing science and the humanities, as well as the fine arts program, including in some cases the study of ballet or drama, each lasts two years. The technical program, offering specializations in industrial, business, and agricultural areas, lasts three years.

Although Costa Rica had some higher education institutions in the nineteenth century, the modern precursor of the University of Costa Rica was established in 1940. It was the nation's sole higher education institution until 1968, when the National Higher Normal School, a teachers college, was founded. There are now five universities, four state and one private.[3] In addition to the University of Costa Rica (UCR), which remains the heart of the system, there are the Technological Institute of Costa Rica (ITCR), the National University (UNA), the private Autonomous University of Central America (UACA), and the State University at a Distance (UNED), an innovative decentralized program, emphasizing correspondence and tutorial courses, that enables students who cannot afford to live in or travel to San José to continue their studies.

UCR, the largest and oldest university, enrolls some thirty thousand students, approximately 75 percent of those eligible to enter a university. (According to 1973 figures, about 33 percent of all students finish all four school cycles, and the governing board for Higher Education recommended that an average of 85 percent of Cycle IV graduates be granted a place in the university system.) Its main campus is in San José, and it has regional centers in Alajuela, Guanacaste, and Cartago. Tuition was about 125 *colones* in 1977—then about $14.50—per credit hour.

The National University, in Heredia, some thirty minutes outside of San José, also offers a variety of liberal arts, sciences, and professional studies. Its School of Education, which incorporated the National Higher Normal School, is based in Cartago, and has a regional center in San Carlos, in Alajuela Province.

ITCR specializes in science and technology, and its curriculum is designed with the country's development goals and needs in mind. It seeks to train personnel for industry, mining, and agriculture. Most of its students are male, live in the populated central region of the country, and come from families with modest resources.

The State University at a Distance, founded in the late 1970s, is modelled after the United Kingdom's Open University and Spain's National University. It offers basic liberal arts courses, usually at the first-year college level. University resources—textbooks, periodic exams, and telephone consultations with instructors—are made available to those students, generally in rural areas, who cannot attend courses in San Jose.[4]

The Autonomous University of Central America, also in San José, is a private college and university. It too offers instruction in sciences, arts and letters, medicine and law, and also stresses competence in foreign languages. Its administration believes that the UACA offers an alternative to public education. It is generally more conservative politically, and its students usually come from fairly prosperous families.

Costa Rica's educational reforms since 1948 have sought to increase all Costa Ricans' access to educational opportunities. In this sense, the system has furthered democratic values. Yet, there have clearly been ulterior political motivations behind educational reforms, just as in other policy areas, that were linked to the institutionalization of the National Liberation Party (PLN) [see Reading 4.2]. Regardless of the political forces behind educational reforms, however, education in Costa Rica serves to strengthen many aspects of the democratic tradition.[5]

NOTES

1. For a detailed study of the Costa Rican education system, see Clark C. Gill, *The Educational System of Costa Rica* (Washington, D.C.: U.S. Department of Education, 1980); and Louis F.

Mirón, "National Plan for Educational Development in Costa Rica: Theoretical and Historical Perspectives" (Ph.D. diss., Tulane University, 1986).

2. In most Latin American countries, universities have, since the early twentieth century, enjoyed legal political autonomy, permitting members of the university community—at least in theory—to speak, meet, publish, or engage in other forms of expression without government interference or persecution. This has not always been observed in other countries in the region, but in Costa Rica, where freedom of expression is relatively unrestricted, university autonomy has been genuine.—EDS.

3. There are also several small, specialized higher education institutions, including the United Nations–sponsored University for Peace and the Inter-American Institute of Agricultural Sciences (*Instituto Interamericano de Ciencias Agrícolas*—IICA). These centers enroll few students, generally at the graduate level, many of whom are from outside Costa Rica.—EDS.

4. In some respects, UNED resembles an American community or junior college. Its graduates have the option of completing their college studies at one of the larger universities.—EDS.

5. The educational system continues to be severely deficient in many respects, however. One recent study found that 80 percent or more of students in the sixth, ninth, and eleventh grades did not obtain minimum passing marks on Spanish language examinations. Costa Rica boasts a literacy rate of 90 percent; the average citizen has an eighth-grade reading level. See *Inforpress Centroamericano* (Guatemala), no. 731 (March 19, 1987): 15.—EDS.

4.7 Problems and Prospects of the Costa Rican Trade Unions*

BY ELISA M. DONATO AND MANUEL ROJAS BOLAÑOS

Even though many early leaders of the National Liberation Party (PLN) were trade unionists, organized labor has been weak in contemporary Costa Rica. Unions have faced formidable legal obstacles; only the few strikes that courts declare legal are subject to the negotiation procedures specified by the Labor Code, and employers can dismiss union organizers at any time. In this respect, as Elisa Donato and Manuel Rojas note here, Costa Rican democracy falls short of ensuring full participation by wage earners. The authors paint a general picture of organized labor as weak and fragmented. Only a few sectors—public employees and banana plantation workers— account for a large portion of union members, and political divisions separating the federations prevent unified action. Rojas and Donato argue that labor must overcome differences if it is to survive strong antiunion pressures from business organizations and the government.

Donato holds a licenciatura *degree in sociology from the University of Costa Rica. Rojas, also a sociologist and the author of Reading 3.2, received his doctorate from the National Autonomous University of Mexico (UNAM) and teaches at the University of Costa Rica.*

*Excerpted from "Problemas y perspectivas del sindicalismo costarricense," *Aportes*, no. 24 (April–May 1985): 30–34.

THE earliest workers societies in Costa Rica, founded in the last decades of the nineteenth century, did not become true unions until they began to collectively negotiate wages and working conditions with employers in the 1930s.[1] In 1920 workers demanding an eight-hour day declared a general strike, and in 1934 laborers on the Atlantic coast banana plantations stopped work in the largest labor action yet held in Costa Rica [see Reading 2.8]. Both marked important advances in the development of organized labor and the popular movement.

With the approval of the Labor Code in 1943 [see Readings 3.1 and 3.2], a number of independent unions formed the Costa Rican Workers Confederation [*Confederación de Trabajadores de Costa Rica*—CTCR]. President Rafael Angel Calderón Guardia attended the CTCR's founding meeting, as did the Mexican Vicente Lombardo Toledano, general secretary of the Latin American Workers Confederation [*Confederación de Trabajadores de América Latina*], and most principal leaders of the Costa Rican Communist Party. By 1945, 125 unions had joined the federation.

The Rerum Novarum Costa Rican Workers Confederation [*Confederación Costarricense de Trabajadores Rerum Novarum*—CCTRN] was also founded in 1943. It was inspired by Archbishop Víctor Sanabria's advocacy of Church participation in the labor movement [see Reading 3.2]. The CCTRN was fundamentally reformist: in its December 1944 convention, it condemned the "errors" of capitalism but expressed the belief that they could be resolved within the existing economic system.

Competition, though not always overt, between the leftist-dominated CTCR and the Church-influenced CCTRN led to a surge of union activity. In his May 1947 state of the nation address, President Teodoro Picado noted that 228 unions were affiliated with the two federations. To win worker support, both federations used all their resources, including those of their international backers. To some degree, the main union organizations have since relied on their international affiliates, sometimes placing such ties above the real needs of the Costa Rican workers.

After the 1948 civil war, the labor movement entered a long period of decline. The CTCR was declared illegal and Communist-supported unions were not permitted to operate at all until after 1953, when the Communists participated in the founding of the Costa Rican General Workers Confederation [*Confederación General de Trabajadores Costarricenses*—CGTC]. In the aftermath of the war the Catholic CCTRN was in control of the field, but various difficulties prevented it from exploiting a potentially favorable situation for developing a mass-based reformist movement.

The first of these obstacles was the 1950 split in the CCTRN, when about 1,500 members quit and founded the National Workers Confederation [*Confederación Nacional de Trabajadores*], which was influenced by the ideas of the charismatic Argentine populist leader Juan Domingo Perón.[2] Second, key CCTRN leaders—including Benjamín Núñez and his brother Santiago,

Luis Alberto Monge, and Armando Araúz—abandoned the labor movement to work full time for the new National Liberation Party [PLN].[3] The PLN benefited from the work of these skilled cadres but the CCTRN did not. The federation's close identification with the PLN hampered its ability to gain workers' backing. Third, after 1948, and particularly following Archbishop Sanabria's death in 1952, the Catholic Church gradually moved away from the CCTRN.

Finally, after 1948, unionism lost strength. Significant labor activity was limited to the banana zones or to groups that traditionally had been organized, such as railroad workers, shoemakers, and printers. Union activity was practically nil in most sectors for a number of reasons, including the state's undertakings in the areas of health, education, and housing [see Reading 4.2], and the new opportunities for upward mobility, which had an enormous impact among the popular classes, strengthening the myth of an egalitarian, "middle-class" society.

State regulation of labor-employer conflict was also greater after 1948. With the introduction of official negotiating procedures, employee-employer debate was less likely to be carried out in factories or other production units than in the tripartite National Salary Council [*Consejo Nacional de Salarios*], where government representatives mediated. Moreover, between 1950 and 1970, minimum wage increases outpaced inflation, which genuinely improved the lot of most workers.

The PLN had no particular interest in creating unions, although it devoted considerable resources to small and medium-sized producers' cooperatives and community development associations [see Readings 4.2 and 4.12]. Although the Labor Code turned out to be a double-edged sword for Costa Rican trade unionists, the PLN has never proposed thorough revisions or lifting the restrictions on workers organizations.

Under these conditions, it was unnecessary, and indeed improbable, that a strong labor movement would develop. . . . In the 1960s, with greater industrialization, factory owners made it clear from the start that unions would not be tolerated.

The Costa Rican union movement since 1948 has generally been highly fragmented, despite numerous attempts at unity and coordinated action. . . . Not even efforts since 1969 to celebrate International Workers Day in a unified fashion have succeeded. The federations all marched together in the May Day parade in 1977 and 1984, but most years at least one organization refrained from taking part. . . .

Recent attempts at labor unity bore little fruit in 1979–80. Divisions grew in 1980–81 with the founding of the Communist-controlled Unified Workers Confederation [*Confederación Unitaria de Trabajadores*—CUT] and the anti-Communist Democratic Workers Front [*Frente Democrático de Trabajadores*].[4] Unity efforts did succeed in 1984, when various groups established a National Council of Federations [*Consejo Nacional de Confederaciones*] that formally complained to the United Nations–sponsored International Labor Organization about restrictions on union rights and collective bargaining. In the complaint, the Costa Rican unionists criticized their government for restricting the right to organize and denounced the International Monetary Fund for imposing economic policies that harmed workers and the popular sectors.

Ongoing, operational union unity, however, has yet to be achieved. The fragmentation does not just arise from programmatic and ideological differences. To a large degree, it grows out of a conception of unionism that assigns too much importance to leaders, thus facilitating games involving individual interests and a preoccupation with short-term goals. The government, business sectors, and international union organizations have also fomented divisions, hoping to further their own interests. Unfortunately, this has meant that most union leaders devote scant attention to labor's role in Costa Rica's future.

According to figures issued by the Labor and Social Security Ministry and the union federations, in 1984 there were 306 unions with a total of 132,501 members. This is equivalent to 15.7 percent of the work force, up from 10.9 percent in 1973. However, this increase is less than that registered in 1963–73, when the proportion of the work force in unions grew from 2.6 to 10.9 percent. As was the case ten years ago, the economic branches with the highest unionization rates are in basic services, including publicly owned utilities, communications, and transport. The unionization rate in the agricultural work force has also increased notably, from 5.7 percent in 1973 to 14.8 percent in 1984 [see Reading 4.13]. In agriculture, the growth stems largely from the formation of unions by small and medium-sized producers, day laborers, and squatters. The banana workers are no longer the main organized group within the agricultural labor force.

In the service sector, excluding utilities, communications, and transport, the proportion of the work force in unions grew from 19.9 percent in 1973 to 28.8 percent in 1984. Increases for the 1973–84 period have also been registered in construction—from 5.5 to 8.7 percent of the work force—and in retail commerce—from 2.1 to 5.5 percent. In industry, however, 4.5 percent of workers belong to unions today, a decrease from the 5.9 percent of 1973.

Although the public and private sectors have about the same number of unions, 63.7 percent of union members are public-sector employees. Within the public sector, 56.2 percent of all workers belong to unions; in the private sector the unionization rate is an extremely low 7.1 percent.[5]

In early 1984, five labor federations existed in Costa Rica: the Authentic Confederation of Democratic Workers [*Confederación Auténtica de Trabajadores Democráticos*—CATD], the Costa Rican Workers Central [*Central de Trabajadores Costarricenses*—CTC], the Costa Rican Democratic Workers Confederation [*Confederación Costarricense de Trabajadores Democráticos*—CCTD], the leftist CUT, and the National Workers Confederation [*Confederación Nacional de Trabajadores*—CNT].[6] These federations included 184 unions (60.1 percent of the national total) and 97,119 (73.3 percent) of union members. In recent years, a larger percentage of unions have joined federations; in 1976, 51.5 percent of unions were independent and did not belong to any federation. The leftist CUT—with 41,069 members (31.0 percent of the unionized workers)—was the largest labor organization in 1984. It was followed by the CCTD (18,138 members or 13.7 percent), the CATD (16,152 members or 12.2 percent), the CNT (12,043 members or 9.1 percent), and the CTC (9,717 members or 7.3 percent).

In recent years, militant unionism—represented in 1976 by the CGTC and FENETRAP (the public employees union) and in 1984 by the CUT—has undergone a notable decline with respect to both the number of affiliates and total membership. The proportion of unions aligned with such militant tendencies fell from 37.0 percent to 29.3 percent in 1976–84, while their share of the total union membership dropped from 64.0 to 42.3 percent. Political-ideological factors played a role in this decline, but the CUT has also been relatively uninvolved in the formation of new unions. Nevertheless, in 1984 the CUT was still the largest federation, partly because of the size of a few of its members, such as National Public Employees Association [*Asociación Nacional de Empleados Públicos*—ANEP].

In the 1970s, union development picked up as economic growth slowed and the state began to reverse its policy of maintaining constant increases in real wages and social services. Both new unions and those created in the 1960s, which had had very modest organizing successes, benefited. Nevertheless, the labor movement has yet to achieve genuine strength or significantly extend its influence.

Costa Rican unionism is strongest among salaried workers in the state-controlled service sector. Elsewhere in the working class, the labor movement has had little impact. The recent approval of the *solidarismo* law [see Reading 4.8], as well as the large number of *solidarista* associations that have already been created even in workplaces where unions traditionally existed, does not appear to augur well for the labor movement. The current antiunion offensive by both government and business may well exacerbate organized labor's problems, leaving it with little more than a "nominal" presence on the Costa Rican scene.

What is to be done? Unionists must give top priority to defending labor's rights, especially the right to collective bargaining. . . . This does not necessarily mean an all-out defense of existing union structures and forms of action. Unionism based on the institutionalization of conflict, on making demands that can be tolerated or absorbed by the system, is becoming obsolete, particularly given the conditions created by the economic crisis and austerity policies. . . .

Labor must modify its strategies for organizing, for connections between leaders and membership, for ties to political parties (and political involvement in general), for cooperation between federations and, finally, for relations between federations and independent unions. Changes in contemporary Costa Rican society demand a new type of unionism, a unionism on the offensive. Though formed to fight for economic demands, unions must now broaden their efforts to include other aspects of working and living conditions, as well as issues related to salary negotiation procedures and employer-employee relations. The labor movement, moreover, must act on questions that concern the whole of society, such as the environment, urban problems, women's rights, land tenure, and so on.

Workers must be permitted and encouraged to participate in the daily life of their unions, in decision making and in reviewing contracts, until now usually the purview of small groups of leaders. Unions cannot continue to operate as appendages of political parties, since this tends to subordinate the interests of labor to those of the parties. Confusion between union and party also impedes the growth of organized labor and the development of fresh perspectives. . . .

Finally, workers and union leaders must understand that today only with unity can they confront the coordinated attack of the business organizations [*cámaras*], government, the media, and their allies. In the face of this onslaught, labor can no longer practice the strategy of "dispersion." But although labor unity is a desirable goal, it will be difficult to achieve without radical changes in existing workers organizations.

NOTES

1. On the early history of the Costa Rican labor movement, see Vladimir de la Cruz, *Las luchas sociales en Costa Rica, 1870–1930* (San José: Editorial Costa Rica, 1980).—EDS.

2. This short-lived federation has no relation to the organization of the same name that exists today.—EDS.

3. Benjamín Núñez, a Catholic priest who helped negotiate an end to the 1948 civil war, was a member of the 1948–49 junta and Costa Rica's first post-1948 labor minister. He later served as ambassador to Israel, as did Luis Alberto Monge, a leader of the National Liberation Party, who was president of Costa Rica from 1982–86. Armando Araúz served as one of Monge's two vice-presidents.—EDS.

4. The CUT was, from its founding, dominated by the Communist Popular Vanguard Party (PVP). In 1984, when factional divisions led to a split in the PVP, the CUT was seriously weakened, especially among the banana workers.—EDS.

5. The public-sector unionization rate is actually higher, because several important government workers organizations, such as the National Educators Association, are legally registered as associations, rather than unions, even though they function like the latter.

6. With the 1984 split in the CUT, yet another small federation appeared on the scene.—EDS.

4.8 The Solidarismo Movement*

BY MANUEL ROJAS BOLAÑOS

The solidarismo *movement consists of a system of unusual worker-employer associations that usually take the place of trade unions. Labor and management both contribute to a common employees' savings fund used to finance health, housing, and educational benefits for workers. Based on ideas developed by Alberto Martén, José Figueres's minister of economy in the 1948–49 post–civil war junta (Reading 4.1),* solidarismo *departs from classic social democratic theory by positing harmony between labor and capital, and by attempting to present an alternative to trade unionism.* Solidarismo *is a peculiarly Costa Rican phenomenon. But particularly after the 1984 approval of a law favoring the organization of* solidarista *associations, attempts have been made to export the model to the rest of Central America. As Manuel Rojas Bolaños argues in this brief article,* solidarista *associations generally benefit management more than labor.*

Rojas, a sociologist at the University of Costa Rica, is the author of Reading 3.2 and co-author of Reading 4.7.

THE *solidarismo* movement has existed in Costa Rica for more than twenty years. It has grown considerably over the last four years and now has a membership of about forty-five thousand workers.[1] It offers a typically managerial solution to the labor-management conflict. As has been shown in the excellent research of sociologists Gustavo Blanco and Orlando Navarro, *solidarismo* seeks to create insurmountable obstacles to the spread of unionization by fostering the growth of employee associations reminiscent of the earlier workers' mutual aid societies, but in this case under management control.[2]

Solidarismo tries to conceal the existence of labor-management conflict, encouraging workers to expect to attain a share in ownership of the business and its profits. The real truth is quite different. In the first place, the capital contributions with which management funds these associations do not come from business earnings; they are taken from severance pay funds that employers are legally obligated to maintain. Second, as the study mentioned above has shown, the likelihood of employees acquiring a share in ownership is very small. As of September 1981, only 6 of the 218 associations that form this movement have been able to acquire significant shares of the stock of the businesses that employ their members.

*Excerpted from "Solidarismo, SEL . . . Utopía," *Aportes,* no. 10 (August–September 1982): 12.

Thus, caught in the misconception that they will participate in management, the workers hand over the leadership of their organizations to management representatives (most of the official posts are held by employees trusted by management). They relinquish their right to struggle for better wages and working conditions and accept a tacit understanding with management that goes beyond what is stipulated in their work contracts, which are in any case tremendously favorable to management's interests.

NOTES

1. According to the Guatemala-based *Central America Report,* by mid-1984 the number of *solidarista* associations had risen to 800, with a membership of 110,000—one-third of the wage-earning work force. These figures may, however, be somewhat exaggerated. Two years later, *solidarista* leaders claimed the same total membership and even though the movement had been growing rapidly, only 816 associations had been registered with the Ministry of Labor. See *Central America Report* 11, no. 45 (November 16, 1984): 357; Gustavo Blanco, "El solidarismo y los padrinos poderosos," *Aportes,* no. 30–31 (August–November 1986): 18.—EDS.

2. Gustavo Blanco and Orlando Navarro, *El movimiento solidarista costarricense* (San José: Editorial Costa Rica, 1984).

4.9 The Popular Church in Chacarita

BY THE NATIONAL CENTER FOR PASTORAL ACTION (CENAP)*

Liberation theology and the Popular Church have probably had less impact in Costa Rica than in any other Central American country. Many of the social problems that in El Salvador or Nicaragua have prompted priests to become revolutionaries have, in Costa Rica, historically been addressed with some degree of effectiveness by government programs. In addition, an earlier variety of Catholic radicalism, the social Christian doctrine articulated by Rafael Angel Calderón Guardia, was highly influential in Costa Rica, particularly during the period of calderonista *rule (1940–48). Not only the state, but much of the Church hierarchy as well, has long been committed to reformist solutions to social problems. Nevertheless, as this reading illustrates, there are still poor communities in Costa Rica where the problems are overwhelming and the state's response has been grossly inadequate. The Popular Church, advocating a "preferential option" for the poor, has stepped into this void with priests who reside in the communities they serve and who share the often dismal living conditions of their neighbors. Using the idiom of liberation theology to communicate with and mobilize their parishioners, they have—as in the Chacarita setting described below—often been able to achieve vastly greater levels of popular mobilization and participation than either political parties or state-sponsored community organizations.*

*Centro Nacional de Acción Pastoral, "La iglesia se hizo pueblo en Chacarita," *Aportes,* no. 4 (June–July 1981): 18–19.

"WE realized that no one was concerned with us. To find housing we had to squat in an abandoned shack in a forgotten section of town, where the garbage piled high and raw sewage flowed freely. The municipal authorities were not interested in solving the problem and didn't treat us like human beings. Once every four years, when elections rolled around, the politicians came to make idle, deceptive promises in exchange for our votes. After each campaign, people became increasingly apathetic and skeptical. Then we began to become aware of our Christian duties and decided to work to build a popular church."

This is the recollection of a young woman, slender and humble, from the neighborhood of Fray Casiano de Madrid in Chacarita [Puntarenas], where residents are creating a Christian way of life linked to the problems of their community. In a Church meeting in the barrio, one man sat at a table made from two long planks and reflected: "We used to think that 'church' meant that one removed oneself from one's daily problems to pray."

However, the pressing problems of this poor community of longshoremen, small fishermen, day laborers, street vendors, lottery sellers, and unemployed workers were too overwhelming and could not be ignored. Prostitution, alcoholism, drugs, and family disintegration forced community members to see Christ and His Church in a different light. Because they are poor and dispossessed, many have been forced to invade land in order to survive. They sought solutions in Christ's liberating message.

They formed fifteen new organizations to address the community's needs: the Chacarita Community Committee, Popular Defense, Progressive Junta, Day-care Committee, Housing Committee, Association of Development, and more. The Church inspired the grass roots to take action, and community action in turn legitimized the Church's message. In this mutually enriching interaction, the Popular Church arose spontaneously as a response to oppressive conditions. Thus, the concept of Christian religious practice has been extended, and now requires not just attendance at Sunday mass, but active commitment to one's community and fellow human beings. This commitment is put into practice through concrete efforts to improve each neighborhood.

The Church itself, however, does not provide an organizational structure for the community. Instead, it advocates a new kind of Christian practice, encouraging community members to form work groups or participate in existing organizations in accordance with their own skills and interests. There is a complementary relation between the Popular Church and the community organizations.

The priests who minister to the people of Chacarita, Santiago Tortosa and Luis Arocena, live in and have become part of the community. They often lead study groups in reflecting about social conditions, theology, the liberating aspects of catechism, and the celebration of the Eucharist. When the Department of Immigration tried [in 1981] to expel the priests, the community mobilized to support them. Obviously, the authorities were unhappy that Christians were engaged in a kind of religious practice that involved working for the good of the community. On some occasions, the interests of the community have not coincided with those of the authorities, and this has led to conflicts. Thus far these differences have not been irreconcilable. But in the future, as popular organization gains momentum, the tension between the community and the government may not be easily defused.

Within the Church a parallel conflict rages. In poor communities, where circumstances have forced people to turn to the Church to help resolve their problems, Christianity is viewed as an active commitment to the oppressed, much as Christ Himself saw His own teachings. At the same time, other groups within the Church argue that the link between God and man is a direct one, and that one's "good works" should be expressed directly to God, not shared among one's brothers. Actually, there are not two separate popular and traditional churches, but there are distinct interpretations of Christian faith. In Chacarita, the Popular Church is concerned with community development, grass-roots organizations, and the people's interests.

4.10 Blacks in Costa Rica: Upward Mobility and Ethnic Discrimination*

By Philippe Bourgois

Costa Rica is often portrayed as ethnically homogeneous, which not infrequently is used to "explain" everything from its pacifism to its democratic system. Although it is true that most Costa Ricans are descended primarily from Spanish and other European immigrants, the range of physical types is large, and ethnic minorities include Amerindians, Chinese, and English-speaking blacks whose distinct culture still reflects their West Indian origin. This reading examines blacks' position in the ethnic occupational hierarchy of Limón Province, where most reside. Many blacks have become landowners employing "white" landless laborers. Despite this upward mobility, they have not assimilated to the same degree as most other immigrant groups in Costa Rica.

Philippe Bourgois, an assistant professor of anthropology at San Francisco State University, is the author of Ethnicity at Work: Divided Labor on a Central American Plantation *(1989) and numerous articles on the Atlantic coast of Central America.*

BLACKS of West Indian descent today constitute Costa Rica's largest ethnic minority.[1] Most blacks in Costa Rica reside in the Atlantic coast province of Limón, where they represent less than 25 percent of the population (nationally,

*A longer version of this article appeared in *New West Indian Guide* 60, nos. 3 & 4 (1986): 149–65. Research in Costa Rica and northern Panama in 1982–83 was supported by the Inter-American Foundation and the Wenner-Gren Foundation for Anthropological Research.

blacks comprise less than 5 percent of the total population). In contrast to the black diaspora elsewhere, blacks in Costa Rica have been dramatically upwardly mobile. Fleeing poverty and economic crisis in the Caribbean, they began arriving in the late nineteenth century. Most were employed by the United Fruit Company in railroad construction and banana cultivation. They formed part of a larger cultural group spanning the entire Caribbean coast of Central America and centered in areas dominated by U.S. transnational corporations. Often the same individuals who planted bananas or harvested cacao in Limón previously shoveled dirt on the Panama Canal or piloted barges along Nicaraguan rivers.[2] By the 1930s, a majority of the West Indian immigrants to Costa Rica had obtained small plots of land or had risen in the banana company's labor hierarchy. Today blacks are better off economically than most of Limón's Hispanic and Amerindian population. Nevertheless, discrimination against them persists.

The first West Indian immigrants reached Costa Rica in 1872, contracted by railroad financier Minor C. Keith, who later founded the United Fruit Company. Keith had previously imported representatives of dozens of different population groups to work on the construction of the Costa Rican Atlantic railroad [see Reading 2.3].[3] Only West Indian blacks, however, tolerated the rigid labor discipline and exposure to the yellow fever, malaria, and poisonous snakes that abounded in the swampy Limón lowlands. It is said that some 4,000 Jamaicans died in the construction of the first twenty-five miles of the Costa Rican railroad. Although Keith imported another 10,000 Jamaican laborers between 1881 and 1891, the subsequent waves of West Indian immigrants arrived on their own, escaping unemployment and poverty on the islands of their birth.[4] By 1927 there were 19,136 Jamaicans in Costa Rica, almost all in Limón Province.

Most historians report, and many contemporary Costa Ricans believe, that the immigrant West Indian laborers in Costa Rica at the turn of the century were so fiercely loyal to their employer—Keith and United Fruit—that they refrained from union organizing or labor disturbances.[5] This faulty image of black passivity has emerged as a racist stereotype among Hispanics in Limón and in northern Panama. Even the publications of the Costa Rican Communist Party and the militant tendency within the union movement fail to note the participation of West Indian immigrants in the early years of labor organizing.

Close scrutiny of primary source material, as well as interviews with elderly West Indian laborers, belie the myth of black labor complacency. Newspaper reports and historical archives from the turn of the century abound with references to violent strikes, labor disturbances, and organizing drives. In fact, reports of bloody confrontations between black workers and management date as far back as 1879.

Costa Rican blacks' resistance to economic exploitation and ethnic discrimination peaked between 1910 and 1930. Their strikes were almost invariably violently repressed, resulting in serious casualties. Much of this resistance was channeled into Marcus Garvey's Universal Negro Improvement Association (UNIA), a worldwide organization that stressed the dignity of blacks throughout the diaspora. The UNIA was exceptionally strong in Costa Rica on the banana plantations. In fact, Limón is one of the few places in the world today where the UNIA still exists. The banana workers used the UNIA to organize against the racist labor hierarchy on the plantation and its message was invoked in several major strikes. Subsequently, however, the UNIA leadership ceased its support of the banana workers. United Fruit Company archives reveal that Marcus Garvey and his associates actually struck deals with management.

From the 1930s to the 1950s, emigration of blacks contributed, somewhat paradoxically, to the upward mobility of those who remained in Limón. During periods of economic crisis, many poor West Indian laborers were forced to leave Limón in search of employment. From 1927 to 1950, according to census data, the Costa Rican black population fell from 18,003 to 13,749. Racist immigration laws and restrictions on black employment outside of the Atlantic lowlands acted as a "one-way valve" during the boom and bust cycles of the banana industry which "pumped working-class Negroes out of the region . . . [leaving behind a] rump of well-to-do peasants and old people concentrated in the best cacao districts."[6]

Blacks who stayed behind during economic crises, when employment on the plantation was no longer available, squatted on uncultivated lands and established themselves as subsistence farmers, often in abject poverty. Once the economy improved, these squatters were able to convert their subsistence plots into commercial cacao or banana farms. At the same time, however, racist immigration laws prevented West Indians seeking employment as wage workers from reentering the country.

In this manner, most of the blacks remaining in Costa Rica by the end of the 1930s depression left plantation employment to become full-time farmers. In the mid-1950s, with the rise of cacao prices on the world market, these formerly marginal black farmer-squatters emerged as comfortable landowners. Since they were the first settlers in the region, they generally occupied the choicest lands closest to roads and ports. The growing number of landless Hispanics immigrating to the Atlantic coast lowlands provided them with a plentiful supply of inexpensive day labor. An ethnic occupational hierarchy emerged that contrasts markedly with the pattern prevalent in the rest of the world: "the Atlantic Zone [is] one of the few places in the world where bourgeois blacks exploit an underprivileged white minority."[7]

Although for the most part comfortable economically, blacks have not emerged as a true upper class in the Limón region. Even at the height of their involvement in the cacao industry in the 1960s, black farms were not large-scale agroindustrial complexes oriented toward capital accumulation. The largest landholdings and the more profitable rural enterprises in Limón have always been owned by Hispanic or North American absentee landlords. Black farmers represent a middle-level local elite operating small or medium-sized farms.

Ironically, upward mobility has now contributed to the demise of black farms. Children of the successful cacao farmers of the 1960s have, for the most part, left agriculture. High school and university graduates do not consider cacao farming a satisfactory life-style, no matter how successful cacao farmers may appear by local rural standards. The better-educated younger generation has—since the mid-1970s—increasingly left agriculture for Panama City, San José, Puerto Limón, or even New York, where they find better opportunities for economic advancement. Indeed, one reason so few young blacks perform heavy agricultural labor in Limón today is that most have emigrated.

Significantly, the elderly cacao farmers encourage their children to leave the agricultural sector. Black parents, even those from the humblest backgrounds, infuse their children with upwardly mobile aspirations. They emphasize not only getting out of wage work, but also escaping agriculture for the big cities. Farming is associated with low status; Limón residents often remark that "chopping bush is ungentlemanly," even on one's own farm. Younger blacks still residing in Limón hire Hispanics to work in their cacao groves, while they attend to more profitable alternatives such as lobster fishing, running bars, selling marijuana to tourists, or working for the government, or they live on remittances sent by relatives in the United States.

Education has played a crucial role in black upward mobility and is part of the West Indian immigrant tradition. Blacks consistently attain higher levels of education than Hispanics. In 1983, while 55.4 percent of Hispanics did not finish primary school in Limón, the same was true for only 38.5 percent of blacks.[8] This advantage over Hispanics has been confined to the middle educational levels, primary and high school, rather than college. Until the 1960s, few blacks reached the university level. In 1964, for example, out of the entire Limón black population of over fifteen thousand, there were only four black lawyers, one civil engineer, and five high school teachers.[9] By the 1970s, with the extended cacao boom, large numbers of cacao farmers' children had entered the professions throughout Costa Rica.

Over the past fifteen years, black rural dwellers have increasingly sold their holdings to Hispanic immigrants and have either emigrated or "died out." This process has been accelerated by a devastating leaf fungus known as moniliales, which has been destroying approximately two-thirds of the harvest since late 1978. Some blacks with devastated cacao farms have been unable to emigrate and now have few alternatives to agricultural wage labor. Nevertheless, they continue to enjoy an above-average economic status, superior to that of most Hispanics in the countryside.

A significant number of working-class and unemployed blacks are concentrated in Puerto Limón, the capital of the province, where there are high levels of unemployment (23 percent in 1981). Nevertheless, urban blacks continue to occupy a slightly higher socioeconomic niche than the average Hispanic, and they shun low-prestige jobs. According to a 1980 survey, 30.5 percent of black workers had white-collar jobs in Puerto Limón, compared to 21.1 percent of Hispanics.[10] Street sweepers, construction workers, and shoeshine men—among the lowest status occupations—are almost invariably Hispanics rather than blacks. Because they are well represented in white-collar and government positions, blacks have benefited from the local patronage system and often have access to preferred jobs, especially in the public sector.

Similarly, those blacks who have remained on the banana plantations represent a miniature labor aristocracy. They generally work in semiskilled jobs, as low-level supervisors, or in the "softer" unskilled tasks. Hispanics have nicknamed them *"la rosca"* [the groove of the screw] because they are so "tight with management." Indeed, blacks are overrepresented as mechanics, clerks, watchmen, and paymasters. Already in the 1940s, blacks were most heavily concentrated in banana company departments that did not require heavy manual labor, such as electricity, transport, engineering, or materials and supplies.

The largest single concentration of black menial laborers is on the docks in Puerto Limón. Dock workers, however, are better paid than farm workers and lead more cosmopolitan, urban life-styles. A close examination of the distribution of jobs among the dock workers reveals that, once again, the "softer" tasks are dominated by blacks, especially elderly blacks. This is true, for example, of the task of "curving," which involves standing at a curve point along the loading machine to make sure that no boxes of bananas fall as they advance on the rollers. Similarly, the worker who sits next to the power switch in order to shut off the electricity in case of an emergency is almost invariably black.

Access to alternative sources of income explains why blacks are underrepresented in menial positions on the plantations. Blacks do not shun agricultural wage work any more than their Hispanic or Amerindian counterparts who are born near the plantations and who own land and/or have access to better jobs through seniority and personal contacts. The only difference between blacks and other local Hispanic or Amerindian residents is that they express their distaste for plantation wage work more vocally. They justify their rejection of agricultural day labor in specifically ethnic terms: "I'm nobody's slave anymore. Let the Spaniards do that class of work. It's their turn now."[11] Blacks also maintain that they avoid unskilled plantation work because of the racism of Hispanic foremen.

Land acquisition and upward mobility have contributed to the development of conservative political attitudes among blacks. The emphasis in black Costa Rican culture is on "proper behavior" and "respect for authority." The pro-U.S., promanagement orientation of second- and third-generation black Costa Ricans contrasts dramatically with the labor militancy of the original immigrants. Even the poorest black families aspire to middle-class respectability. The small minority of blacks who are still at the lower end of the local occupational hierarchy (performing machete work in the fields) identify with the conservative political values of the more privileged members of their ethnic group—the cacao farmers and skilled workers. Participation in unions and antagonism toward management are viewed as alien to black ethnic identity. Strikes and—worse yet—"Communist ideas" are abhorred as satanic values introduced by immigrant "Spaniard" day laborers of a "lower cultural level."

This conservative orientation has been reinforced by the racism of Costa Rican society. Until 1949, even second- and third-generation West Indian descendants were denied Costa Rican citizenship. During the 1930s, the threat of deportation made Costa Rican–born blacks reluctant to participate in labor organizations. Their ambiguous nationality status became a "Damocles sword" that the United Fruit Company used against them during labor disturbances.[12] This vulnerability to deportation, together with age-old ethnic antagonisms, has inhibited black workers from joining the Hispanic-dominated national labor organizations. In fact, over the years, the United Fruit Company systematically employed an ethnically based "divide and conquer" antiunion strategy pitting blacks against Hispanics, and both against Amerindians.[13]

Costa Rican hostility toward blacks increased during periods of economic crisis such as the 1930s depression and World War II. On numerous occasions, blacks were forced to appeal to United Fruit (which either employed them or purchased their produce) for protection from racist local authorities. Blacks' reliance on the "goodwill" of this U.S. company and their inability to find salaried jobs outside the plantation enclave brought about a transformation in their attitudes toward management. In fact, during the 1930s and 1940s, laws were passed forbidding the employment of blacks outside of the Atlantic zone. This increased their dependence on the United Fruit Company, the principal employer in Limón Province.

The upward mobility of the black population has been precarious. Those who were small farmers usually did not have legal title to their land and sold all their cash crops (cacao and bananas) to the United Fruit Company. They had to remain on good terms with the company in order to stay in business. Those blacks who remained in the company's employ, in the "soft" privileged positions, lived with the fear that they might be demoted at any moment should their loyalty to management be questioned. In order to maintain their position within the plantation hierarchy, blacks emphasized their "reliability and obedience" and contrasted it with the unruliness and political volatility of "Communistic" Hispanics. Today, blacks' reputation for apolitical passivity is their best recommendation for continued access to the better plantation jobs.

Another important ideological influence on blacks in Limón has been the emigration of so many of their relatives to the United States. Many Costa Rican blacks regularly receive letters and/or visits from relatives now living in New York, California, or Miami. The dramatic wage differentials between Central America and the United States make life in the north appear almost utopian from a dollars and cents perspective. Photographs and descriptions of U.S. technology and of large urban centers exacerbate the impression of U.S. omnipotence. Many Limón blacks perceive the United States as the land of golden opportunity.

There are two contradictory matrices of ethnic discrimination in Limón. On the one hand, blacks consider themselves more cultured than Hispanics. On the other hand, Hispanics are convinced of their racial superiority over blacks. Black landowners employing Hispanic migrant laborers ascribe to the same racist constructs typical of landowners anywhere in the world who employ day laborers of a different ethnic group. Blacks claim that "whites are treacherous, lazy, shiftless drunkards" with "nomadic tendencies." Whites are even reputed to "smell bad" and have "cooties" [*piojos*] in their hair. It is not unusual to hear black farmers explain in patronizing tones how they have to be careful never to pay their white workers on Saturday evening lest they spend all their money on liquor before Sunday morning.

Even blacks who work side by side with Hispanics as day laborers on banana plantations consider their Hispanic fellow workers "less civilized." They criticize them for being loud, violent, alcoholic, and abusive to their women. In a somewhat more poetic vein, anthropologist Trevor Purcell quotes a black woman's racist impression of Hispanic workers: "Dey looks to me laik dey were barberians, laik dey wud kil an' iit piiple, datz di wey dey looks. Deze piiple wur illiterate an ignorant an wii wuz ahlweys afreeid av dem. If yu goin along de striit an yu si dem yu waak on di odder sa'id. Dey always kiari dier kutlas [machete] wid dem."[14]

Nevertheless, white supremacist ideas are so powerful that blacks' superior economic position in the local class hierarchy has not overshadowed the racism directed at them by lighter-skinned peoples. Even impoverished landless Hispanics who have worked all their lives for black landlords remain convinced that blacks are racially inferior. For example, the other side of blacks' assertion that Hispanics are "dangerous, violent, alcoholic savages" is that blacks are "cowards who run at the sight of blood." The fact that blacks do not perform menial agricultural wage labor is cited by Hispanics (and Amerindians) as proof that they are "lazy, ambitionless" and "afraid to sweat." Hence the Costa Rican adage, "Where there is work, there are no blacks."

Ironically, one effect of the persistence of ethnic discrimination against blacks is the preservation of black culture. The obvious skin-color difference between West Indians and the rest of the Costa Rican population has prevented the second and third generations of blacks from blending into Costa Rican society, even though they have risen in the local class structure. Under similar circumstances of dramatic upward mobility, other immigrant ethnic groups would have assimilated. Although professional blacks tend to marry Hispanics and often forbid their children to speak Creole English, the racism of Costa Rican society limits their assimilation. Were it not for this physically based discrimination, blacks would probably no longer exist as a distinct ethnic group in Costa Rica.

NOTES

1. Although there was a small population of African slaves in Costa Rica during the colonial period, these early blacks mixed with the European and Amerindian inhabitants and no longer constitute an identifiable ethnic group.

2. More recently, many have emigrated to New York City to work as orderlies in hospitals.

3. In addition to small "experimental" numbers of Canadians, Dutch, Swedes, black North Americans, Carib Afro-Amerindians, Syrians, Turks, East Indians, Egyptians, and Cape Verdians, Keith imported "one thousand healthy, robust Chinese of good customs and addicted to work" (Costa Rican National Archives, Historical Section, no. 1055, April 6, 1872), and 1,500 "good, humble, thrifty . . . [Italians] . . . of a superior race." (Ibid., no. 1131, February 23, 1888, p. 3). See Charles Wilson, *Empire in Green and Gold* (New York: Henry Holt and Company, 1947), pp. 52, 61; and José Rodríguez Bolaños and Víctor Borge Carvajal, "El ferrocarril al Atlántico en Costa Rica" (*Licenciatura* thesis, University of Costa Rica, San José, 1976), p. 227.

4. A veritable depopulation of able-bodied laborers occurred in the West Indies at the turn of the century. For example, from 1900 to 1910, 40 percent of all adult males left Barbados in search of employment in Central America and Panama. In Barbados, a day's wage was twenty cents at the turn of the century. United Fruit Company labor contractors were offering to pay the same amount per hour. The unemployed were so desperate that riots erupted outside the recruiting stations of the Panama Canal Company in Barbados. See David McCullough, *The Path Between the Seas* (New York: Simon and Schuster, 1977), pp. 170, 476.

5. Many historians and anthropologists have reported that Costa Rican West Indians were passive laborers. This erroneous conclusion stems from reliance on company reports and pro-management local newspapers, which intentionally emphasized West Indian laborers' supposed passivity in order to persuade Costa Rican authorities to allow their importation in larger numbers. Furthermore, the comfortably established second- and third-generation descendants of these immigrants prefer to forget their grandparents' history of exploitation and struggle.

6. Charles Koch, "Ethnicity and Livelihoods: A Social Geography of Costa Rica's Atlantic Coast" (Ph.D. diss., University of Kansas, 1975), pp. 378, 385.

7. Ibid., p. 378.

8. Marta Elena Vargas Villalobos and Gabriela Requeyra Edelman, "Un estudio sobre la participación del grupo negro en el empleo: sus oportunidades y limitaciones 1981–1982, Centro Provincia de Limón" (*Licenciatura* thesis, University of Costa Rica, San José, 1983), p. 44.

9. Lewis Mennerick, "A Study of Puerto Limón, Costa Rica" (Associated Colleges of the Midwest, Central American Field Program, San José, 1964, Typescript), p. 50.

10. Vargas and Requeyra, "Un estudio sobre," pp. 43, 113.

11. In Atlantic Costa Rica, Hispanics are referred to as "Spaniards" or "whites."

12. United Fruit Company took full advantage of blacks' ambiguous nationality, as suggested in this 1943 report by a United executive about a plantation on the Panamanian–Costa Rican border: "Division has not been living up to the laws as regards accident pay, severance pay, and other social privileges to which laborers are entitled by law. Apparently these payments were not made . . . mostly on the assumption that the Company wished to save money and *was safe in not making these payments, as most of the negroes around* [here] *do not have cédulas* [nationality identity cards] *and cannot bring action against us in the courts."* R. H. Hamer to A. A. Pollan, February 1, 1943, United Fruit Company Archives, Almirante [emphasis added].

13. Philippe Bourgois, *Ethnicity at Work: Divided Labor on a Central American Plantation* (Baltimore: Johns Hopkins University Press, 1989).

14. Trevor Purcell, "Conformity and Dissension: Social Inequality, Value and Mobility among West Indian Migrants in Limón, Costa Rica" (Ph.D. diss., Johns Hopkins University, 1982), p. 79.

4.11 Agrarian Reform in Costa Rica*

BY MITCHELL A. SELIGSON

Despite Costa Rica's reputation as a country of yeomen farmers (see Chapter I), land ownership has historically been highly concentrated. Nevertheless, after 1948 agrarian reform was not high on the list of the National Liberation Party's objectives. The small-holding peasantry, especially in the central coffee-growing regions, enthusiastically backed National Liberation. Agricultural laborers, particularly those in the Communist-controlled banana workers' unions, were inalterably opposed to many aspects of the new political model. Unorganized landless laborers and squatters generally participated little in politics and did not constitute a significant pressure group at the national level. Thus, there were few political reasons to make land reform a priority.

This changed with the 1961 founding of the Alliance for Progress. Concerned about the impact of the Cuban revolution in the rest of the continent, U.S. policymakers began to encourage Latin American governments to carry out agrarian reforms as a means of undercutting more radical change. In this reading, Mitchell A. Seligson describes the achievements of the Costa Rican agrarian reform after 1961 and also notes some of the obstacles that have prevented it from having a greater impact.

Seligson is director of the Center for Latin American Studies and professor of political science at the University of Pittsburgh. He has authored or edited several books, including Peasants of Costa Rica and the Development of Agrarian Capitalism *(1980).*

THIS little country has been traditionally known for its strong class of yeomen and its democratic tradition. . . . However, the distribution of land in Costa Rica is highly unequal as has been consistently revealed by the four agricultural censuses conducted in the second half of the present century. The latest census, conducted in 1973, highlights the situation . . . 36.9 percent of the

*Excerpted from longer essays that appeared as "Agrarian Reform in Costa Rica, 1942–1976: The Evolution of a Program," *Land Tenure Center Paper* (University of Wisconsin, Madison) no. 115, (1978), and "The Impact of Agrarian Reform: A Study of Costa Rica," *Journal of Developing Areas* 13 (1979): 161–74. This article forms part of a larger study on Costa Rican peasants that has received generous support from the Social Science Research Council, the Danforth Foundation, the Ford and Rockefeller foundations, and the Institute of Government Research of the University of Arizona. The author gratefully acknowledges the institutional support he received from the *Instituto de Tierras y Colonización* (ITCO) and from its director, Lic. José Manuel Salazar N.

landholders own only 1 percent of the farmland and the entire bottom half of the owners (57.6 percent) own only slightly less than 4 percent of the land. At the other end of the spectrum, the top 1 percent of all the largest farm owners own over a quarter of all the land. At the very top are the eighty largest farms which collectively own 463,754 hectares of land. The Gini Index of the overall distribution of land for 1973 is .86, which ranks it sixth most unequal of the fifty-four nations studied by Taylor and Hudson.[1]

While the problem of concentration of land among the landholders is acute, the problem of landlessness is even more serious. Only 22 percent of the economically active peasant population are landholders.

The explanation for the deterioration of the land-tenure situation in Costa Rica is complex and is reported on extensively elsewhere.[2] Suffice it to say that relative equality in landholding began to change with the introduction of coffee cultivation in the early part of the nineteenth century. By the beginning of the present century, after the rapid expansion of banana plantations, the Costa Rican yeoman was fast on the retreat. The situation did not reach crisis proportions until the closing of the frontier sometime in the 1960s, when virtually all land was either in private or in state hands. Landless peasants, a growing number of whom were being mechanized out of their jobs, have increasingly turned to the state for the resolution of their problem.

This reading examines the evolution of agrarian reform in Costa Rica from 1948 to 1976. The evidence reveals the limited nature of all but the most recent efforts. Nevertheless, the evidence also demonstrates that those peasants who have received land under the reform programs have benefited substantially, both monetarily and psychologically. The conclusion is drawn that reform is an imperative for future stability of the Costa Rican countryside.

For many years the Costa Rican government flirted with the idea of agrarian reform, but two central factors inhibited decisive action. First was the fact that the government remained heavily influenced by the large landowners. Serious efforts at reform had to overcome this group's fears that an agrarian reform might eventually force them to relinquish some of their properties to land-hungry peasants.

But it would be totally incorrect to argue that the landlords were involved in a death struggle with peasant masses; pressure for reform from below was minimal. Peasants traditionally had the alternative of taking advantage of laws that provided virgin land in remote regions for those who wanted it. . . . When the first effort at reform appeared in the 1940s, it was a "back-door" one. The Costa Rican state, as a result of the serious economic dislocations produced by World War II, began to take steps to modernize its structure. In 1942 the Ministry of Agriculture and Livestock was organized, and within it the Office of Colonization and Distribution of State Lands was created to administer state forest reserves. Since sections of these reserve lands were being illegally occupied by private individuals (both large landholders and peasants alike), the office was inexorably drawn into the business of settling land disputes. The

Office of Colonization was not equipped to handle the problem . . . and very little was accomplished.

By 1949 it had become clear that a more effective bureaucratic structure had to be evolved to deal with the land problem. . . . Unfortunately the reform effort was stillborn; no legislative action occurred. . . . The impetus that finally pushed Costa Rica into passing an agrarian reform law came primarily from external factors. Costa Rican land barons looked with fear at the swift moving Cuban revolution: *Fidelismo* was alive in the hemisphere and who would be next? There is some evidence that the U.S. AID mission was attempting to encourage some sort of reform.[3] The U.S. position on the need for reform became crystal clear in August 1961, when the Conference of Punta del Este laid the foundations for the Alliance for Progress, a major component of which was the promulgation of agrarian reforms in participating states. Internal pressure for reform began to grow. . . . As talk of agrarian reform grew, peasants became encouraged to invade land in the hope that their possession would be legalized under the anticipated law. As a consequence, landholders whose property had been invaded put pressure on the government to pass the law so that they could receive compensation for their loss. A few months after Punta del Este the logjam was broken and the agrarian reform law came into being on October 14, 1961. . . .

The goals of the law were ambitious: (1) to better the socioeconomic conditions of peasants; (2) to conserve natural resources; (3) to promote an increase in the productivity of the land; (4) to avoid the concentration of land in the hands of those who would use it for speculative purposes; (5) to support the development of small and medium-sized farms; (6) to avoid the creation of *minifundios;* and (7) to promote cooperatives. Critics have argued, however, that even in the unlikely event that all of these goals were eventually met, the peasantry would not find relief. . . . The key to understanding criticism of the law lies in the area of compensation for expropriation. The law places heavy emphasis on "respect for private property." . . . The legislators wanted to do all they could to prevent peasants from interpreting the new law as an open ticket for further land invasions. . . . Incidents of squatting did increase after the law went into effect. The second reason for the emphasis on respect for private property lies at the heart of the controversy. The law provided for *prior* full compensation, based on the owner-declared value of the property for tax purposes, for expropriated land. Hence, the extent of the expropriations (and consequently the scope of the entire agrarian reform) was directly and inexorably tied to the financial ability of the state. For every *latifundio* that was expropriated, funds had to be found to pay the owner in full for his property or bonds had to be issued for payment. Either way, each expropriation had a direct impact on national indebtedness. . . . Hence, the scope of the reform program, despite the best intentions of those whose job it was to implement it, was severely restricted.[4] . . . The *Instituto de Tierras y Colonización* (Lands and Colonization Institute), established in November 1962 . . . went through several stages in its evolution. The first was characterized by an emphasis on colonization schemes. The object was to settle substantial numbers of landless peasants on virgin lands. Given the limited financial resources of the institute and its desire to benefit the largest possible number of peasants, it was felt that only by buying land in remote areas would there be sufficient funds to permit the purchase of any sizable plots. In all, 1,272 peasant families were located on eleven colonies with a total of 35,412 hectares among them.

At first blush the colonization idea seemed like a good one. There were, however, extraordinarily high hidden costs. The institute did not fully appreciate the fact that a peasant had to have more than a plot of land and his two hands. Roads were essential: Roads make it possible to obtain seed, fertilizer, and tools for the production of crops and also provide access to markets once the crop has been harvested. Roads also permit the sick to be transported to hospitals and make it possible for agricultural extensionists to visit the farms and provide technical advice. Upon their establishment, most of the ITCO colonies had neither roads linking them to the outside world nor roads linking one farmer to his neighbor. The regions chosen for the colonies were often so remote and so inaccessible that even fifteen years after their establishment some still did not have all-weather roads connecting them to the outside world. ... It is not that ITCO did not want to provide roads in these areas, it is simply that it did not have the means to do so. ...

Other kinds of infrastructure were needed as well. Houses had to be erected for the colonists; water systems had to be installed. ITCO argued that other government agencies responsible for housing and potable water should take over these projects. These agencies in most cases replied, however, that these were ITCO projects and ITCO's responsibility. ... As a result, ITCO was saddled with the responsibility of being a road builder, house builder, water system builder, etc. ... All in all the colonization program was not particularly successful. In 1966 the final two colonies were established. After that time no new colonies were created. The eleven extant colonies went through some very rocky times, and in some cases large numbers of colonists abandoned their farms. In the 1970s, however, as national development proceeded, many of these remote areas were finally linked to the national highway system. Crops began to be harvested and sold. However, it generally was agreed that the costs of the colonization program were too great to make it a viable alternative. ...

By late 1966 serious reexamination of ITCO's programs was under way. ... Officials with the institute began searching for a new role that would be compatible with its economic situation. The role selected was the settlement of squatter conflicts. ... The 1961 law emphasized this aspect of the program since squatting conflicts were a source of considerable tension in the nation. The squatters steadfastly refused to be evicted, while the landowners demanded eviction or compensation. In addition, a large number of squatting conflicts developed on public domain land. ... In the years 1966 to 1969 ITCO dedicated itself to the resolution of these conflicts. The cost to the institute was minimal, since all that was required was the utilization of the legal and administrative staff ITCO already had on its payroll. Capital expenditures were largely unnecessary. The program met with some success. . . . The entire four-year period saw the granting of 2,093 titles, compared to only 224 titles in the previous four years.

Despite some success, the overall effort was a fruitless one. The problem was that the program sought to deal with the consequence of inequality in land distribution rather than its cause. . . . It became evident that such a program was not acceptable to either the peasants or the political elites. The peasants wanted land and preferred to get it legally. They preferred to avoid the risks involved in squatting if at all possible. Political elites, on the other hand, sought to avoid rural unrest, and tranquility could only be achieved by providing land to peasants before serious conflicts erupted and squatting occurred. . . .

By the end of the 1960s, ITCO had accumulated enough experience from its past efforts to embark upon a program that promised greater success. ITCO had learned from the colonization programs that the total cost of setting up colonies in remote regions was far too high and that, while the initial costs of purchasing land in more developed regions were higher, the total costs promised to be much lower. ITCO had also learned that potential recipients of land had to be self-motivated and fully aware of the realities of the project at hand rather than be misled by pie-in-the-sky promises that could not be fulfilled. Finally, ITCO had learned that it needed to deal with peasant hunger for land before it developed into rural violence. ITCO planners began evolving new principles for guiding their reform efforts in the 1970s. First, settlements should all be accessible to some major marketing center. Second, the settlement should be located in an area with the highest possible level of infrastructure already present. ITCO tried, whenever practicable, to establish the projects on established farms rather than in virgin territory. In many cases the farms had been abandoned before ITCO took them over; the internal roads, wells, storage sheds, flood control systems were usually in place and required little additional investment to put them in working order. . . . Third, ITCO projects were required to show signs of potential economic viability. Each new project was carefully studied by a team of agronomists and economists. Crop yields were estimated and market prices were calculated. . . . The final principle guided the selection of beneficiaries. ITCO became actively involved in the stimulation of groups of peasants who were seeking land so that wherever possible the peasants who ultimately settled in a project were first organized into a group. In this fashion, peasants self-selected themselves for ITCO projects. In the past, ITCO had shied away from such groups, fearing that by assisting them it might end up encouraging a land invasion. ITCO now prefers to have at least minimal contact with these groups so that it can give them guidance and, at the same time, have some feel for their mettle. ITCO does not make it easy for these groups to get land, for to do so would only invite disaster for those not willing to put up with the hardships of initiating a settlement. The struggle for land helps build camaraderie. The likelihood of mutual cooperation once the project became established is thus increased considerably.

Two types of projects were developed under the new guidelines. The first of these was the "self-run communal enterprise program" (*empresas comunitarias de autogestión*). The other was the individual parcel program, much like the colony in its land-tenure pattern. . . . Essentially, the difference between the individual parcel program and the communal enterprise is that under the former the land is given in parcels to individuals, while under the latter system the land is *owned* and *worked* in common. Common land is viewed as of critical importance to the project's success. . . . Since no one peasant alone has sufficient capital to convert his plot into a modern, efficient farm, the entire reform program often turns out to be highly inefficient. The only inexpensive source of extra labor under these reform programs is family labor. Thus, there is a strong incentive to have large families. The communal enterprise, in contrast, operates all land in common and therefore has the potential of becoming an efficient operation with a relatively high level of capital investment and technology. In this sort of operation family labor is replaced by communal labor on the part of members and by mechanization.

Reform in the 1970s has moved ahead with much greater speed [and] . . . ITCO has made intensive efforts to revitalize what had become a stagnant reform program.[5]

Not only have the recipients as a whole benefited from the reform, but some of the reform peasants have made great strides in improving their incomes. The impact of reform is even more noticeable among those beneficiaries who have held their land for at least four years. Those peasants have incomes that average 9 percent higher than the entire sample of beneficiaries [in a survey of 753 ITCO project members]. As the years go on, the individuals who receive land from ITCO are able to increase the yields on their farms and hence increase income. Probably a major factor in producing these higher yields is the technical assistance and credit programs made available to the peasants. . . . Peasants who have received land from ITCO feel significantly more trusting in government, more positively oriented toward the future, and more politically efficacious than the landless peasants. . . .

Nevertheless, the disease of inequality in land distribution in Costa Rica has festered so long and its magnitude has become so great that vast amounts of capital and human energy will be needed before any significant impact will be felt. Costa Rica is a small country, measuring 50,900 square kilometers. Of this area, some 61 percent (3,122,546.1 hectares) was owned as farmland according to the 1973 agricultural census. ITCO's efforts through 1976 have resulted in the granting of 66,859 hectares (2 percent) of the farmland. In 1973 there were 145,255 landless peasant families of which 2,574 (1.7 percent) have received land from ITCO. Quite clearly, much more needs to be done for the landless peasant.

NOTES

1. Charles L. Taylor and Michael C. Hudson, *World Handbook of Political and Social Indicators,* 2d ed. (New Haven: Yale University Press, 1972).

2. Mitchell A. Seligson, *Peasants of Costa Rica and the Development of Agrarian Capitalism* (Madison: University of Wisconsin Press, 1980).

3. John Riismandel, "Costa Rica: Self-Images, Land Tenure and Agrarian Reform" (Ph.D. diss., University of Maryland, 1972), pp. 207–8.

4. In 1982, ITCO was renamed the Institute for Agrarian Development (*Instituto de Desarrollo Agrario*—IDA). While the law that created the IDA did much to place the agrarian reform agency on a firmer financial footing, serious budgetary problems continued to limit IDA's effectiveness. —EDS.

5. By 1980, ITCO had established fifty agrarian reform projects—with a total area of over 111,000 hectares (296,400 acres)—that directly benefited some 4,200 peasant families. See Jorge A. Mora Alfaro, "La estructura agraria y la capacitación campesina," *Revista de Ciencias Sociales,* nos. 19–20 (1980): 76.—EDS.

4.12 Agrarian Cooperatives in Costa Rica*

BY GERMÁN MASÍS

Cooperatively owned enterprises have been an important mechanism employed by the Costa Rican state both to defuse conflict and to increase poor and working people's economic stake in the existing order. While cooperatives are potentially an important form of participation and contribute to the democratization of society, they have not always lived up to their potential. This reading by Germán Masís suggests that while some rural co-ops are prospering, others have suffered for lack of adequate financial and technical support from the state. He argues that there is a growing gap between wealthy cooperatives involved in producing export or luxury goods and those oriented toward subsistence agriculture.

Masís is a frequent contributor to Aportes, *the publication of the National Center for Pastoral Action (CENAP).*

RURAL cooperatives are a relatively recent phenomenon in Costa Rica. In the early 1960s, following the Punta del Este Conference [in Uruguay that founded the Alliance for Progress], Latin American policymakers began to view the cooperative as a symbol of participation and democratization and the ideal form of organization for solving the socioeconomic problems of the poor.[1] Such considerations appeared to be of the utmost urgency at a time when the

*Excerpted from "Cooperativismo agrario en Costa Rica," *Aportes,* no. 11 (November–December 1982): 20–22.

Cuban revolution's efforts to transform economic dependency were creating enormous expectations throughout the continent.

The cooperative model was thus adopted by the early 1960s as part of state policy. Peasants' demands for and occupation of land in various parts of the country called into question the country's unequal system of land tenure. When the Lands and Colonization Institute (ITCO) was created to carry out agrarian reform, cooperatives became a convenient method of organizing its peasant beneficiaries. ITCO initiated the formation of several cooperatives and began to provide administrative and financial assistance to various others as well.

However, in a number of cases, ulterior motives lay behind the founding of these ITCO-sponsored ventures, including the derailing of squatter groups and nascent peasant unions. ITCO created production cooperatives, as well as cooperatives for marketing agricultural inputs and equipment, but in many cases the peasants understood little about the importance and possibilities of co-op organization or its potential for resolving their economic difficulties. Many of these cooperatives lacked collateral for loans and access to credit and technical assistance. In addition, they typically had little administrative experience and possessed few means of marketing their output. Perhaps most important, these cooperatives have been involved almost exclusively in the production of nonexport goods, leaving them without secure markets, subject to extreme price fluctuations, and with only a marginal share in the country's economy.

ITCO organized its cooperatives into a federation—called *Fedeagro*—which, after ten years, separated from the agrarian reform agency and became an independent organization. In the period in which ITCO directed *Fedeagro,* a number of peasant cooperativists, dissatisfied with the agency's policies, established an alternative co-op federation—*Fedecopa*—that they themselves administered. Nevertheless, *Fedecopa* member co-ops generally were involved in the same kinds of production as those in *Fedeagro*—basic grains, vegetables and other staples—and were generally in a similar, economically marginal situation.

By the 1970s, rural cooperatives occupied a significant place in the economy.[2] But the legislation governing cooperatives did not distinguish between poor co-ops dedicated to subsistence agriculture that lacked institutional backing and those wealthier, export-oriented, agroindustrial co-ops that functioned like true capitalist enterprises. These two blocks of cooperatives are characterized by contrasting orientations, interests, and expectations, as well as differing capacities for affecting policy decisions.

This gap between wealthy and poor co-ops was not diminished by the founding [in 1973] of an autonomous institution designed to promote and direct the cooperative movement, the Cooperative Development Institute [*Instituto de Fomento Cooperativo*—INFOCOOP]. It is even possible that the gap has widened in recent years. Unrestricted state technical and financial support has allowed some cooperatives to achieve ever higher levels of capitalization, while leaving further behind those that have not been able to take advantage of such opportunities.

The economically successful cooperatives formed an umbrella organization—the National Cooperative Union [*Unión Nacional Cooperativa*—UNA-COOP]—that has become a powerful political pressure group. UNACOOP in turn created a National Cooperative Council [*Consejo Nacional Cooperativo*—CONACOOP] that includes all cooperatives in the country, including *Fedeagro* and *Fedecopa,* and which defines policy goals for the entire movement. UNACOOP has sufficient economic clout to have helped found a bank to provide financial support to cooperative enterprises. Politically, it has used its influence to encourage the formation of a Ministry of Cooperatives.

Many Costa Ricans consider cooperatives an adequate means of assuring participation and of democratizing society. Nonetheless, from the point of view of the dominant groups, cooperativism has frequently served as a sedative in the face of popular mobilizations, including those by the same sectors that have embraced cooperative forms of organization. There is no doubt that some cooperatives—generally the modern, efficient enterprises that employ land, labor, and capital much as any other business—have come to occupy important positions in Costa Rica's productive structure. For the poor, however, cooperatives founded on a top-down basis have not reflected their needs, particularly when credit and technical assistance are lacking. Cooperatives could have provided the popular sectors useful experiences in reflecting on ways of solving their problems and in group decision making and collective work. But this would have required both a reorientation of existing cooperatives and greater commitment to agrarian reform on the part of the state.

Some rural cooperatives have managed to operate as capitalist enterprises, engaging in practices that make a mockery of their philosophy. At the same time, others painfully limp along, a form of peasant organization that is scarcely able to guarantee its members' survival.

NOTES

1. There were, however, a number of earlier experiences with co-ops. The country's first co-ops were founded in the 1920s and 1930s to provide members with low-cost housing and loans. In the 1940s the number and variety of cooperative enterprises grew substantially, and in 1947 the National Bank of Costa Rica (BNCR) formed a special cooperative section that established sixteen co-ops, some of which still exist today. In 1953, at the beginning of José Figueres's first elected term, the BNCR's cooperative section was upgraded and became a full department of the bank, with significantly greater financial resources and more personnel. See Instituto Nacional de Fomento Cooperativo (INFOCOOP), *Ocho temas básicos para un curso de cooperativismo* (San José: INFOCOOP, 1980), pp. 52–56.—EDS.

2. By the early 1980s, cooperatives accounted for 15 percent of Costa Rica's gross national product, 33 percent of its coffee production, and nearly 75 percent of its milk output. With some 200,000 members (who with their families totaled about 800,000), the cooperative movement included as members an estimated one-fourth of the country's work force. See Farid Ayales Esna, "La neutralidad de Costa Rica y la guerra en Centroamérica," *Relaciones Internacionales* 4, no. 6 (1983): 28.—EDS.

4.13 Costa Rican Peasants and the Politics of Quiescence*

BY A. DOUGLAS KINCAID

In this reading, sociologist A. Douglas Kincaid briefly outlines Central American peasants' responses to modern agrarian capitalism and explores why Costa Rican peasants have not mobilized politically to the same extent as their counterparts elsewhere in the region. He reviews several theories that have attempted to explain the absence of widespread rural mobilization in Costa Rica and finds them incomplete. A comparison of rural conditions in Costa Rica and the rest of Central America leads him to conclude that the key to the Costa Rican peasantry's different political behavior lies in the reformist policies of the National Liberation Party, dominant in Costa Rica since the 1948 civil war. Reforms—though far from satisfying all of the campesinos' *needs—have undercut other efforts at mobilization. After the economic crisis began in 1980, however, Kincaid notes signs of change. The peasantry is far from developing a revolutionary movement or temperament. But it has begun to organize around selected issues in a manner that suggests that peasants no longer see acquiescence and PLN-sponsored reform as their only options.*

Kincaid is associate director of the Latin American and Caribbean Center at Florida International University in Miami. He holds a Ph.D. in sociology from the Johns Hopkins University.

WITH regard to peasant politics, Costa Rica stands as a case apart in Central America. Throughout the region, the postwar expansion of agrarian capitalism, along with rapid population growth, created a large, expanding rural labor force with declining access to land and insufficient alternative rural employment. Many peasants migrated to the city to flee this predicament. Others, however, sought solutions in the countryside, often through mass or community organizations. Peasant movements have played major roles in the contemporary revolutionary situations in El Salvador, Nicaragua, and Guatemala. In Honduras, mass-based peasant organizations have pressured the government to implement or expand agrarian reform for more than twenty years. But in the Costa Rican countryside, neither revolutionary nor reformist movements have prospered.

This image of Costa Rican passivity must not be overstated. Costa Rican

*Research for this article was carried out during 1982–83 with support from the Inter-American Foundation, the Institute for the Study of World Politics, and the Central American University Confederation (CSUCA).

peasants do frequently participate in local community organizations and development projects, and they vote regularly in national elections.[1] More significantly, they have engaged in illegal land occupations, or squatting, on a massive scale. Figures from the Institute of Agrarian Development, Costa Rica's land-reform agency, show that between 1963 and 1982, the institute dealt with more than 1,000 cases of alleged illegal occupations encompassing some 15,600 squatter families on 415,000 hectares (1,025,465 acres) of land. By the 1973 census totals, the latter figure comprises more than 10 percent of the country's total farmland. Many more cases were suppressed by police and judicial authorities or were simply uncontested by landowners. Finally, peasant and rural workers organizations have surged during the economic crisis that began in 1980. The percentage of the rural labor force in unions, for instance, was only 5.3 percent in 1973 and 6.3 percent in 1977, but by 1984 had climbed to 14.8 percent.

This new wave of organization, should it endure, would constitute an important social and political development. It does not alter, however, the distinctive quiescence of the Costa Rican peasants in the post-1948 period. The low degree of organization of Costa Rican peasants through the 1970s may be compared to figures of around 25 percent of the rural labor force in countries like Honduras, Venezuela, and Colombia. Moreover, much of that organized minority in Costa Rica was to be found among the relatively privileged permanent employees on large, foreign-owned banana plantations.

The task, then, is to explain why the Costa Rican peasant has offered such a relatively weak organized response to the pressures of agrarian capitalism. A number of explanations have been offered, variously emphasizing economic, sociocultural, and political factors regarded as unique to Costa Rica. It is difficult to judge these hypotheses on evidence from Costa Rica alone, however, because it is hard to determine which specific traits of the Costa Rican rural population are fundamental and which are circumstantial to the question of mobilization. A better procedure is to evaluate the Costa Rican case in light of what is known about peasant movements elsewhere in Central America.[2] Competing explanations may then be examined and an alternative put forward.

Before turning to these explanations, one might ask whether Costa Rican peasants were sufficiently well-off, so that collective action was unnecessary. Although rural conditions lag behind those in urban areas, it is true that by many standards—including average levels of income, education, and health care—Costa Rica ranks well above the rest of Central America. Relatively few Costa Rican peasants live at the thin margin of subsistence. Yet poverty is by no means rare. A study based on 1973 census returns (and thus prior to the recent economic decline) led to a conservative estimate that 32 percent of all rural families were poor, with an annual household income (including nonmonetary sources) of under $165.[3] Thus, regardless of whether peasants elsewhere were even worse off, there was clearly room for organized action on the part of Costa Rican peasants, particularly within a context of increasing land-lessness among rural families and growing conflicts over ownership and posses-sion.

One explanation holds that displaced peasants in Costa Rica failed to orga-nize because they had alternatives, such as claiming land in the extensive, unoccupied frontier regions or seeking work on banana plantations. This view argues, too, that the relatively high degree of ethnic homogeneity inhibited peasant radicalism.[4] Yet neither argument is very persuasive. Sparsely settled agricultural frontiers did not forestall frequent rebellions of peasant communi-ties against the early encroachments of export agriculture in the nineteenth century. More recently, open frontiers of unclaimed lands larger than that of Costa Rica failed to impede massive mobilization of Honduran peasants or social revolution in Nicaragua. On the other hand, labor on banana plantations has served more to stimulate than hinder organization, first through the bitter unionization struggles of plantation workers themselves and subsequently as workers with experience in those organizations filtered through to other rural areas. This has been most pronounced in Honduras, but can also be found in Costa Rica, where banana workers' unions have been among the most militant labor organizations and the backbone of radical political parties.

The ethnic homogeneity argument is also problematic. Prior to 1900, nearly all Central American agrarian movements pitted Indian peasants against Spanish, *criollo,* or *ladino* elites. However, this is a poor basis on which to construct an argument for contemporary Costa Rica. Strong peasant move-ments in El Salvador and Honduras have arisen despite the decline or disap-pearance of Indian ethnicity as a salient feature of agrarian social relations. It is also doubtful that contemporary Costa Rica, with its important Atlantic coast black population, is more ethnically homogeneous than its neighbors. Finally, while ethnic divisions between landlords and peasants may strengthen the latter's resistance, such divisions within working classes have often been exploited by dominant groups to weaken labor movements, including those in rural areas [see Readings 2.8 and 4.10].

Other scholars argue that the individualistic smallholder mentality preva-lent among Costa Rican peasants impedes collective action.[5] Sturdy individual-ism was supposedly the legacy of landholding patterns in the coffee regions, where relative labor scarcity and land abundance gave rise to small and me-dium-sized coffee holdings and wage labor rather than the large estates and coerced labor that were common elsewhere.[6] Nevertheless, this argument too, with its stress on individualistic over collective action, is a weak explanation of contemporary Costa Rican peasant politics. Costa Rican labor is no longer scarce and land no longer readily available. The postwar expansion of capitalist agriculture and state power has tended to weaken the strong internal cohesive-ness of peasant communities, in Costa Rica and throughout Central America. Nearly all contemporary Central American peasant organizations have thus had to struggle against peasant individualism in order to create cooperative or organizational structures. In some cases, as in El Salvador, smallholders themselves have been successfully organized.

Yet another view maintains that the lack of popular organizations in general is the result of a particular mix of state policies implemented by the bourgeoisie, which combine the co-optation of small farmers and the urban middle class with repression of organizational efforts among the rural landless and the urban proletariat [see Reading 4.2]. This distinction corresponds perfectly to the particular bases of electoral strength and weakness of the National Liberation Party (PLN) which, with its precursors, has—even when out of power—been the country's dominant political force since 1948. Yet, this argument, too, is incomplete.

Co-optation through reforms and the provision of state services may have "demobilized" smallholding peasants, but the argument does not address why and how such measures were implemented. It treats as one and the same the interests of the bourgeoisie and the state, and accords little or no importance to the nature and outcome of disputes among Costa Rica's ruling elites. Furthermore, antilabor legislation and other repressive measures may have hindered urban and rural unionization, but the repression certainly pales in comparison to the brutality routinely visited on popular movements elsewhere in Central America, where peasants and others were nonetheless organized.

What lessons may be gleaned from those other countries? Three basic forms of peasant mobilization may be discerned across the Central American region's modern history. The first may be called "community solidarity" situations, in which peasant villages have resisted or rebelled against dominant-class efforts to expropriate their lands, appropriate their labor, or incorporate them into larger market structures. In the past, this localized, semiautonomous organized response has been common in Central American villages that retained a significant Indian identity. Such movements have been rare in Costa Rica because of the absence of an Indian labor force and the peculiar geography of coffee expansion, which was based on the outward dispersion of a relatively small population rather than the conversion or creation of large landed estates. In Costa Rica, the nineteenth-century privatization of Church, municipal, and Indian landholdings was largely uncontested, while elsewhere in Central America it was an important element of localized peasant solidarity and the immediate cause of numerous rebellions.

In the twentieth century, "community solidarity" movements have waned throughout the region. As once remote communities have been integrated into expanding agricultural commodity and labor markets, linked to urban centers by road and communications networks, and penetrated by national political institutions, the scope of autonomous local action has been sharply reduced. Only among the highland Indians of Guatemala does traditional community solidarity remain an important force, and there it has been closely circumscribed by a vigilant authoritarian state. Thus, while the internal relationships of rural communities may still be analyzed as a help or a hindrance to the formation of peasant movements, they are not a sufficient basis for contrasting Costa Rican quiescence with mobilization elsewhere.

The second type of mobilization involves rural labor unions, formed by agricultural wage laborers. In general, agricultural enterprises are resistant to unionization, given such typical characteristics as low skill requirements, mechanization, seasonal variations in labor demand, and volatile market prices. In Central America, the major exception to this rule is the banana industry, where a set of unusual conditions—large, concentrated labor forces employed year-round on plantations owned by foreign corporations enjoying near-monopolistic control over world markets—fostered the emergence of a labor movement in the 1930s. Such movements produced strong banana worker unions in both Honduras and Costa Rica [see Reading 2.8]. Costa Rica, in this respect, is not an exceptional case.[7]

The intervention in the countryside of external, generally urban-based social actors has led to a third type of peasant mobilization. The same circumstances that have weakened local community ties and reduced peasants' potential for autonomous local solidarity have increased their contact with outsiders possessing the resources (as well as a variety of motives) to foster peasant organizations. Such organizations generally represent smallholding, renting, and landless peasant families seeking state intervention on their behalf. They have been especially weak in Costa Rica.

What, then, are the principal forces behind these contemporary Central American peasant organizations, and what have they done in Costa Rica? First and foremost, perhaps, stands the Church. Religious and lay activists of the Catholic Church have been involved in creating large-scale peasant organizations in Guatemala, Honduras, El Salvador, and Nicaragua. In each case, these organizations have been among the most militant, often revolutionary, defenders of peasant interests. But in Costa Rica, the Church has been minimally involved with peasant mobilization. An oft-cited reason for this is the conservative attitudes of the Costa Rican Church hierarchy. But Catholic hierarchies nearly everywhere have opposed progressive social movements within the Church's institutional boundaries. In fact, the original motivation for forming peasant organizations elsewhere was profoundly conservative: to combat the spread of Communist and Protestant ideas. In Costa Rica, however, events followed a different course.

In Costa Rica, simply put, the state got there first. Beginning with the *calderonista* reformist policies of the 1940s, and greatly amplified by the PLN after 1950, programs and services in education, health care, social security, community development, and small producer credit gradually extended into the countryside. These programs forestalled the emergence of similar efforts under Church or other private sponsorship. Elsewhere in Central America, in the absence of much state commitment to social welfare, it was precisely this pattern of Church activity—radio schools, literacy campaigns, cooperative promotion, self-help groups, housewife clubs, and so forth—that provided the mass base of "Catholic Left" social movements. Progressive religious activists have not been lacking in Costa Rica, but they generally have not had the same popular constituency [see Reading 4.9].

Another external force behind Central American peasant organizations is labor unions. National and international labor federations, with diverse leftist, Catholic, and U.S. labor ties, have often supported peasant groups of corresponding ideological sign. This effort has usually reinforced existing organizations, however, rather than stimulated new ones.

In both Costa Rica and Honduras, the initial movement for national peasant organizations came in regions surrounding the banana plantations and was sparked by ex-banana workers linked to Communist labor organizations. The contrast between the two countries is instructive. In Honduras, the Communist presence in both union and peasant organizations was subject to continual attack by the government, which typically either replaced militant leaders with pliant ones or, when that failed, sponsored parallel organizations to siphon off popular support. These tactics were supported by substantial U.S. material and political assistance. The original Honduran peasant organization was quickly destroyed, but the parallel movement gradually spread throughout the country during the late 1960s.

In Costa Rica, however, despite frequent harassment and the exclusion of the Communists (the Popular Vanguard Party, or PVP) from the electoral arena during the 1950s and 1960s, leftist labor dominance in the banana zones was not directly challenged. Parallel labor and peasant organizations were formed but remained small and were not accorded great importance by either the Costa Rican government or U.S. allies. Nevertheless, in spite of numerous organizing efforts, congresses, and clarion calls, the Left was unable to establish a significant peasant movement beyond the banana zones. The explanation of this situation takes us to the next set of peasant organizational sponsors—the political parties.

Leftist, rightist, and centrist political parties and related organizations have all sought to organize peasants in the other Central American nations. The relatively open Costa Rican political arena has posed the fewest obstacles to these campaigns, such that their dearth becomes all the more curious.

The confinement of leftist peasant mobilization to the banana zones is symptomatic of a larger failure throughout the region. Surprising as it may seem amidst current revolutionary upheavals, nowhere in Central America has a Communist or other leftist party been able to create a mass-based peasant organization.[8] Only in part can this failure be attributed to repression, since Church-based movements have also been hard hit. Marxist groups have often emphasized proletarian class struggles at the expense of attention to peasants' problems. In Costa Rica, this insensitivity is indicated in the complaints of local peasant groups that initial PVP organizational assistance in land conflicts rapidly deteriorates into little more than electoral manipulation. The lesson from other Central American processes is that the radicalization of peasant groups has not resulted from direct ideological appeals, but rather from local organization and conflicts over issues of immediate concern.

Though certainly less common, right-wing political organizations have also sought to mobilize peasants, most notably in El Salvador. Such efforts invariably have been attempts to control threatening mobilizations of a more progressive nature. Since the latter have not yet become a significant force in Costa Rica, the absence of rightist mobilizations needs little further explanation.

The absence of centrist mobilizations is more perplexing. Specifically, the social democratic PLN has dominated Costa Rican politics for more than three decades and pursued social reform. Why has such a party not sought to organize peasants as a force behind agrarian and other social reforms, or at least as an electoral tactic?

One possible answer points toward the class interests of the PLN's leaders, who are prominent in the ranks of large estate and agribusiness owners and managers of state-sponsored agroindustrial projects.[9] Yet this perspective on the power of the dominant class is not a sufficient description of the PLN or an adequate explanation for nonmobilization. In other contexts, support for peasant organizations has not proven incompatible with large-scale, modernized agriculture.

The crucial factor is that, alone among the centrist parties of Central America, the PLN was able to implement its reformist and state-centered development model without having to confront the entrenched interests of a dominant landholding class. While the 1948 civil war indicates that this model did not take shape without significant conflict, its success was not contingent on breaking the control of a landed oligarchy over the peasantry. The relative weakness of large landowners made it possible to enact reformist programs and win peasant votes without prior collective mobilization in the countryside.

On the other hand, the PLN has not faced any serious competition on its own reformist turf. Specifically, the absence of a strong Christian Democratic party has obviated any need for competitive peasant mobilization among rival centrist parties. The Christian Democrats encountered in politics an obstacle similar to that which Church activists faced in the field of community welfare: the PLN and its policies have preempted the available space. In conclusion, the relative passivity of Costa Rican peasants in the post–civil war era can be attributed to their lack of external allies. This is the result of the comparatively easy implementation of a reformist development model, which elsewhere has been stymied or weakened by the persistent power of landed-class interests. The PLN did not need peasant organization to implement this model, while at the same time, state-sponsored reformism greatly reduced the desire and ability of other actors—the Church, labor unions, political parties, etc.—to organize peasants for other purposes.

Nevertheless, while the absence of an oligarchical ancien régime is a matter of history, the viability of the PLN development model has been called into question in the wake of the post-1980 economic crisis. Popular mobilization, including that of peasants and rural workers, may be becoming a more important strategy in Costa Rican politics, for both the PLN and its opponents.

It appears that the recent surge in peasant organization is mainly the result of two distinct processes. One stemmed from the banana companies' decision to cut production, shift to nonlabor intensive African palm cultivation, or close plantations altogether in the face of weak demand and low international prices [see Reading 5.4]. The resulting unemployment in plantation zones gave renewed impetus to peasant organization, again with the active collaboration of the banana worker unions and the Left. That, in turn, created some stirring of interest in the U.S.-supported parallel union structure, although it remained a low priority among the Reagan administration's targets for assistance.

The second process was less visible but more novel. Around 1980, small farmers in and around the Central Valley began to organize, aided by PLN activists dissatisfied with the regressive direction of social policy under the Carazo government and, after 1982, under their own party's administration. While the movement initially focused on such limited issues as the price of fertilizer or diesel fuel, by 1983 it had begun to include demands and actions on behalf of landless peasants in that region.

Whether this new wave of mobilization is a momentary response to the current economic crisis or represents a more enduring alteration of Costa Rican politics cannot be foretold. Despite the respite afforded by U.S. economic aid, the outlook for the PLN's expansive, state-led development model is not bright. The potential for translating peasant discontent into organization is thus greater, particularly for PLN activists and probably for the Left as well. While such a trend in the short run would undoubtedly increase the level of rural conflict, in the long run Costa Rican democracy likely would be the better for it.

NOTES

1. John A. Booth and Mitchell A. Seligson, "Peasants as Activists: A Reevaluation of Political Participation in the Countryside," *Comparative Political Studies* 2 (1979): 29–59.

2. A. Douglas Kincaid, "Agrarian Development, Peasant Mobilization and Social Change in Central America: A Comparative Study" (Ph.D. diss., The Johns Hopkins University, 1987).

3. See Manuel J. Carvajal, David T. Geithman, and Patrick R. Armstrong, *Pobreza en Costa Rica* (Gainesville, Fla.: Center for Tropical Agriculture, University of Florida, 1977), pp. 134, 135.

4. Mitchell Seligson, *Peasants of Costa Rica and the Development of Agrarian Capitalism* (Madison: University of Wisconsin Press, 1980), pp. 153–62.

5. Francisco Barahona Riera, *Reforma agraria y poder político: el caso de Costa Rica* (San José: Editorial Universidad de Costa Rica, 1980), pp. 425–28.

6. Land tenure in the coffee industry and the question of the Costa Rican "yeoman farmer" are addressed in detail in Readings 1.1, 1.2, 1.3, 1.4, and 1.6.—EDS.

7. Banana workers are generally regarded as belonging to a different class (the proletariat) than peasants, typically defined as controlling at least a small plot of land. While class distinctions

among rural workers are important, it is useful to consider the two together. Banana unions have periodically sought to organize peasants beyond the boundaries of the plantations. There has been considerable mobility between the roles of landless laborer, smallholder, and plantation worker. A few years of work on a banana plantation is a common way for a poor peasant to save enough to purchase land. Alternatively, plantation layoffs may force large numbers of workers to return to small-scale agriculture.

8. This judgment excludes the cases of postrevolutionary Nicaragua and the regions of El Salvador under the control of the Farabundo Martí National Liberation Front (FMLN) guerrillas. Control of state power by the Left (albeit de facto in the Salvadoran case) obviously constitutes a very different set of conditions.

9. See Mayra Achío Tacsan and Ana Cecilia Escalante Herrera, "Los grandes empresarios azucareros: Costa Rica 1960–1978," *Cuadernos Centroamericanos de Ciencias Sociales* 9 (1982): 65–88; and Mylena Vega, *El Estado costarricense de 1974 a 1978: CODESA y la facción industrial* (San José: Editorial Hoy, 1982).

CHAPTER V

The 1980s Economic Crisis

Editors' Introduction *

In August 1981, a year before the "Mexico weekend" that is now widely regarded as marking the onset of the Latin American debt crisis, Costa Rica became the first country in the region to cease payment on all its international obligations. Two years later, the United States stepped in with massive economic assistance and engineered a partial recovery. Many of the Costa Rican economy's structural weaknesses, however, were unaffected by the post-1983 upturn and economic stability remained tenuous.

Even though the advent of the crisis in the early 1980s seemed sudden, signs of trouble had been accumulating for almost a decade. By the early 1970s, industrialization policies based on import substitution and regional integration (see Readings 4.4 and 4.5) were contributing to growing trade deficits—for every $100 of industrial output, the country imported $80 of machinery and inputs.[1] When oil prices soared in 1973, the situation worsened and growth slowed. The increased social spending of the 1960s and 1970s, while resulting in impressive advances in health and education (see Readings 4.6 and 5.5) had been financed largely with foreign loans.

Throughout the 1970s, the government tried to maintain existing levels of production and employment through direct investments financed for the most part through foreign borrowing. By 1980 the public sector employed

*Part of this introduction is adapted from Marc Edelman, "Back from the Brink: How Washington Bailed out Costa Rica," *Report on the Americas* 19, no. 6 (1985): 37–48.

20 percent of the labor force and produced 24 percent of all goods and services.[2] The availability of inexpensive foreign loans that permitted increased public spending and the sudden quadrupling of coffee prices in 1977 meant that it was easy to ignore disquieting signs of stagnation and impending crisis.

As Helio Fallas explains in Reading 5.1, the sudden deterioration of 1980–82 was not only the result of these structural factors, but of several immediate circumstances as well. In 1978 coffee prices plummeted and the following year oil prices again rose sharply. The 1979 insurrection in Nicaragua interrupted overland traffic, slowed commerce with the rest of the Central American Common Market, and also led to capital flight. The worldwide recession of the early 1980s also had a negative effect on foreign demand for Costa Rican exports.

The policies of the administration of President Rodrigo Carazo (1978–82) also contributed to the growing crisis. Faced with an expanding public-sector deficit, the government began to absorb a growing share of bank credit and to print money in order to meet its debts. In 1980, when interest rates were rising sharply, the government increased its reliance on more expensive commercial bank financing. The country's currency, the *colón,* fixed for years at 8.6 *colones* to the dollar, was overvalued, making imports and travel abroad artificially cheap and Costa Rica's exports overly expensive by regional standards. The artificially high value of the currency further exacerbated the trade deficit.

The *colón* was finally allowed to float in September 1980. At the end of the year its value against the dollar had nearly been halved. In 1981 the currency plummeted to 39 per dollar, and in July 1982 it reached a low of 65 to the dollar, before stabilizing at 44 to the dollar in 1983.[3] Together with the devaluation, inflation soared to nearly 100 percent in 1982. Unemployment more than doubled from 1979 to 1981—from 4.1 to 8.3 percent of the work force—and climbed to 8.5 percent in 1982. Much higher levels of underemployment and drastic declines in real wages brought a sudden impoverishment of much of the population and threatened political stability. Costa Rica had no army, but it was widely believed that powerful upper-class groups were working to destabilize the Carazo government, angered at the president's refusal to make agreements with the International Monetary Fund (IMF) that he considered damaging to the country's sovereignty. Alarmed political analysts warned that Costa Rica might follow the route of Uruguay, another social welfare state, where a parliamentary democracy was replaced with a military dictatorship in 1973.

But dire predictions proved unfounded. When the National Liberation Party administration of Luis Alberto Monge was inaugurated in May 1982, one of the new president's first priorities was to reach agreement with the IMF. The objective obstacles were formidable, however. Already topping $4 billion, Costa Rica's foreign debt was, on a per capita basis, one of the highest in the world. In terms of two key indicators—the ratio of debt to gross domestic product (GDP) and of debt to exports—Costa Rica was *(and still is)* among the Latin American countries least able to meet payments and remain afloat. The Monge administration, with the help of the IMF, achieved two reschedulings of the foreign debt. Inflation was brought down from nearly 100 percent in 1982, to 33 percent in 1983, and 12 percent in 1984. Economic growth reached a respectable 6 percent in 1984, fell to 2 percent in 1985, and climbed slightly to 3 percent in 1986. In return for the new loans that fueled this turnaround, the IMF demanded a series of austerity measures designed to increase exports, decrease imports, and slash government spending. But Costa Rica has not met one IMF target since it began negotiations with the fund in 1981.[4]

How then to understand the continuing indulgence of the IMF and other international lending institutions and how to explain the slow economic recovery that began in 1983 and quickened after 1984? Costa Rica has come to play a strategic role in U.S. Central American policy, as a base for Nicaraguan *contras,* a neighbor to the Panama Canal, and a democratic, pro-U.S. showcase in a region historically dominated by military regimes. Because the Costa Rican economy is small—with a GDP (in 1985) of just over $4 billion—relatively limited injections of U.S. aid have had an immediate, perceptible effect, permitting temporary relief from the debt crisis not possible in the larger Latin American countries. U.S. assistance to Costa Rica remained at relatively modest levels until 1981, totaling less than $200 million in the eighteen years between 1962 and 1979. In 1982, however, the U.S. Agency for International Development (USAID) began to supply Costa Rica with Economic Support Funds (ESF) under a new program of loans and grants of which the "primary objective . . . is to support U.S. economic, political and security interests and to advance foreign policy objectives."[5]

Total ESF assistance and the proportion of USAID funds that are donated outright have grown dramatically since 1982. In 1985 Costa Rica received a $160 million grant under the ESF program, in addition to other economic assistance. By assuring a flow of credit to the private sector and subsidizing imports from the United States, USAID grants provide the edge that allows Costa Rica to make debt payments *and* to retain politically acceptable living standards. Costa Rica became the second largest recipient of U.S. aid in Latin America, after El Salvador, and at one point was the second highest per capita recipient of U.S. assistance worldwide after Israel. U.S. economic assistance between 1983 and 1985 was equivalent to a staggering 35.7 percent of the Costa Rican government's operating expenditures, one-quarter of export earnings, and around 10 percent of the country's GDP.[6]

But U.S. economic assistance comes with strings attached. In broad terms, U.S. aid has been tied to the same kind of conditionality posed by the IMF. The goal is to create export-oriented, internationally competitive economies, unprotected from world market forces by tariff barriers. Wage rates should favor capital rather than labor and, indeed, real wages (adjusted for inflation) in 1986 had fallen to 1971 levels.[7] U.S. economic assistance has also been part of an implicit—and at times explicit—political quid pro quo. Not long after pro-neutrality President Oscar Arias (see Reading 7.16) took over in 1986 from the more pro-Washington Luis Alberto Monge, the United States held up $80 million in U.S. and international credits, forcing Costa Rica again to temporarily suspend payments on most of its interest obligations. Later, the Tower Commission revealed that the U.S. refusal to disburse aid was directly linked to Arias's reluctance to permit Nicaraguan *contras* to operate on Costa Rican territory (see Chapter VII).[8]

According to the Reagan administration, salvation lies in the open access to the U.S. market assured by the Caribbean Basin Initiative (CBI). In the short run, garment and assembly plants located in free-trade zones are seen as a partial solution to the crisis. The export of "nontraditional" items such as flowers, spices, and tropical plants are viewed as the key to continuing long-term economic growth. Increasingly, advocates of this model of development articulate the vision of a Central American Taiwan or South Korea.

With its relatively educated work force and developed infrastructure, Costa Rica is one of the countries likely to benefit most from the CBI program. Nevertheless, Costa Rica's initial experience with the CBI indicates that CBI-type incentives are far from a panacea. While nontraditional exports have grown rapidly, duty-free exports to the United States under the CBI totaled only $33.9 million in 1984 and three-quarters of this was accounted for by beef, one of Costa Rica's four main traditional exports (along with coffee, bananas, and sugar). Of the dozen companies drawn to Costa Rica by the CBI as of June 1985, four planned to start or expand tropical fern and flower production. But only 362 new jobs were created by the three tropical plant companies for which data were available. And in late 1986, the U.S. Commerce Department slapped a 19 percent tariff on cut-flower imports from Costa Rica, severely dampening interest in this new investment line. Official U.S. figures claim that in 1985, some ninety CBI export-oriented foreign garment companies created 2,428 new jobs, but this estimate is likely based on plants reaching their as yet unattained full capacity.[9] Textile exports rose dramatically by 1986, and industry and government sources claimed that the garment sector employed between 30,000 and 40,000 workers.[10] But in the 1980s it is estimated that the Costa Rican economy must create over 27,000 new jobs *each year* just to keep pace with the natural growth of the work force.[11]

But ferns and flowers and even blue jeans do not constitute a modern industrial sector. Redirecting industry to the world market is a major undertaking requiring immense financial resources. Such a transformation of the industrial sector remains a weak point in U.S. designs for Costa Rica. Service on the $4.6 billion debt absorbs a large share of available resources and little is left to make the nation's industries competitive with East Asia or lower wage areas of the Caribbean Basin. If Costa Rica had not received an eighteen-month IMF standby loan in mid-1987, it would have had to devote more than 80 percent of its export earnings to debt service.[12]

Implementing export-oriented growth in Costa Rica has required aggressive efforts to change the country's institutions and to reach a new elite consensus. USAID and IMF plans for Costa Rica had long been the cause of divisions within the upper class. Industrialists, who had relied on subsidized credit and prospered behind high tariff barriers, generally opposed liberalizing the economy, while agroexport interests usually favored IMF programs.[13] By channeling funds directly to the private sector and withholding disbursements at critical moments in order to gain legislative approval of economic changes it considered essential, USAID has been able to begin the process of restructuring the Costa Rican economy. This has meant limits on government spending, reductions or eliminations of subsidies on food and low-cost credit for peasant farmers, sale of state-owned enterprises, changes in currency and banking laws, and the establishment of incentives for exporters.[14]

Not all Costa Ricans, of course, agree with this effort to dismantle the country's traditional social welfare institutions and emphasize exports over the domestic market. As Helio Fallas points out in Reading 5.1, any administration faced with a serious economic crisis has to make decisions about which social sectors will pay the costs of resolving the problem. He proposes efforts to reach a new political consensus around a development model that will have as a top priority the needs of Costa Rica's poor majority. In Reading 5.2, Juan Manuel Villasuso suggests that Costa Rica may be headed for a more concentrated, "socially unacceptable" income distribution pattern. Villasuso has been an outspoken advocate of basing economic recovery at least in part on a revival of domestic demand.

In spite of the severe economic decline of 1981–82, organized popular protest was relatively muted and the Costa Rican state continued to be able to defuse conflict using compromise rather than heavy-handed repression. Reading 5.3 describes the 1983 movement against electric rate increases, the first significant effort to organize popular resistance to the government's economic austerity program.

The 1985 decision by the major foreign banana companies in Costa Rica to shift many of their operations elsewhere (see Reading 5.4) is one of the more serious recent setbacks in Costa Rica's efforts to regain solvency. Bananas have accounted for approximately one-quarter of export earnings in recent years and have employed a large portion of the rural work force. The health effects of the crisis, analyzed by medical anthropologist Lynn Morgan in Reading 5.5 have been less severe than anticipated, although adequate statistics are often lacking. Morgan warns, however, that a model system of primary health delivery is now being undermined by increased dependence on foreign aid from donors who favor Reagan-style, fee-for-service medicine over state administered universal care.

The tenuous economic recovery that began in 1983 is the subject of Reading 5.6 by *Miami Herald* reporter Tim Golden. Even as improvements were registered in Costa Rica's economic indicators, questions remained about how long the country could continue to depend on U.S. largesse, especially if it took more independent foreign policy positions. Lezak Shallat analyzes the price of U.S. assistance in Reading 5.7 and examines the charge that AID funds have been used to construct a "secret parallel state" of private-sector groups that duplicates and undermines welfare-state institutions. She describes the irony that once Economic Support Funds were deposited in the Central Bank, Costa Rican taxpayers had to make such large interest payments to the United States that their country was unable to meet IMF deficit-reduction targets. The United States employed the interest income not only for promoting private-sector activities, but for constructing AID's lavish new headquarters.

The durability and the social costs of the post-1983 economic recovery are among the most important issues raised in this chapter. Since the low point of 1982, growth has been restored and inflation has been cut in recent years to between 10 and 25 percent, a low level by regional standards. Real wages remain basically stagnant, but social upheaval on the scale that threatened in 1982 is no longer likely. Yet the structural weaknesses of the economy persist and the costs of recovery for the country's social welfare institutions, economic independence, and political sovereignty continue to be severe. These issues will not only remain important subjects of debate in Costa Rica in the coming years; they are essential for understanding the country's role in the Central American crisis and its relations with the United States.

NOTES

1. Claudio González-Vega, "Fear of Adjusting: The Social Costs of Economic Policies in Costa Rica in the 1970s," in *Revolution and Counterrevolution in Central America and the Caribbean,* eds. Donald E. Schultz and Douglas H. Graham (Boulder, Colo.: Westview, 1984), p. 356.

2. Oficina de Planificación Nacional y Política Económica [OFIPLAN], *Evolución socio-económica de Costa Rica 1950–1980* (San José: Editorial UNED, 1982), pp. 318–19.

3. In recent years, the government has declared frequent "mini-devaluations" of the *colón.* In mid-1987, $1 (U.S.) was worth about 57 *colones* at the official rate and 62 *colones* on the black market.

4. Sol W. Sanders, "Costa Rica Milks the U.S. to Nurture Its Welfare State," *Wall Street Journal,* 21 March 1986.

5. USAID, *Congressional Presentation Fiscal Year 1985.*

6. Based on "Costa Rica: Key Economic Indicators" (San José: U.S. Embassy, 1985); *Latin American Regional Report: Mexico and Central America* (London), 30 November 1984; *Tico Times* (San José), 1984 Review.

7. U.N. Economic Commission on Latin America figures cited in *Latinamerica Press* (Lima), 10 July 1986.

8. *Christian Science Monitor,* 8 May 1986.

9. *Caribbean Basin Initiative Business Bulletin* (Washington, D.C.: U.S. Department of Commerce, June 1985); *New York Times,* 1 February 1987; U.S. Department of State, *The U.S. and Central America: Implementing the National Bipartisan Commission Report,* DOS Special Report No. 148 (Washington, D.C., 1986), p. 13; *Inforpress Centroamericana* (Guatemala), 2 October 1986.

10. Lowell Gudmundson, "Costa Rica's Arias at Midterm," *Current History* 86, no. 524 (1987): 419.

11. Helio Fallas, *Crisis económica en Costa Rica: un análisis económica de los ultimos veinte años* (San José: Nueva Década, 1981), p. 57.

12. *Central America Report* (Guatemala), 1 May 1987; *Latin American Weekly Report* (London), 7 May 1987.

13. The continuing fragility of the elite consensus on economic policy was illustrated by the resignation and subsequent reappointment in 1987 of Central Bank director Eduardo Lizano (author of Reading 4.5). Before resigning, Lizano blasted proprotectionist business sectors, politicians, and organized labor for lacking "responsibility and maturity" and for blocking austerity measures necessary for an IMF agreement. But less than two months after he stepped down, an IMF accord was signed and Lizano was back at his old post. In 1987 manufacturers also manifested opposition to Costa Rica's proposed entrance into the General Agreement on Tariffs and Trade (GATT), a move that would lower or remove most protection from local industry.

14. For more details, see Marc Edelman, "Back from the Brink: How Washington Bailed out Costa Rica," *Report on the Americas* 19, no. 6 (1985); and Roberto Artavia, Forrest D. Colburn, and Iván Saballos Patiño, "La experiencia con exportaciones en Costa Rica," *Centroamérica: estrategias de desarrollo,* ed. Forrest D. Colburn (San José: EDUCA, 1987).

5.1 Economic Crisis and Social Transformation in Costa Rica*

BY HELIO FALLAS VENEGAS

This reading by economist Helio Fallas, written at the height of the economic crisis in 1982, argues for a new model of development for Costa Rica. Though critical of both unplanned public-sector growth and the free-market prescriptions proposed by the International Monetary Fund, Fallas eschews single-factor explanations and summarizes the various theories about Costa Rica's economic problems. Even though the symptoms of crisis abated after this essay was written (see Reading 5.6), the structural problems described here remain much the same today. The discussion of the role of the news media in shaping debate about the crisis and in influencing consumption patterns is a particularly original aspect of this selection. Fallas also argues that any economic program administered by any government will have to address the problems raised by the "exhaustion" of Costa Rica's development model, as well as the social and political implications of different development choices.

*Excerpted from Helio Fallas Venegas, "Crisis económica y transformación social en Costa Rica," in *Costa Rica hoy: la crisis y sus perspectivas,* ed. Jorge Rovira Mas (San José: Editorial UNED, 1983).

Helio Fallas is a graduate of the University of Costa Rica and the University of the Andes in Bogotá, Colombia. He works with the Inter-American Institute of Agricultural Cooperation (IICA) and has taught at the University of Costa Rica and the National University in Heredia.

COSTA RICA is experiencing its most profound economic, social, cultural, and political crisis since 1948. The situation is one of generalized crisis. Because of its very nature and depth, its duration, and the absence of a political group that unites the country's principal social forces around a program for meeting the needs of the majority of Costa Ricans, we find ourselves facing a crisis that calls into question the present model of development and threatens the social and political peace the country has enjoyed in the last three decades. In this sense, the crisis is no longer a transitory one but a structural one, raising doubts about the present economic structure as well as the social and political ones. . . .

There is certainly consensus that the crisis exists, but not about its causes. Various explanations have been offered such as:

1. Problems in the external sector, which are exemplified in the following quotation from ex-President Rodrigo Carazo: "Let them buy more from us, abolish the quotas and the tariff barriers, and pay us just prices."[1]
2. Government intervention has brought us a giant state apparatus, added to inadequate incentives for the productive sectors.
3. Dependent capitalism in Costa Rica entered a critical phase in recent years as a result of multiple contradictions in the country's socioeconomic structure, the recent recessions in the developed capitalist countries, and the policies regarding foreign capital investment.
4. The crisis originated from errors of the Carazo government and the situation of the country will change with the new government. . . .
5. The economic and social system is "exhausted" and requires major transformations within a framework of political democracy and independent, nonaligned development. This last approach considers interrelated internal and external factors together, without falling into those interpretations that blame all our problems on the industrialized countries and the transnational corporations, or exclusively on specific sectors, such as the government or overprotected industry.

It is important to point out that these diverse interpretations are based on different ideological paradigms which are supported or encouraged by different social groups. The main communications media, for example, are engaging in a persistent ideological campaign that claims the only thing responsible for the deep crisis is the uncontrolled growth of the state. From this oversimplification, they suggest that with a drastic reduction in the size of the public sector and minimum government interference with "natural" economic laws all the problems of underdevelopment would disappear as if by magic. The hidden agenda of this approach is to obscure the Costa Rican economy's weaknesses and the limited capacity for self-sustained growth and job creation that grow out of its extreme economic, technological, and political dependence. It also ignores the effects of this economic structure on income distribution. . . .

The most important elements of the crisis are structural in origin, although it must be recognized that there exist other, more recent factors that have helped make the situation even worse. The structural elements of the economic and social crisis include:

1. A series of problems caused basically by the type of productive structure and which have brought us low or zero economic growth and low growth in productive employment, especially after 1980, and a chronic deficit in the balance of payments.
2. A lack of vertical integration in the productive structure, characterized by excessive dependence on imported inputs and excessive economic and technological dependence in general.
3. Rapid, unplanned expansion of the public sector, particularly in the 1970s, in large part as a result of the inability of the productive structure to generate sufficient growth or employment. This has led to growing fiscal deficits and an elevated level of indebtedness, which together constitute an enormous burden for an economic system, especially one in such precarious circumstances.
4. Generalized poverty, which has been worsening, in large part as the result of concentration in the ownership of the means of production, a growing inflation rate, and growing unemployment and underemployment resulting from economic stagnation.

Some of the more recent elements that have contributed to the crisis are:

1. Increases in the price of petroleum and its derivatives.
2. The world recession which limits appreciably the export possibilities of underdeveloped countries such as Costa Rica.
3. The Central American political situation.
4. The flight of national and foreign capital.
5. Insufficient availability of credit and increases in interest rates.
6. The application of a neoliberal economic policy that has created disequilibria in the areas of exchange rates, prices, and interest rates and that has heightened inflation and the public-sector deficit, while diminishing production, workers' purchasing power, and the size of the domestic market. . . .

Costa Rican society has become an imitator of the cultural values and the consumption, production, and technological patterns of the highly industrialized countries, thinking that this type of development is what is most appropriate for us. This means that the prevailing consumption patterns are based on highly sophisticated, imported models and are not in accord with the country's development possibilities and needs. They benefit instead certain social classes and contribute to increased external dependence. In this process, the communications media play a determining role in supporting foreign cultural penetration, miseducating and encouraging the adoption of foreign consumption patterns. This in turn has a negative effect on the balance of payments, since luxury goods and the intermediate goods required to produce them are imported. In the same way, it affects the allocation of productive resources by conditioning what is produced. . . .

The economic crisis, together with the spreading poverty and the unencouraging prospects as regards economic growth and employment, raises serious doubts about the functioning of the present Costa Rican model of development. This model was based on a social pact that especially favored the emerging industrial class, sectors of the old agroexport oligarchy, and middle and bureaucratic strata. The state assured that the weakest groups in society would participate to some degree in the growth of production through the application of labor laws and the provision of greater basic services. Although few workers had opportunities to accumulate capital, many of them enjoyed acceptable living conditions.

With the exhaustion of the development model and its inability to offer minimal living conditions for many workers, it may be possible to define a new political pact around a development model based on principles different from the present ones. This new model must provide answers about development options in six broad areas that will define how the crisis will be faced and which sectors of the population will pay the costs of solving it.

These areas are:

1. Consumption patterns: imitative and consumeristic as we have had them until now or seeking fundamentally to satisfy the basic necessities of the entire Costa Rican population.
2. The beneficiaries of development: maintaining the present patterns of concentration and poverty or reversing these tendencies through reforms, . . . including genuine agrarian reform.
3. The degree of external dependence: whether to seek greater autonomy through controls on foreign investment.
4. The definition of proportions and equilibria between different sectors and branches of production.
5. The function and size of the state.
6. The orienting mechanism of the socioeconomic system: leaving the market to decide what is produced, how it is produced, and for whom, or having a plan that orients the economy. For our country, the most

beneficial system would be required planning for the public sector and agreed-upon planning for the private sector.

In this context, a nonliberal strategy, as an alternative to that advocated by the neoliberal economists and the International Monetary Fund, would be one that favors a pattern of consumption that permits the satisfaction of basic needs. It would seek to reverse the tendencies toward income concentration through policies that promote real economic democracy, greater autonomy in the conduct of foreign affairs, and realistic proportions between the different productive branches, in accordance with the priorities that are established, so that the state might be the principal promoter of development, without this signifying that it may decide everything or ignore the necessities, dignity, or liberty of human beings.

NOTE

1. *La República* (San José), 24 February 1982.

5.2 The Impact of the Economic Crisis on Income Distribution*

BY JUAN MANUEL VILLASUSO ETOMBA

In this 1983 article Juan Manuel Villasuso examines one of the most alarming aspects of the economic crisis: the increasingly regressive distribution of income and wealth. Several aspects of the deteriorating economy—including inflation, devaluation, and the worsening employment situation—have contributed to eroding the "socially acceptable" distributive pattern that historically was typical of Costa Rica. Villasuso, who has advocated stimulating domestic demand (rather than exports) to generate recovery, addresses here a series of problems related to the economic crisis that are rarely considered by his more orthodox colleagues or by the international lending institutions.

Villasuso holds a licenciatura *degree in economics from the University of Costa Rica and a master's from Louisiana State University. During the administration of Luis Alberto Monge, he served briefly as minister of planning and economic policy.*

THIS essay offers a few observations and reflections on the economic crisis Costa Rica is experiencing, particularly its effect on the distribution of income and wealth between the various groups within Costa Rican society. Let us

*Excerpted from Juan Manuel Villasuso Etomba, "Evolución de la crisis económica en Costa Rica y su impacto sobre la distribución del ingreso," in *Costa Rica hoy: la crisis y sus perspectivas,* ed. Jorge Rovira (San José: Editorial UNED, 1983), pp. 201–15.

begin by describing the process of deterioration of the national economy that began in 1978. We have chosen this particular year, because it was then that the two most distinctive elements of the phenomenon began to manifest themselves: the drop in production (recession) and the increase in prices (inflation). This of course does not mean that we will not refer to trends that have been evident for longer periods. . . .

CHARACTERISTICS OF THE CRISIS

The disequilibrium in the Costa Rican economic system is fundamentally seen in three areas: decreased production, trade imbalances, and the budget deficit. These imbalances have brought maladies that, until very recently, were relatively unknown in this country: inflation, unemployment, and devaluation. These problems, in turn, affect the distribution of income and wealth, and provide the motive for application of economic policies that also modify the distribution structure. . . .

Beginning in 1977 when the gross domestic product (GDP) rose by 8.9 percent, the rate of growth began to fall drastically. By 1980 growth had slowed to 0.8 percent. The trend continued, and in 1981, for the first time in several decades, production fell, in absolute terms, on the order of 4.6 percent. It is estimated that in 1982 the fall of the GDP will be much greater (around 5 or 6 percent).[1]

This deterioration in national production has not affected all sectors equally. Some, like construction and certain service and industrial activities (nonmetallic minerals and metal machinery), have experienced a much sharper drop in production. Various factors may account for the drop in production strength. They include:

1. Decrease in credit in the private sector. The correlation between production and credit in Costa Rica is so close that one could go so far as to say that if there is no credit, there is no production. In recent years (particularly 1978–81), both domestic and foreign credit suffered a marked decrease. This occurred with domestic credit as a result of bank financing to the public sector, which deprived private activity of needed resources; with foreign credit because of the loss of confidence in Costa Rica and the general tightening of credit in international financial markets.
2. Increasing production costs as a consequence of domestic inflation, which made raw materials and other national inputs more expensive, devaluation that raised the price of imports, and the rise in interest rates, that is, the cost of capital, locally and in international markets.
3. Contraction of aggregate demand because of inflation and wage policy, which caused a substantial drop in real salary levels. This reality, of course, negatively influences domestic demand.

4. The general economic uncertainty produced by inflation, devaluation, and the lack of clarity and consistency in government policy led to recessionary actions on the part of the business community, which was trying to protect itself. The principal consequences of this climate of uncertainty and the shift in the expectations of the industrial sector were: a decrease in the private investment rate (the result of higher financial risk and a likely decrease in profitability); an increase in the rate of decapitalization of businesses (the result of less investment, and the inflation/devaluation that substantially raised debts of companies with dollar loans and reduced their working capital/liquidity); and capital flight to the international market as a means of personal protection (in response to the unstable Central American political situation and uncertainty about the national economy).

5. Finally, it is significant that financial activities suddenly became more attractive than the production of goods and services. If the behavior of the foreign exchange market, where the tendency toward devaluation can be predicted with a certain level of accuracy (although short-term speculative oscillations may be unpredictable and on occasions quite severe), it is still evident that "dollarizing" production or industrial resources—that is, carrying accounts in dollars rather than *colones*— was more profitable than production itself, especially with the more liquid resources (working capital, inventories, etc.).

The problems presented by the foreign-oriented sector of the Costa Rican economy, though multiple and complex, can be summed up under two broad categories: deficit in the trade balance and the large foreign debt. The trade deficit has been an endemic problem. Since the mid-1950s, the figures indicate that the value of imports far outweighs that of exports. In 1970, for instance, exports represented 23 percent of GDP. By 1980 this figure had grown to 30 percent. Nevertheless, in this same period, imports increased from 25 percent to 40 percent of GDP. The commercial deficit, for its part, rose from 40 percent of exports in 1970, to almost 60 percent in 1980.

This situation is structural in character, and arises from various factors:

1. An industrial production system highly dependent on imported raw materials and capital goods, and oriented toward internal consumption [see Reading 5.1].
2. A consumption pattern with a propensity to import (possibly the result of the tendency to revalue currency to maintain an exchange system with fixed parity).
3. Terms of trade that contributed to long-term deterioration.
4. A hesitant attitude toward increasing exports, particularly of nontraditional products, which can be explained both by high protectionism (including the Central American Common Market) that minimizes

risks and assures an attractive profit margin, and by the characteristics of the companies themselves and the behavior of businessmen [see Reading 4.5].

The two mechanisms used to finance the trade deficit have been foreign investment and foreign debt—the latter unquestionably the most important in recent years. The public-sector foreign debt rose from less than $900 million in 1978 to more than $2.7 billion in 1982. Loan conditions became more stringent. Payment terms were shortened, interest rates rose, and debt service increased at an exaggerated rate (reaching approximately 35 percent of the value of exports).

In 1980 both the trade deficit and the debt reached a crisis level. Largely because of the impressive decline in terms of trade (around 30 percent between 1977 and 1980) and the revaluation of the *colón* (a consequence of fixed exchange rates that did not permit adjustments for inflation), imports exceeded exports by 20 percent in the 1970s. The debt ballooned as the Carazo administration borrowed to make up for the trade gap and cover the costs of consumption.

This imbalanced situation meant that hard currency reserves were depleted, and a devaluation of the *colón* was required. But devaluation, at this point, was presented as a process of "floating" or continual adjustments rather than as a one-step measure as had been customary before. Devaluation has multiple effects, but the most significant impacts are in the areas of domestic inflation, public finance, import and export levels (in theory exports should rise and imports fall) and, most importantly, redistribution of income. As domestic prices are adjusted, which could take an indefinite amount of time or not occur at all if the exchange rate remains floating at an artificially high level, income distribution shifts to the benefit of exporters and the detriment of consumers, producers for the local market, and other socioeconomic groups.

In the fiscal sector, the imbalance between the central government's revenue and spending began to increase at an accelerated rate for several reasons. Regarding spending:

1. The increasingly active role of the state in the economic and social sphere.
2. Fixed expenses and a manner of establishing them (via the national budget) that requires increases in government spending.
3. The policy (conscious or unconscious) of absorbing workers who would otherwise be unemployed.
4. The likelihood that resources are squandered in certain activities and institutions. This may be a question of their size (diseconomies of scale), or of the poor control and supervision, administrative vice, prebends, sinecures, and corruption that have come to be firmly implanted in public administration.

With respect to revenue:

1. The inability or lack of will (for the sake of giving it a name) to generate new resources.
2. The proliferation of exemptions (from duties, income taxes, etc.). Such incentives have been conceded indiscriminately. There are no clear criteria about the type of activities and companies that in fact require such state support.
3. Tax authorities' inefficient enforcement and lax pursuit and prosecution of tax evaders.
4. Legislation flawed with loopholes and subterfuges for avoiding income reporting.

All this contributed to the soaring budget deficit. To finance it, the Central Bank resorted to printing money with no backing, which aggravated inflationary pressure and modified the bank credit structure. The government, moreover, turned to executive decrees as an expedient way to increase indirect taxation and raise revenues. It is important to note that in 1977, 66 percent of revenue was derived from indirect taxation. Now, the percentage has risen to 82 percent, and the tax structure has become more regressive.

THE DISTRIBUTIVE STRUCTURE IN COSTA RICA

The prevailing structure has been "socially acceptable." This means, first, that no political group has realistically or convincingly proposed the need for revolution to transform the income structure or the ownership of the means of production. Second, it means that very possibly the majority of the Costa Rican population would not choose to take up arms to change the distributive scheme.

This climate of social acceptance stems not from repression or deception but from a socioeconomic system that in recent decades has made possible general improvements for important sectors of the population [see Chapter IV]. The system, moreover, has been sufficiently flexible to permit social mobility. Compared with other countries, our distribution situation is much more equitable, especially the distribution of wealth. A glance at other Central American countries will suffice to corroborate this.

Yet to complete the analysis and place the problem in its proper perspective, two important factors must be recognized. First is that in Costa Rica important and visible inequalities still exist. The second is that the tendency toward concentration is clear and defined.

1. Approximately 5 percent of the wealthiest families received 26.5 percent of family income in 1977. The poorest 40 percent received only 12.4

percent of the total. The situation has been deteriorating; in 1971 the percentages were 25.6 percent and 14.1 percent respectively.

2. More than 75 percent of the population presently depends on a salary or daily wage and does not possess means of production. In addition, in the last thirty years the percentage of salaried workers has increased by 10 percent and the number of employers (with means of production and employees) dropped from 10 to 3 percent.

3. In the mid-1970s, it was estimated that in Costa Rica the poorest half of the population set aside 31.7 percent of its income to pay taxes, while the richest 10 percent reserved only 21.9 percent for that purpose. This situation surely has further deteriorated, as indirect taxes place a relatively greater burden on the poor.

4. In 1982 the unemployment rate reached 9.4 percent, and the underemployment rate hit 22.4 percent. This contrasts sharply with statistics of just a few years ago (1977), when the rates, respectively, were 4.6 and barely 11 percent.

5. Of the smaller farms, 40 percent occupy a mere 1.3 percent of the land used for farming and livestock, while 5 percent of the largest farms covered 59.3 percent of this land.

6. Between 1950 and 1973, land distribution had been concentrated in large holdings. In this period, the number of ranches or farms of less than ten hectares (twenty-five acres) rose from 54.0 percent to 57.6, while the percentage of farmland they encompassed fell from 4.8 percent to 4.0 percent.

7. The industrial sector, where development really began in the 1960s, emerged highly concentrated. In 1964, 3.1 percent of industrial establishments were located in "very highly concentrated" branches and generated 44.0 percent of the value added of this sector. And 83.5 percent of the businesses were in "low concentration" branches, producing 30.4 percent of the value added.

8. But high concentration did not only characterize this early manufacturing activity. It is also characteristic of its evolution, during which concentration became more accentuated. Between 1964 and 1975, the value added produced by the "highly concentrated" branches grew by 35.5 percent, while the value generated by the "sparsely concentrated" areas dropped by 37.5 percent. The number of businesses in different branches also shifted, showing ever-higher concentration.

At the start of the 1970s, great efforts were made, especially by the public sector, to "close the social gap" between affluent and poor. New agencies were created [see Readings 4.2, 4.3, 4.4, 4.11] and diverse programs were founded to improve Costa Ricans' quality of life. No data exist to permit an accurate evaluation of the results of this effort. Nevertheless, a comparison of the available data on income distribution between 1971 and 1977 indicates a deterioration, despite the resources the state set aside to improve the conditions of the weakest economic groups. . . .

THE ECONOMIC CRISIS AND THE DISTRIBUTIVE STRUCTURE

The recession has generated unemployment among the salaried population. In two years (July 1980 to July 1982), the jobless rate has practically doubled, from 5.9 percent to 9.4 percent, and the ranks of the unemployed have swelled by more than forty thousand. This phenomenon, practically unknown in the country's recent history, has brought about changes in the distribution of income. The less-qualified, less-educated wage earners, with less work experience, already on the lowest rung of the salary ladder, are the most easily dismissed.

The case of professionals also warrants attention. For them, the crisis seemed to manifest itself not only through unemployment (the rate has tripled from 1980 to 1982) but also in underemployment. This is particularly worrisome when we note that more than fifty thousand students are enrolled in universities and that the government, the primary employer of this work force, has frozen the number of positions and may restrict hiring in coming years. Inflation, the policy of limiting increases in nominal salaries, and the lack of automatic income adjustment mechanisms (indexing) have unleashed a drastic plunge in real income. Between March 1979 and July 1982 this reduction has been on the order of 45 percent.

These changes have not affected all categories of workers equally. The impact depends on job category, type of economic activity, negotiating power, etc. For example, laborers and artisans have seen their real earnings reduced more than professionals and technicians, and the decline of agricultural-sector wages has been significantly greater than in the industrial sector.

These discrepancies in real wages are transforming distribution patterns in two senses: first, among the salaried or wage workers themselves; and second, between that population and other economic groups. While the average real salary has fallen by 45 percent, per capita GDP in the same period did not drop more than 10 percent. This clearly indicates the relative impoverishment of salaried workers in comparison to other groups.

The process of devaluation has itself had important repercussions on distribution. On the one hand, export activities with high value added—coffee, sugar, meat, bananas, etc.—have seen a remarkable increase in their income in *colones,* with inflation trailing behind and production costs rising at a lower rate than devaluation. These agroexporter groups are already at the top of the distributive pyramid, and they are benefiting from devaluation (which generates the inflation that harms the salaried workers and wage earners). Obviously, devaluation is damaging the distributive structure in Costa Rica and widening the gap between rich and poor.

And the process has had other effects. In certain branches of the economy, devaluation has displaced resources, which are then invested in lucrative financial speculation. It is said, though not yet proven, that currency exchange houses and traders have amassed enormous fortunes.

The impact can be seen, too, on ownership of the means of production. In terms of foreign currency, devaluation cheapens domestically produced goods and services, as well as capital and land. This reduction in the price of buildings, farms, equipment, and machinery can cause the means of production to pass from domestic to foreign hands. This is precisely what seems to have happened. . . .

In summary, it would seem that the acceleration of the process of concentration of income and wealth is caused by a combination of factors, which are still operating. The policies that will be followed in confronting the crisis in the future will not help bring about better distribution, but rather will reinforce these trends. The effect on the social, economic, and political structure of Costa Rica in the next few years and through to the end of the century is difficult to predict. But an enormous danger exists that in the not very distant future, the distribution system will no longer be "socially acceptable." At that time, Costa Rica's social harmony, which for decades has been an example for Central America and the world, may be brought into question.

NOTE

1. In 1982 GDP fell 7.3 percent, according to the United Nations Economic Commission for Latin America.—EDS.

5.3 Electricity Rates: From Discontent to Organized Resistance*

In 1983, as part of the austerity program demanded by the International Monetary Fund (IMF), the state-owned utility companies began sharply raising their rates. Light bills soared, and many poor people found themselves barely able, or unable, to pay. With prices rising for food and other basic goods and services, discontent was growing. It finally led to an unusual organized movement. Starting in poor communities like Hatillo, on the outskirts of the capital, people began to organize and protest against the electricity price hike. Soon it became a national movement, uniting rural and urban communities, poor and middle-class neighborhoods. By June 1983 neighborhood committees erected barricades in protest and the government was forced to roll back the rates.

This article about the movement was written by the staff of the progressive Catholic magazine Aportes. *It is based on discussions with the national committee that coordinated the protests, and on materials provided by various community groups.*

*"Tarifas eléctricas: del descontento a la lucha organizada," *Aportes,* no. 14–15 (June–September, 1983).

The discontent in our community began months ago. As soon as the hikes in public-service rates, already approved by the government, went into effect we saw how various other neighborhoods were organizing to put a stop to the increases. Two volunteers in our community formed a committee and called on everyone to attend a neighborhood meeting. It was well attended, and a protest committee with the task of fighting the government and the electric companies was formed as a result. —Protest Committee of San Rafael Arriba de Desamparados

In April 1983 one of the most significant protest movements in recent Costa Rican history was born. When electric bills began to reach the hands of housewives, workers, small businesses, and educational institutions, voices demanding a payment strike were heard. The 24.25 percent surcharge on the bills, based on the previous month, could not be allowed. The movement against the rise in electricity rates was gestating and seemed irreversible, as this was the most outrageous of a whole set of rate increases not only for electric service but also in the cost of living in general.

In its negotiations with the International Monetary Fund, the government of Luis Alberto Monge had promised to "reduce the global deficit of the nonfinancial public sector in 1982 and 1983 to a maximum of 9.5 percent and 4.5 percent of the GDP [gross domestic product]." One measure initiated to strengthen Costa Rica's finances was an increase in public-service rates.

In November 1982, as Costa Rica's agreement with the IMF to raise electricity rates 92 percent went into effect, the surcharges applied under the system of cumulative monthly increases began to be felt more acutely.

The people began to protest through the usual channels for dissent: conversation in buses and *pulperías* [small grocery stores], on street corners, among women in the neighborhood, or even during personal visits to the electric company to make some kind of individual deals. On finding that the utility companies had no interest at all in solving the problem, people began to understand that the only possible solution would be collective action.

By November meetings were taking place in the communities that would later become the movement's center: Hatillo 5 and Hatillo 6, where "struggle committees" [*Comités de Lucha*] were formed to fight the electricity rate hikes.[1] As a result of the May 2 march toward the SNE [National Electricity Service] headed by these communities, the fight took shape and extended to other communities. Light bills were burned during the demonstration, and protesters stood their ground until the SNE's president agreed to receive a committee, which conveyed a message about the injustice of the decreed increases. Nothing positive resulted from this encounter. ICE [Costa Rican Electrical Institute] argued that the increases in electricity bills had been approved by the utility, the government, and the IMF in order to correct conditions that were contributing to the institute's great indebtedness. Remember that ICE's debt amounted to $618.7 million (that is, 12.4 billion *colones*), the largest debt of any public-sector institution.

The very day of the march the government formed a commission to study what had happened. It attempted to move rapidly, to block any further strengthening of the popular movement. But that same afternoon, the "Integral Association of Hatillo" called a General Assembly for May 4, to form a National Coordinating Committee against electric rate hikes. In this assembly, which brought together numerous community organizations, the slogan I DON'T PAY MY ELECTRIC BILL was born. It came to be almost an identity badge for all those in the movement and it could be seen in the windows of thousands of Costa Rican homes.

The assembly also called for struggle committees to be established nationwide. Conditions were ripening to make the achievement of this goal a reality, as communities took steps to see that their neighbors wouldn't pay their light bills. In the words of the struggle committees themselves:

> The discontent in our community [San Rafael Abajo de Desamparados] was noted many months back, by the comments on the bus and among the housewives. In our community, it was necessary to channel the struggle through meetings in the center of Santa Ana and here in Piedades, forming in this way a District and Cantonal Struggle Committee, with representation in the canton, carrying the spark of protest to each home, each family.
>
> The struggle in San Rafael Abajo de Desamparados began, motivated by the attitude of other organized communities. It began to identify with the struggle as put forth by the National Committee, and then it organized public gatherings and formed its own committee.
>
> First, those affected by the hikes went to the companies in person and to ICE to register their discontent and request a review of their bills. But the situation they encountered was very difficult, and they were closed off by the personnel that attended them. Not finding a solution through dialogue, they began to organize the Struggle Committee based on the work of the National Coordinating Committee and the Civic Committee of Alajuela.

Once formed, the committees undertook various measures in the neighborhoods. They formed vigilance committees in each sector to collect light bills, house to house, not only to deliver them to the companies, but also to make sure that many people who still did not have confidence in the movement didn't pay their bills. Megaphones, posters, and banners became instruments for keeping the community motivated and informed.

THE GOVERNMENT NEGOTIATES WITH THE GHOST COMMITTEE

On May 9 the government reached an agreement with a committee made up of some union leaders, which had no popular support. According to the agreement, the rates would be set at their February 1983 levels, and nobody's electricity would be cut off for lack of payment. Many people, confused by these negotiations, wanted to give in; nevertheless many committees did not let themselves be fooled. A flyer that circulated in Hatillo said:

As you can see for yourselves, the bills for the month of May have only been lowered minimally, and in most instances are still rising. Let's not fool ourselves, let's return the bills to the National Power and Light Company through our representatives on the Struggle Committee. The strike continues and grows stronger; this reduction is a new governmental insult to the workers and housewives and forces us to choose between paying our electric bill and eating.

That agreement did not have the desired effect, and the companies began cutting off the strikers' electricity. This measure only led to the creation of teams in the communities that reconnected the power. Defense committees, made up in large part by women, stood watch to prevent electricity service from being suspended in those houses or commercial centers that were part of the movement. In this manner, the communities began to create new forms of defiance for confronting governmental sanctions. These groups, directed by the National Coordinating Committee, organized a march on May 10 from the Legislative Assembly to the *Casa Presidencial.*

The thousands of protesters delivered a preliminary proposal to the government that would raise the ceiling on rates to four hundred kilowatts, that the amount of the bills return to December 1982 levels, and be frozen there for a guaranteed two years. In addition, they demanded that each inspector, after reading the meters, leave customers a written record of kilowatt usage, and that a preferential two thousand kilowatt tariff be fixed for school cafeterias, nutrition centers, and education centers.

By the end of May, twenty-nine deputies from various political parties had declared themselves friends of the movement, and fifty-seven municipalities openly manifested their support. Despite these important advances, the government maintained its firm position of not meeting the movement's demands, and tried to discredit it, saying that it was made up of "a few people driven by the Communists who are trying to make things difficult for the current administration."

THE BARRICADES SPEAK

Patience ran out. June 7 dawned with blockades of roads entering the cities of Puriscal and Los Lagos de Heredia, which opened the way for other communities to follow suit. On June 8 barricades went up in both Hatillos, Ciudad Colón, Santa Ana, Cañas, Guápiles, San Ramón, Siquirres, and elsewhere. More than forty communities joined the blockades. This situation so alarmed the government that it had no choice but to negotiate with the communities, which would take down the barricades only if their demands were met. On June 9 the government announced it had reached an agreement with the communities. The people had triumphed.

THE STRUGGLE TO LOWER THE ELECTRICITY RATES: A LESSON IN PARTICIPATION AND GRASS-ROOTS ORGANIZATION

This movement, which [the government] tried so hard to discredit, managed to fuse together diverse sectors: students, housewives, children, professionals, and workers, in addition to distinguished politicians. People who had never before participated in a demonstration were seen blocking roads, carrying obstacles to the barricades, attending meetings, delivering their bills to struggle committees in order to become one more payment striker, pasting slogans in their windows, and fundraising for the struggle.

The organized protest to reduce electric tariffs was a school for grass-roots organization and participation: this was confirmed by the struggle committees themselves just days after their triumph. As the committee from Concepción de Tres Ríos declared:

> The lesson for us from this struggle is the great experience of knowing that if we fight, we triumph, and triumph teaches us to struggle and struggle for our rights. We believe that if all Costa Ricans struggle together, supporting each other, this country would be a truly democratic country and not a country that has been managed at the whim of its rulers.

The Committee from Hatillo 5 noted that its members had

> learned several lessons: (1) The people must struggle in an organized manner. (2) We must fight together, without any political or religious distinctions. (3) The struggle committees have to support their position in the communities, keep alert, keep the community correctly and fully informed about the situation, and not leave that to the communications media that have no interest whatsoever in effectively supporting communal struggles. (4) That only an organized people can save the people.

The Committee from Montserrat de Alajuela pointed out that

> the lesson this struggle leaves is one of great transcendence, because we learned that only through organization and unity will we be heard and our just petitions answered. We learned to struggle with the people, and saw that even an economically weak class through unity becomes strong. This is our starting point for the importance of learning how to fight.

NOTE

1. These are two poor communities on the outskirts of San José.—EDS.

5.4 The Declining Banana Industry*

By Tim Coone

For decades, bananas and coffee have been Costa Rica's top sources of export earnings. Yet as the economic crisis struck, the U.S.-owned banana companies began to cut back their operations or diversify into crops, such as African oil palm, that absorb little labor. In spite of currency devaluations that brought windfall profits, the companies charged that Costa Rican taxes and wages were too high. Scaling back banana production led to an immediate increase in unemployment and reduced export earnings at a time the country could little afford it. In this reading, Tim Coone describes the factors that influenced the companies' decision and some of the human costs involved.

Coone covers Latin America for The Financial Times *of London.*

THE banana industry in Costa Rica is again set to become a critical political and economic issue. With exports of around fifty million boxes per year, Costa Rica is the second biggest exporter of bananas in the world. Banana exports represent 23–25 percent of the country's export earnings and the industry employs almost forty thousand people. It is a key sector in the economy and the ever-delicate relationship between the multinational banana companies, the government, and the banana workers is again on the boil.

All the foreign banana companies operating in Costa Rica—Standard Fruit, United Fruit, and Del Monte—claim that Costa Rica is the highest-cost producer in the world. They cite higher wages and high disease control costs, but the biggest irritant of all for the companies is the $1 export tax per box. The Union of Banana Exporting Countries (UPEB) agreed to impose the tax in 1974 to secure a fairer return for the exporting countries from the expanding banana trade. However, only Costa Rica has ever imposed the tax fully, and then not until 1981, while all the other UPEB countries have successively succumbed to pressure from the companies to reduce the taxes. Costa Rica is now feeling the pinch. Besides the tax, the companies are also complaining of poor infrastructure, high port tariffs, and inefficient loading facilities at the new banana terminal at Moín Port, and are either tacitly or openly threatening to cut back production.

United Fruit has already grubbed out three thousand hectares of plantations

*This article originally appeared as "Turbulent Times in Costa Rica's Banana Plantations," *Financial Times* (London), 15 February 1984; and "Banana Town Closedown Divides Costa Ricans," *Financial Times* (London), 3 January 1985.

on the Pacific coast and is replacing them with African oil palm. The remaining three thousand hectares are to go the same way, says Mr. Richard Johnson, director of United Fruit in Costa Rica, because their Pacific coast operations cannot compete with Ecuadorian and Nicaraguan bananas to the U.S. West Coast market, or with Colombian bananas to the Gulf and European markets.[1] He said that, as a result of the transfer to oil palm production: "Our banana output will probably fall by five million boxes this year."

Production cost figures are hard to obtain, however. Mr. Rafael Bolaños, head of a social science research unit at the University of Costa Rica and a former Standard Fruit employee, said: "Even within the company it is practically impossible to obtain figures on true production costs. They are a closely guarded secret because the companies like to claim that every country is a high-cost producer in negotiations with the governments."

Señor Carlos Rojas, Costa Rica's representative in UPEB, agrees. He said: "With the devaluation of the currency here, it is just not true to say that Costa Rican production costs are any higher than those in Panama for example."

United Fruit's shift to oil palm has produced violent clashes in the past year with the banana workers' union over heavy job losses (oil palm requires a third of the labor input of bananas) and with workers who have invaded abandoned banana lands.

Señor Rojas said: "Exports this year will remain at around fifty million boxes. They cannot be allowed to fall." He said negotiations are presently under way between the government and United Fruit over possible arrangements to buy out the Pacific coast plantations and turn them over to workers' cooperatives or to run them as joint enterprises with United Fruit. "I don't think they are interested in selling their plantations though," Señor Rojas said. "What they really want is to remove the tax and that is what the battle is about."

The tax has already been reduced temporarily to seventy-five cents per box, in spite of a high in the banana market. The reduction will be reviewed in March and clearly the companies are hoping for a further reduction.

The government is in a bind. Banana export taxes bring in revenue of almost $50 million per year. The country is undergoing a foreign exchange crisis and is under heavy pressure from the International Monetary Fund to cut government spending, increase tax revenues, and fuel, electricity and other tariffs. Sharp price rises last year caused widespread protest, causing the government to backtrack. The Costa Rican Communist Party (PVP), which is powerful among the banana workers, is committed to a much more militant line this year after a serious division in its ranks. This could lead to confrontations in the plantations.

Negotiations on all fronts are still being held behind closed doors, but after the annual cycle peaks out in two months another turbulent period lies in wait for Costa Rica's banana industry.

*   *   *

The town of Palmar in southern Costa Rica is a classic banana town, owned and built by United Fruit, a local subsidiary of the United Brands Company. The lives of its inhabitants are dependent on the fortunes of the company.

At the height of production, eight million boxes of bananas per year were shipped to California. Exports have now fallen to nothing as the company has decided to pull out of Palmar, effectively ending its involvement in banana production in Costa Rica.

There are several reasons why. Mr. Richard Johnson, vice-president of United Fruit, cites stiff competition from both Nicaragua and Ecuador for several years, and a local banana export tax of seventy cents a box.

With the closure of Palmar, the company will still be exporting some fifteen million boxes per year, but purchasing from local producers, rather than running its own plantations, which occupied sixteen thousand hectares of land in the 1950s.

The company's decision to end its own production in Costa Rica has provoked opposition from both the Costa Rican government and its workers. Under a contract signed in the 1950s, the company is obliged to maintain four thousand hectares of bananas in production until July 1988, or face government expropriation of its property.

United Brands has offered to sell the remaining 2,370 hectares of plantations to the government for $15 million; in reply, the government has offered to lease the plantations for three years and continue negotiations on the purchase price.

While offers go back and forth, the company has been quietly dismantling its production facilities. Most easily removed items, such as fertilizers, chemicals, and packing materials have already been shipped out of the country, surprisingly with government consent.

Railway spurs and irrigation piping have been taken up in the plantations and machinery, such as excavators and tractors, has been moved to the nearby company-built port of Golfito, ready for shipment. The work force has been cut in half and local union officials fear that the rest will be laid off within the next month or so. In Golfito "for sale" notices are appearing on many homes not owned by the company.

The union itself, the workers' union of Golfito (UTG) has to bear a major share of the blame. A seventy-two-day strike for salary increases which finished in September paralyzed production, which has not been resumed since. "The strike was the final blow," said Mr. Johnson.

Some union officials say, however, that the strike was the excuse the company had been waiting for to close down Palmar. "It was a disastrous mistake," said Señor Gustavo López, a Golfito dockers' union official who was sacked without compensation.

A division in late 1983 in the local Communist Party, which has a powerful influence among the banana workers, lay at the root of the problem. The moderate wing of the party was against the strike, accurately believing that the company would close if it went ahead.

The militant wing proceeded regardless.

The strike was declared illegal by the government because the union had not gone through all the necessary procedures. All the union militants were subsequently sacked, leaving a bitter and disillusioned work force which now faces the prospect of prolonged unemployment.

Señor Paulo Zúñiga, the union's legal adviser, criticizes the government for helping to destroy the union during the strike, on the promise that the company would continue production afterward. "The company had broken its contract by pulling out before 1988, and the government should expropriate the lands without compensation," he said. "The government is turning Costa Rica into a classic banana republic."

The UTG still has some leverage. Land invasions have become a popular method of forcing the government into action over the problem of unemployment in rural areas. Communist Party officials in Golfito say that if the government does not act quickly against the company, the dismissed workers and landless peasants in the region will take matters into their own hands.

The company and the government will wish to avoid this as the company could lose its $15 million for Palmar and the government would need to use the security forces against the unemployed laborers. Two workers were shot and killed in confrontations with the police during the strike.

Señor Benjamín Piza, the minister of security, said that if it came to a land invasion, "we will have to act." The government is also worried that arms might be used by the workers in future confrontations.

One further factor also faces United Brands. It still has a healthy share of the California market, with around fifteen million boxes of bananas coming from its plantations in Panama, despite fierce Ecuadorian and Nicaraguan competition.

Señor Rafael Bolaños, a professor of social sciences at the University of Costa Rica and a specialist on the foreign fruit companies' operations, said: "If United Brands stops production in Costa Rica it would be a grave commercial error. All their production for California would then come from Panama, and just one fifteen-day strike there would lose them the entire California market."

For that reason alone, United Brands will be aiming to maintain buying contracts on Costa Rica's Pacific coast. But if it pushes too hard a bargain, it might find that the tensions and bitterness simmering in the steamy tropical heat of Palmar and Golfito might explode. The company there might lose more than it was hoping to gain.

NOTE

1. After the 1985 U.S. trade embargo against Nicaragua, Nicaraguan bananas were no longer sold in the U.S. market. They continued to be exported to Canada, however.—EDS.

5.5 Health Effects of the Costa Rican Economic Crisis*

By Lynn M. Morgan

At the height of the economic crisis in 1981–82, Costa Rica had already spent a decade establishing a model health care system. Because of this experience and the existence of programs, personnel, and infrastructure, the immediate health effects of the crisis were probably not as severe as many people anticipated. Nevertheless, the long-term effects of the crisis and the austerity programs imposed by international lending organizations have already begun to undermine one of the developing world's most remarkable health care systems, resulting in growing foreign dependence, worsening of some important health indicators, and postponement or cancellation of plans to expand primary care programs.

Lynn M. Morgan, assistant professor of anthropology at Mount Holyoke College, holds a Ph.D. in medical anthropology from the University of California, Berkeley and San Francisco. She did dissertation research in Costa Rica on community participation in government health care programs.

IN the early 1970s, the Costa Rican government vowed to overhaul the nation's health system before the end of the decade, creating a low-cost primary care network accessible to the entire population. By 1980 the government had nationalized all the hospitals and nearly all of its health professionals.[1] It had extended social security health coverage to almost all citizens regardless of income or occupation and provided the first systematic medical attention to rural regions. Between 1970 and 1980 infant mortality dropped by 69 percent (from 61.5 to 18.6 per 1,000 live births); deaths from infectious and parasitic diseases fell by 98 percent (from 13.6 to 1.7 per 10,000); and communicable diseases such as polio and diphtheria were completely eradicated. In Latin America, Costa Rica's health indicators were second only to those of Cuba. Internationally, Costa Rica was widely cited as a "health care success story" and a model for primary health care programs.

But that was before the economic crisis. In the health sector, the effects of the crisis can be seen in four areas: (1) deterioration in health status, as poverty

*A longer version of this article appeared as "Health without Wealth? Costa Rica's Health System under Economic Crisis," *Journal of Public Health Policy* 8, no. 1 (Spring 1987): 86–105. Research was funded by a Fulbright-Hays Dissertation Fellowship, the Robert H. Lowie Fund of the Department of Anthropology, University of California, Berkeley, and a Tinker Foundation grant through the Center for Latin American Studies at Berkeley.

contributed to higher disease rates; (2) reductions in the government's ability to maintain public health and medical services; (3) increased reliance on foreign aid to finance the health system; and (4) growing debate over the state's role in health care. As a result of the crisis, health services were reduced and the health model called into question, just after an expensive health infrastructure was erected and when people most needed health services.

By 1986 the health effects of the crisis were still being debated. Statistical indices of health improvements had leveled off but had not declined precipitously the way many experts had predicted. Some speculated that the figures had been altered to convey greater optimism, while others praised the health sector for weathering the crisis. Large influxes of foreign aid after 1982 might have mitigated the health effects of the crisis, but it is also likely that available health statistics have not been broken down sufficiently to show which sectors of the population have suffered most from the crisis. To evaluate these trends, national figures must be disaggregated to compare persons by categories such as occupation, region, income, or ethnicity. Such data were not as available in 1986 as they were in 1981. For example, with four research institutes monitoring nutritional levels, by 1986 the nutritional data collected in 1982 had not yet been released by the Ministry of Health.

Increased poverty inevitably produced deteriorating nutritional and health status. In 1982 nutrition experts estimated that 111 percent of the average monthly salary would be required to feed a family of six. Numbers of children hospitalized with severe malnutrition rose from a 1981 low of 152 cases to 322 cases in 1982.[2] Per capita consumption of meat and milk products dropped between 1978 and 1982.[3] Rates of moderate (second-degree) malnutrition in rural areas rose between 1978 and 1982.[4]

The agricultural sector fared worse than others. Rural workers in 1982 would have had to earn 71 percent more than their actual salaries just to afford the government's basic market basket.[5] Even among banana workers, whose salaries are high relative to other agricultural laborers, 15.6 percent of children under six suffered from some degree of malnutrition, compared to 8.6 percent nationwide.[6]

Some infectious disease rates showed increases in the early 1980s. Malaria—which had been well controlled during the 1970s—began to rise alarmingly, from 189 cases in 1981 to 569 cases in 1984, with refugees from neighboring countries accounting for over half the cases in the latter year. Rheumatic fever, whooping cough, viral hepatitis, and cutaneous leishmaniasis also showed significant increases between 1981 and 1984. In late 1985, a government report pointed to increases in intestinal parasitic diseases, rheumatic fever, drug-dependent psychosis, and alcoholism, and cautioned that deteriorating social conditions could be to blame.[7]

Infant mortality rates for the nation as a whole increased only slightly between 1980 and 1984. Nevertheless, in certain municipalities sharp increases were recorded, prompting concern from health officials who cited deteriorating living standards and difficulties in extending health services.[8] One detailed longitudinal study of nutrition and infant mortality in rural Puriscal canton showed that increases in numbers of low birth-weight babies, prematurity, and lack of access to prenatal care were outcomes of the crisis.[9]

The extensive medical infrastructure developed during the 1970s was extremely expensive to maintain. Between 1972 and 1979, the budget of the Social Security System *(Caja Costarricense de Seguro Social)*, the agency responsible for most health care programs, rose by 689 percent. The *Caja's* budget deficit amounted to over one-third of its operating budget—$26 million in 1982—and contributed to the government's overall debt problem.

Measures designed to alleviate the deficits fueled public dissatisfaction with the Social Security System. At the beginning of 1983, payroll taxes were raised, with the employer's share rising from 6.75 percent to 9.25 percent. This provoked an angry response from business leaders, who argued that the increase would make Costa Rica uncompetitive in international markets. Another measure required the 22,000 *Caja* employees to begin paying 4 percent of their salaries to the fund, whereas until late 1982 they had benefited from social security health coverage without being taxed. Employee benefits were cut back, a hiring freeze was imposed, and workers were offered incentives to resign voluntarily.

In April 1982, social security doctors went on strike, demanding a $45 per month pay increase. Prior to 1980, a *Caja* physician's salary of 15,000 *colones* ($1,744) per month had been considered high. After the devaluation the same salary was worth only $278, which did not allow doctors to maintain their formerly high standard of living. To terminate the forty-two-day strike, the *Caja* worked out an agreement granting many of the doctors' demands. The strike's divisive impact was evident in comments made by the *Caja* president, who told a 1983 graduating medical school class that the salary increases won as a result of the doctors' strike would otherwise have been spent to create jobs for his audience.[10]

Doctors and patients alike were exasperated by the scarcity of supplies resulting from the crisis. A 400 percent rise in prices of imported goods since the 1980 devaluation drastically limited the *Caja's* ability to buy medicine, equipment, and hospital supplies. By late 1982, $6.5 million worth of drugs and medical supplies lay unclaimed in customs warehouses because the *Caja* could not pay for them. In an effort to cut costs, the *Caja* reduced from one thousand to four hundred the number of drugs that could be imported, much to the dismay of health professionals, patients, and pharmaceutical companies.

The crisis prevented further extension of health services, according to the minister of health.[11] Health officials had predicted in 1980 that 94 percent of the population would be incorporated into the social security program by 1982, yet in 1982 just 78 percent of the population was covered, the same as in 1979. The Ministry of Health announced the reduction or elimination of latrine building, water and sanitation improvements, and pollution surveillance. A shortage of trained health auxiliaries forced the closing or understaffing of several rural health posts, even though this program was the centerpiece of the country's health system. Ironically, the surplus of unemployed nurses which existed at the time could not be used to staff those posts, because the Ministry of Health could not afford the higher salaries they commanded. No new auxiliaries were trained between 1980 and 1983, until the United Nations Children's Fund (UNICEF) provided training scholarships for rural health workers.

From its inception the Ministry of Health's primary health care program had been heavily dependent on assistance from abroad, but by 1977 the original contracts with foreign aid organizations had expired. Even the U.S. Agency for International Development (USAID), the most consistent source of aid for the country, took Costa Rica off its health aid eligibility list because the country had gotten "too healthy" for USAID to justify health assistance. The Ministry of Health boldly declared in 1977 that henceforth the rural health program would be supported entirely by the government. In 1982, despite a changed economic climate, the health minister continued to champion self-sufficiency: "We should not hope for foreign salvation through the cooperation of countries or international organizations. This would be a grave error, since the solution to our problems must be a matter of national action. We must resolve the health crisis with our own resources, and by seeking solutions in new and simpler strategies."[12]

By early 1984, Costa Rica had to abandon its plan to wean the health sector from outside aid. Costa Rican health officials and other Central American health planners met with representatives of twenty international organizations to ask for a total of $640 million in health aid for the region. The Costa Rican ministry proposed a $207 million national health budget in August 1984, $148 million of which would have to come from external funding agencies. By 1985 the Inter-American Development Bank, the Kellogg Foundation, UNICEF, and USAID were providing technical and financial assistance to the health sector.

Primary care in the 1970s had been actively supported by all international health agencies. Paradoxically though, the changing priorities of these agencies in the 1980s no longer favored a Costa Rican–style health system. The most recent (1982) USAID Health Sector Policy Paper reflects Reagan-era fiscal and social conservatism. It assails government-subsidized health services and promotes government austerity, private-sector medical care and fee-for-service medicine.[13] Similar trends are evident in health policy documents issued by the World Bank and the United Nations Development Programme.[14] The austerity measures imposed on Costa Rica in the 1980s by the International Monetary Fund (IMF) offer further evidence of the health sector's reliance on policies set outside the country. The IMF limited public-sector spending, restricting the government's ability to respond to health and nutrition problems brought on by the economic crisis.

In 1982 the health sector became the focus of a nationwide debate that encapsulated many of Costa Rica's ideological and political schisms. Representatives of the agroexport sector, who generally favor free-market solutions to Costa Rica's economic troubles, formed one extreme. They lobbied for "reprivatization" of medical care through elimination of mandatory social security and encouragement of free-market competition among health providers. Underlying their argument was a plea for class-based medical care, with access to services contingent on ability to pay. Groups committed to the expansion of the welfare state formed the other extreme of the debate. The health workers' and public employees' unions, social democratic loyalists, and the Communist Party all argued (albeit for different reasons) that the post-1970 system of universal primary health care had allowed Costa Rica to reduce social inequalities in health and to improve the national health profile. They said that "reprivatization" of medicine would return Costa Rica to unequal medicine, with one system for the rich and another for the poor, and they urged more, rather than less, state involvement in health care.

The government attempted to defuse the conflict by offering concessions to both camps. The first group was placated by a *medicina mixta* program, which gave patients the option of choosing their own physicians and paying doctors' fees while the *Caja* covered costs of drugs and medical tests. The government also started a program that assigned doctors to the workplaces of large companies, thereby reducing sick leave and cutting employers' costs. Welfare state enthusiasts were pleased when the government passed legislation forcing delinquent businesses to pay their outstanding debts to the *Caja*. They were also pleased when the *Caja* again took steps to universalize social security coverage by committing itself to tracking down, signing up, and paying the fees of indigent citizens.

Two dilemmas have undermined the Costa Rican state's ability to maintain primary health care programs. First, the government's attempts to nationalize health services have been sidetracked by debate over the "acceptable" degree of state involvement in providing social services. Second, the search for stable, ongoing sources of funding is frustrated by the shifting, sometimes capricious policies of international health agencies. Costa Rica's health programs are not self-supporting, and the agencies that initially offered support are now becoming disenchanted with the approach on which the entire program was constructed. The Costa Rican government's challenge will be to perform a political high-wire act. It must maintain state control over the health system developed during the 1970s while not exceeding the austerity budget of the 1980s. And it must do so without reducing services at a time when people need them most.

NOTES

1. With the exception of one hospital that was nationalized in 1984.

2. María Cecilia Fernández Saborío, "Deterioro de la condición socioeconómica y sus consecuencias para la familia y la niñez" (Report prepared for UNICEF by the Ministerio de Planificación), p. 24.

3. *La República* (San José), 11 May 1985.

4. C. Díaz Amador, "Estudio comparativo del estado nutricional de la población menor de 6 años entre 1978–1982" (Paper presented at the Congreso Nacional de Salud Pública, San José, Costa Rica, March 27, 1985).

5. Fernández Saborío, "Deterioro de la condición socioeconómica," p. 24.

6. A. Guerra, "Estudios antropológicos de clasificación funcional: análisis comparativo del poder adquisitivo del salario del obrero bananero," *Boletín Informativo del S.I.N.* [Sistema de Información en Nutrición], no. 10: 11–16.

7. J. Jaramillo, *Los problemas de la salud en Costa Rica* (San José: Ministerio de Salud, 1984); Ministerio de Salud, *Memoria de 1984* (San José: Ministerio de Salud, 1984), p. 14; Caja Costarricense de Seguro Social, *Indicadores de Servicios de Salud* 5 (1985).

8. *La Nación* (San José), 1 December 1984.

9. L. Mata, "Estado nutricional del niño en Puriscal durante la crisis" (Paper presented to the Congreso Nacional de Salud Pública, San José, Costa Rica, March 27, 1985).

10. *La Nación,* 16 February 1983.

11. Jaramillo, *Los problemas de la salud,* p. 47.

12. *La Nación,* 20 October 1982.

13. USAID, *Health Sector Policy Paper* (Washington, D.C., 1982).

14. World Bank, *Health Sector Policy Paper* (Washington, D.C.: World Bank, 1980); United Nations Development Programme, *Advisory Note: Primary Health Care, with Special Reference to Human Resource Development* (UNDP Bureau for Programme Policy and Evaluation, Technical Advisory Division, 1983).

5.6 After the Bitter Pill, Costa Rica Improves*

BY TIM GOLDEN

After the Costa Rican economy bottomed out in 1981–82, massive infusions of U.S. economic assistance, new agreements with international lending institutions, and fiscal austerity programs permitted a significant recovery. Much of the improvement, however, was attributable to increased U.S. aid. As Tim Golden points out in this article, the amount of such aid may be inversely proportional to the Costa Rican government's independence in international affairs, especially around the question of U.S. support for the Nicaraguan contras. Meanwhile, the country's debt is larger than ever and Costa Ricans ask how long they will be able to rely on U.S. largesse.

Tim Golden is a staff writer for the Miami Herald.

THERE seemed to be little disagreement about the applause that thundered through the National Stadium here [San José] as Luis Alberto Monge handed

*Reprinted from the *Miami Herald,* 19 May 1986.

over the presidential sash eleven days ago. The send-off, political analysts said, had more to do with the low-key president's unusual economic success story than any vaunted political achievements.

Unlike most of his Latin American counterparts, Monge was able to get the austerity prescribed by international lending agencies down the throats of his countrymen. Pointing to sharp drops in unemployment and inflation since 1982, some economists said in retrospect that Monge even made it seem as though the infamously bitter pill hadn't tasted so bad.

But Monge bequeathed more to successor Oscar Arias than a rebounding standard of living and the daunting task of moving Costa Rica's economy from shaky stability to recovery.

Even before Arias took office, it became clear that his legacy would also include tougher access to the American cash that helped Costa Ricans accept their austerity program.

The World Bank, citing noncompliance with several Costa Rican economic commitments, has withheld disbursement of $40 million in promised credits.

STAYING ON TRACK

The U.S. Agency for International Development, first citing Washington budget delays and later Costa Rica's failure—as shown with the World Bank—to stay on the proper economic track, has held up another $40 million in balance-of-payments aid, Central Bank president Eduardo Lizano said.

With Costa Rica's economy gasping under a $4.6 billion foreign debt—one of the world's largest per capita—the shortfall has had a quick, sharp impact.

The Central Bank already is straining under an acute cash-flow crisis. Lizano said in a telephone interview Friday that Costa Rican finance officials would meet with creditor-bank representatives Saturday in Miami to press Costa Rica's request for a postponement of some $20 million in interest payments due last month. Thus far, the banks have said no.

Meantime, the government has transferred funds out of bank accounts abroad as a precaution against the assets being frozen. Lizano, a highly respected veteran of the Monge administration, confirmed that money had been pulled out but declined to specify how much.

The backlog of requests to the Central Bank for foreign exchange has increased in sixty days to over $30 million.

Lizano and other officials said they are hopeful that differences with the World Bank can be ironed out in meetings this week. Costa Rican officials and foreign diplomats said they expected the aid spigot to be turned back on as soon as World Bank conditions are met, but few expected to see new money before mid-June.

CLIMATE OF UNCERTAINTY

That prospect already has some Costa Rican economists worried that the attractions of their economy's hard-won stability may start to fade into a climate of uncertainty.

Beyond the stricter U.S. attitude, there appears to be dwindling patience with Costa Rica's slow progress in getting its economic house in order. Specifically, U.S. officials want to see the government cutting back its considerable bureaucracy and cutting out its inefficient corporations and protective import duties.

The prescription is the same for the World Bank and the International Monetary Fund, with which Arias will have to negotiate a new standby agreement later this year.

But as for the continued flow of U.S. aid, there was also another, more ominous signal for Arias in the Reagan administration's unusual tight-fistedness.

Although prominent U.S. and Costa Rican officials have categorically denied any pressure, some Costa Rican officials and other informed sources said privately that U.S. officials at least for a time linked the disbursement delay to their anger over Arias's open opposition to U.S. aid for Nicaraguan rebels.

At the Reagan administration's strong urging, U.S. and Costa Rican sources said, Arias has carefully avoided restating his stance.

Some Costa Ricans say the episode has sent their government one of the strongest signals yet that Arias will not receive U.S. help in tackling Costa Rica's debt without paying a political price.

Just over a year ago, the lawyer-economist told *Forbes* magazine that "as long as there are nine [Sandinista] *comandantes* in Nicaragua, we'll be able to get $200 million more or less" in annual economic aid from Washington.

This year, however, even the Sandinistas weren't able to keep the aid total high.

The Reagan administration requested $150 million in cash economic support funds for 1986. When the foreign aid authorization came back from Capitol Hill after newly mandated budget cuts, the total was down to $120 million. State Department and congressional sources have predicted that the cuts will only deepen in the future.

The U.S. squeeze doesn't come at the worst of times.

Rising world-market coffee prices propelled by Brazil's drought are expected to bring in an additional $165 million this year for Costa Rica's top export. The economy's saving from the drop in world oil prices is an estimated $100 million. The windfall from falling interest rates abroad is calculated at $25 million.

Nonetheless, said one Costa Rican economist, the bonanza can be counted on for two years at the most.

It can be expected to only lighten Costa Rica's debt-service burden slightly, and give little if any room for Arias to work toward his pledges of a hundred thousand new private-sector jobs and eighty thousand homes over his four-year term.

"We are getting a little greater margin," the analyst said, "but not full independence."

5.7 AID and the Secret Parallel State

BY LEZAK SHALLAT

In early 1988, a secret U.S. AID-funded private-sector development network was uncovered in Costa Rica. It quickly became known as the "parallel state." The intent was to undermine Costa Rica's state-directed development strategy, creating an alternative structure more in line with the Reagan administration's private-sector orientation. The ensuing scandal provoked charges that AID had exploited Costa Rica financially, trampled on its sovereignty, and scorned the development strategy that had evolved through Costa Rica's democratic political processes.

Lezak Shallat, a U.S. free-lance journalist who writes for a number of U.S. and Latin American publications, has lived in Costa Rica for many years and has reported extensively on the "parallel state."

TWO new office buildings completed in the fall of 1988 dwarf surrounding mansions in a San José suburb favored by Costa Rica's nouveaux riches. On a main avenue the new United States Embassy—an incongruous mix of bunker and park—makes its unabashed statement of American presence. Looming nearby, the U.S. Agency for International Development's mammoth new headquarters stands as a monument to what has become known as the parallel state.

The term "parallel state" was introduced by top advisers of President Oscar Arias to describe the network of AID-funded, private-sector organizations that they claim duplicate and undermine existing Costa Rican government institutions and development agencies. In its fervor to restructure the local state-oriented economy, critics said, the United States quietly built a parallel structure of private banks, schools, and commercial agencies to receive the $1 billion allocated to Costa Rica since 1983. At the same time, U.S. AID was charging Costa Rica high interest rates on undisbursed grants and channeling these funds into an AID-controlled discretionary account in the Costa Rican Central Bank.

The interest Costa Rican taxpayers paid into this "special account" from

1983 to 1987 could have paid for twenty thousand houses—the Arias government's top domestic priority. Exempt from local oversight, this money was used for an array of projects never aired before the Costa Rican people—including construction of U.S. AID's $10 million headquarters, an appropriate "capitol" for the "parallel state." As Deputy José Miguel Corrales, a respected member of Arias's National Liberation Party, put it in a letter to Presidents Arias and Reagan, "The people of Costa Rica, their economy in shambles, have built office quarters for the richest and most powerful nation on earth."

The 1979 Sandinista victory in Nicaragua and the Costa Rican economic decline had led Washington to revise its low-priority status for Central America's most stable democracy. Costa Rica's commitment to state-financed development and extensive social welfare programs had spawned borrowing policies that saddled it with a large foreign debt. Following the recommendations of the president's National Bipartisan Commission on Central America, led by Henry Kissinger, the U.S. Congress authorized AID to, in the words of a senior U.S. official in San José, "support Costa Rica in a big way."

While development assistance increased relatively little, AID began pouring unprecedented sums into the Central Bank to finance balance of payments and imports. These Economic Support Funds (ESF) grew from an initial $20 million in 1982 to a total of $731.8 million, mostly in grants, by 1987. These U.S. dollars were given to the Central Bank for its foreign obligations and for resale at local currency equivalents to dollar-hungry private importers. The *colones* produced in this exchange were deposited in AID's special Central Bank account, ostensibly earmarked for local development.

This standard AID arrangement came with an expensive twist in accords signed between 1983 and 1987. The Central Bank was to pay market interest rates—averaging 21 percent—on funds transferred into AID's account but not yet disbursed. As ESF transfers multiplied 36-fold over five years, AID collected 41 billion *colones* in interest. This money was plowed back into the "special account" as supplemental funds controlled entirely by AID. (Costa Rica wrested control of the fund and eliminated $90 million in interest payments in the 1988 AID accord.)

Fluctuating exchange rates and account balances make it difficult to calculate the dollar equivalent for interest paid. Its magnitude can be illustrated in other terms. In 1986, the year Arias took office, interest payments of 2 billion *colones* accounted for nearly one-third of the Central Bank's 6.5 billion *colón* deficit. And while payments to AID were generating Central Bank losses equal to slightly under 1 percent of gross domestic product, the International Monetary Fund was admonishing Costa Rica to reduce its public-sector deficit to a maximum of 5.5 percent of GDP.

According to Ottón Solís, an economist then serving as minister of planning, the AID arrangement was a stumbling block in the IMF negotiations, despite strong U.S. advocacy of an accord. "The IMF sets targets for public-sector deficits," Solís explained. "If Central Bank losses are increased by interest payments, then expenditures have to be reduced in other fields, such as development. The IMF doesn't mind where."[1]

In July 1987, Dick McCall, an aide to Massachusetts Democratic senator John Kerry, visited Costa Rica to probe charges that AID was withholding ESF funds in order to pressure Costa Rica to privatize certain state enterprises. "It's a Catch-22," he later said. "You demand cuts in government deficits and then institute a system that creates a deficit."[2]

Economically unsound from the Costa Rican point of view, the AID agreements also invited legal questions about ownership of the account. Under U.S. law, several sources agreed, the funds belonged to Costa Rica, as the 1988 AID agreement finally spelled out. If so, as Deputy Corrales charged in a little-noticed 1987 bid to repeal the accords, the expenditures should have been subject to the approval and control of Costa Rica's Legislative Assembly. The accords, negotiated directly with the executive branch, sidestepped this requirement. For the United States, this was Costa Rican money. For Costa Rica, with no access to the account, it was U.S. money.

Either way, critics noted, these public funds from U.S. and Costa Rican taxpayers were financing private companies that supplanted democratically created public institutions. Many Costa Rican and even some U.S. officials privately expressed misgivings over an arrangement that allowed AID to dodge public debate of its controversial overhaul of the Costa Rican development sector. The widespread objections to privatizing state-run banks and enterprises such as ICE (the Costa Rican Electrical Institute) suggest that AID's privatizing agenda would not have fared well had it been subject to public scrutiny.

But Costa Rica's extreme dependence on U.S. funds kept public expression of these misgivings to a discreet minimum. In January 1988, Planning Minister Solís guardedly aired his concerns in an opinion piece in the leading local daily, *La Nación*. "It would be deeply disturbing if, given the impossibility of doing things openly and thus democratically, subterfuges and economically inefficient Machiavellianisms were adopted. The principles of productivity would be grotesquely contradicted if attempts were made to wear down and bankrupt state institutions via the creation of parallel structures organized as private entities." (Solís later resigned to protest reforms favoring U.S. AID-promoted private banks over the nationalized system.)

Solís was wise to couch his criticism in general terms. A few months later, top Arias adviser John Biehl attacked the Reagan administration for constructing a "parallel state" of private-sector groups. Biehl, a Chilean-born economist, was hounded out of the country for casting aspersions on Costa Rican sovereignty.

Biehl made the remark to the Chilean magazine *APSI* in a 1988 interview later excerpted by Costa Rica's *La Nación*. A close friend of Arias's since their university days in England, Biehl had long been a target of the conservative newspaper for his advocacy of Arias's regional peace effort. In the resulting uproar, such groups as the Chamber of Commerce and the ultrarightist Free Costa Rica Movement [see Reading 7.8] demanded his expulsion, and U.S. pressure led to his dismissal as a local officer of the United Nations Development Programme. Biehl returned to Chile.

Other than Arias himself, few public figures jumped to Biehl's defense. Those who did noted that AID's strategy for Costa Rica was "parallel" in more ways than one. In quietly building a private development network to undercut that of the government, it "paralleled" similarly undemocratic U.S. efforts to subvert Costa Rican neutrality in the Reagan administration's covert war against Nicaragua's Sandinistas.

An organization of intellectuals and cultural figures called *Soberanía* (Sovereignty), for instance, took out advertisements emphasizing the political dimensions of the "parallel state." The advertisements mentioned an array of U.S. activities along the Nicaraguan border, including the installation of a Voice of America radio transmitter, the establishment of the Murciélago military training base, and the construction of a secret CIA airstrip [see Readings 7.13 and 7.14].

Just as the "fight against communism" gave the Reagan administration its rationale for illegally battling the Sandinistas, Reaganomics provided the framework for AID's high-handed privatizing zeal. In principle, Reaganomics called for reduced government spending, a return to free-market forces, and the transfer of resources to a more efficient private sector. As applied to Costa Rica, however, it meant selling off state enterprises and funneling U.S. public funds to private Costa Rican enterprises.

"They ended up with the fiction," economist Biehl explained. "When something is financed with Costa Rican taxpayers' money, it's public sector and inefficient. When the same thing is financed by U.S. taxpayers' money, it's private sector and efficient."[3]

AID offshoots, often duplicating existing Costa Rican public-sector programs and institutions, reach into every facet of Costa Rican development— building roads, supplying venture capital, promoting exports and investment, spurring agroindustry, even providing technical education for agronomists and tropical scientists. FINTR, a trust fund, administers AID's $174 million buy-out of the state development corporation CODESA [see Reading 4.4]. Credit insurance programs, rediscount credit facilities, and special credit lines made millions of U.S. foreign aid dollars available to private banks and to a host of export-oriented, private-sector initiatives.

Many Costa Ricans support AID's programs to privatize the national educational and banking systems. Certainly, few disagree on the need to modernize and keep solvent government enterprises. But, critics maintain, reform should be compatible with the style and priorities of the state-dominated development model for which Costa Ricans have repeatedly voted over the past forty years. "The creation of a 'parallel state' of private initiatives is rooted in the political desire to dismantle the state systems that Costa Rica has built to promote public welfare," commented former University of Costa Rica rector Fernando Durán, who witnessed an attempt to have an AID project known as EARTH (Agricultural School for the Humid Tropics) duplicate the university's own highly regarded School of Agriculture.

In Durán's view, billion dollar bailouts have lulled Costa Ricans into a false sense of economic well-being and the conservative local media, promoting the political and economic agenda of a wealthy minority [Reading 7.3], have misled them about the virtues of transferring resources from the government to private hands.

"The word 'parallel' is an unfortunate misnomer," explained one government economist. " 'Parallel' assumes equal growth in equal conditions. The more exact term is 'parasitic,' because duplicated efforts detract from the public sector by redirecting its potential resources to the private sector."

Local officials say they are particularly galled at the AID-backed private network's seduction of public-sector professionals at salaries that the Costa Rican government cannot hope to match. Such practices detract from the government's own development effort, Biehl charged, and "undermine the possibility of public-sector efficiency."

Furthermore, Biehl added, AID's parallel network offers neither public-sector controls nor private-sector efficiency. The Costa Rican Coalition for Development Initiatives (CINDE), an AID creation that duplicated the government's Center for Investment and Export Promotion (CENPRO), was a case in point. When U.S. newspapers revealed an internal AID memo charging the San José mission with creating a development agency—CINDE—that largely benefited local politicians, the Costa Rican Legislative Assembly investigated. At first, CINDE refused to cooperate, claiming that it was a private company. But the possibility that CINDE had received public funds via interest payments to the "special account" gave lawmakers grounds to demand that it open its books.

The confidential AID memo leveled charges of cronyism and legal irregularities against the local AID office, reserving much of its criticism for mission chief Daniel Chaij, who was subsequently kicked upstairs to Washington. (Among its revelations were U.S. college scholarships awarded to children of rich and influential Costa Ricans.) But according to Costa Rican and U.S. sources, problems with Chaij were evident long before the October 1987 internal audit.

Dick McCall, the Senate aide who investigated withheld AID funds, had returned to Washington satisfied with local explanations for the aid disbursement delays. But he also uncovered tensions between Costa Rica and AID arising out of Chaij's confrontational style, the intense pressure to modify Costa Rica's economy, and reluctance on the part of AID officials to view Costa Rican democracy as more than "just holding elections." The officials, he said, failed to appreciate that Costa Rica's "basic social safety net" arose as a "compact this democracy has made with its people." By imposing policies to restructure these institutions without evaluating the social consequences, as Costa Rican officials were charging, U.S. AID was in fact threatening Costa Rican democracy, McCall was told.

"Nobody in AID had ever thought about the reason for Costa Rica to have a nationalized banking system," McCall concluded. " 'If the nationalized banking system is inefficient,' I asked them, 'why not spend time and resources making it more efficient?' The private sector has a role to play, but we can't tamper too much with a system that has created stability. If the Reagan administration is interested in creating stability in the region, it shouldn't beat Costa Rica over the head but use it as a model."

This model Central American democracy meanwhile was finding that its own attempt to bring peace and stability to the region had not won it any favors from President Reagan. ESF funds, so abundant in the last years of the pliant Monge administration, were significantly reduced under Arias (see Table).

Linking loan payouts to specified economic performance targets is a standard AID practice that may have played a role in the rhythm of funding. But political observers attribute the marked drop in aid to Arias's foreign policies, not his economic ones. Though neither government openly acknowledges U.S. pressure, sources within both governments point to the Reagan administration's private annoyance with the Arias regional peace initiative as a possible factor in the reduction of funds.

The Arias government finally tackled its AID-imposed economic dilemma the same way it handled the *contras*—unilaterally withdrawing its support. Several months before the 1988 AID accord was drawn up, Costa Rica stopped interest payments to the U.S. agency. Housecleaning within the U.S. Embassy and AID mission, meanwhile, brought in new personnel with greater finesse. Costa Rican control over the "special account" was formalized and negotiations undertaken to return interest payments to the Central Bank. The "parallel state" denounced by concerned Costa Ricans still exists, but at least Costa Rica isn't paying for it.

NOTES

1. Interview, San José, September 1988.

2. Telephone interview from Washington, July 1988.

3. Interview, San José, March 1988.

UNITED STATES AID TO COSTA RICA
(IN MILLIONS OF DOLLARS)

	1946–61	1962–81	1982	1983	1984	1985	1986	1987	1988†
AID and predecessor agencies	21.4	158.0	11.5	28.5	15.9	25.9	12.9	17.2	11.6
Loans	10.9	126.0	9.7	20.2	11.6	10.7	6.3	8.3	—
Grants	10.5	32.0	1.8	8.3	4.3	15.2*	6.6*	8.9	11.6
Food commodity assistance	1.1	20.5	18.3	27.3	22.4	21.1	20.9	21.6	15.0
Economic Support Funds	—	—	20.0	155.7	130.0	160.0	123.6	142.5	90.0
Loans	—	—	15.0	118.0	35.0	—	—	—	—
Grants	—	—	5.0	37.7	95.0	160.0	120.6	119.8	85.0
Other**	31.0	47.8	2.0	2.0	1.1	1.7	3.7	N.A.	N.A.
Security assistance	.1	6.9	2.0	2.6	9.2	9.2	2.5***	1.7	N.A.
Total	53.6	233.2	53.8	213.5	169.4	208.7	163.6	181.3	116.6

†Preliminary estimate
N.A. = not available
*Includes Central America Peace Scholarship Project.
**Peace Corps, Narcotics Program, and others.
***Does not include $9 million request for antiterrorist training.
Source: U.S. Department of State

CHAPTER VI

Costa Rica and the Nicaraguan Revolution

Editors' Introduction

In the early 1960s, after the Cuban revolution, Latin America had a prominent place on the U.S. foreign policy agenda. But by the late 1960s and early 1970s, Washington's attention began to wane, as the Vietnam War, détente, and renewed contact with China became the central concerns. Few people outside the region paid much attention to Central America, let alone quiet Costa Rica. Few reports appeared on Costa Rica in the U.S. press. Those that did were generally innocuous features about American retirees, or on the latest exploits of Robert Vesco, the fugitive financier who found refuge in Costa Rica from 1972 until 1978.[1] It was an era of general prosperity and peace, a time when many of Costa Rica's clichés about itself had a ring of truth.

In 1977 Jimmy Carter entered the White House, bringing with him a new attitude toward human rights. His administration began openly criticizing tyrants and juntas and negotiated the treaty that would gradually hand over control of the Panama Canal to Panama. During his presidency, such repressive regimes as General Augusto Pinochet's in Chile and General Anastasio Somoza's in Nicaragua saw their U.S. economic aid whittled down. For other relatively repressive governments, such as those in Haiti, Bolivia, and Guatemala, aid packages were redesigned in an effort to channel resources to the poorest sectors without propping up the regimes. By fiscal year 1979, countries with relatively open political systems—Costa Rica among them—saw their U.S. assistance packages rise significantly.[2]

The climate in Washington was favorable toward human rights advocates' efforts to strengthen the hemisphere's institutional framework for redressing abuses. The Organization of American States had established the Inter-American Human Rights Commission in the 1960s and granted it greater powers in the 1970s. In 1969 OAS members meeting in Costa Rica signed the American Convention on Human Rights, also known as the Pact of San José. The treaty, which provided for an Inter-American Human Rights Court as a sister institution to the commission, entered into force in 1978. In a gesture recognizing Costa Rica's respect for human rights, the OAS established the court in that nation's capital.

The contrast between Costa Rica and its neighbor to the north had never been more acute. Somoza's Nicaragua presented the Carter administration with a human rights situation that required more than an adjustment in its foreign-aid budget. During 1977, the Nicaraguan Church hierarchy voiced strong criticism of the Somoza regime, and the Sandinista National Liberation Front (FSLN) stepped up its attacks. On January 10, 1978, Pedro Joaquín Chamorro, the publisher of the Nicaraguan opposition paper *La Prensa* and longtime Somoza foe who had been part of early Costa Rican–based efforts to oust the Somoza family (see Reading 6.1) was assassinated. A general strike ensued. Many Nicaraguans joined the opposition, or rallied behind the FSLN, which for the first time since its founding some fifteen years earlier began to garner broad-based support. The dictator's days were numbered.

Costa Rica played a pivotal diplomatic, political, and logistical role in the Sandinista revolution. The motivation was in part historic, as Charles Ameringer notes in Reading 6.1. Lingering bitterness over Costa Rica's annexation in 1824 of the Nicaraguan province of Nicoya, border disputes along the Río San Juan, and various parochial squabbles in the nineteenth century established a historical framework for mutual suspicion. So did the assistance that one government or the other sporadically offered to revolutionary or conspiratorial groups. By the late 1940s, however, the old antipathy took on new dimensions. Anti-Somoza activists on several occasions staged abortive invasions from Costa Rican territory, while leaders of the losing side of Costa Rica's civil war launched their own attacks in 1948 and 1955 with Somoza's assistance. A pattern of cross-border strikes and counterstrikes followed by outraged appeals to international opinion and OAS fact-finding teams was set.[3] The scenario would be replayed in the 1970s, during the Nicaraguan revolution, and in the 1980s, during the counterrevolution.

On one level, the post-1948 friction between the two countries stemmed from personal rivalry between President José Figueres of Costa Rica and the Somoza family. On another, it reflected the widening ideological gap between Costa Rica, which was disarming and strengthening a democratic social welfare state, and Nicaragua, which under the Somozas was militarizing and institutionalizing a tyranny.

As anti-Somoza sentiment grew in the late 1970s, the Sandinistas established training camps in northern Costa Rica and Nicaraguan opposition figures began openly using San José as their headquarters. Costa Rica's relations with Nicaragua deteriorated. In October 1977 Costa Rican security minister Mario Charpentier went to a remote section of the border to investigate personally Nicaragua's charges that the Sandinistas had staged an attack from the zone. Charpentier, accompanied by two civil guards and a dozen local reporters, was traveling on the Río Frío in a small boat when Nicaraguan armed forces opened fire. The bombardment and shooting went on for ninety minutes, as the minister told San José by radio to try to phone Nicaragua and get them to stop.[4] Less than a year later, in September 1978, the Nicaraguan air force raided the Costa Rican town of La Cruz, its bombs falling near uniformed school children practicing for an Independence Day parade. In November two civil guards were killed by Nicaraguan troops. Costa Rica broke relations with Somoza's government and began encouraging other countries to follow suit.

In the next few months Costa Rica, Venezuela, Panama, and Mexico led the diplomatic campaign against Somoza. By some accounts, Costa Rica was the prime player, particularly after March 1979, when Venezuelan president Carlos Andrés Pérez, a social democrat with great international stature and considerable disdain for Somoza, stepped down and a conservative administration, less friendly to the Sandinistas, took over. Some Mexican experts believe that it was Costa Rican president Rodrigo Carazo who convinced President José López Portillo to break ties with Managua on May 20, 1979—just nine days before the Sandinista southern front launched its final offensive from Costa Rican territory.[5]

In the meantime, a prominent group of Nicaraguan establishment figures—doctors, priests, educators, and businessmen—began their own campaign to convince the world that the corruption, brutality, and repression of the Somoza regime had reached levels that could no longer be tolerated. They were called *Los Doce* or the "Group of Twelve." Starting in the fall of 1977, they operated out of Costa Rica, where some had long associations with President Figueres, a foe of the Somozas since his days in the Caribbean Legion in the 1940s (see Chapter III). One of the Twelve, Carlos Tunnermann, who later served as Nicaragua's minister of education and then ambassador to the United States, recalled: "The Group of Twelve undertook the international work, to visit governments and international organizations, to make known that the boys of the [Sandinista] Front were not terrorists, that they had taken up arms because it was necessary and that the terrorist was the government and the *somocista* system."[6]

In the summer of 1978, Somoza, in a conciliatory mood induced by pressure from Washington, allowed the Twelve to return home. There, *Los Doce,* which included individuals closely aligned with the Sandinistas as well as political centrists, joined other political and labor organizations to form the

Broad Opposition Front, known by its Spanish acronym FAO. Within months, many of these opposition leaders were forced to return to Costa Rica, where they remained until their triumphant homecoming in July 1979.

But Costa Rica did more than lend its democratic prestige in diplomatic circles, open its heart to the opposition, and shelter refugees. It gave the Sandinistas virtually free rein in northern Costa Rica, particularly the Pacific province of Guanacaste. Local farmers allowed Sandinistas to train on their land and covered up the Sandinista presence when OAS observers came to investigate (see Readings 6.5, 6.6, and 6.7). Except for occasional crackdowns during international mediation efforts or for appearances' sake, officials turned a blind eye to the Sandinistas' activities and later actively assisted them. Arms shipments from Venezuela, Panama, and Cuba were allowed through Costa Rica, provoking a major scandal in the early 1980s, when a Legislative Assembly investigation charged that many of the weapons never reached the Sandinistas, but were kept by corrupt officials and later smuggled—for a profit—to the Salvadoran guerrillas (see Reading 6.8).

As the conflict heated up, Costa Rican territory ceased being a mere training ground and became the rear guard for the Sandinistas' southern front. In later years, villagers in northern towns would freely recall their own involvement, how they gave food to the guerrillas and cared for their wounded. Numerous young Costa Ricans, including one of Figueres's sons, took up arms alongside the Sandinistas. Virtually all Costa Ricans adopted the Sandinista cause as their own. Luis Burstin, a prominent doctor, political conservative, and former information minister, recalled the mood in San José in June 1979:

> I was living in London at the time, and I came back for a few days in June. I was astonished to find one of my closest friends here, a conservative physician of impeccable anti-Communist beliefs, completely absorbed in the task of aiding the Sandinistas. The Costa Rican government, which gave generous support to the revolutionaries, told Somoza, in all honesty, that it lacked the military capability to control the Sandinistas. Communists, government officials, democratic politicians, citizens of the right, the left, and the center were all thrown together in the same enterprise. The overthrow of Somoza became a national fiesta.[7]

By this time, of course, there was no longer even a pretense of neutrality. Carazo might have campaigned in 1977 on a "boot Vesco" platform, but by the time of his May 1978 inauguration, Nicaragua was without doubt the single biggest issue. Nor was the issue a divisive one. Polls that year showed that Costa Ricans were overwhelmingly opposed to Somoza; 96 percent of those expressing an opinion thought the Sandinistas' fight was just.

Costa Rica's decision to support the Sandinistas was not without risks. Although Venezuela and Panama had given Costa Rica some arms and small aircraft, it had no army to speak of—certainly not one that could withstand an assault by Somoza's National Guard. And Somoza often threatened to retaliate (see Reading 6.7).

The guerrillas on the southern front were politically heterogeneous, including Marxists, social democrats, and even some supporters of Nicaragua's anti-Somoza Conservative Party. Press coverage of the war was also concentrated on the southern front, and this contributed to an image of Sandinista moderation that was congenial to many Costa Ricans. But Costa Rican support for the revolutionaries was not without a note of ambivalence. Though wholeheartedly behind the struggle to oust Somoza, many Costa Ricans polled voiced concern about Communist influence within the Sandinista movement.

For Washington, of course, fear of communism was a top concern. Until the last minute, the Carter administration was trying to get rid of Somoza without letting the Sandinistas take power. For the forty hours between Somoza's departure and the Sandinistas' triumphant march into Managua, Carter even backed as provisional president Somoza's handpicked successor, Francisco Urcuyo, a former speaker of the lower house of the Nicaraguan Congress.[8]

President Carazo also wanted to shape the outcome of the revolution but he was more realistic about the popularity and strength of the Sandinistas. While Carter was searching for a conservative or centrist who would take into account the influence of the Left, Carazo took the opposite tack. As Mitchell Seligson and William Carroll note in Reading 6.7, Carazo allowed the Sandinistas to set up a government in exile in San José, while pushing them to broaden their base to include moderates and conservatives. At first, the Sandinistas did include some prominent moderates, such as Violeta Barrios de Chamorro and Alfonso Robelo, on the governing junta. But as the revolution became more radical, the moderates moved into the opposition. Even Carazo, in July 1980, refused to attend the revolution's first anniversary celebrations on the grounds that Cuban leader Fidel Castro would be in Managua. "I am not fond of walking on the same platform as dictators," Carazo said.[9]

When counterrevolutionary groups began to form, it was the more moderate forces—the disillusioned ex-southern-front Sandinistas—that found sympathy in Costa Rica. Although small right-wing groups of former Nicaraguan national guards and *somocista* politicians were also at times active in Costa Rica, these forces found their main support in Honduras. As Chapter VII illustrates, Costa Rica again became involved in its neighbor's conflicts. But Costa Ricans' aid to the *contras* was far more limited, and given with far less enthusiasm, than their help to the Sandinistas had been. Though many became disillusioned by the Sandinistas, few Costa Ricans ardently supported the *contras,* or placed much trust in their promises to bring democracy, Costa Rican-style, to Nicaragua.

NOTES

1. The most comprehensive account of Vesco's stay in Costa Rica, and his questionable dealings with José Figueres and other leading politicians, is Julio Suñol, *Robert Vesco compra una república* (San José: Trejos Hermanos, 1978).

2. Lars Shoultz, *Human Rights and United States Policy toward Latin America* (Princeton, N.J.: Princeton University Press, 1981), pp. 205–6.

3. In fact, the first OAS fact-finding commission was established in December 1948 to study conflict on the Nicaraguan–Costa Rican border. It chastised both sides for harboring armed opposition groups. See Tord Hoivik and Solveig Aas, "Demilitarization in Costa Rica: A Farewell to Arms?" *Journal of Peace Research* 18, no. 4 (1981): 338–39.

4. *Tico Times,* 21 October 1977.

5. Mario Ojeda, "Mexican Policy toward Central America in the Context of U.S.-Mexico Relations" in *The Future of Central America: Policy Choices for the U.S. and Mexico,* ed. Richard R. Fagen and Olga Pellicer (Stanford: Stanford University Press, 1983).

6. Shirley Christian, *Nicaragua: Revolution in the Family* (New York: Vintage Books, 1986), p. 49.

7. Luis Burstin, "Costa Rica Teeters," *New Republic,* 18 June 1984.

8. In a separate incident just over a week before the Sandinista victory, the U.S. Air Force sent two helicopters to the northern Costa Rican city of Liberia. Washington said this was a precautionary measure in case U.S. citizens had to be evacuated from Nicaragua. But the Liberia airport was also the main receiving point for Cuban and Panamanian arms shipments to the Sandinistas and the U.S. presence aroused suspicion. The Costa Rican Legislative Assembly voted 29–20 to expel the American contingent.

9. *Miami Herald,* 15 June 1980.

6.1 The Thirty Years War Between Figueres and the Somozas*

BY CHARLES D. AMERINGER

José Figueres came to power in Costa Rica in the 1948 civil war with the backing of the Nicaraguan anti-Somoza opposition. Nicaraguan president Anastasio Somoza García supported repeated efforts to topple Figueres in the late 1940s and 1950s. The enmity between the two was deep and lasting; "Tacho" Somoza went so far as to challenge "don Pepe" Figueres to a duel in 1955. Yet the antagonism between their two countries cannot be explained solely as a consequence of their leaders' personal hatred. The two men lived, and governed, as Central America confronted the cold war, and later, under Tacho's sons Luis and Anastasio Somoza Debayle, faced the Cuban revolution. Figueres, with his Caribbean Legion against dictatorships and espousal of social democracy, professed belief in the viability of a non-Communist Left in the region. To the Somozas, for whom "non-Communist Left" was a contradiction in terms, Figueres posed a subversive threat to their family's dynasty in Nicaragua.

*Excerpted from *Caribbean Review* 8, no. 4 (Fall 1979): 4–7, 40–41.

The two men, as Charles Ameringer indicates here, were not merely symbols of democracy and dictatorship, "good" caudillos and "bad." They also represented the two ways the United States countered the so-called Communist threat in Central America. Costa Rica's Figueres (albeit with CIA assistance) sought to support peaceful social change. Nicaragua's Somozas helped the CIA overthrow Guatemala's progressive president Jacobo Arbenz in 1954 and assisted in the Bay of Pigs invasion of Cuba in 1961. While Figueres and the Somozas sparred with and conspired against each other, both were also allies of Washington and thus came to represent what Ameringer calls "a paradox of U.S. policy."

Charles D. Ameringer teaches history at Pennsylvania State University. He has written extensively on Costa Rica, including Don Pepe: A Political Biography of José Figueres of Costa Rica *(1978).*

IT seems characteristic of Central American countries that they get involved in one another's affairs. Exiles from one state find refuge in another, where they continue their political activities and even prepare revolutionary expeditions. Filibustering, arms trafficking, alliances between political factions of one state with those of another have kept the region in turmoil for over a century. The Central American states have never really separated when it comes to political intrigue and revolutionary activity. These periods of political conspiracy are particularly acute when specific countries are governed by strong-willed and ambitious leaders. . . . The situation becomes especially explosive when such leaders are contemporaries and when, moreover, they are guided by sharply differing political views. Such a situation existed in the post–World War II era when José Figueres dominated Costa Rican affairs and Anastasio Somoza García ruled Nicaragua.

These two men were very different in nature and ideology and looked upon each other as a threat to survival. In fact, Figueres had come to power with the aid of Somoza's rivals and had pledged himself, in return, to the overthrow of Somoza. In his book *By Whom We Were Betrayed . . . and How,* Rosendo Argüello, Jr., a Nicaraguan exile, tells of meeting Figueres during his exile in Mexico in 1942, and of the two concluding that dictatorship was a common malady in the isthmus for which a common remedy ought to be sought. . . .

In December 1947, only two months before the Costa Rican elections, Figueres entered into the "Caribbean Pact" wherein he joined forces with exile elements of Nicaragua, Honduras, and the Dominican Republic under the sponsorship of Guatemalan president Juan José Arévalo. Figueres had persuaded these exiles that Costa Rica was the "weakest link" in the dictatorial chain and that once it was broken Costa Rica might be the staging area for revolutionary movements against the other dictators of the region. Somoza was to be the first target [see Chapter III for background on the civil war]. . . .

Once in power, however, Figueres did not seem as anxious as before to carry out his end of the Caribbean Pact. The Caribbean Legion had been born, and Figueres provided Argüello with a training camp and funds for the preparation of a Nicaraguan Army of Liberation, but nothing serious happened. Whether the responsibilities of office sobered "don Pepe," as Figueres was known, or whether he betrayed his allies—as Argüello later charged—is a matter of speculation. . . .

Somoza, however, was concerned. During the Costa Rican civil war, he had intervened on the side of Calderón and Picado, but withdrew under sharp protests by the U.S. Department of State, which warned both Nicaragua and Guatemala against becoming involved. Subsequently, Somoza kept a close watch on don Pepe's Founding Junta. He was not pleased over its reported collaboration with Nicaraguan exile elements. He allegedly placed spies in Argüello's training camp and gathered intelligence from other sources, which convinced him that an invasion of Nicaragua was being prepared. As a result, he gave assistance to Calderón to prepare an invasion of his own.

On December 10, 1948, a small force of *calderonista* exiles based in Nicaragua crossed the frontier and penetrated a few miles into Costa Rica. Figueres reacted quickly and sent volunteers to the front to contain the invaders, but relied principally upon the neophyte Organization of American States to bring hostilities to an end. The OAS, indeed, responded to Figueres's call, by requesting both parties to observe their treaty commitments with reference to hemispheric solidarity and by dispatching an observer group to prepare an on-site investigation. The action of the OAS prevented further action by Somoza, but at the cost to Figueres of pledges to disband the Caribbean Legion and expel prominent Nicaraguan exiles. For a polite slap on the wrist, Somoza had managed to remove a potential threat from his doorstep.

THE U.S. ROLE

The role of the United States in this affair is an important consideration. The cold war had begun, and the United States had demonstrated to its tiny neighbors that it wanted no disruptions in the Caribbean area. This policy was reinforced in June 1949, when the Caribbean Legion undertook yet another action, this time using Guatemala, with the support of Cuba, as a springboard for an attack against Rafael Trujillo of the Dominican Republic. The United States, acting through the OAS, admonished the governments of Guatemala, Cuba, and Costa Rica against abetting exile revolutionary movements and encouraged the normalization of relations with the governments of Nicaragua, Honduras, the Dominican Republic, and Venezuela. A premium had been placed upon stability in the Caribbean. . . . Nevertheless, the enmity between don Pepe and Tacho (Somoza) had been established, and the future was predictable.

When José Figueres became constitutional president on November 8, 1953, one could sense trouble ahead for Costa Rica and Nicaragua. By this time,

Figueres had become a recognized leader of the non-Communist or democratic Left in the Caribbean, and the political refugees of the region flocked to his protection. Venezuela's Rómulo Betancourt led a virtual parade of Venezuelan, Cuban, Honduran, Nicaraguan, and Dominican exiles to San José. The situation was complicated by events in Guatemala, where Jacobo Arbenz had established an allegedly pro-Communist regime, which made the United States even less sympathetic toward Figueres's antidictatorial policy. It did not take long for trouble to arise.

In early April 1954, a small band of Nicaraguan exiles under Pablo Leal entered Nicaragua clandestinely from Costa Rica and attempted to assassinate Anastasio Somoza García and his two sons, Luis and Anastasio (Tachito). Somoza was furious and immediately accused Figueres of aiding Leal. He claimed that Leal and his men were transported to the frontier in trucks from Figueres's finca at *La Lucha* and under escort by principal officers of the Costa Rican Civil Guard. Figueres denied the charges and called for an OAS investigation, but Somoza would accept nothing less than a personal apology from Figueres, the expulsion of Betancourt (whom Somoza labeled the new chief of the Caribbean Legion), and the dismissal of the "guilty" Civil Guard officers. Although Betancourt did, in fact, leave Costa Rica, Figueres refused to meet any of the other demands, and for the remainder of 1954 tension between Costa Rica and Nicaragua mounted.

Somoza began to enlarge his air force, and rumors circulated that he was again helping Calderón to prepare another invasion of Costa Rica. The Venezuelan dictator Marcos Pérez Jiménez also joined the plot, reportedly because of his irritation over the sanctuary provided Venezuelan exiles in Costa Rica and because he resented Figueres's boycott of the Tenth Inter-American Conference in Caracas in March 1954. Somoza aided Calderón because he supposedly believed Figueres was involved in a vast Communist plot to take over Central America. He linked the April plot to assassinate him with two additional events that occurred in May: a banana workers' strike on the north coast of Honduras (allegedly with Guatemalan support) and the shipment of arms to Guatemala from behind the Iron Curtain. Somoza reasoned that since Leal had come to Costa Rica from Guatemala in December 1953, before proceeding to Nicaragua, all these events were connected and, in fact, were supposed to occur simultaneously, in order to plunge the region into turmoil and facilitate a Communist takeover. For this reason, Somoza aided Carlos Castillo Armas and the U.S. Central Intelligence Agency in the overthrow of Arbenz in Guatemala and then prepared to seek his revenge against Figueres.

On January 11, 1955, a group of *calderonista* exiles calling itself the Authentic Anti-Communist Army and led by Teodoro Picado, Jr., the ex-president's son and West Point classmate of Tachito Somoza, invaded Costa Rica from Nicaragua. . . . Figueres immediately called upon the OAS for aid, claiming that his country had been the victim of aggression by Nicaragua. The OAS responded quickly, and the United States, with the authorization of the OAS, put an end to the hostilities by selling four F-51 Mustang fighters to the Costa Rican government for a dollar each.

During the few days that the fighting lasted, Somoza angrily denied Figueres's charges that Nicaragua was involved and even challenged don Pepe to a duel. . . . However, Figueres denied that the affair was simply a personal feud and insisted that it was a serious matter of democracy versus dictatorship. Figueres has claimed that his ability to convince a number of leading North American liberals, among them Adolf Berle and Illinois senator Paul Douglas, that the dictators of the region were ganging up on one of the few remaining democracies in Latin America swung popular opinion to his side and induced the U.S. State Department to take decisive action.

However, although Figueres was grateful to the United States for his rescue, he had "mixed feelings," because he did not feel that the United States fully sympathized with his cause. He was upset over a remark by Assistant Secretary of State Henry F. Holland that described him as a "troublemaker" and he was disappointed that the United States refused to impose sanctions upon Nicaragua as an aggressor. Moreover, Figueres believed that the United States was partially responsible for the attack in the first place.

In a confidential memorandum, Figueres accused the U.S. ambassador in Managua, Thomas Whelan, of being implicated in the affair. He related that on three occasions prior to the invasion he had furnished evidence of the plot to CIA agent Thomas Flores and that Flores, after traveling to Managua, assured him that no such plot existed. Figueres also appealed directly to the Department of State to investigate his charges and received similar assurances that no invasion was being prepared. "One may assume," Figueres wrote, "that these investigations were entrusted to Whelan." Figueres charged that Whelan and Somoza were intimate "buddies," and that Whelan was an apologist for the regime and an agent for its lies.

Specifically, Figueres accused Whelan of spreading the false story that the Pablo Leal affair was a simple assassination plot and that he, Figueres, was implicated. Figueres asserted that Leal's movement was a legitimate revolutionary action involving Nicaragua's most respectable opposition leaders. . . . Figueres claimed that, because of Whelan, he had been discredited in the State Department—looked upon as a troublemaker—and his appeals went unheeded. This, despite the fact, Figueres added, that Whelan once boasted, "perhaps under the influence of alcohol," that he had personally reviewed "the mercenary troops which invaded Costa Rica in 1955." . . .

As serious as these charges were, Figueres added another more sinister. He accused the CIA of aiding Somoza in the attack upon Costa Rica in repayment for his support of the CIA-sponsored invasion of Guatemala. "The same North American mercenary aviators who took part in the attack upon Guatemala," Figueres asserted, "later came from Nicaragua and machine-gunned eleven defenseless towns in our territory." Figueres was referring especially to Jerry DeLarm, a North American adventurer, who flew for Castillo Armas and the

CIA and who was related to Calderón by marriage. This charge presents a paradox of U.S. policy, with its covert side trying to topple Figueres, and its overt side rescuing him.

Whatever may be the truth of these charges, one cannot deny the critical role of the United States in this affair. The United States was still able to maintain the peace in Central America. Although it appeared to respect its pledges of nonintervention and operated within the OAS structure, its sale of warplanes to Figueres was the principal signal to all concerned. At the same time, the exigencies of the cold war were giving rise to a "new interventionism" characterized by covert action. The CIA had already enjoyed success in Iran and Guatemala, although its fumbling and bumbling in this episode foretold some of its later disasters. . . .

The invasion of 1955 was the last incident between Figueres and Tacho Somoza, because the dictator was gunned down at a Saturday night dance in León in September 1956. There is no evidence that Figueres was involved. He was in Italy at the time and, although he showed little remorse, he expressed surprise. He told representatives of the Associated Press in Florence that he hoped the Nicaraguan people might now be able to establish "honest and representative government." However, the continuation of the Somoza dynasty under Tacho's sons Luis and Anastasio (Tachito) frustrated such hopes, and the relations between them and Figueres remained strained. Tachito, especially, did not forgive the troubles between his father and Figueres and he probably suspected that Figueres had something to do with his father's death. It did not take him long to show his feelings.

In May 1957, three Cuban gunmen were arrested in San José and charged with plotting against the life of President Figueres. According to the investigation by Costa Rican authorities, the three had been promised $200,000 for the job. Although they had apparently been hired by Dominican agents—the notorious Johnny Abbes García and the sinister Félix Bernardino—they had come from Managua, where Anastasio Somoza Debayle (Tachito) had allegedly agreed to facilitate their action.

Just a few months later, in August, Figueres alleged that he had uncovered a new plot by *calderonistas* to launch an attack upon Costa Rica from Nicaragua and charged that Tachito, now chief of the Nicaraguan National Guard, was supporting the plan. Although nothing came of this episode, Figueres remarked that Ambassador Whelan was up to his old tricks and that "he was continuing to encourage the subversive activities of Tachito Somoza against Costa Rica." . . .

The relations between Figueres and the Somozas entered an acute stage in 1959 in the context of Fidel Castro's takeover in Cuba. Even though Figueres was no longer president, he felt obliged to assist moderate Nicaraguan exile elements in a plot against President Luis Somoza in order to preempt similar plans by radical groups based in Cuba. Figueres aided moderate leaders Enrique Lacayo Farfán and Pedro Joaquín Chamorro, who undertook an airborne invasion of Nicaragua at the end of May 1959 from Punta Llorona, a base in the south of Costa Rica. In a lengthy communication to Figueres after the failure of the invasion, Chamorro described what went wrong and left no doubt that Figueres and elements of his National Liberation Party had supported every phase of the operation, including planning, the providing of the base, and the acquisition of arms and aircraft. Figueres himself had traveled to Washington and Caracas in the hope of securing support for the movement; the United States demonstrated its sympathy (within the OAS) by delaying a response to Nicaragua's invoking of the Rio treaty until the movement had a chance to fail or succeed on its own; Venezuela (now governed by Rómulo Betancourt) stood ready to airlift arms to the insurgents in the event the movement gained momentum. The failure of this invasion, plus a number of others that occurred in the turbulent summer of 1959, coupled with the fear of additional Castro-style revolutionary movements in the Caribbean and Central America, led to a new, nonviolent phase of Figueres's effort to unseat the Somozas.

Figueres became the recipient of covert funding by the CIA as part of a policy in support of the non-Communist Left in Latin America. Figueres and his allies were no longer troublemakers; instead, they were a possible alternative to Castroism in the face of growing economic, political, and social unrest. CIA official Cord Meyer came to Costa Rica and collaborated with Figueres in financing democratically oriented, progressive organizations. He and Figueres channeled funds to political parties, newspapers, and individuals. In late 1959, in collaboration with the democratic Left parties of the region, Figueres established the Inter-American Institute of Political Education in San José, which was designed to train young leaders in democratic political organization and tactics and to provide a point of contact for parties of the democratic Left. Nicaraguan exiles affiliated with the Independent Liberal Party and the Nicaraguan Revolutionary Movement, among others, took part, and the CIA provided financial backing through the Kaplan Fund and the Institute of International Labor Research, both of New York. The CIA, however, was working both sides of the street, as demonstrated by its close collaboration with Tachito Somoza in the Bay of Pigs affair. As a result, don Pepe's antidictatorial efforts (with CIA backing) gave greater priority to cooperation with Juan Bosch and other Dominican exiles for the ouster of Rafael Trujillo.

On the overt side, don Pepe became a favorite of the Kennedy administration. His policy of economic and social change within the framework of representative democracy fit in very well with the Alliance for Progress scheme of accelerated evolution, and Figueres established close ties with such New Frontiersmen as Chester Bowles and Arthur Schlesinger, Jr. In March 1962, Adolf Berle, a top adviser on Latin American affairs under Kennedy and an intimate friend of Figueres's, tried to persuade Figueres to help him arrange a peaceful political solution in Nicaragua. He asked Figueres to serve as a mediator between Luis Manuel Debayle, representing the Somozas, and Fernando Agüero, a Conservative Party leader, with a view to establishing the ground rules for free elections in Nicaragua in 1963. Figueres was willing to help, but after several fruitless months lost heart: "Things do not seem to move," he told Berle in August of that year. "I am of the impression that Somoza will want to impose a successor regardless of what happens."

This remark revealed a sense of resignation on the part of don Pepe and a general decline in his rivalry with the Somozas. The efforts by the democratic Left to promote peaceful revolution had not been effective and, with some exceptions, it suffered an eclipse in the decade of the sixties. . . .

United States support of Figueres's activities also diminished. Cord Meyer left Costa Rica in mid-1962, and CIA funds dried up shortly afterward, although small amounts continued until 1967, when *Ramparts* magazine exposed such CIA funding activities. . . . For his part, Anastasio Somoza Debayle consolidated his position in Nicaragua, and, particularly after the death of Luis in 1967, Tachito became the new Tacho. He attempted to improve his image internationally and the regime was probably less repressive, at least until the reaction against his unsavory handling of Managua earthquake relief funds and supplies in 1972.

During Figueres's second presidency (1970–74), relations between Costa Rica and Nicaragua remained peaceful. Figueres displayed no hostility toward the new leader of the Somoza clan. In fact, early in his administration he declared, "We are not conspiring. We are not going to hold the son responsible for what his father did or did not do." Figueres's attitude toward Latin American military dictatorships, in general, had changed. . . . Figueres even met with Somoza several times in this period, and the two leaders, as if they were old friends, discussed such matters as the Central American Common Market and tried to promote a reconciliation between Honduras and El Salvador in the aftermath of the [1969] Soccer War.

One may only speculate about the reasons for this changed attitude, but new international conditions and political styles and the conservatism associated with age may offer some explanation. Figueres was not sympathetic toward the political activism of the sixties and he deplored the tactics of terrorism and skyjacking employed by radical groups. In one of the most sensational events of his presidency, Figueres not only stopped an airplane hijacking by a group of Sandinista guerrillas at the international airport outside of San José, but he extradited the surviving members to Nicaragua, in total disregard of the constitution.

Because of don Pepe's conduct during his presidency, one might assume that he played little or no role in the overthrow of Anastasio Somoza Debayle in July 1979. This is not the case. . . .

When the situation began to deteriorate in Nicaragua following the ugly disclosures of the corrupt handling of Managua earthquake relief and the eventual murder of Pedro Joaquín Chamorro, many of the Nicaraguan moderates turned to Figueres for aid. If Somoza were to fall, Figueres preferred their success to that of the Sandinistas, or at least the installation of a regime that would embody his commitment to social democracy. According to one of the members of *Los Doce,* Figueres was a "formidable friend." Nicaraguan exiles operated openly and freely on Costa Rican soil, leading to a rupture in relations between the two countries. It is unlikely that they would have had so free a hand without Figueres's support. Figueres even patched up his quarrel with President Rodrigo Carazo, in order to facilitate these activities. It may be noted that the Sandinista group which fought in the south, advancing on Rivas from Costa Rica, was the most moderate of the guerrilla factions. Moreover, don Pepe's own seventeen-year-old son, Mauricio, volunteered for service with the rebels in the civil war. Finally, Figueres apparently helped break the impasse between the Nicaraguan Junta of National Reconstruction and the U.S. special envoy in Costa Rica. Instead of appearing to yield to U.S. pressure for guarantees against extremism, Figueres suggested that the junta request the OAS to establish a commission for monitoring the actions of the post-Somoza government.

The events of the recent struggle are dramatic enough, but one can only imagine what they would have been like if the old Tacho were still alive and don Pepe were in his prime. Nonetheless, it appears that the Thirty Years War between Figueres and the Somozas is over.

6.2 The Somozas' Properties in Northern Costa Rica*

BY MARC EDELMAN

The Somozas' acquisition of vast properties on the Costa Rican side of the border was one element in the growing friction between Costa Rica and Nicaragua during the 1960s and 1970s. Motivated by both business and strategic considerations, the Nicaraguan dictators created what many termed "a state within a state" and even gained control of Hacienda Santa Rosa, where Costa Rican forces defeated William Walker's invaders in 1856 (see Reading 1.5). This reading describes the construction of the Somozas' empire in northern Costa Rica, which began during the 1940s, and their ties with local landlords and Costa Rican politicians.

Edelman, an editor of this volume, is assistant professor of anthropology at Yale University.

*Research for this article was supported by the Inter-American Foundation, the Social Science Research Council, the Institute for the Study of World Politics, and the Sigma Xi Scientific Research Society. The author thanks Jeff Gould for helpful comments.

THE Somoza family first gained a foothold in Costa Rica during the presidencies of Rafael Angel Calderón Guardia (1940–44) and Teodoro Picado Michalski (1944–48). Although Calderón and Picado were allied with the Communists [Readings 3.1 and 3.2], dictator Anastasio Somoza García feared the Costa Rican social democratic opposition's ties to his opponents within Nicaragua.[1] Somoza also had compelling business reasons for establishing ties to Calderón and Picado. In 1932, during the depression, Costa Rica had imposed tariffs on cattle imports to stem hard-currency expenditures and make the country self-sufficient in beef production. In retaliation, Nicaragua prohibited livestock exports to Costa Rica, although the ban was never enforced until Somoza came to power. Consolidating what was to become a near-monopoly on Nicaraguan livestock marketing, Somoza employed his National Guard to force small ranchers to sell him cattle at artificially low prices. Beginning in the mid-1930s, many of these animals were exported illegally to Costa Rica, where—because of the protectionist legislation—livestock prices were rising rapidly. With this access to cut-rate cattle, Somoza was better able than other Nicaraguan exporters to pay high Costa Rican duties. Nor did he always pay. Many more head were certainly smuggled across the border. As William Krehm notes in his important yet long-neglected *Democracies and Tyrannies of the Caribbean,*[2] Somoza's animals

> went to Víctor Wolf, close ally of the Costa Rican ruling house of Calderón Guardia, who fattened them on his ranch at Chomes near Puntarenas. These exports did not exist so far as Nicaraguan statistics were concerned, but turned up in Costa Rican records. The Costa Rican Statistical Report for 1943 gave cattle imports for 1942 as 8,652 head. But the Nicaraguan Year Book for 1942 placed the total exports from Nicaragua for the same year (not only to Costa Rica, but to Panama and Peru) at 1,467. The 7,185 head that entered Costa Rica from Nicaragua, but didn't leave Nicaragua for Costa Rica, were one of the many miracles of the Somoza regime.[3]

Probably in connection with his contraband cattle business, Somoza García had expressed interest at the beginning of the Calderón administration in acquiring property in the northwestern Costa Rican province of Guanacaste, the main livestock region. There—in contrast to the central part of the country—large estates or *latifundios* predominated [see Reading 1.2]. In 1940 Casimiro Sobrado García, owner of the 19,232-hectare (47,503 acre) Hacienda El Tempisque—situated forty-two miles south of the border along Guanacaste's major inland waterway—traveled to Nicaragua, where he offered to sell Somoza the property.[4] Sobrado, whose Spanish immigrant father had built a sugar mill at El Tempisque and turned the hacienda into one of the best-administered and most lucrative properties in Guanacaste, was accompanied to Managua by Luis Brenes Gutiérrez, whose family had recently entered ranching and had close ties to national government officials.[5] While Somoza's interest in the Tempisque property was clear, the reason the sale was never finalized cannot be ascertained.

During the 1948 Costa Rican civil war, Somoza supported Picado's *calderonista* government against José Figueres's social democratic insurgents [see Chapter III]. With the insurgents' triumph, Somoza gave Calderón and Picado asylum in Nicaragua. In part as a result of Somoza's longtime feud with Figueres [see Reading 6.1], the dictator found his access to Costa Rica's cattle market closed. Somoza was by now expanding his control over other sectors of the Nicaraguan economy. In any case, Costa Rica's livestock imports largely ceased after 1950 as it attained self-sufficiency in beef production.

It is clear that the dictator's sons and successors, Luis and Anastasio Somoza Debayle, shared the interest in northern Costa Rican real estate, albeit for different reasons. The younger Somozas' acquisition of extensive properties in northern Costa Rica in the 1960s was probably motivated in part by speculative considerations and the desire to diversify their investments outside Nicaragua. But the paramount concern was almost certainly strategic. As early as 1944, Nicaraguan exiles based in northern Costa Rica had attempted to overthrow the Somozas.[6] In 1959 and 1960 larger incursions took place under the direction of Nicaragua's Conservative Party.[7] A key leader of these efforts was Indalecio Pastora, whose family controlled Hacienda Verdún and other properties that spanned both sides of the border. In addition, dissident Nicaraguan general Carlos Pasos, treasurer of the anti-Somoza forces, had acquired the Guanacastecan haciendas Paso Hondo in Cañas in 1957 and Santa Rosa in the border canton of La Cruz in 1958.[8] With several actual or potential exile bases near their southern border, the Somozas began to establish a presence of their own in northern Costa Rica.

Their allies in this effort were Guanacastecan landlords, some of Nicaraguan nationality or descent, who were sympathetic to the Somozas' Nicaraguan Liberal Party and members of the family and administration of former Costa Rican president Picado, who were exiled in Nicaragua. During the 1944 exile attack on Nicaragua, Picado's government coordinated military operations with Somoza and even permitted Nicaraguan guardsmen to operate on Costa Rican territory.[9] Functionaries of the Picado government were also said to be involved in Somoza's cattle smuggling.[10] Through his second wife, who was from La Cruz, Picado had close ties to large landowners in the border area, including some who were later partners of both his son, Teodoro Picado Lara, and General Somoza's son, Anastasio Somoza Debayle—who graduated from West Point together in the class of 1946.[11] Picado's labor minister, Miguel Brenes Gutiérrez, who with his brothers had acquired an extensive section of Hacienda El Viejo (adjacent to El Tempisque), had remained in Costa Rica after the war and was one of the largest Costa Rican beef exporters in the late 1950s.[12] During his presidency, Picado himself had also been interested in purchasing at least one hacienda in Guanacaste and was privately accused by the owner of fomenting a squatter invasion when his offer was rejected.[13]

In 1962 Picado's son, a lawyer, brought together a group of investors that included his mother, his American wife, and his cousins René and Alvaro

Picado Esquivel and formed a corporation called *Compañía Agro-Pecuaria La Esperanza.* [14] Less than three months later, Picado Lara, who was registered as company director, stepped down and "in substitution of the resigner and for the rest of the legal period . . . the Director appointed [was] señor Anastasio Somoza Debayle, of age, once-married, General of the Army of Nicaragua, resident of Managua."[15]

The same day Somoza, with Picado Lara's assistance, was also named director of *Murciélago, Limitada,* a company founded the previous year to administer the hacienda of that name in La Cruz.[16] In a 1963 meeting at the hacienda, *Agro-Pecuaria La Esperanza* was made owner of half of *Murciélago, Limitada,* while Somoza retained the other half of the shares in his own name. Also in 1963, Picado Lara founded a company with Alfonso Salazar Céspedes, who in 1943 had been part of a group that briefly owned Murciélago. The purpose of this venture, however, was to exploit Hacienda El Viejo, which Salazar had recently acquired. Picado Lara contributed 250,000 *colones* (then approximately $37,000) in cash and Salazar supplied the land.[17] In 1964, five months after founding the company, a revision of the statutes that followed a board meeting in the border town of Peñas Blancas noted that Alfonso Salazar and Anastasio Somoza Debayle were "the only partners."[18] Picado once again had sold out to Somoza or had been representing him from the beginning.

With the purchase of Hacienda Santa Rosa in 1966 by a company owned by Luis Somoza Debayle, the Somozas controlled about 31,000 hectares (76,570 acres) in Guanacaste: approximately 10,500 (25,935 acres) in Santa Rosa; 16,431 (40,585 acres) in the adjacent Murciélago;[19] and 4,118 (10,171 acres) in El Viejo.[20] The strategically located Murciélago and Santa Rosa haciendas included nearly forty-five miles of coastline on the Santa Elena Peninsula and Descartes Point, which jutted into the Pacific just a few miles from Nicaragua. El Viejo was along the Tempisque River, the major inland waterway. All three properties had airstrips suitable for large planes. The Somozas were also reported in 1966 to be seeking control of the Pastora family's holdings along the border and were said to possess an additional 30,000 hectares (74,100 acres) spanning twelve miles of the frontier near Los Chiles in Alajuela Province.[21]

The Somozas' presence in Guanacaste aroused considerable opposition. The widely disliked Nicaraguan dictators were said to have created "a state within a state," infringing on national sovereignty. On at least two occasions Costa Rican newspapers charged that uniformed Nicaraguan national guards were brought into Murciélago and Santa Rosa to evict squatters.[22] On annual visits to El Viejo in the 1960s and 1970s, according to former hacienda employees, Anastasio Somoza was always accompanied by twenty or thirty Nicaraguan national guards and by armed men in civilian dress.[23] In 1968 Costa Rican fishermen in waters off Murciélago reported that they had been attacked from machine gun emplacements on shore.[24] Costa Rican authorities found undocumented workers, including a Nicaraguan National Guard lieutenant, laboring on Murciélago, as well as farm machinery that had apparently been smuggled into the country.[25] The Association of Wood Industries accused the Somozas of smuggling huge quantities of lumber into Nicaragua.[26]

It was also reported in 1971 that the Somozas were providing military training at Hacienda Murciélago to Cuban exiles who intended to invade Cuba. Then-President Figueres, while declaring that he did not believe the reports, lent them a degree of credence by stating that ships sighted off the coast of Murciélago "might have to do with the Cubans or contraband."[27]

Although these reports were never proven, the Somozas' ties to Cuban exiles were clearly close. When Teodoro Picado Lara withdrew as a director of Murciélago, Limitada, in 1977, he was replaced by a Cuban, Manuel Porro, who actually ran the farm.[28] At El Viejo, there were no press reports of Cuban exile military activities. Residents of the area, however, say that when "the General" was there he always received visits from the Cuban owners of the nearby Guinea sugar mill who were partners of Costa Rican ultrarightist Hubert Federspiel.[29] On one occasion described by residents a plane "from Cuba" landed on the hacienda runway. There it was painted, covered with branches, and the registration number (matrícula) was changed.[30]

These apparent violations of national sovereignty were all the more significant since many were near Santa Rosa, a site of great historical and symbolic importance to Costa Ricans. It was here that Costa Rican troops first clashed with U.S. pro-slavery filibusters led by William Walker in 1856 [see Reading 1.5] and where an anti-Figueres invasion force composed of supporters of former presidents Calderón and Picado was defeated in 1955.[31] In 1966 Luis Somoza, hoping to placate his Costa Rican opponents, offered to donate 25 hectares (62 acres) surrounding the main house of the hacienda to the Costa Rican state for a museum. Conflicts with squatters in 1966 and again in 1969–70, however, sustained anti-Somoza feeling in Costa Rica at a high pitch and led to the expropriation in 1970 of over 10,000 hectares (24,700 acres) of Santa Rosa which were to be used for a national park. The peasant families who had occupied the hacienda were relocated in agrarian reform projects elsewhere in Guanacaste.

The anti-Somoza mood in Costa Rica intensified in 1978 as opposition to the dictatorship within Nicaragua spread [see Readings 6.1, 6.5, 6.6 and 6.7]. Somoza anticipated expropriation of his holdings and quietly resigned as a director of El Viejo in August 1978.[32] Murciélago, however, had attracted more negative attention in Costa Rica and was of significantly greater strategic importance because of its coastline and proximity to the border.[33] Somoza was also in effect the only owner and thus found it more difficult to simply withdraw. In 1978 President Rodrigo Carazo signed an executive decree expropriating Murciélago and a similar legislative decree followed in June 1979.[34]

Even so, it took some time to gain control of the hacienda. As late as September, government guards charged that Murciélago was "totally full" of cattle belonging to Luis Gallegos, son of a former partner in Santa Rosa and owner of the nearby Hacienda Los Inocentes. The guards reported that Gallegos and his employees had keys to the Murciélago gates and were using a truck that had been expropriated from Somoza to travel around the hacienda. The guards claimed to be powerless to stop them. A report to the provincial ranchers' association also claimed that many of the cattle were contraband from the property of Manuel Centeno, which straddled the border.[35]

The last recorded meeting of *Murciélago, Limitada,* was held on July 12, 1979, in Managua, exactly one week before the triumph of the Sandinista revolution. Somoza's cousin, Alberto Bermúdez, stepped down as director in favor of a Nicaraguan resident of Miami, Renaldy Gutiérrez Solano, who had represented Somoza on the board since 1978.[36] Those present agreed to modify the bylaws so that "the corporation will be able to hold ordinary and special assemblies of shareholders outside of the territory of Costa Rica, indicating expressly for that effect the city of Asunción, Republic of Paraguay."[37]

When Somoza fled Nicaragua for Miami on July 17, 1979, it was unclear whether he intended to remain in the United States, whose government he considered to have "betrayed" him. The Murciélago statutes indicate that even before leaving Managua, Somoza had considered Alfredo Stroessner's Paraguay as a possible refuge. It was there that the deposed dictator was assassinated by Argentine guerrillas the following year.[38]

NOTES

1. Anastasio Somoza García became general of the National Guard in 1934 and was president during 1937–47 and 1951–56. He was assassinated in 1956 and his son Luis Somoza Debayle served out the remainder of his father's six-year term and an additional term that ended in 1963. Succeeded by supporter René Shick, Luis Somoza died of a heart attack in 1967. Anastasio Somoza Debayle was president-elect at the time of his brother's death and remained in power until the 1979 Sandinista victory.

2. William Krehm, *Democracies and Tyrannies of the Caribbean* (Westport, Conn.: Lawrence Hill, 1984). This work was widely read in Spanish after it was published in 1959. It did not appear in English until 1984.

3. Ibid., pp. 112–13.

4. *El Guanacaste* (Liberia, Costa Rica), 18 November 1940. Size information on El Tempisque is from an uncatalogued plan in the *Catastro Nacional,* the Costa Rican cadastral survey office.

5. Luis Brenes Gutiérrez's brother Miguel was minister of labor in the Picado government.

6. Eugenio Rodríguez, *De Calderón a Figueres* (San José: Editorial UNED, 1980), p. 101.

7. Jesús M. Blandón, *Entre Sandino y Fonseca* (Managua: FSLN, 1981), pp. 82ff., 141ff.

8. In 1933, when the departing U.S. Marines selected a commander of the new Nicaraguan National Guard, Pasos was one of two candidates passed over in favor of Anastasio Somoza García. He broke with Somoza and left Nicaragua in 1944, returned in 1947, was briefly in jail, and then went into exile. See Bernard Diederich, *Somoza and the Legacy of U.S. Involvement in Central America* (New York: E. P. Dutton, 1981), pp. 26–27; Anastasio Somoza, *Nicaragua Betrayed* (Boston: Western Islands Publishers, 1980), pp. 88–89.

9. Rodríguez, *De Calderón,* p. 101.

10. Diederich, *Somoza*, p. 28; Richard Millet, *Guardianes de la dinastía* (San José: EDUCA, 1979), p. 282. After 1948, Picado was a frequent contributor to the Somoza family newspaper, *Novedades*. See Ligia Estrada Molina, *Teodoro Picado Michalski: su aporte a la historiografía* (San José: Imprenta Nacional, 1967), pp. 203, 252.

11. Picado Lara was also accused by one of the most prominent figures in the Nicaraguan opposition of joining his former classmate Anastasio Somoza Debayle in the 1954 torture of anti-Somoza activist Jorge Rivas Montes, who was reportedly hung by his testicles. See Pedro Joaquín Chamorro, *Estirpe sangrienta: Los Somozas* (Buenos Aires: Editorial Triángulo, 1959), pp. 51, 87.

12. It was Miguel Brenes's brother Luis who was involved in the 1940 effort to sell the elder Somoza the Hacienda Tempisque.

13. Author's interview, 1981. Calderón, who had virtually no property upon assuming the presidency in 1940, left office in 1944 owning a large cattle ranch in the northwestern part of Costa Rica, as well as other properties in the central part of the country. See Krehm, *Democracies and Tyrannies*, p. 134.

14. Information on this company is from the records of the San José *Registro Público, Sección Mercantil* (hereafter *RP SM*), number 8101. *Registro* citations followed by a single number refer to microfiche records of individual companies. Other citations are to bound volumes and refer to *tomo* (volume), *folio* (page), *asiento* (entry), and year.

15. RP SM, T52, F291, A186, 1962.

16. RP SM, T52, F290, A185.

17. RP SM, T56, F137, A102.

18. RP SM, T56, F541, A422.

19. *Catastro Nacional* (hereafter CN) G1-2-1-43, 1952. Catastro plans are cited according to province, canton, district, farm number, and year. This total of 31,049 hectares is close to Diederich's (p. 76) estimate that the Somozas controlled 223,000 acres (30,283 hectares) in Costa Rica in 1966.

20. CN G5-1-1-557, 1975.

21. *La República,* 25 April 1966. See also Julio Suñol, *Insurrección en Nicaragua: la historia no contada* (San José: Editorial Costa Rica, 1981), p. 59.

22. *La República,* 25 April 1966; *Libertad,* 27 January 1973.

23. Field interviews, 1982. Former employees at El Viejo reported that "the General" liked to rest on the porch of the hacienda house in a hammock embroidered with the initials AS. Somoza's partner Alfonso Salazar had the same initials and also used the hammock.

24. *La Prensa Libre,* 26 March 1968; *Libertad,* 30 March 1968.

25. *La República,* 26 April 1966.

26. *La Prensa Libre,* 25 April 1966.

27. *La Nación,* 16 January 1971. In Nicaragua, the Somozas provided bases for Cuban exiles from the time prior to the 1961 Bay of Pigs invasion until 1975. See William M. LeoGrande, "Cuba and Nicaragua: From the Somozas to the Sandinistas," in *The New Cuban Presence in the Caribbean,* ed. Barry B. Levine (Boulder, Colo.: Westview, 1983), p. 45.

28. RP SM, T184, F532, A652.

29. *Libertad,* 17 August 1963; Mayra Achío Tacsan and Ana Cecilia Escalante Herrera, "Los grandes empresarios azucareros: Costa Rica 1960–1978," *Cuadernos Centroamericanos de Ciencias Sociales,* no. 9 (1981): 74–75; RP SM, 7687, 1963.

30. Field interviews, 1982.

31. Miguel Acuña, *El 55* (San José: Librería Lehmann, 1977).

32. RP SM, T201, F77, A68.

33. Ironically, recognition of this area's strategic importance later led to its use for training Costa Rican civil guards and for a secret *contra* air base [see Readings 7.11, 7.13, and 7.14].

34. *La Gaceta Oficial,* 12 June 1979.

35. Cámara de Ganaderos de Guanacaste, Actas (meeting minutes), Liberia, Costa Rica, vol. 9, p. 21.

36. Gutiérrez was a key figure in the Monrovia-based Bavaria Land Development Company which in March 1980 acquired El Viejo from Somoza-partner Alfonso Salazar (RP SM, T215, F335, A323; T214, F539, A481). This maneuver may have been intended to obscure the fallen dictator's continuing control of the property.

37. RP SM, T212, F507, A474.

38. On the assassination of Somoza, see Angel Luis de la Calle, "Yo maté a Somoza: entrevista con Gorriarán Merlo," *El País Semanal* (Madrid) 8, no. 331, 2a época (August 14, 1983): 10–17.

6.3 Springing Sandinista Prisoners in Costa Rica*

By Plutarco Hernández

Plutarco Hernández is a Costa Rican who fought alongside the Sandinistas and later became disillusioned with the revolution. A leftist from his youth, he was influenced in the 1950s by anti-Batista Cuban exiles in Costa Rica and later studied at Moscow's Patrice Lumumba University. He joined the Sandinistas in the mid-1960s. Later, accused of ultraleftism, he broke with them within weeks of the revolution's triumph. This break seems to have been motivated by ideological differences and a long-standing personal conflict with Humberto Ortega, now Nicaragua's defense minister and brother of President Daniel Ortega. Hernández later declared that he remained "an independent and critical Marxist-Leninist" who believed that socialism must be preceded by social democracy in all of Central America. Revolution, he said, "is not made by decree."

This reading describes a 1969 attempt to spring from a Costa Rican jail Sandinista leader Carlos Fonseca (who was killed in combat in Nicaragua in 1976). Like other episodes of political violence in Costa Rica (see Reading 7.6), the operation had tragicomic aspects. There were several casualties, and the guerrillas ended up in jail with Fonseca. The bloodshed outraged Costa Ricans; even the Costa Rican Communists termed it a maneuver to sabotage their efforts to take part in elections. Fonseca, Hernández, and the others finally won their freedom when Sandinista commandos hijacked a plane carrying the president of United Fruit and three other company executives. Hernández would be recaptured years later, but pardoned after two months by President Rodrigo Carazo.

LET'S say our situation was not very enviable. Our recent assault on the bank in La Uruca carried out by a Sandinista cell had turned out badly and the San

*Excerpted from *El FSLN por dentro: relatos de un combatiente* (San José: Trejos Hermanos, 1982), pp. 40–44.

José police were really hunting down the FSLN [Sandinista National Liberation Front]. As a result, *compañero* Carlos Fonseca was caught, surprised in the house of a German friend of Erick Ardón's where he was hiding at the time.[1] He was immediately held responsible for the La Uruca holdup, and moved to the prison at Alajuela.

The Sandinista *compañeros* devoted themselves to devising a plan to rescue their highest leader. On my return from Managua I became totally involved in planning and eventually carrying out the rescue of Carlos Fonseca. I got to work with *compañeros* like Julián Roque, Rufo Marín, Germán Pomares, Antonio Rodríguez Mairena "El Corso," and others. And therein lies another story. . . .

The rescue operation took place in the early morning of December 23, 1969. The group that carried it out was divided into two squads. The first was composed of *compañeros* Humberto Ortega, Julián Roque, Rodríguez Mairena, Rufo Marín, and myself. Néstor Carvajal, Tito, *compañero* "Gonzalo," and Germán Pomares made up the second group.[2] The action was conceived in terms of a commando-style attack against the Alajuela prison and the idea was very simple. We would enter the prison on a clever pretext, rapidly subdue the guards, rescue *compañero* Fonseca, and disappear without leaving a trace.

In order to make sure that the guards would open the door for us without suspecting our real motive for being there, Rodríguez Mairena ("El Corso") and I pretended we wanted to hand over a thief (Rufo Marín) whom we ourselves had captured in a house in El Carmen, a neighborhood in Alajuela. The guard suspected nothing unusual. He consulted with his immediate superior and opened the door for us. This accomplished, we immediately released Rufo, who carried a .45 pistol, at the same time as Humberto Ortega rushed in armed with a machine gun. The guards, nine in all, were completely taken by surprise. Five of them were in the same waiting room while the rest were dispersed among the passageways of the jail.

According to the rescue plan, when our two vehicles approached the prison, *compañero* Roy Pineda, pretending to be drunk, would begin to sing a song on the sidewalk outside. This would be the signal for Carlos to ask permission to go to the bathroom so that he could be out of his cell when the rescue operation began. Up to this point everything went as planned.

The guards' surprise didn't last for long. Recovering from their initial shock, they took out their weapons and began to fire. And a real battle began, one that lasted some eight or ten minutes—long, interminable minutes that tore the whole neighborhood out of the peace and quiet typical of that time of night, 1:00 A.M.

That's when our plans started to come apart. I was supposed to return immediately to the vehicle I was driving, which had carried the first squad, keep the windows open and the motor running, and be ready to escape with the *compañeros* once the rescue had been performed. The second vehicle was to stay parked a few meters behind; its occupants were to lend support to the *compañeros* who had already entered the prison. But when the firing began the *compañeros* got confused and decided to make their getaway ahead of time. Only *compañero* Germán Pomares got out of the second vehicle and threw himself into the action. The premature departure of the second car further complicated the situation. This was the car that Carlos was supposed to escape in. So Carlos had to get into my car, which I had rented eight days before in the Hotel Presidente, beginning his escape in the wrong vehicle and headed in a different direction than we had planned. *Compañero* Humberto was seriously wounded in the chest and forearm. I practically had to drag him into the car while Pomares and Rufo Marín stayed inside the jail covering our escape. *Compañeros* Julián Roque and El Corso did the same. In the end Marín was left lying in the park in Alajuela, wounded in the exchange, while Pomares escaped in the car stolen from the Ministry of Agriculture and Livestock, and El Corso and Julián Roque managed to take refuge in safe houses in Alajuela.

Meanwhile, we sped toward the site planned for the transfer, an old bridge about five kilometers from Alajuela on the old highway, where Carlos was supposed to get into another, safer, vehicle. We were very surprised when we arrived at the bridge and didn't find, or didn't see, the transfer vehicle. Making a quick decision, we headed toward the capital, passing through Heredia where five police patrol cars tried to intercept us by blocking the way. We managed to get through under a rain of gunfire and the terrible wail of the sirens. We continued toward Llorente, where we ran into a huge roadblock of some fifteen patrol cars scattered along and across the road. I consulted with Carlos. We had a few Molotov cocktails and Humberto's submachine gun in the car. Humberto was virtually at death's door. Carlos was against taking any action that involved running the barricade and risking all our lives. He was very concerned about the condition of our *compañero*. So we decided to stop the car. I signaled with the lights, and we opened the doors and came out with our arms up over our heads.

We were put into different patrol cars and taken straight to San José, not without first seriously warning the Civil Guard that *compañero* Humberto urgently needed to be taken to a hospital. Once in the capital we were put in the Third Company's lockup, in very tiny cells, just one by two meters. They handcuffed our hands and feet. It was about four in the morning. Two hours later they took us away to begin interrogations. They gave us the paraffin test. They found traces of powder on my hands even though I hadn't carried any weapons. What happened was that during the flight from the prison, since Humberto was badly wounded and bleeding, I had picked up his submachine gun and one of his ammo clips. When the interrogations, intense and violent, were concluded, they took us back to the lockup, convinced we would not tell them anything about the identity of the other participants. We spent that whole day without eating. All we had was a bit of water they gave us in the morning. They didn't let us go to the bathroom, so we had to use the cell. That was unbearable. We were kept under those conditions until December 27, when we were transferred to the Central Penitentiary.

That same day Rufo Marín was also transferred after being captured, bleeding, in the park in Alajuela and later secluded in the San Juan de Dios Hospital. The next day they transferred Humberto from the same hospital to the penitentiary. So on December 28 we were all reunited, the newly captured with the recaptured *compañero* Fonseca.

NOTES

1. Sergio Erick Ardón was later a founder and congressional deputy of the Revolutionary People's Movement (MRP), which became the Movement for a New Republic in the early 1980s [see Reading 7.7].

2. Germán Pomares was an FSLN fighter killed in the war to overthrow Somoza. Rufo Marín is an FSLN fighter's nom de guerre; it was the name of Augusto César Sandino's second-in-command during the 1927 attack on the U.S. Marine garrison at Ocotal.

6.4 A Rebel in the Wings: Edén Pastora in 1976*

BY STEPHEN SCHMIDT

Around 1975, an unknown Nicaraguan who called himself "Pedro" settled in a remote Costa Rican fishing village. In August 1978, the world would come to know "Pedro" as Edén Pastora. He was the "Commander Zero" who led the seizure of the Nicaraguan National Palace, an audacious move that invigorated the flagging Sandinista movement. During the next year, as the revolution against dictator Anastasio Somoza gained strength, Pastora was a key commander on the southern front. After the 1979 victory over Somoza, he served as deputy defense minister and head of the Sandinista militia, but later broke with the revolution. Costa Rica again became his base, as he tried to build an anti-Sandinista force. His relations with the CIA and more conservative contra *rebel groups were always strained, and although Costa Ricans—and their press—found Pastora appealing, his movement failed to grow and he finally laid down his arms in 1986.*

In this 1976 article, Tico Times *reporter Stephen Schmidt recounts his meeting with "Pedro." Schmidt later became the central figure in a dispute with the Costa Rican Professional Journalists Association* (Colegio de Periodistas) *over the licensing of journalists. He now edits a newsletter for the Center for Science in the Public Interest in Washington.*

"TO fight, you've got to give up your tranquility, your liberty, your way of life, and sometimes your life itself."

The man speaking is not a typical resident of this sleepy little town of 250,

*Stephen Schmidt, "A Home for a Rebel," *Tico Times,* 9 April 1976.

for it is hard to imagine anything but utter contentment here at the mouth of the San Juan River.

Pedro—which is not his real name—is a guerrilla. He's Nicaraguan and a member of the outlawed *Frente Sandinista.* Pedro fled Nicaragua a little over a year ago, and now finds himself in Barra [de Colorado, a northern village].

Sprawling across a bench on the porch of the town's only cantina, a small group of men takes shelter against the burning sun. It's Sunday, and the men drink beer, and talk of fishing, sharks, and the weather. Pedro talks of revolution.

"It's inevitable, Somoza will fall within the next four or five years," says the short, stocky forty-year-old. Dressed in a baseball cap, T-shirt, shorts, and sneakers, the avid admirer of Fidel Castro says he began his revolutionary activities in 1957, "when I realized that crime, corruption, and prostitution were overrunning my country."

By the time Pedro took up the revolutionary banner, Augusto César Sandino—the man who has become a modern legend throughout Latin America—had been long dead. But his story still lives in the hearts of men like Pedro.

Born in 1893, Sandino was a farmer and mining engineer who took part in the 1926 liberal revolution against Adolfo Díaz and Emiliano Chamorro. He later broke with the liberal leadership over the continued presence of U.S. Marines in Nicaragua. The U.S. expeditionary force first came into Nicaragua in 1912, and four years later, paid $3 million for an option in perpetuity on building a canal across the isthmus.

Sandino continued his guerrilla fighting against U.S. influence until 1933, when the marines were brought home. Never captured, but reconciled after the withdrawal, Sandino headed a farm cooperative until he was suddenly seized and executed in 1934.

"Sandino's death was masterminded and paid for by the U.S. government, and everybody recognizes it," says Pedro with a faint smile. "The U.S. people are so warm and sincere, I don't understand why their leaders always support and maintain repressive regimes."

When Pedro "became politically conscious" in 1957, he took to the hills of southern Nicaragua "to fight, organize, and conspire." He doesn't like to give specifics of his activities, because that might endanger comrades still battling the government of General Anastasio Somoza. He says he has been arrested three times, but was released each time through a general amnesty.

He is not being sought by the Nicaraguan courts, "because we have no real courts there. Justice is carried out by that bastard dictator. He'd like to get me back, but you can be sure I'll never enter a courtroom after he gets his hands on me. I'll end up at the bottom of some river," Pedro says bitterly.

When things got too hot for him in 1974, Pedro came over the border with his wife and three children. In that short time, he has become one of Barra's most prosperous citizens.

He says he works "twenty-five hours a day," and that his year has been so intense, it seems like ten. He has become a successful shark fisherman, and operates Barra's largest electric generator (thirty-seven kilowatts), for which he charges a monthly fee of five *colones* per light bulb.

At first, his house was constantly buzzed by Nicaraguan warplanes, "which were violating Costa Rican air space." But Pedro went running into town one morning when a Nicaraguan delegation was just arriving for some official business.

"I'm going to get me a bazooka and shoot that damn plane down the next time it flies over my house," he said loud enough for the suddenly nervous delegation to hear. "They ran home quicker than you can imagine, and the plane hasn't been back since," he says with a hearty laugh.

Pedro says he is not afraid of an attempt to kidnap him and take him back to Nicaragua—just twelve miles north of Barra.

"I feel safer here than in San José," he says. "In San José I could disappear for three or four days without anybody missing me, but here everybody knows me, and I'm sure they would protect me."

Now that Pedro is so well established in Barra, he is thinking of making his life here, even though he is convinced Somoza "can't last five more years."

According to the guerrilla, four conditions have come together for the first time, and these spell Somoza's downfall.

"You've got the political, military Sandinista group, which has never been stronger; the clergy, which has turned against him for the first time; the United States, which is beginning to realize that it can't maintain him forever; and the fact that Somoza's economic power is plunging," Pedro maintains.

But even if and when Somoza goes, Pedro will stay. "I'm forty years old and have a wife and children to think about," he says. "It's not because I'm tired, but the circumstances are such that I feel I should be here."

Though he is no longer an active member of the Sandinistas, "my heart and my soul are across the border with my people, who are fighting the most noble fight—for their freedom."

6.5 Aiding the Muchachos. An Interview with María Kautz de Coronel

BY JULIO SUÑOL

María Kautz de Coronel is, in the words of journalist Julio Suñol, "a grand old woman of the Sandinista struggle." A Nicaraguan of German ancestry and the wife of José Coronel Urtecho, a celebrated poet, she has lived near Los Chiles, a small Costa Rican border town, for over thirty years. Her ranch, known as Las Brisas, was a center of

*Excerpted from Julio Suñol, *Insurrección en Nicaragua: La historia no contada* (San José: Editorial Costa Rica, 1981), pp. 55–59.

Sandinista activity during 1977–79, the final years of struggle against the Somoza dictatorship. In this interview with Suñol, she describes how her family initially befriended and then turned against the Somozas and how she assisted the Sandinista guerrillas who attacked the National Guard border station at San Carlos in October 1977. Two of her sons later remained part of the Sandinista government, while two grew disillusioned and left.

THE Las Brisas ranch is in Costa Rican territory, some five kilometers [three miles] from the San Juan River in Nicaragua. One can walk just a kilometer on ranch property and then get in a boat up the Río Medio Queso, which runs into the Río San Juan and then into Lake Nicaragua at the Nicaraguan town of San Carlos. The *tercerista* faction of the Sandinista rebels was in charge of the attack on the San Carlos fort in October 1977.[1] This would be another of the apparent FSLN defeats that were to be transformed into triumphs by later events. Soon the battle against *somocismo* would be growing rapidly.

Doña María Kautz de Coronel—cattle rancher, mechanic, successful farmer, carpenter, tractor driver, and a woman who knows how to use firearms—struggled tirelessly against Somoza at the age of seventy-three. Doña María has a wide, beautiful, and honest smile, and offers her important historical testimony with pride.

MKDEC: The boys met at our hacienda. Most of those who had started the movement on this side of the border were present. Edén Pastora, my son Carlos Coronel, my nephew Richard Lugo Kautz (now a commander). . . . They would all show up out of nowhere, then go back to San José, and come back here again and that went on for about a month. Suddenly they began to show up carrying packages they said were no big deal, but they were arms. How they got hold of their weapons, I don't know. But they'd show up, come in the house, go up to the attic of the hacienda, and leave the stuff there for safekeeping, with boxes of bullets and everything. These sorts of preparations went on for about six months. Right in the middle of it all we were notified that the Organization of American States (OAS) was coming to visit, because people were already saying a lot of things about Costa Rica, about how it was helping bring life to the Sandinista movement. The OAS people were going to arrive and my sons, who were quite worried about this, began to remove the weapons in the middle of the night, so they wouldn't be found in our house. They worked like slaves, two days of terribly difficult work. But when the gentlemen from the OAS arrived, they came inside and questioned the ranch hands. Everyone said they didn't know anything and so these gentlemen simply left and reported they had found nothing.

I calculate there were more than five hundred huge rifles, and then there were plenty of cartons of bullets, and some little rifles, I don't know what they were called. Our ranch hands were in complete solidarity with the Sandinistas: they knew nothing and they knew everything. They became very cross when they were questioned, because all of them were the sons of our former servants, my father's staff, and they had lived on the border for many years.

The attack was directed by my son Carlos Coronel, Marvin [José Valdivia], Richard Lugo, Daniel and Humberto Ortega, and others I can't recall.

JS: And your husband, the famous poet José Coronel Urtecho, what was he doing while all this was going on?

MKDEC: Nothing, he didn't even notice, because he spent his life writing. Whenever he heard a ruckus, he'd just ask, "What's going on?" His sons would call back, "Nothing."

When this boy Marvin was wounded, when the boys left San Carlos—defeated, because the truth is their attack was strongly repelled—they took our boat, the *Coronel Kautz,* and retreated very quickly with the plan of hiding out on the Río Medio Queso, crossing the border, and getting back to Las Brisas. But before they got to Las Brisas, the boat broke down. So they came back on foot along the edge of the plain, which was flooded by the river. My son Luis was carrying Marvin, who was badly wounded, on his shoulder. He got him to the airport, put him on an express plane, and the man is still alive. He was one of the commanders, the chief of the militia.

JS: And what did you do personally for the war against Somoza?

MKDEC: I helped with whatever I was asked to do. I went out with my car to take arms to Los Chiles, to bring people food. All that time I went around helping, and playing dumb. Because right there in Los Chiles was a very good Costa Rican commander, very intelligent, friendly, a supporter of the war. I told him I knew nothing and I knew everything. I don't remember his name, but he was a magnificent person. It's a shame my memory is so bad, the truth is that I'm already quite old enough, seventy-three years old, and a load of years as big as mine isn't such a cinch to carry around.

The daily aggression of the Nicaraguan National Guard's planes against Costa Rican territory had already gone right on above me. Even over Los Chiles, especially the town of Los Chiles, and from there they came right through the middle of the Medio Queso plain and flew over the houses, my house. They didn't fly right overhead because they were afraid, since I was prepared to give them a scare. And, of course, I had what it took to do that.

And worst of all was the helicopter of "the Kid," *"el Chigüín"* [Anastasio Somoza Portocarrero, son of the Nicaraguan dictator]. Every day he would show up between one and three in the afternoon—el Chigüín in person in his own helicopter—a beautiful machine, absolutely stunning—and he came in low across the plain and made low circles out there in front. They never came right over the top of the house.

They never bombed us, absolutely not. They flew and flew and they never found anyone, or saw anything. But they were always very careful with us. El Chigüín knew very well that Las Brisas was a center of Sandinista activity. But he didn't attack Las Brisas, because he knew that if he did, he would be in big trouble since it was in Costa Rican territory. That was why he didn't attack us, and because he knew us personally. We actually had been friendly with his grandfather, the first Somoza, General Anastasio Somoza García, nicknamed Tacho. We knew his son Tachito [Anastasio Somoza Debayle] when he was a little kid. I had even given him a little jaguar I'd caught. I was hunting and killed the jaguar cub's mother, but I caught the cub alive and I gave it to Tachito as a present when he was fifteen years old. Later he took me to see the jaguar, which had become really beautiful. This was more than forty years ago. We were quite friendly with Tacho, the first Somoza. Later José and I realized that this man was a real problem for Nicaragua, especially his sons. Tachito is a monster.

JS: How far is it from Las Brisas to San Carlos?

MKDEC: Well, it depends on which launch you take. If you take a fast one, like they have today, it takes an hour and a half or two hours. You have to cross the border on the Río Medio Queso, a tributary of the San Juan River, which is where our ranch is. The river is part Costa Rican and part Nicaraguan. Just like the Río Frío, which comes out in front of San Carlos, the Medio Queso goes toward Los Chiles and crosses the border, in the famous spot where Somoza's forces attacked the then-minister of security of Costa Rica Mario Charpentier [in October 1977, see introduction to this chapter]. . . .

JS: Was taking San Carlos strategically important for the Sandinista guerrillas?

MKDEC: Of course, in the sense that it would permit them to control the border zone. Also Somoza owned a very large ranch there, with runways, soldiers, and five hundred or a thousand national guards based on his private land. He couldn't keep them all in San Carlos, because it was very small. That was where el Chigüín trained the members of the Basic Infantry Training School [EEBI]. There was an enormous concentration camp there, basic infantry, planes, boats. El Chigüín had everything at his disposal.

JS: Is San Carlos a poor town?

MKDEC: It's not poor. There has always been rubber, beans, rice, they have everything. It's ugly, but it isn't poor. The Somoza ranch alone produced six thousand hectares [about 14,800 acres] of rice. All of that was expropriated, now it belongs to the state. The zone is large and there are great expectations for it in the future, because it has everything, even cattle. Now they're developing sugarcane plantations. Everything grows in that part of the Atlantic zone.

JS: How many Sandinistas set out to capture San Carlos?

MKDEC: Two hundred to two hundred fifty, I think. Since it was done by boat, it was very difficult to get them there. The planned capture of San Carlos was supposed to be coordinated with other attacks. But that part failed for reasons

I simply don't know. It was to be part of a series of attacks that never took place and San Carlos was isolated. But in reality San Carlos became the first shot that made people understand the problem. Two or three months later the Sandinistas began to gather support and they kept on amassing support until they achieved total victory.

NOTE

1. In 1975 disagreements within the Sandinista Front over the best strategy for toppling Somoza led to a division into three factions: the Prolonged Popular War group, which concentrated its efforts in rural northern Nicaragua; the Proletarian group, which argued that urban workers were the key constituency to organize; and the "third" or *tercerista* group, that attempted to build a multiclass coalition and wide international support for the anti-Somoza movement. The *terceristas* operated mainly in southern Nicaragua, near the Costa Rican border. By 1978–79, as the anti-Somoza movement grew, the rift in the FSLN was resolved with two proclamations of unity by representatives of the erstwhile factions.—EDS.

6.6 *Costa Rica Supporting Sandinistas**

BY WARREN HOGE

Perhaps the worst-kept secret of the 1979 Nicaraguan revolution was the extent of Costa Rican involvement in the southern front. Costa Ricans offered strong support to the Sandinistas, who could virtually do as they pleased in northern Costa Rica, particularly in Guanacaste Province. As the interview with María Kautz de Coronel indicates (Reading 6.5), the rebels had training camps and arms caches in the north. This reading gives an overview of Costa Rican involvement—and hints of the arms scandal to come (see Reading 6.8).

Warren Hoge, formerly Rio de Janeiro bureau chief of the New York Times, *also reported on Central America in the late 1970s and early 1980s. He later became the* Times's *foreign editor and is currently an assistant managing editor of the newspaper.*

COSTA RICA, a country with no army of its own, is actively aiding the Sandinista rebels in neighboring Nicaragua while just as actively seeking to hide its involvement.

The government of President Rodrigo Carazo Odio has severed relations with the government of President Anastasio Somoza Debayle in Managua and has expropriated a farm and airstrip the dictator owned in Costa Rica. It is concerned at the same time that its support of the rebels not become public enough to goad General Somoza into taking action in reprisal.

The Nicaraguan Provisional Government of National Reconstruction,

**New York Times, 29 June 1979.

named three weeks ago by the Sandinistas, is based here [San José] in a comfortable parquet-floored house in an upper-class section of the capital. It is distinguishable from other residences in the area only by the number of autos with blue-and-white Nicaraguan license plates parked in its driveway.

Thousands of middle- and upper-middle-class Costa Ricans here and in towns to the north have set aside rooms for guerrillas on rest and recuperation between periods on the front lines in Nicaragua.

CLANDESTINE TRAINING CAMPS

Many of the rebels have received their training in clandestine training camps, reportedly in the northern province of Guanacaste, and Costa Rica has provided the rebels with access to Nicaragua from the south. Two Costa Ricans have served on . . . the Sandinist military coordination arm. The rebels' best-known commander, Edén Pastora, is a naturalized Costa Rican who operated a power plant in the Atlantic port of Barra del Colorado before returning to fight in his native country.

Mauricio Figueres, seventeen-year-old son of former president José Figueres of Costa Rica, is fighting with the guerrillas in a continuation of what has become something of a vendetta between the Figueres and Somoza families.

Costa Rica, with a population of 2.2 million, has the highest per capita income level in Central America and a history of stable democratic government. There are some who complain about the large numbers of Nicaraguans here—the streets of downtown San José are filled with Nicaraguan refugees—partly out of concern that they will bring poverty to a country that has little of it and partly out of bias against Indians. Costa Rica's population is largely of European descent.

Nonetheless, the overwhelming majority of Costa Ricans are passionately in the rebels' corner and support their government's assistance to them. The foundation for this sentiment is hatred of General Somoza, in comments about whom the words "devil" and "monster" often figure.

The government denied accounts by witnesses that Costa Rican civil guards patrolling the border fired yesterday on troops they believed to be Nicaraguan government soldiers. The government said that the guards fired into the air to alert guerrillas to the presence of Somoza troops on Costa Rican soil.

Earlier this week Costa Rica was at pains to dissociate itself from the activities of two Costa Rican pilots captured Sunday on a beach in El Salvador where their C-47 transport, which had taken off from Juan Santamaría Airport here loaded with arms and ammunition, had landed for lack of fuel.

6.7 The Costa Rican Role in the Sandinista Victory*

BY MITCHELL A. SELIGSON AND WILLIAM J. CARROLL III

The Costa Rican government's support of the Sandinistas in 1978–79 was clearly a factor in the downfall of the Somoza dynasty. Mitchell A. Seligson and William J. Carroll III argue in this reading that Costa Ricans were motivated not only by antipathy toward the dictatorship but by long-standing hostility toward their northern neighbor. The antagonism can be traced back to the early years of independence. As early as 1824, Nicaragua and Costa Rica were in conflict over the Nicaraguan province of Nicoya, which Costa Rica annexed. In the mid-nineteenth century, Costa Rica fought Nicaraguan troops loyal to the freebooter William Walker (see Reading 1.5) and nearly went to war with Nicaragua over rights to the San Juan River, a dispute settled by the Jerez-Cañas Treaty. More recently, the first Somoza to rule Nicaragua, Anastasio Somoza García, and Costa Rican statesman José Figueres hated each other and supported various efforts to topple one another in the 1940s and 1950s (see Reading 6.1).

Mitchell Seligson, also the author of Reading 4.11, is director of the Latin American Studies Center at the University of Pittsburgh. William Carroll III holds a doctorate in political science from the University of Arizona.

THE first indications of Costa Rican support for the Sandinistas came during Augusto C. Sandino's struggle against the U.S. Marines' occupation of Nicaragua. During this period, Costa Rica frequently served as a jumping-off point for armed incursions northward. The failure of the Costa Rican government to prevent such activity was attributed to problems of effectively patrolling the difficult terrain along its northern border. No doubt there is an element of truth to this claim, but in the context of the historically strained relations between the two countries, it is difficult to accept it as the complete explanation. . . . By the late 1960s, clashes between the Nicaraguan National Guard and Sandinista units became frequent along the Costa Rican border. Civilians in the border region often claimed that the Nicaraguans were being overly zealous and were illegally crossing the border into Costa Rica. Then Nicaragua began harassing truckers crossing the Nicaraguan–Costa Rican border, and tension mounted. . . . Then in October 1977, after a lull of almost a year following the combat deaths of two of its principal leaders, the FSLN went on

---

*Excerpted from Mitchell A. Seligson and William J. Carroll III, "The Costa Rican Role in the Sandinista Victory," in *Nicaragua in Revolution,* ed. Thomas W. Walker (New York: Praeger, 1982), pp. 332–36.

the offensive, attacking the National Guard barracks in the remote San Juan River town of San Carlos, near the Costa Rican frontier [see Reading 6.5]. National Guard reinforcements already in the area were able to force the Sandinistas to retreat across the border, but not before a much more serious incident took place. Claiming "hot pursuit," the Nicaraguan air force strafed three Costa Rican boats inside the latter's national territory. Aboard one of the boats was Costa Rican security minister Mario Charpentier, accompanied by a group of journalists. The hostile act immediately received wide media coverage and led to a vigorous protest by Costa Rica, which further strained the worsening relations between the two countries.

COSTA RICAN POLICY TOWARD THE INSURRECTION: 1977–1979

Following the San Carlos raid, the Costa Rican government granted asylum to eleven members of the FSLN who had participated in the operation and had escaped to Costa Rica. While such a humanitarian gesture on the part of Costa Rica was not unprecedented, the action brought immediate charges from Nicaragua that its southern neighbor was providing sanctuary for Sandinista guerrillas. The Somoza newspaper, *Novedades,* claimed that the invasion of San Carlos occurred with the knowledge and acquiescence of the Costa Rican authorities. The situation failed to improve when a meeting of Central American heads of state in Guatemala City, called on October 31 to discuss the border conflict and other topics, was conspicuously not attended by Costa Rica's president Daniel Oduber.

As Oduber's term in office drew to a close in May 1978, the FSLN guerrillas began to have doubts about the availability of Costa Rica as a safe haven under his successor, Rodrigo Carazo Odio. As a candidate for office, the firm anti-Communist Carazo had pledged to recall the Costa Rican ambassador to Moscow. Later, as president-elect, it was reported that he promised the Nicaraguan foreign minister that he would take action against those FSLN elements operating in Costa Rica. Once in office, however, Carazo seemed to have a change of mind, granting asylum to a high-ranking FSLN leader in June 1978. He may have begun to have second thoughts, though, when Somoza responded to this action by sending reinforcements to the Costa Rican border in a show of strength.

As the year wore on, the strategic importance of Costa Rica as a nearby sanctuary for continuing the struggle against Somoza was further underscored by the return of influential Nicaraguans who had been exiled there. *Los Doce,* a group of prominent and well-respected intellectuals and professionals, arrived in Managua from San José in July, having been allowed back by Somoza who hoped "to improve his image in the United States." However, matters did not improve for Somoza since the group immediately called for an antigovernmental front to include the Sandinista guerrillas, causing popular outbreaks of violence in major cities. But perhaps the most significant exile to return was Edén Pastora Gómez, who as *"Comandante* Zero" led a force of twenty-five guerrillas in attacking and holding the Nicaraguan National Palace for forty-eight hours in late August [see Reading 6.4]. Costa Rica acted at this time in a somewhat ambiguous role as it offered to have its ambassador in Managua mediate between Somoza and the guerrillas, while publicly announcing that Pastora Gómez would be free to return to Costa Rica whenever he wished.

Costa Rica's concern that a total Sandinista victory in Nicaragua could have a decidedly destabilizing effect on its welfare, and that instability along the northern border would grow, resulted in offers from Costa Rica in September 1978 to mediate the Nicaraguan crisis. This diplomatic effort had little chance to unfold, however, as the gesture was withdrawn by mid-month following new violations of Costa Rican territory by Nicaraguan aircraft in "hot pursuit" of suspected guerrillas. The fact that Somoza denied these violations to the news media did not prevent Costa Rica from calling for an OAS team to investigate its complaint. Concurrently, as the mood in Costa Rica swung away from efforts at mediation, the opinion that Somoza must go at any cost became more prevalent. This increased hostility is illustrated by the official Costa Rican decision at the time to expropriate a 15,000-hectare Somoza estate in Guanacaste, and by ex-president Figueres's call for arms to be shipped to the Sandinistas.

Costa Rican fears of a Communist takeover in Nicaragua again surfaced in November 1978. Official policy toward the guerrillas became at best ambivalent as the government in San José initiated cleanup operations to rid the northern border areas of the FSLN. . . . The change in policy by San José was seen to damage the chances of the FSLN unleashing a planned new offensive against Somoza from the Guanacaste region. Yet during this same period, Costa Rica's official line regarding the guerrillas became even more ambiguous as Costa Rica broke off diplomatic relations with Nicaragua in response to a serious armed conflict between Costa Rican and Somoza forces at the border.

As the year 1978 waned, the final offensive hinted at by the FSLN still failed to materialize. There is sufficient information to suggest that this inaction was due in large part to the intermittent cleanup operations Costa Rica continued to conduct in the border regions. The policy at this time, however, may not have been entirely of Costa Rica's own choosing. On December 26, angered by increased cross-border attacks, Somoza closed the frontier with Costa Rica, threatening to invade the country unless the government in San José stepped up its anti-Sandinista operations. This action precipitated a Costa Rican call to the OAS asking for protection against Nicaraguan invasion. It also led to serious discussions in San José as to whether or not the country should build up its armed forces. Its realization that the Civil Guard was no match for an armed attack begs the question of how the Carazo administration realistically expected these same forces to contain or eradicate an ever-growing and more professionally organized guerrilla force. . . .

The ambivalent nature of Costa Rican priorities concerning the Somoza crisis continued on into 1979. Early in the year, "Operación Jaque Mate," aimed at ridding the frontier environs of the FSLN, was launched by San José. But like those that preceded it, the action lacked serious content and was largely ineffective and symbolic. For Costa Rica, the real concern was still the disruption that the continued presence of Somoza brought to the entire region. Short of the unlikely event that mediation would force the dictator out, the Carazo administration realistically concluded that the FSLN was the only viable means of terminating the dynasty.

By never effectively eliminating the Sandinista presence along the border with Nicaragua, whether by design or inability, Costa Rica did provide a valuable asset to the guerrillas in the final takeover of the country. Because he could never be certain that a new and larger offensive was not about to break over the southern border, Somoza found it impossible to concentrate entirely on retaking the cities captured by the guerrillas. He could no longer collect and employ his forces against the rebel centers one by one, as he had done so successfully during the rebellion of the previous September. Whenever this strategy was attempted, FSLN units would invade from Costa Rica, obliging Somoza to detach his special 3,000-man force to prevent the loss of the southern provincial capital of Rivas.

One large guerrilla column of about three hundred troops, which crossed over from Costa Rica in May 1979, caused Somoza to call for an emergency meeting of the OAS. Angered by the continued transgressions, and by Carazo's attempts to persuade other Latin American nations to break all ties with Managua, Somoza threatened to invoke the Inter-American Treaty of Reciprocal Assistance in order to obtain military help from other OAS members. Pressure originating from within his own cabinet as well as from segments of the private sector encouraged Carazo to back off from his self-appointed diplomatic initiative; these elements feared the possibility of Somoza lashing out against Costa Rica in retaliation.

By June, as matters rapidly deteriorated for Somoza, the FSLN was allowed to set up a governmental junta-in-exile in San José. What normally would have been a diplomatically deplorable maneuver by Costa Rica, that of openly fomenting the downfall of a sitting government outside its own territory, now brought immediate recognition for the junta by various nations, so low was the international public opinion of the Somoza regime. Costa Rica was among the first to extend formal recognition to the junta, first as a belligerent force to be considered on an equal par with the Somoza government, then as the rightful representative of the Nicaraguan people. Until the final FSLN military victory, however, Costa Rica never forgot its underlying preoccupation that a Communist power might fill the vacuum that an ouster of Somoza would create. As late as the downfall itself, on July 17, the Carazo administration still pursued the ambiguous policy of providing a public base of operations for the rebel Nicaraguan government while trying to convince the junta that it should toe the official Washington line and broaden its base to include conservatives.

Once Somoza was out, Costa Rica no longer had a hostile force threatening to invade across its northern frontier. Attention could be turned from matters of armed strength to more pressing political and economic considerations. Despite the internal criticism Carazo faced because of his handling of the Nicaraguan crisis, Costa Rica could be content that it had played an important role in removing the hated Somozas from the region. Without the continued use of sanctuaries along the border, and the moral support of the majority of the Costa Rican people, the FSLN might have been denied victory altogether.

6.8 Costa Rica Is Pipeline for Weapons*

BY SHIRLEY CHRISTIAN

One aspect of support for the Sandinista revolution came back to haunt Costa Rica: arms trafficking. In 1981 a Costa Rican legislative investigations committee charged that President Rodrigo Carazo's administration had covered up its involvement in arms trafficking, and had tried to obstruct the congressional investigation. The committee further charged that some Cuban weapons—perhaps as many as half—that entered Costa Rica for the Sandinistas during the revolution never reached the insurgents. Rather, it said, the arms remained in Costa Rica. Officials later sold the weapons, which were then smuggled to the Salvadoran guerrillas. Coming in for particularly harsh criticism was Juan José "Johnny" Echeverría Brealey, who by then had been forced out of his post as Carazo's minister of public security. [1] While the eleven-month congressional investigation was under way, Shirley Christian reported on the origins of the arms network. She examined whether the arms operation, inspired in the late 1970s because of support for the Sandinistas' goals, had become a source of official corruption and black marketeering by the time the Salvadoran Left launched its ill-fated "final offensive" in early 1981.

Christian, later a Buenos Aires–based New York Times *correspondent, formerly covered Latin America for the Associated Press and the* Miami Herald. *She won a Pulitzer Prize in 1981 for her reporting from Central America, and is the author of* Nicaragua: Revolution in the Family.

BIT by bit, Costa Ricans are discovering how their country has served as a conduit for tons of arms on their way to Central American guerrillas. The tangled tale of intrigue, smuggling, and corruption has become a national scandal with international repercussions involving Nicaragua, El Salvador, Panama, and Cuba.

*Miami Herald, 15 February 1981.

The growing number of Costa Ricans implicated in the scandal includes President Rodrigo Carazo and several other past and current government officials.

Concern over the flow of arms into Central America—with war-torn El Salvador the ultimate destination for most of them—took on added urgency late last week, heightening interest in the Costa Rican connection.

Reports from Washington said the Reagan administration had evidence that Communist governments, including Cuba, had pledged beefed-up arms support to El Salvador's leftist guerrillas. Based on that evidence, the administration was said to have decided to increase sharply military and economic aid to El Salvador's right-wing government. . . . Costa Rica's role as part of the arms pipeline to the guerrillas is still murky. But enough facts have emerged to support an interesting thesis that has gained credence here.

The first part of this thesis holds that during at least the first half of 1980, and possibly much later, arms that had been left in Costa Rica by the Nicaraguan Sandinistas were delivered by plane to guerrillas in El Salvador, probably more for money than from ideological considerations.

More recently, according to this thesis, the Costa Rican planes and pilots, long known and trusted by the Sandinistas, flew into Nicaragua, with arms runs into El Salvador continuing from there. This coincides with the evidence Washington claims to have that arms are now reaching the Salvadoran guerrillas via Nicaragua.

The thesis also holds that Nicaragua, which is threatened with a cut-off of U.S. aid if it assists revolutionary movements in the region, hopes to deflect such charges by using the Costa Rican planes and pilots.

At least three clandestine flights into El Salvador since last June have been linked to Costa Rica because the planes involved were either loaded there, registered there, or piloted by Costa Ricans.

DOCUMENTATION

That these flights occurred has been documented. One plane crash-landed in El Salvador last June and was photographed by military authorities. Salvadoran military officials have presented evidence of having attacked and destroyed the others, in November and in January.

Also documented is that the pilots involved—two Panamanians and several Costa Ricans—were among those who ran arms into Nicaragua during the fighting there. . . . These episodes added that much more confusion to the already Watergate-like attempts to investigate the arms business—investigations that many Costa Ricans are convinced are going nowhere.

Congressional and executive-branch inquiries were opened about seven months ago after a businessman and his son, a former captain in the Costa Rican Civil Guard, put together a report on the arms traffic through Costa Rica during the 1978–79 Nicaraguan war.

The father and son, Alberto and Daniel Lorenzo, placed much of the blame on the then-minister of public security, Juan José Echeverría, who subsequently resigned. It is not clear, however, whether the apparently forced resignation of a man very close to the president was the result of the arms accusations or of Carazo's disapproval of Echeverría's divorce and remarriage.

Echeverría and [disgraced civil aviation director Roberto] de Benedictis have been among the many stars of National Assembly hearings that have so far produced a thousand pages of testimony, most of it concerning Costa Rica's role in the Nicaraguan war. What was only rumored then is acknowledged now, even by President Carazo.

A NATIONAL FERVOR

Costa Ricans, who love their own freewheeling democracy and hate dictators, threw themselves into the mission to overthrow Nicaragua's Somoza dynasty with a national fervor. They processed huge quantities of arms, ammunition, and other supplies (the exact amount is unknown) while giving the Sandinistas sanctuary and free run of Guanacaste Province, which borders Nicaragua.

"We were all imbued with the enthusiasm of the moment," said a Guanacaste resident who is now having second thoughts. The Sandinistas "seemed like such nice people . . . Costa Ricans got involved in the Nicaraguan affair because they thought it was the thing to do. When we realized how it was going to be, it was too late."

One of the hundreds of Sandinistas who moved in and out of Guanacaste in those days was Edén Pastora, who apparently charmed everybody in sight. Known to the world then as *Comandante Zero,* Pastora showed up here twenty days after the end of his daring takeover of the Nicaraguan national legislative palace in August 1978. Soon, the arms were flowing through Costa Rica.

"We thought that anything was better than Somoza and that whatever happened farther down the road could be taken care of later," said Elio Espinar, a Guanacaste landowner who himself has been linked to the arms trade. Espinar added that he is still convinced Pastora does not want a totalitarian, Communist state for Nicaragua.

In effect, it was patriotic to help the young men and women of red and black, the Sandinista colors. Whether it was also good business for some Costa Ricans is one of the missing facts. Missing as well are proof of the origin of the materiel passing through Costa Rica and evidence showing to what extent weapons were skimmed off for the Civil Guard and various individuals here.

A businessman named Fernando Trejos, whose daughter reportedly was close to Sandinista *comandante* Humberto Ortega during the time the Sandinistas were operating out of Costa Rica, has accused President Carazo himself of taking a $30 million payoff for aiding the Sandinistas.

When the accusation was leaked to the press, Carazo filed suit against Trejos for slander and defamation. Ortega, now the commander in chief of the Nicaraguan armed forces, sent a sworn statement denying that there had ever been such a payoff involving him and Carazo but not denying it on behalf of the entire Sandinista movement.

Carazo has taken general responsibility for the arms traffic through Costa Rica during the Nicaraguan war, saying that it was done out of national commitment but that he did not want it to set off commercial arms trafficking from here. Carazo also has denied reports that his son, Rolando, since killed in a motorcycle crash, participated in the Nicaraguan arms network.

Elio Espinar had a different view.

He said that Rolando Carazo was "a great guy" who had been a key player in the Nicaraguan activities, "getting permits, dealing with his father and so on."

The Lorenzos, in their written accusations, said the normal procedure for handling the arms pouring through Costa Rica for the Sandinistas had been for the local Civil Guard and key individuals to skim off about 25 percent of the weapons to sell or use. They believe the earlier rifles going to El Salvador probably came from this supply, which the Lorenzos estimated to have totaled about five thousand Belgian FALs. . . .

WITNESSES' STORIES

Some of the witnesses called by the National Assembly investigating commission have denied that as many as five thousand weapons even passed through Costa Rica. However, the man who says it was his job to receive the weapons bound for Nicaragua—Willie Azofeifa, chief of staff in the Security Ministry—has acknowledged that he never counted the weapons or opened the boxes in which they came.

Another thing that nobody apparently did was to question where the weapons were coming from. The Costa Rican public, traditionally and strongly anti-Communist, had the vague notion that they originated in either Venezuela or Panama, two friendly countries whose governments also supported the Sandinistas.

Though it is accepted that the ammunition did come from a Venezuelan factory, investigators claim the weapons themselves entered Panama from Cuba and later were brought directly to Costa Rica.

Colonel Guillermo Martí, who resigned last July as head of criminal investigation because of what he claimed was high-level pressure on him to halt one aspect of the arms investigation, said that he had realized the arms were coming from Cuba when he heard Cuban accents on one of the arms flights.

Martí said one of the Costa Rican pilots who flew the planes from Cuba was Roberto Kohkemper, the man who flew the Piper Aztec to Managua two days before it was destroyed by the Salvadoran military last month.

Kohkemper told the investigating commission he had never flown to Cuba in his life.

NOTE

1. For an account of the congressional report, see Alan Riding, "Arms Scandal Is Charged in Costa Rica," *New York Times,* 16 May 1981.

CHAPTER VII

The Approach of War and the Search for Peace

Editors' Introduction

The 1980s witnessed remarkable swings in Costa Rican foreign policy. The former champion of the Sandinista cause became embroiled in the Reagan administration's crusade to oust the Nicaraguan revolutionaries. *Contras* roamed through northern Costa Rica, U.S. intelligence agents ran covert operations, and Costa Ricans themselves were contemplating an unprecedented military buildup. Yet as the prospect of regional war grew ever more likely, Costa Rica stepped back. In the 1986 presidential elections, the nation rallied behind Oscar Arias, who would win a Nobel Prize for his peacemaking efforts. With the disintegration of the Reagan administration's Central America policy amid the Iran-*contra* scandal and the 1987 signing of the Arias Peace Plan, Costa Rica emerged as both a symbol and an active advocate of Central American peace.

When the Sandinistas entered Managua on July 19, 1979, hundreds of Nicaraguan national guardsmen fled. Most headed for Guatemala, Honduras, or El Salvador, but small numbers settled on farms in northern Costa Rica where landowners, some of them Nicaraguan, were sympathetic to the Somozas. This marked the beginning of Costa Rica's problems with the *contras*. [1]

Some of the ex-guardsmen formed the Fifteenth of September Legion, and staged periodic raids from Honduras against Nicaragua. The budding *contra* forces in Costa Rica lay low. In late 1980, apparently at the behest of their backers in the Argentine military, *contra* commandos staged attacks on a leftist Costa Rica–based shortwave station—*Radio Noticias del Continente*—that broadcast programs against the Southern Cone dictatorships and was reportedly linked to exiled Argentine Montonero guerrillas.[2] Several of the ex-guardsmen were captured and jailed. A year later, fellow *contras* hijacked a domestic Costa Rican airline flight, swapped their hostages for the prisoners in San José, and flew to El Salvador.

By the end of 1980, the U.S. Central Intelligence Agency was providing funds to support the political activities of an anti-Sandinista organization headquartered in Costa Rica, the Nicaraguan Democratic Union (*Unión Democrática Nicaragüense*—UDN).[3] Directed by José Francisco Cardenal and Edmundo and Fernando Chamorro Rapaccioli, the UDN was linked to one faction of the Conservative Party, a long-established Nicaraguan party that had opposed the Somozas. The UDN was beginning to organize what it called the Nicaraguan Revolutionary Armed Forces (*Fuerzas Armadas Revolucionarias Nicaragüenses*—FARN). In the summer of 1981, the CIA welded the Honduran-based anti-Sandinista forces, such as the Fifteenth of September Legion, into one organization. It was to become the main *contra* army, the Nicaraguan Democratic Force (*Fuerza Democrática Nicaragüense*—FDN).

Both the FARN and the FDN had by late 1981 established bases in northern Costa Rica, which were used for small raids across the border.[4] Between the February 1982 election of the new Costa Rican president Luis Alberto Monge and his May inauguration, traditionally a period of transition and weakened state authority, the anti-Sandinistas consolidated their logistics networks. In April 1982, an FDN unit attacked the main Nicaraguan southern border post at Peñas Blancas, on the Pan American Highway. Though the raid caused little damage, it appeared to be coordinated with two simultaneous FDN attacks along Nicaragua's northern border with Honduras. Two months later, Costa Rican security officials estimated there were up to three hundred FDN *contras* training at eight haciendas in the north.[5]

On April 15, 1982, three weeks before Monge's inauguration, former Sandinista guerrilla commander Edén Pastora, who had not been seen publicly since resigning his Nicaraguan Defense Ministry post the previous summer, held a news conference at a posh resort outside San José.[6] He revealed his break with the Sandinistas and his decision to fight his former comrades. Pastora had long been a popular figure in Costa Rica, and his message that he was the "authentic" Sandinista and that the *comandantes* in Managua had betrayed the revolution was greeted with great fanfare in the press. By June, the Costa Rican National Security Agency (ASN) believed that as many as two thousand anti-Sandinista combatants, mostly followers of Pastora, were in the country.[7] In September Pastora formed the Democratic Revolutionary Alliance (ARDE). It incorporated Pastora's fighters, some of whom were veterans of his 1979 campaign against Somoza, and the forces of Miskitu

Indian leader Brooklyn Rivera and UDN-FARN chief Fernando "El Negro" Chamorro. Former Nicaraguan junta member Alfonso Robelo also brought his followers under the ARDE umbrella. Led largely by disillusioned San-dinistas and political centrists, ARDE became the main anti-Sandinista group on the "southern front" and attempted to maintain some distance from the ex-*somocistas* who formed the backbone of the Honduras-based *contras.* In April 1983, ARDE began offensive military activities along Nicaragua's border with Costa Rica.

The presence of Pastora's forces confronted the new Monge administration with a quandary. On the one hand, Monge sought to keep Costa Rica out of regional conflicts. On the other, key members of his government and increasingly powerful right-wing sectors sympathized with the Nicaraguan rebels (see Readings 7.3 and 7.8), as of course did Washington, which Monge felt he could not afford to antagonize given the depth of the economic crisis. Publicly, his response was to formally codify Costa Rica's traditional pacifist and isolationist tendencies by announcing in September 1983 that he would declare Costa Rica's "perpetual, unarmed neutrality." At the same time, Monge was vulnerable to rightist domestic and U.S. pressure. Though secu-rity forces occasionally conducted a raid or a crackdown on anti-Sandinista groups, Monge turned a blind eye to most armed *contra* activities, especially if this was the implicit price for the massive U.S. economic aid that began in 1983.

Monge flew to Washington for a state visit just after his inauguration, and in December 1982 Reagan stopped in Costa Rica, the first U.S. president to do so since John F. Kennedy in 1963. U.S. influence in Costa Rica during Monge's 1982–86 presidency grew rapidly and reached its zenith in his last two years in office. At the beginning of his term, the conflict between the desire for neutrality and the need for critical U.S. aid led to contradictions and ambivalence in Costa Rican policy. Major disagreements between key ministers—such as the bellicose foreign minister Fernando Volio and the proneutrality public security minister Angel Edmundo Solano—also contri-buted to the inconsistent policy toward the *contras,* Nicaragua, and the United States.[8] Volio, for example, eagerly cooperated with Reagan adminis-tration efforts to diplomatically isolate the Sandinistas, while Solano actively sought to defuse tensions with Nicaragua over navigation rights on the San Juan River.

In his first two years, Monge rejected a U.S. offer to send "combat engi-neers" to build roads along Costa Rica's northern border. He also denied the U.S. Navy permission to hold maneuvers in Salinas Bay on the Nicaraguan border and shunned U.S. invitations to train Costa Rican civil guards in Honduras, to participate in the U.S. Big Pine military maneuvers in Hon-duras, and to send observers to the newly revived Central American Defense Council (CONDECA).[9] Monge also mediated in some tentative, little-publi-cized contacts between the Salvadoran government and the Farabundo Martí

National Liberation Front guerrillas, which could hardly have been to Washington's liking.

In the second half of his term, however, Monge did send civil guards to Honduras for training by U.S. advisers and the pace of military instruction within Costa Rica itself was dramatically stepped up (see Reading 7.11). "Combat engineers" did not build roads in the north of Costa Rica. But they did work in other regions and completed a coastal highway which would, in case of war, permit military equipment to be transported from U.S. bases in Panama to the Nicaraguan border without ever passing through Costa Rica's major population centers (see Reading 7.2). Meanwhile, the road network in the north is being built under the auspices of the civilian U.S. Agency for International Development.[10]

"If something happens in Congress," the CIA's Latin America covert operations chief told *contra* leaders in May 1984, "we will have an alternative way, and to assure that, here is Colonel North. You will never be abandoned."[11] In March 1984, the *contras* had spent the last authorized covert funds provided by the CIA. As the CIA operations chief feared, Congress, angered at CIA involvement the previous year in mining Nicaraguan harbors, cut off all *contra* aid in October. But the commitment to the *contras* and the introduction to *contra* leaders of the NSC's Lieutenant Colonel Oliver North, had serious implications for Costa Rica and its relationship with the United States.

When *contra* raids from Costa Rican bases provoked Nicaraguan counterattacks along the border, the Monge government urgently appealed to Washington for increased arms assistance (see Reading 7.1). The State Department saw the request as a golden opportunity to undercut San José's neutrality and enlist it in the anti-Sandinista cause. The United States granted Monge's military assistance request—plus an additional $2 million tacked on by the State Department. Not long after, a private association of conservative Costa Rican investors built a powerful transmitter near the northern border and signed a secret agreement with the U.S. Information Agency to broadcast anti-Sandinista programs produced by the Voice of America.[12]

On the diplomatic front, the Monge administration also showed increased willingness to toe the U.S. line. In the fall of 1984, Nicaragua—in a surprise move—offered to sign the Contadora draft peace agreement that Monge had previously endorsed. Costa Rica, along with Honduras and El Salvador, rapidly withdrew its support for the accord, raising objections that were widely believed to have originated in Washington. In April 1985, Monge flew to Washington shortly before a congressional vote on *contra* aid and appeared at Reagan's side voicing support for renewed assistance to the rebels. Although he later retracted those statements under pressure from within his government, he had undoubtedly lent legitimacy to the Reagan administration's campaign.

The U.S. Embassy in Costa Rica had, in the first years of Monge's term, been directed by Curtin Winsor, a political appointee best known for arrogant, undiplomatic gaffes; he called Monge's neutrality declaration "bullshit" and labeled former president Rodrigo Carazo "a certified nut."[13] Removed from his post in February 1985, Winsor was succeeded by Lewis Tambs, an author of the Santa Fe Document that served as a blueprint for Reagan policy toward Central America. Tambs had previously been ambassador to Colombia and, since 1982, a consultant to the NSC.[14] As conservative as Winsor, but with greater sophistication as a diplomat, Tambs later acknowledged to the Tower Commission probing the Iran-*contra* affair that his main mission as ambassador to Costa Rica was to "open the southern front" against Nicaragua.[15]

"Opening the southern front" meant that military concerns related to the *contra* war rapidly took priority over other aspects of U.S.–Costa Rican relations. In mid-1985, U.S. Green Berets began training civil guards on a farm twelve miles south of the Nicaraguan border that had formerly been the property of Nicaraguan dictator Anastasio Somoza (see Readings 6.2 and 7.11). Right next door, covert U.S. operatives, with the support of Costa Rican officials and security forces, began building an airstrip for use in supplying the *contras* (see Readings 7.13 and 7.14). Costa Rican paramilitary groups and foreign mercenaries, some of them American, assumed a greater role in *contra* operations (see Readings 7.8, 7.9 and 7.10). Nevertheless, in spite of the immense resources expended on their behalf, the southern front *contras* were beset by serious problems of morale, corruption, and political factionalism. As even NSC operatives conceded, many key *contra* leaders were involved in profiteering and drug running or had little will to fight (see Reading 7.12).

By late 1986, the Reagan administration's policy of secret and illegal backing of the Nicaraguan *contras* was unraveling. In the 1986 presidential elections, Oscar Arias of the National Liberation Party (PLN) easily defeated conservative Rafael Angel Calderón Fournier, who had taken a more belligerent stance toward Nicaragua.[16] From the start his position was clear. Shortly after his February 2 election, Arias told U.S. television newsman John McLaughlin, "If I were Mr. Reagan, I would give money to Guatemala, El Salvador, Honduras, and Costa Rica for economic aid and not military aid to the *contras.*"

Arias criticized the Sandinistas—at times harshly—and he did not move immediately to close down *contra* operations. But in September 1986, following reports of mysterious flights near the Nicaraguan border, he dispatched the Civil Guard to occupy a secret air base that had been built by the U.S. National Security Council's "private" *contra* aid network (see Reading 7.14).

Less than a month later, Sandinista gunners downed a *contra* supply plane over southern Nicaragua and captured Eugene Hasenfus, a U.S. cargo handler who, wearing a parachute in violation of orders, was the only survivor of the four-man crew. While the Reagan administration denied any connection to the aircraft and sought to portray it as part of a "private" *contra* aid effort, documents found in the wreckage and statements by Hasenfus himself suggested the involvement of high U.S. government officials.

In late November, following revelations of covert U.S. arms sales to Iran, Attorney General Edwin Meese announced that he was investigating the diversion to the *contras* of profits from the Iran sales. The ensuing furor led to the appointment of a special presidential review panel under John Tower, former Republican senator from Texas. Even before the Tower Commission issued its report in February, the Reagan administration's covert operatives in Costa Rica felt its impact. In December Ambassador Tambs resigned for "personal reasons." The following month, the CIA's San José station chief, Joe Fernández (a.k.a. Tomás Castillo), was recalled, supposedly for aiding the *contras* at a time when the CIA was prohibited from doing so (see Reading 7.15).[17]

President Arias faced similar quandaries as his predecessor, but he increasingly focused on alternative solutions. Like Monge, Arias had to rely on U.S. aid and private foreign investment for continuing Costa Rica's tenuous economic recovery. Yet Arias was clearly outraged at U.S. efforts to draw Costa Rica into the war against Nicaragua. Despite his vulnerability, Arias was able to resist White House pressure in part because the international situation was changing.

The most important change was the near certainty of regional war. Heightened conflict in the rest of Central America, especially in Nicaragua, was sure to spill over into Costa Rica given the large number of *contras* along the northern border. With only modest security forces and no genuine military, Costa Rica had relied for its national security on its right under the 1947 Rio Mutual Defense Treaty to seek hemispheric support against any external threat and on its reputation as an unarmed democracy. Yet Costa Rica's increasingly open collaboration with the Reagan administration's war against Nicaragua had severely undermined its international credibility just when the danger of war was most acute. With a pending World Court suit brought by Nicaragua, the Monge administration's tilt toward Washington threatened irreparable damage to efforts to win economic and political support in Western Europe and Latin America.[18] For many Costa Ricans, Monge's abdication of sovereignty forced a painful reappraisal of whether the country was willing to live up to its traditional neutralist and pacifist ideals. Finally, the prolonged wars in the region were limiting the new foreign investment viewed as essential for Costa Rica's economic recovery.

In October 1986, just after the clandestine airstrip became public knowledge (see Reading 7.14), CIA director William Casey had flown to San José and demanded that Arias meet him secretly in the U.S. Embassy. Arias refused. In early December, in the midst of the burgeoning scandal, Arias met with President Reagan in Washington. The White House, dissatisfied with the Costa Rican president, had more than once postponed such a visit. But now, Reagan's popularity was at an all-time low and his Central America policy a shambles. Seeking to recover congressional support, he strove to project the image of a peacemaker and thus welcomed Arias. But Arias had his own agenda and used the opportunity to argue forcefully for peaceful solutions to the region's conflicts, particularly in Nicaragua. Arias did receive promises that $40 million in frozen USAID funds for Costa Rica would be disbursed. His calls for U.S. cooperation in seeking a negotiated settlement in Nicaragua, however, went largely unheeded.

The Central American Peace Plan for which Arias received the 1987 Nobel Peace Prize had improbable origins (see Reading 7.16). Weeks after Arias's Washington trip, Costa Rican foreign minister Rodrigo Madrigal Nieto met in Miami with U.S. Assistant Secretary of State Elliott Abrams and special envoy Philip Habib (who later resigned in disagreement with Reagan administration policies). Not surprisingly, the Miami meeting focused on changes to be demanded of Nicaragua. But Vinicio Cerezo's new civilian government in Guatemala, anxious to conserve its much-vaunted neutrality, refused to back Madrigal's proposals. The Contadora Group and the Support Group, comprising eight Latin American democracies, refused to go along with Costa Rican positions that they saw as too close to those of the Reagan administration.[19]

In a February meeting in San José, Arias presented to the presidents of Guatemala, El Salvador, and Honduras a formal peace proposal. With the unwieldy title of "Procedure for Establishing a Firm and Durable Peace in Central America," it included measures that later became the heart of the Esquipulas II or Arias plan: cease-fires in all conflicts in the region, suspension of outside military aid to antigovernment guerrillas, general amnesties for political prisoners, free elections, and negotiations between governments and unarmed opposition forces. Nicaragua was not invited to that meeting, but Arias and Cerezo pushed to include Managua in the next talks planned for June in Guatemala.[20]

In March the U.S. Senate voted 97–1 to support the Arias plan. El Salvador and Honduras, both highly dependent on U.S. economic and military aid and sensitive to White House pressures, balked at holding the five-country June summit. When Salvadoran president José Napoleón Duarte objected to the "insufficient preparation," the meeting was postponed until August. Reagan administration officials, who believed the conference would benefit Nicaragua, were clearly pleased. They were also, however, seeking to placate critics who argued that the administration was not doing everything it could to seek peaceful solutions in Central America.

Arias, in the United States for an unofficial visit to Indianapolis in June, was called unexpectedly to the White House for what Costa Rican officials expected would be a brief handshake and photo opportunity aimed at reassuring skeptics about administration intentions. Instead, the Costa Rican president was met by a phalanx of high U.S. officials, including President Reagan,

Vice-President Bush, National Security Adviser Frank Carlucci, White House Chief of Staff Howard Baker, Assistant Secretary of State Elliott Abrams, Deputy Secretary of State John Whitehead, and special envoy Philip Habib. While the U.S. side charged that the peace plan was soft on the Sandinistas, Arias apparently stood his ground and argued for the viability of peaceful solutions. Costa Rican officials described the sixty-five-minute exchange as "sharp, tense and blunt."[21]

In August 1987, all five Central American presidents signed the peace plan. It was a victory for Costa Rican diplomacy and a defeat for Reagan administration attempts to pursue military "solutions." Reagan and Democratic House Speaker Jim Wright had offered their own peace plan just before the Esquipulas meeting, but this effort to pull the rug out from under the Central American presidents had only momentary impact. Arias had seemingly achieved the impossible, cajoling El Salvador's Duarte, Honduras's Azcona, and Nicaragua's Ortega into signing an agreement under which all committed themselves to making significant changes in their political systems (see Reading 7.16).

Arias had succeeded where the large countries of Latin America in the Contadora and Support groups had made little headway, in spite of their greater resources and more sophisticated diplomatic establishments. But his main triumph was not only in getting his four Central American colleagues to sign the Esquipulas II accords and in creating a framework that might someday lead to the resolution of the region's conflicts. The signing of the peace agreements dramatically shifted the terms in which Central American issues would be debated, both in the region and in Washington. Particularly after Arias was awarded the Nobel Peace Prize in October 1987, even the most committed Reagan administration ideologues (and their supporters in Costa Rica's powerful right wing) were reluctant to argue their position solely in terms of national security and military threats. While many still insisted on viewing Central America through an East-West geopolitical prism, the Arias Peace Plan—elaborated and agreed to by all of the region's leaders—now enjoyed virtually unquestioned legitimacy and provided the key reference point for evaluating progress toward peace, national reconciliation, and human rights.[22]

NOTES

1. Although the *contra* war did not assume significant proportions until late 1981, anti-Sandinistas took up arms immediately after the revolution. On these events and their implications for Nicaraguan security planners, see Marc Edelman, "Soviet-Nicaraguan Relations and the Contra War," in *Vital Interests: The Soviet Issue in U.S. Central American Policy,* ed. Bruce D. Larkin (Boulder, Colo.: Lynne Rienner, 1988).

2. After the attacks, Costa Rican security forces raided and closed *Radio Noticias,* alleging violations of weapons laws.

3. Edgar Chamorro and Jefferson Morley, "How the CIA Masterminds the Nicaraguan Insurgency: Confessions of a 'Contra,' " *New Republic* 193, no. 6 (August 5, 1985): 19–20.

4. In this period, one bank robbery and a number of attacks on isolated northern farms were attributed by Costa Rican security minister Arnulfo Carmona to "ex-*somocista* criminals." See *La Nación,* 27 January 1982.

5. *La Nación,* 8 April 1982; *La Nación Internacional,* 4–10 June 1982.

6. Pastora attained fame for leading the Sandinistas' August 1978 capture of the National Palace in Managua. Following the Sandinista victory in 1979, he served as vice-minister of defense and chief of the militia. He left Nicaragua in July 1981 after renouncing his military positions and writing an affectionate letter to Humberto Ortega (modeled on Che Guevara's 1965 farewell letter to Fidel Castro) in which he hinted at his desire to fight as an "internationalist" elsewhere in Central America.

7. *Tico Times,* 4 June 1982; *La Nación,* 1 June 1982.

8. Fernando Volio resigned as foreign minister in November 1983 to protest Costa Rica's United Nations vote condemning the U.S. invasion of Grenada. His resignation also coincided with Monge's neutrality declaration. Volio was replaced by the more moderate former justice minister Carlos José Gutiérrez.

Angel Edmundo Solano, who as security minister favored a strict interpretation of neutrality and periodically cracked down on *contra* camps in the north, was forced out in an August 1984 cabinet shake-up. The pretext for the dismissal was Solano's charge that right-wing "extremists" were plotting to destabilize Costa Rica. But Monge was under pressure to dump Solano, especially after the powerful Chambers of Commerce and Industry gave him a thirty-day ultimatum in July. Solano was replaced by Benjamín Piza, a founder of the ultraright Free Costa Rica Movement (MCRL) and an ex-president of the Chamber of Commerce.

9. The Central American Defense Council (CONDECA) was founded in 1963 under U.S. auspices with the goal of creating a bulwark against extraregional "threats." It fell apart following the 1969 "soccer war" between El Salvador and Honduras.

10. On AID road building in the north, see Carlos Granados and Liliana Quezada, "Los intereses geopolíticos y el desarrollo de la zona nor-atlántica costarricense," *Estudios Sociales Centroamericanos* 40 (1986): 47–65. On the U.S. military role in general, see Patricia Flynn, "U.S. Military Moves in Costa Rica and Honduras," *CENSA's Strategic Reports* (Berkeley: Center for the Study of the Americas, 1985).

11. *New York Times,* 21 January 1987.

12. This agreement was ironic, since for two years Monge had campaigned in the press for "radio sovereignty," complaining that Nicaraguan broadcasts received in northern Costa Rica constituted "cultural penetration."

13. *Washington Post,* 4 February 1984; *Latin America Weekly Report,* 30 November 1984.

14. On Tambs's NSC connections, see *La República,* 15 May 1985.

15. Quoted in Peter Kornbluh, *Nicaragua: The Price of Intervention* (Washington: Institute for Policy Studies, 1987), p. 132.

16. Arias's aides reportedly discovered after the election that Calderón had received CIA money funneled from Cuban organizations in Miami. See the *Miami Herald,* 9 March 1987.

17. Fernández was not the first CIA station chief to be recalled from Costa Rica. In 1971 the United States withdrew Earl J. Williamson because press reports charged that the agency was involved in "rumors of an attempt to overthrow" President José Figueres. Figueres suggested the allegations lacked proof, although the head of the House Foreign Affairs Subcommittee, Democrat John S. Monagan of Connecticut, indicated that there had been "overzealous actions" by some U.S. officials. See the *New York Times,* 11 February 1971.

18. Nicaragua later dropped the suit, which had accused Costa Rica of harboring *contras,* when it appeared that Arias was making a serious effort to limit the rebels' activities.

19. The Contadora Group, founded in 1983 with the goal of seeking a negotiated settlement in Central America, includes Panama, Colombia, Venezuela, and Mexico. Argentina, Uruguay, Brazil, and Peru founded the Support Group in 1985 to back Contadora diplomatically. With little progress to show by 1987, many of these governments' concerns had shifted away from Central America to issues of debt and development. The stagnation of the Contadora process contributed to Arias's success in offering an alternative peace plan.

Arias's success in brokering the plan can probably be attributed, at least in part, to his sidestepping of pro-U.S. foreign minister Rodrigo Madrigal and his direct management of both negotiations between the Central American presidents and communications between San José and the Costa Rican Embassy in Washington. See *La Nación,* 24 April 1988.

20. The Arias Peace Plan is also frequently referred to as the Esquipulas II (or the Guatemala) Accords. The talks leading to the agreement began in Esquipulas, Guatemala, near the Honduran border and the site of the Black Christ shrine revered throughout Central America. The five presidents had also met there in 1986, thus the peace plan signed in 1987 is termed Esquipulas II.

21. *New York Times,* 18 June 1987.

22. A useful analysis of the different governments' compliance with the accords as of January 1988 is the *Preliminary Report of the LASA Commission on Compliance with the Central American Peace Accords* (Pittsburgh: Latin American Studies Association, 1988).

7.1 Secret Memo: U.S. Response to Costa Rica's Urgent Request for Security Assistance

BY THE U.S. DEPARTMENT OF STATE

This internal State Department memo—classified secret—was leaked to the press in the spring of 1984 and was the subject of articles in several major dailies. It is published here for the first time. The document's authors view recent Nicaraguan–Costa Rican border clashes as "an opportunity to help shift the political balance in [the United States'] favor of Nicaragua's southern flank" and as a way of weaning Costa Rica from its "neutralist tightrope act, and push[ing] it more explicitly and publicly into the anti-Sandinista camp." The arms aid request could, they say, help "keep open the southern [contra] front." Of particular interest is the memo's description of the border incidents. The clear pattern, it says, is ARDE attacking first, a Nicaraguan response, followed by Costa Rican outcry. ARDE's provocations, the memo's authors warn, could cause public relations difficulties. They argue that the United States should "try to demonstrate that pattern of Sandinista incursions, shellings and intimidation predated ARDE's establishment of an effective military response." When finally approved, the Costa Ricans' request for $7 million in military aid was increased to $9.6 million by the Reagan administration.

SECRET

FIRST DRAFT MAY 5, 1984

**U.S. RESPONSE TO COSTA RICA'S URGENT REQUEST
FOR SECURITY ASSISTANCE**

A. *Overview and Key Issues*

Nicaraguan attacks against Costa Rican border posts at El Castillo and Peñas Blancas, April 29 and May 3, are events with serious potential implications for the two countries and for U.S. strategy toward the region. The precise motivation for the Nicaraguan attacks is unclear. They may be part of a concerted pressure campaign to force Costa Rica to clamp down on the Nicaraguan armed opposition forces operating out of Costa Rica under ARDE; or, they could be simply retaliation against specific ARDE actions. Further events on the ground are likely to show whether they represent part of a GRN [Government of Nicaragua] strategy of intensified pressures—or are simply the latest of a long series of border flare-ups destined to subside in a flurry of diplomatic activity followed by common agreement to reduce tensions.

In either event, Costa Rica's formal, written request to the United States for immediate delivery of approximately $7 million in small arms to help counter the Nicaraguan border activity is potentially an important milestone in our relations.

The specific issue we face is how to respond to Costa Rica's request. There are two major considerations: (1) the impact of this action on the regional balance, particularly on Costa Rica's willingness to stand up to Nicaraguan pressure tactics; and (2) its implications for the crucial Congressional debate on Central American funding, including our supplemental requests for military aid to El Salvador and for covert activities. Beyond that, we must also consider its diplomatic and public relations impact, in Europe, in other parts of Latin America and domestically in the United States.

B. *Situation on the Border*

Draft to be provided Monday. Assessment to include: (1) severity of recent incidents; (2) disposition and relative strength of Nicaraguan and Costa Rican forces (e.g., brief comment on overall superiority of Nicaraguan armed forces and summary of available information on deployments near Costa Rica, including any indications of recent ESP [*sic*] [EPS, *Ejército Popular Sandinista* or Sandinista Popular Army] buildup, or lack thereof); (3) analysis of possible relationship between ARDE operations and GRN border attacks and (4) prospects for future incidents. *(Request to CIA)*

C. *Costa Rican Security Requirements*

First draft below covers: (1) Costa Rica's specific request list; (2) initial comments on availability, appropriateness and costs of items requested. SOUTHCOM [U.S. Southern Command, Panama] and JCS [Joint Chiefs of Staff] are scrubbing CR list. Final draft also will review ——— requirements beyond the immediate request to help determine what charges, if any, should be made in the FY'84 supplemental or FY'85 request should the situation be judged to be more critical or higher priority than when these programs were developed. (PM, with input from DSAA, JCS and ISA [Intelligence Support Activity, U.S. Army])

1. Analysis of Costa Rican Request.

   (a) *Summary GOCR* [Government of Costa Rica] *Request:* Preliminary analysis indicates a very modest initial request list for the most basic defense items, such as M-16 rifles, 81MM mortars; .50 caliber machine guns and ammunition. The request may be summarized as follows:

—	4,000	M-16 rifles and ammunition (5,000)	$3.01 million
—	200	M-79 grenade launchers	.14
—	120	M-60 machine guns and ammunition (200)	.27
—	600,000	7.62MM ammunition (1,000,000)	.19
—	18	K90MM recoilless and ammunition	.55
—	24	81MM mortar and ammunition	.56
—	23	.50 caliber machine gun and ammunition	.45
—	20	various tool kits	.05
			$5.24 million

— 15% (add on for concurrent spare parts)	
— 24% (add on for air transportation)	$2.04
— (or, 17% if surface transportation)	
— Probable MIT to train in use of weapons	.30
— Total preliminary estimated cost, without SOUTHCOM scrub	$7.58 million

   (b) *Need:* The GOCR request for military equipment is in keeping with its overall military needs. The Public Security Forces are extremely poorly trained and equipped. Their troops lack such basic items as uniforms, load bearing equipment, helmets, flak vests, individual weapons and mortars. The list submitted by the GOCR attempts to address their basic deficiencies. If the GOCR is to conduct even an elementary self-defense, the types of equipment they have requested are vital. The sooner it is shipped and the Security Forces are trained to use it properly, the sooner they will be able to present a more credible defensive posture.

   (c) *Availability:* Most of the items requested by the GOCR can be made available either through regular army stocks or drawdowns from Army war reserve stocks. Although many of the items will have to come from this latter category and will no doubt not make the US Army happy, the items can be identified and shipped. The two problems are with the 90mm recoilless rifles and tool kits. There are currently no 90mms in stock or on the rebuild line. The Salvadorans have first priority on the next batch from the rebuild line. We can adjust that priority to give some of the 18 requested to the Costa Ricans, but we will have to determine whether El Salvador or Costa Rica has the greatest need. Tool kits are also in extremely short supply. We will try to identify some to ship to Costa Rica but that may be difficult.

(d) *Cost:* The cost of the request will probably run between $7.5 and $10 million, determined in part by availability, mode of transportation chosen and full identification of support items. For example, certain items have been left off the GOCR list, such as magazines for the M-16 rifles. SOUTHCOM will provide a realistic assessment by Monday of what the GOCR request entails. As soon as that is available, we will be able to determine a more accurate total cost figure. We can then make a decision as to what level of assistance we are able/willing to fund. . . .

2. *Current MAP* [Military Assistance Program] *Program for Costa Rica.* Appropriated funds under the FY-84 CR totaled $2 million in MAP. Of this amount, $600,000 has been obligated for ammunition, training aids, repair and rehibilitation [*sic*], MTT and other basic supplies and equipment. In addition, there are a few items which have been on order from previous year's MAP, as well as this year's, which we may be able to expedite since they are scheduled for delivery relatively soon (press reports some have just arrived). They include jeeps, trucks and generators.

Of the remaining $1.4 million: (1) $800,000 will be used to repair patrol craft at the Swift Ships facility in Louisiana. This repair price has been quoted by Swift Ships as part of a repair package which includes several Salvadoran vessels as well. Were Costa Rica to pull out of the deal to use the money elsewhere, for small arms for example, they would not only raise the ultimate cost of the repair for themselves, but also raise costs for the Salvadorans. (2) The final $600,000 is for a Bell helicopter to replace one which crashed and has gone unrepaired due to continuing difficulties with its manufacturer, the Hiller Company, which is now bankrupt. The Costa Ricans have placed an extremely high priority on the repair or replacement of this helicopter and frustration over negotiations with Hiller has been a constant constraint [*sic*] in bilateral relations in the recent past. The current deal with Bell has alleviated those tensions. It is recommended that we stick with the plan to purchase the Bell helicopter rather than divert the money to other uses. In addition, both the patrol boats and helicopter will help the Costa Ricans address the border problem more effectively. . . .

D. *Analysis of Available Legal Authorities*

Insert here draft from Mr. Thessin, L, covering (1) *506(a) of the FAA* [Foreign Assistance Act] and (2) *21d of the AECA* [Arms Export Control Act]. This issue is picked up again in Congressional section below:

3. *Reprogramming* of MAP funds from other countries to Costa Rica would be very difficult at this late stage of the fiscal year and could cause serious foreign policy problems in other parts of the world. We have recently informed the Congress in connection with the 21(d) decision on El Salvador that reprogramming was not possible. To reprogram now would cast doubt on the credibility of our earlier statement. The use of 21d authority or 506(a) would avoid jeopardizing relations with other countries.

   Reprogramming requires a 15 day notification period on the Hill although this can be waived by a Presidential determination under section 614(b) of the FAA. This is a cumbersome and time consuming process and could cause problems on the Hill.

E. *Diplomatic/Geopolitical Context*

1. *Recent patterns of border conflict.* The recent chronology of Costa Rican–Nicaraguan border incidents (attached at Tab C) follows a clear pattern: a) ARDE attacks an EPS garrison, b) Nicaragua attacks Costa Rica, c) Costa Rica rushes a few hundred troops to the border—with appeals on occasion for U.S. military assistance, d) both sides exchange harsh protest notes, e) both appeal to world opinion, f) conciliatory gestures are made, g) status quo ante. Key incidents:

   (a) *Conventillos/February 18.* A major incident; began on February 18 and 22, when anti-Sandinista forces attacked EPS troops near the town of Conventillos. EPS forces retaliated by machine gunning a Costa Rican Rural Guard patrol in the area. It is unlikely the Guardsmen were mistaken for ARDE. The GOCR reinforced the border and asked the U.S. for .50 caliber machine gun ammunition (the ammo arrived six weeks later). Protest notes went back and forth, Costa Rica withdrew its Ambassador, a sub-cabinet "mixed commission" meeting was postponed, and the GOCR protested to the OAS. A month later, Nicaragua sent the GOCR a conciliatory note which Costa Rica accepted with relief. Costa Rica's Ambassador returned to Managua and a mixed commission meeting was tentatively set for after Holy Week.

   (b) *San Juan del Norte/April 15.* The next round of border problems began with ARDE's brief capture of San Juan del Norte April 15. On April 17 and 19 EPS forces attacked GOCR security forces in the general area of San Juan del Norte. Again, there was little chance the Sandinistas mistook their target, according to Embassy San José.

(c) *El Castillo/April 29.* Following a reported ARDE attack on an EPS garrison at El Castillo *(verify whether there was any such attack)*, Nicaragua retaliated by rocketing and strafing two Costa Rican border towns. There was no mistaking the towns as populated by Costa Rican civilians.

(d) *Peñas Blancas/May 3.* As the protest notes started to fly, another border incident occurred on May 3 when a brief Nicaraguan mortar attack on a Civil Guard observation post at Peñas Blancas was met by rifle fire from the Costa Ricans. The GRN claimed the attack was a hoax perpetrated by ARDE. The Costa Rica's [*sic*] believe EPS forces were responsible. (Bill T: expand this section, if not covered by earlier section of paper.)

Since the capture of San Juan del Norte, events have followed a pattern similar to the Conventillos incident but at a much higher intensity level. The Costa Ricans have reinforced the border and asked for U.S. military assistance. This time, however, the GOCR clearly regards it as a more serious incident, coming on the heels of El Castillo. Protest notes have been exchanged. The GOCR invited the Contadora countries to send observers to the border, held a meeting of all Ambassadors from OAS countries resident in San José, and asked Panama, Venezuela and Israel to assist in meeting urgent security needs. Interestingly, the GOCR neither withdrew its Ambassador from Managua, nor protested (as yet) to the OAS in Washington, as in the past.

Now that Nicaragua has again made its point that ARDE must be more tightly controlled in Costa Rica, Managua seems to be moving to calm the situation. Nicaraguan Foreign Minister D'Escoto asked to meet with his Costa Rican counterpart. Gutiérrez countered by insisting any meeting include a Contadora representative. The GRN quickly agreed. We do not know when or whether this meeting will take place. If the pattern holds, Nicaragua will soon make other conciliatory gestures. Costa Rica wants a quiet northern border and presumably will act to calm the area while moving quietly to bolster its woefully inadequate security situation. Under normal circumstances, a mixed commission meeting would be the next step. But on this occasion Costa Ricans may prefer to underline the gravity of the situation and indicate domestically the stiffness of its response by being colder toward Nicaragua and quietly focusing on real, but modest, improvements in its capability to meet such incidents in the future.

ARDE remains a sticking point. President Monge has continued his delicate balancing act in recent weeks by giving ARDE some leeway, but not enough to provoke a large scale Nicaraguan attack. When ARDE becomes inconvenient, as it did following the New York Times bribery story, the GOCR has shown no reluctance to crack down hard.[1] Nicaragua knows that it can count on San José to restrain ARDE as long as the EPS keeps up the military pressure on the border. However, the significance of these events may be less in Nicaragua's intention than in Costa Rica's reactions.

2. *Political assessment.* There are signs that recent events have underlined for Costa Rica's leadership the government's great political and security vulnerability. The GOCR has always recognized, of course, the obvious and very significant disparity of military force between Nicaragua and Costa Rica. And it knows that a growing and well-equipped ARDE force presents another dimension to Costa Rica's security problem that is, at best, only partially within their control. What seems to have happened with the most recent clashes is an intensification of a trend within GOCR thinking that took it across the threshold from almost exclusive reliance on diplomatic positioning to the clear decision on the need to take some initial actions to strengthen basic security. GOCR concern over Sandinista belligerency is not new. Monge has consistently maintained (in private) that his country's security is at risk as long as the Sandinistas are in power.

Whether this trend continues, or the GOCR reverts again toward more traditional "neutrality," is an unknown. However, this could be a turning point in Costa Rica's role in the Central American conflict. Heretofore, the GOCR has sought to defuse tensions, avoid confrontation, and fall back on the moral protection of its unarmed neutrality. This latter course still retains its strong attraction for many Costa Ricans, including an important sector of the body politic. However, Monge and his principal advisers, based on their latest discussions with us, may now be persuaded that traditional policies can no longer be counted on as the best protection against Nicaragua.

If indeed the Costa Ricans have been brought around to this conclusion, it could lead to a significant shift from the GOCR's neutralist tightrope act, and push it more explicitly and publicly into the anti-Sandinista camp. This could pay important political and diplomatic dividends for us. On the other hand, it could up the ante as well if, in return, Cuba and Nicaragua move to destabilize Costa Rica, with strikes and covert moves to create unrest. With the grave economic situation that exists in Costa Rica, there is ample ground for Cuban/Nicaraguan adventurism and political unrest.

On the international plane, a Costa Rican shift as a result of a clear Nicaraguan threat 1) could force many European and Latin American governments to take a new, more critical look at Nicaragua; 2) could produce a stronger Core Four voice in the Contadora process supporting our policy interests—a trend on Costa Rica's part that has already begun; and 3) could present to the world another clear victim of Sandinista aggression to stand beside El Salvador and Honduras, giving greater credibility and moral support to those two nations.

While difficult to evaluate, such shifts could also change the GOCR's approach to ARDE; strengthening its base of operations. (This could play the other way, of course, with the GOCR trying to buy time by further overt acts to clamp down on ARDE, but that now seems less likely.) While there is some chance ARDE operations may be shifting to Honduras as part of its evolving, more cooperative arrangements with the FDN, a shift in attitude by Costa Rica could keep open the southern front.

However this plays, a visible shift in Costa Rica's position will strengthen our position in Central America. This is the principal argument for responding positively, quickly and in full to the GOCR request.

Neither the GOCR nor we now plan to build up Costa Rican security to the point that it can withstand serious Nicaraguan aggression by itself. That would be enormously costly and probably not feasible politically within Costa Rica. We can, and should, however, give the GOCR the political and psychological boost that a quick response would represent. That is the only way to stiffen their resolve and prevent a backsliding into neutrality.

Moreover, if managed properly, our provision of assistance and accompanying public and background statements can help to focus the spotlight on Costa Rica as the victim of Nicaraguan aggression. Beyond that, our favorable action would send another clear signal to the Sandinistas, to our friends in the region, and others, that we mean it when we say we are going to protect our friend [*sic*] and our security interests in Central America. Our active military involvement in Honduras clearly caused the Nicaraguans to pull back from their more blatant attempts to subvert and intimidate that country. There is no reason to believe the Sandinistas will not also take heed if they see a similar signal of commitment by us and the GOCR in Costa Rica.

F. *Domestic/Congressional Considerations*

1. In public relations terms, the latest attacks would seem to help our position:
   — They portray the GRN in an aggressive, militaristic state whose leadership is prepared to set aside legal constraints to intimidate a weaker neighbor. They justify current U.S. policy of responding vigorously in Central America to Cuban/Nicaraguan efforts to subvert other countries. They help make our case in El Salvador, where our charge of Nicaraguan aid for subversion have [*sic*] been challenged in public.
   — Those incidents give weight to our basic theme in the Congress on the need to stop the Sandinistas. They demonstrate why we must aid the Contras.
   — Costa Rica, the aggrieved party, wears a white hat. Its commitments

to democracy and regional peace are not challenged. Attacks against a small democracy with no standing army put Nicaragua in a bad light. In addition, recent Costa Rican actions to strictly limit ARDE activities should help ward off the obvious GRN rationale for its actions.

— These incidents also should be helpful in strengthening our case in Europe and Latin America, where we are making a major diplomatic/psychological effort to win support for our policy.

On the other hand, there is a public relations danger that must be avoided. A major theme of our critics is that this Administration is "militarizing Central America," that we have introduced east-west considerations artificially, and that we always select military over diplomatic solutions. Despite the obvious distortions and inaccuracies of these charges such themes must be reckoned with in planning our political and public affairs strategy on this issue.

To deal with this, we should try to keep the spotlight on Nicaragua as the aggressor, rather than on our reaction to Costa Rica's request. We should construct a response that is not seen as "overreacting." This means that it is important to have the message of Nicaragua's aggressive behavior clearly understood and to portray our response as measured and appropriate to the circumstances. This argues against rushing in and in favor of being seen clearly to be responding to Costa Rican initiatives for assistance, to us and to other countries.

ARDE activities from Costa Rican territory present a complicating factor. To the extent Nicaragua succeeds in portraying its activities as a response to armed provocation by anti-Sandinista guerrillas, our gains will be limited and potential political backing for our response will not materialize. For public relations, it is important to neutralize "the ARDE factor": to demonstrate that the pattern of Sandinista incursions, shellings and intimidation predated ARDE's establishment of an effective military response. Thus the story should be Nicaragua-vs-Costa Rica, not GRN-vs-armed opposition. To the extent that ARDE operations are demonstrated to have occurred in proximity to the Sandinista attacks, the diplomatic, Congressional, and public affairs rationale for a vigorous U.S. response is obviously weakened.

Thus far, the current incidents and the GOCR's reaction have received routine media attention. Ambassador Winsor's reported statements on the U.S. response and the White House statement that we were considering an urgent Costa Rican request received headlines in Washington. Whether or not there is sustained press interest will depend on the extent of further incidents or a dramatic GOCR move on diplomatic fronts. An effective rationale for urgent U.S. military supplies could be dissipated somewhat if there are no further attacks and press stories focus on mediation and lessened tensions.

Basically, however there is a strong case for helping Costa Rica, that may be enhanced by a continuation of incidents or by dramatic Costa Rican appeals. Even without that Costa Rica commands widespread support and sympathy in Congress and, more broadly, in a world jaded by Central American conflict and in quarters where El Salvador and Honduras are dirty words.

2. *U.S. Congressional attitudes* in this context are dominated by the same reservoir of goodwill toward Costa Rica as outlined above—plus a degree of political skepticism on the other side of the aisle regarding Administration policy. It should be relatively easy for us to help the GOCR, especially in a situation that is clearly seen as a crisis. At the same time, Congressional critics of the Administration will be on guard against any move that suggests we are "militarizing Costa Rica." There will also be those on the Hill ready to listen to the GRN side of the story that Costa Rica's hands are not entirely clean because of ARDE's military attacks on Nicaragua from Costa Rican territory. It is essential that we undertake early and thorough Congressional consultations once our basic decisions have been made.

The key element in the Congressional equation will be the impact of our action on Congressional consideration of the Administration's supplemental security assistance requests for El Salvador and for covert activities—as well as its impact on our overall revised Central American assistance package. These are critical to the timing and extent of our response to Costa Rica. It is still too early to tell how these will play.

Funding authorities. There are two principal authorities under which we can provide the assistance needed, Sections 506(a) of the FAA and 21d of the AECA. 506(a) requires no reimbursement or reprogramming. On the other hand, it does require that all previously allocated funding be exhausted, which may take weeks in this case. It also requires advance Presidential notification to Congress accompanied by a determination that an unforeseen emergency exists.

Section 21d depends—insofar as it has been tested—on reimbursement via a supplemental. Its employment again, on the heels of use for El Salvador, could evoke charges that we are trivializing and abusing the authority. On the other hand, there is no prerequisite that other funds be exhausted. Additionally, its use would create a certain parallel between Costa Rica and El Salvador which accentuates the common danger from Nicaragua, reinforcing the validity of our concerns. These considerations argue strongly for 21d as the preferred vehicle.

Given anticipated Congressional action on our Central American legislation May 9–10 and the likelihood that notification to the Congress of further military shipments under 21d to El Salvador will begin on May 10 or soon thereafter, we recommend a phased approach to

Congressional action on Costa Rica involving (a) notification of the GOCR as soon as the decision is made (b) active lobbying of the Costa Rican case on the Hill in the context of overall lobbying efforts (c) notification in conjunction with the El Salvador 21d notification and (e) shipment and public announcement almost immediately thereafter.

H. *Conclusions and Recommendations:*

Under current circumstances, we clearly have a strong interest in providing the GOCR the emergency security assistance it has requested. Except for the avoidable danger that we could come to be seen as pushing the GOCR into militarization, or that precipitate action could confuse the delicate Congressional picture, there are no appreciable downsides. The public and Congressional problems are obviously manageable. And the political and security advantages of responding positively to Costa Rica's modest request—together with the distinct weakening of our position in Costa Rica and throughout Central America if we fail to respond promptly in this case—argue strongly for immediate authorization of the Costa Rican request.

Recommendation:

(1) That you authorize us to inform President Monge promptly that the United States will meet his request for military assistance (as modified) in the amount of $9.6 million;

(2) that we notify the Congress in a manner that best meets our overall Central American legislative requirements, presumably together with the El Salvador 21(d) notification during the period May 10–15; and

(3) that the GOCR and we coordinate public statements concerning our actions, with the announcement and shipment coming immediately after conclusion of the Congressional notification.

Approve_____ Disapprove_____

. . . .

Chronology of Events Concerning Costa Rica–Nicaragua Border Incidents

Feb. 18
[1984]   – Anti-Sandinistas attack EPS forces near Conventillos.
Feb. 22   – Anti-Sandinistas attack again near Conventillos.

Feb. 22 – EPS forces machine gun and mortar Rural Guard patrol near Conventillos.

Feb. 28 – GRN issues communiqué condemning border incidents near Conventillos as a CIA provocation. No criticism of Costa Rica.

Feb. 28 – GOCR sends protest note to GRN over Conventillos incident, recalls Ambassador; postpones mixed commission meeting set for early March.

Feb. 29 – Costa Rica protests to the OAS in Washington.

Mar. 9 – Two Junta members fly to San José and give conciliatory verbal response to Feb. 28 protest note.

Mar. 12 – GRN issues communiqué protesting CIA support of ARDE activities in Costa Rica.

Mar. 13 – GRN sends protest note to GOCR over alleged attacks on El Papaturro Mar. 11, Los Chiles Mar. 12, and Peñas Blancas Mar. 13, claiming attacks came from Costa Rica. ARDE confirms attacks, GOCR denies attacks came from Costa Rica.

March 14 – Monge rejects Mar. 9 verbal apology for Conventillos incident.

Mar. 16 – GRN slams GOCR at meeting of non-aligned countries for complicity in ARDE attacks.

Mar. 20 – Ortega sends Monge a letter in response to Feb. 28 GOCR protest urging Monge to work for peace in CA.

Mar. 28 – Monge protests GRN threats to mine CA harbors. Also rejects Mar. 20 Ortega letter as inadequate.

April 2 – GOCR Security Council reaffirms Feb. 28 measures against Nicaragua.

April 4 – Ortega sends conciliatory letter on Conventillos incident. Claims ARDE activities take place behind GOCR's back. Calls Costa Rica a "fraternal country."

April 6 – Press reports DC-3 crashed in northern Costa Rica on or about March 28 carrying supplies for ARDE.

April 10 – GRN sends GOCR protest note over ARDE attacks on San Juan del Norte from Costa Rica.

April 11 – Monge accepts Ortega's April 4 letter. Mixed commission meeting rescheduled for after Holy Week.

April 12 – Fourteen Costa Rican fishermen seized by GRN and returned 24 hours later.

April 14 – Costa Rican Ambassador returns to Managua despite fishermen incident supposedly because of embarassment [*sic*] over DC-3 incident.

April 15 – ARDE captures San Juan del Norte.

April 17 – GOCR rejects GRN April 10 protest note.

April 17   –   EPS forces machine gun Civil Guard patrol near San Juan del
                Norte.
April 19   –   Nicaraguan plane rockets Civil Guard outpost near San Juan
                del Norte.
April 24   –   GOCR raids ARDE offices in response to New York Times
                bribery story.
April 29   –   Two Nicaraguan planes rocket and strafe two Costa Rican
                border towns near the site of an ARDE attack on EPS garrison
                at El Castillo.
May 2   –   GOCR and GRN exchange protest note on April 29 attack.
                GOCR requests Contadora observer mission.
May 3   –   EPS forces reportedly mortar and machine gun Civil Guard
                border post at Peñas Blancas.
May 3   –   GRN sends GOCR protest note saying that incident earlier in
                the day was an ARDE hoax. FonMin Gutiérrez tells us GRN
                story is ludicrous.

NOTE

1. This refers to an article in the April 23, 1984, *New York Times*. According to this report,
the CIA was providing ARDE with "hundreds of thousands of dollars in covert aid, much of it
in cash" and that this was being used to bribe both "senior government officials in San José" and
"Rural Guard members in areas where the Nicaraguan rebel group operates." Costa Rican press
reports linked Interior Minister Alfonso Carro and his vice-minister Enrique Chacón to the
ARDE-CIA money. Costa Rica's Rural Guard is administered by the Interior *(Gobernación)*
Ministry.—EDS.

7.2 Costa Rica Journal: In the War on Want, Is There a Military Front?*

BY JAMES LEMOYNE

*North central Costa Rica has been a prime target for U.S. development assistance: it
is poor, lacks infrastructure, has underutilized agricultural resources, and is close to
Nicaragua. By 1982 Americans, Costa Ricans and—according to columnist Jack Anderson—Israelis were involved in drawing up a multi-million-dollar land development plan
that would address the region's economic needs while putting in the roads and airstrips
that could someday prove useful to an army on the move.*

*Anderson reported in a 1983 column that then-U.S. Ambassador Francis McNeil in
a confidential cable said that because of the tensions along the Nicaraguan border, the
so-called Northern Zone Infrastructure Development project "has become a number one
priority" of the Costa Rican government. According to Anderson's account, the plan at*

*New York Times, 14 July 1987.

that time called for buying up land and moving in thousands of settlers which, with Honduras to the north, "would create a giant strategic pincers physically isolating Nicaragua." He quoted McNeil as cautioning: "It is essential that the land purchases be expeditiously and quietly carried out to . . . avoid land invasions organized by leftists which would nullify the project's geopolitical objectives."[1]

By 1987, under the supervision of the U.S. Agency for International Development, key roads had been built and basic services had been brought into communities. The scheme, as James LeMoyne reports here, "appears intended to deal with security matters while offering economic and political development for a remote area" deemed too close for its own good to the Sandinistas.

LeMoyne, formerly El Salvador bureau chief for the New York Times, *has reported extensively on Latin America for* Newsweek *and the* New York Times.

THE red clay roads, newly cut into the jungle, are still being smoothed by bulldozers. Logging trucks and farmers with their herds of cattle will not be far behind.

The tropical savanna of northern Costa Rica seems to roll on forever, but from a high point you can see it end, falling abruptly to the shore of Lake Nicaragua. There it forms a volatile frontier that has often been fought over in recent years by Nicaraguan rebel units and Sandinista patrols.

In this wilderness area, the Reagan administration and the Costa Rican government have carried out what appears to be one of the most successful American-backed development projects in Central America.

The project, estimated to cost $20 million, appears intended to deal with security matters while offering economic and political development for a remote area that the Costa Rican government and American officials fear is susceptible to Sandinista influence. This concern has grown as tens of thousands of Nicaraguan refugees fleeing the war in their homeland have moved into the region.

"It's a key area for Costa Rica," said an American official here. "We are doing good development work where it is needed."

USED BY THE SANDINISTAS

Although American officials do not mention it, the work also appears to offer rapid military access to frontier airports and a key stretch of border if ever hostilities with Nicaragua grow or if the United States should one day decide to invade that country.

The large area affected stretches along the border with Nicaragua from the Pacific coastal highway almost to the town of Los Chiles and then south into the swampy, fertile jungle and plains of Guatuso.

In the late 1970s, it was a center for secret Sandinista guerrilla training camps and supply lines used to attack and eventually overthrow the Somoza family dictatorship in Nicaragua. In the final push across the border, Cuban supply planes landed at night near the border laden with weapons and Cuban advisers slipped into Nicaragua with Sandinista units, according to several former Sandinistas who fought here.

As American hostility and resistance within Nicaragua to the Sandinistas' Marxist policies grew, the border once again became a military zone. Between 1982 and 1985, the rebel leader Edén Pastora Gómez dotted the frontier with guerrilla camps, backed by the Central Intelligence Agency.

The Costa Rican government finally closed the camps a year ago, and Mr. Pastora disbanded his force, but there is a lingering sense that this is a region where authority was imposed by men with guns and civil government is still a somewhat novel concept.

BASIC SERVICES FOR THE PEOPLE

American-backed development work was planned in 1983 and the years since have been spent driving roads into the area and bringing basic services to its isolated and impoverished communities. The prime objective, according to American and Costa Rican officials, is to bring the zone under the control of the central government and to enable Costa Rica's paramilitary rural police to monitor it. The rural police have been trained and armed in recent years by the United States.

The region has several small airstrips and larger ones at Liberia, Upala, and Los Chiles, as well as a once-secret landing field on the Pacific coast built for the *contras* with the help of American officials. The airstrip at Los Chiles was extended and paved in recent years and would appear to be easily able to take military planes.

American officials deny that any U.S. funds went into the construction, but local residents recall that the American ambassador and the commander of American regional military forces landed at the airstrip on a visit three years ago.

There is also a deepwater port on the coast at Murciélago. The coast route south to Panama is in poor condition, but troops and equipment could probably be moved by land from the main regional American base in Panama up to the Nicaraguan border within twenty-four hours.

American army engineers have built or improved at least fifteen bridges in one of the worst parts of the coastal route to Panama, near the village of Dominical to the south. A spokesman for the American Embassy said the bridges were built in a "civic action" project purely to aid impoverished Costa Rican communities in an area that in the past was cut off for days when the rainy season swelled the rivers.

But the bridges, like the development project on the northern border, appear to address both security concerns and political and social needs, offering military access if needed while satisfying local demands for long-needed improvements.

AID OFFICIAL OVERSEES WORK

A key element in the success of the work along the border is that it is being overseen by an official from the Agency for International Development, the operating arm of American economic aid in developing countries.

Now that almost one hundred miles of primary roads have been opened, according to the official, Harry Peacock, the next step is to build access roads to small villages and begin community development by helping in land distribution and tasks such as building wells and rural clinics. The villages are asked to contribute to and help plan what they need, a demand that they have eagerly accepted, Mr. Peacock said.

"I see a real change in local attitudes," he said in an interview near the border. "They want development—it's a very significant signal when people become future oriented."

Eighty percent of the land in the region is believed to be arable and government officials now expect Costa Ricans to begin moving in and local young people to stay, instead of looking for work in the cities.

But there may be one lasting cost for what otherwise appears to be a highly beneficial development project. The border region contains some of the most extensive tracts of Central America's rapidly dwindling virgin jungle.

The trees and wildlife almost certainly will not survive the easy access now offered to local lumber companies whose sawmills are already hard at work slicing giant trees that cannot be replaced into boards for the construction projects now springing up in the region.

NOTE

1. Jack Anderson, "Land Scheme," *San Francisco Chronicle,* 14 February 1983.

7.3 U.S. and Contras *Find Ally in Costa Rica's Three Major Dailies**

BY JEAN HOPFENSPERGER

Discovering the conservative bias of the Costa Rican media requires little subtlety. The nation enjoys a relatively free press, and some fine journalists have produced frank and thorough investigative reports on such topics as corruption and drug trafficking.[1] But coverage of such issues as Nicaragua, U.S. foreign policy, Communist participation in the labor movement, terrorism and, perhaps most important, contra *breaches of Costa Rica's neutrality has often been slanted, and the facts less than fully exposed. After one incident, in which* La Nación *(which denied the editors of this volume rights to use its articles on*

*Christian Science Monitor, 18 August 1986.

poverty and on contra *drug trafficking) published a doctored photograph, prominent intellectuals formed a group to push for more objective coverage. As noted in this reading, both former* contra *leader Edgar Chamorro and the editor of the leftist university weekly Carlos Morales, have charged that the CIA pays off reporters. The allegations have not been fully substantiated, but readers of the Costa Rican media may sometimes wonder whether, given the obvious sympathy for the* contras, *the CIA may have been paying the already converted.*

Hopfensperger has reported for the Tico Times *and several U.S. newspapers. She is now a staff reporter for the* Minneapolis Star Tribune.

IN its battle for support in Central America, the United States has a powerful advocate: the Costa Rican press.

Over the past five years, Costa Rica's three main dailies—*La Nación, La República,* and *La Prensa Libre*—have become unabashed supporters of President Reagan's economic and foreign policies, many Costa Ricans say.

Through their articles and editorials, these privately owned papers promote the U.S.-backed Nicaraguan rebels, Costa Rican militarization, International Monetary Fund programs, and most U.S. State Department policies, these analysts say. The fear at these newspapers is that the leftist political system of its northern neighbor, Nicaragua, will spread into Costa Rica.

The Costa Rican government is officially neutral in the Central American conflict, though it admits reluctantly that its territory has been used by the rebels. It does not publicly admit that there are *contra* bases in northern Costa Rica.

Editors say they are not manipulating public opinion. They say the complaints are sour grapes from people who disagree with the newspapers' political views.

However, a wide array of people have criticized the press: President Oscar Arias Sánchez, several former presidents, Archbishop Román Arrieta of San José, peace activists, academics, artists, intellectuals, and members of the legislature.

"The democratic system demands that its citizens and journalists comment, debate, and criticize the actions of its public figures," President Arias said shortly before his inauguration May 8. "However, the democratic system suffers when its citizens and journalists guard silence [or] slant facts or words, thereby confusing public opinion."

Of Costa Rica's Spanish-language newspapers, the only one that isn't editorially conservative is the University of Costa Rica's newspaper, *Universidad.*

Two years ago, according to *Universidad* editor Carlos Morales, then-U.S. Ambassador Curtin Winsor indicated he would like to see *Universidad* shut down. Mr. Winsor encouraged the creation of an alternative student publication, but the attempt failed because of lack of student cooperation, according to Mr. Morales.

Interviews with Costa Rican politicians and academics indicate that pro-U.S. coverage is a result of several factors:

- Scholarships to journalists. The United States Agency for International Development has awarded twenty-one Costa Rican journalists all-expense-paid, six-week tours of various media centers in the United States. Although AID is not usually involved in journalist training, it is giving the awards this year, for the first time, because it was recommended by the Kissinger Commission on Central America as a means to counteract similar Soviet programs.
- *Contra* connections. According to many foreign correspondents and other observers, many newspaper reporters and editors reportedly are friends—and some, advisers—of U.S.-backed Nicaraguan *contra* leaders.
- Alleged payoffs to reporters. Former *contra* leader Edgar Chamorro said last year that Central Intelligence Agency money was used to bribe journalists in Costa Rica and Honduras. Morales, former president of the Costa Rican Journalists' Union, claims that about eight journalists continue to receive such funding. When contacted in Washington, a CIA official said the agency had no response to these charges.

These factors inhibit citizens' freedom of information and curb public debate on major issues, says Gonzalo Ramírez, a National University economist who was a member of the Committee for the Defense of Freedom of Information, a short-lived Costa Rican media watchdog organization that folded under media pressure last year.

"If you don't have cable television, a shortwave radio, or can't read English, you don't know what's really happening in Costa Rica," Mr. Ramírez said. The major U.S. newspapers and magazines are available in Costa Rica.

There is also one Costa Rican–based English-language paper, the *Tico Times,* which is editorially centrist to somewhat liberal.

"The problem is the people's right to know," Interior Minister Guido Fernández says. "Are the newspapers consciously preventing them from knowing because it is against their [the newspapers'] self-interests?"

Yes, says *Universidad* editor Morales.

His newspaper has reported several discrepancies in the coverage of *La Nación.*

Following a demonstration in front of the Nicaraguan Embassy last year, for example, *Universidad* discovered that *La Nación* had published a doctored photograph that erased the insignia of the Free Costa Rica Movement paramilitary group from the shirts of some demonstrators.

The assistant director of *La Nación* José Sánchez Alonso, is the vice-president of the Free Costa Rica Movement, a right-wing civic group with a paramilitary branch.

When questioned about the photograph tampering, Mr. Sánchez said it was the work of an individual at the paper and not a result of the newspaper's policy. He insisted that being an officer in a political group did not represent a conflict of interest with his profession.

"We try to be objective, especially in informational material," Sánchez said. "But because we're human beings, it's difficult."

Regarding coverage of Nicaragua, Sánchez says objectivity is difficult. "We're convinced that the [Nicaraguan] regime is a threat to us."

NOTE

1. Costa Rica does have a licensing law for journalists, which many Western-oriented press groups find incompatible with a fully free press. Particularly frustrating for its critics is the law's lack of a clear definition of what constitutes a qualified journalist. In practice, virtually the only way a journalist can be licensed is to graduate from a five-year journalism program at the University of Costa Rica.—EDS.

7.4 The Refugee Problem and the Tradition of Asylum

The Salvadorans*

BY JOANNE KENEN

The Nicaraguans**

BY SANDRA DIBBLE

For decades Costa Rica was a haven for political refugees from throughout Latin America. Venezuela's Rómulo Betancourt and Carlos Andrés Pérez, Peru's Víctor Raúl Haya de la Torre, Guatemala's Jacobo Arbenz, the Dominican Republic's Juan Bosch, and even Cuba's Fidel Castro followed the steps of independence leaders José Martí and Antonio Maceo to Costa Rica.[1] Less illustrious refugees have come as well. Cubans fleeing Batista were followed, a generation later, by those escaping Castro. In the 1970s, Chileans and Argentines sought sanctuary in Costa Rica after brutal military takeovers in their homelands. Some 50,000 Nicaraguans sat out the worst of the 1979 war in northern Costa Rica; in the 1980s, estimates ranged up to an extraordinary 250,000 undocumented Nicaraguans in Costa Rica. Relatively few Guatemalans have come; most headed north to Mexico. But tens of thousands of Salvadorans have settled in Costa Rica.

*"Costa Rica, Refugees Still Seeking Solutions," *Tico Times,* 26 June 1982.

**"Nicaraguan Refugees Straining Costa Rica," *Miami Herald,* 1 March 1987.

For the most part throughout its recent history, Costa Rica has welcomed the refugees. In the last few years, however, the record has been mixed. After the first terrorist incidents in Costa Rica in 1981, against U.S. Embassy marine guards and the Honduran Embassy (see Reading 7.6), Costa Rica expelled thirty-six prominent exiles, including Salvadoran and Guatemalan opposition leaders. Officials also raided human rights offices, and foreign priests working with the refugees complained of harassment.[2] So did some ordinary Salvadorans, as the first of these two readings makes clear. There were several central reasons for Costa Rica's ambivalence about its own traditional hospitality. One was clearly a fear that the presence of the foreigners would pull Costa Rica into the worsening Central American maelstrom. A related concern was that the presence of revolutionaries would somehow "contaminate" Costa Rican democracy, particularly at a time when the system was already being tested by a grave economic crisis. Finally, there was the sheer size of the problem, and the fact that the refugees were no longer coming for a few weeks or months to sit out a battle or await a U.S. visa. They were coming for the duration of the turmoil in their homelands; many expected to stay for years, if not for good. As the second reading indicates, by some counts in 1987, one out of every ten people in Costa Rica was a Nicaraguan.

Joanne Kenen, one of the editors of this anthology, lived in Costa Rica from 1980 to 1983. Sandra Dibble is a reporter for the Miami Herald.

THE SALVADORANS

The Monge administration last weekend appointed its members to the National Commission on Refugees. They are new faces on an old committee, whose task is to find new solutions to old problems.

The problems facing the 15,000 refugees in Costa Rica—above and beyond the trauma of displacement and, in many cases, bereavement—are mundane but pervasive. How to find, and pay for, a home. How to clothe themselves and their children. How to support themselves in a country that, struggling with its own mounting unemployment crisis, denies refugees permission to work.

Refugees interviewed recently also complain of run-ins with local immigration inspectors who, they say, confiscate their identification cards and later harass or detain them for being "undocumented foreigners."

"A lot of refugees just don't know what their rights are, or how to complain," explains one Salvadoran.

Some also fear that the Monge government's evident concern over national security may lead it to close the frontier to new refugees, or even to evict some or all of the 10,000 Salvadorans now residing here.

Coordinators of refugee programs at the U.N. High Commission on Refugees (ACNUR in Spanish) believe such fears are unfounded. They are aware of problems Salvadorans encounter with immigration agents. But, for the moment at least, they discount theories that the refugees are being "persecuted."

More likely, they say, the refugees—in most cases—are just encountering the same bureaucratic hurdles that all other foreigners face when they try to process their documents here. (The new administration has not yet defined its immigration policies, leading to confusion on the part of immigration officials, foreign residents, and tourists alike.)

"There are problems, but they can be solved," says ACNUR's Sergio Calle. "That's one of the tasks of the government commission," which includes representatives from ACNUR and the ministries of government, public security, labor, foreign relations, and justice.

"The rights of documented refugees are recognized by Costa Rica, and they have nothing to worry about, as long as they obey Costa Rican laws," says Minister of Justice Carlos Gutiérrez. "The undocumented ones—about 10,000 of 15,000, we think—present a different situation."

Before May 1980, Salvadorans fleeing their war-torn country to Costa Rica were automatically granted refugee status. Now they must apply for it.

Usually, says Calle, the Salvadoran recounts his tale—which often includes being a victim of, or a witness to, torture, murder, and persecution—and receives a refugee identity card, renewable every six months. But until the petition is processed, his troubles with Immigration can range from minor inconveniences to a stay in jail.

The need for identity cards—which weren't used during previous deluges of refugees—points up the nature of the Salvadoran problem.

In the spring of 1979, there were about 50,000 Nicaraguans living in refugee camps near Liberia, Guanacaste, recalls Calle. Their presence here was a crisis, but a brief one, he says. The revolution triumphed, and the refugees went home.

Many Salvadorans, however, have been here for more than two years. It's anybody's guess as to how much longer they will stay here.

Only 350 live at the Los Angeles camp in Guanacaste, although ACNUR hopes to transfer 400 more there this year, and make the camp economically self-sufficient through agricultural and artisan projects, says Colón Bermúdez, a spokesman for the Nobel Peace laureate organization.

Another 9,650 live elsewhere in Costa Rica, primarily in the San José area. Most are poor and many are unskilled. All but 2,000 rely heavily on ACNUR, the Red Cross, and religious relief agencies.

When the ACNUR program began here in April 1980, 2,500 refugees lived in urban areas of Costa Rica, with some 500 more streaming in every month. The monthly influx has slowed by some 85 percent, but even ACNUR staff members disagree about what the migration rate will be in coming months.

Some ACNUR sources think last week's earthquake will be the last straw for many of El Salvador's long-suffering poor. Others figure that if they've stuck out the war this long, the earthquake damage won't convince them to move either.

The ACNUR staff notes that extremely heavy fighting in El Salvador during the last few weeks, which has included some of the fiercest battles of the war, may also cause another wave of immigrants. How the Monge administration will react to that—or to an influx of Guatemalans or Nicaraguans—is still unclear.

The biggest day-to-day problem that the refugees face is money. They aren't allowed to work at any jobs in which they could displace a Costa Rican worker, a situation which some refugees interviewed resent, yet understand.

"We've got experience and skills in certain fields," comments a former college instructor. "We should be permitted to start businesses, or agricultural projects that could help us be self-sufficient, and help Costa Rica at the same time."

ACNUR is trying to develop exactly those kinds of small businesses, says Juan Manuel Castro. Some of the eighty-one projects started, like a soap factory, a ceramics workshop, bakeries, a carpentry shop, and an electronics repair service are thriving, letting the five or six families participating in each become independent of ACNUR's assistance.

Other businesses, like an educational toy factory employing fifty refugees in Heredia, failed.

"It shut down because the people didn't have any experience in that field and ACNUR didn't give them the right kind of counsel or advice," complained a refugee familiar with the factory.

"We gave them all the advice, moral and economic support we could," responds ACNUR's Castro. "We invested 776,000 *colones,* and the Red Cross bought 300,000 *colones'* worth of toys for the refugees' Christmas party.

"It was a lovely idea, and it's sad it didn't work," he adds. "It should have done fine—the problem was entirely internal. The families involved didn't agree on anything, and they ended up suing each other in local courts."

Several months ago, some ACNUR officials predicted that large numbers of Guatemalans would join the Salvadoran and Cuban refugees here. So far that hasn't happened, as Guatemalans seem to be adopting a "wait and see" attitude toward the new government that took over in a coup in March. But there are already several hundred Guatemalan refugees in Honduras, note ACNUR spokesmen, and some may eventually arrive here.

Also in doubt is the status of Nicaraguans. Calle notes that the anti-Sandinistas active in Costa Rica—whether planning an armed insurrection or only talking about one—don't qualify for refugee status. "According to the treaties under which we operate," he explains, "people who are actively fighting a sovereign state aren't refugees."

A few hundred Nicaraguans were granted refugee status here after complaining of persecution by the Sandinistas. But recent reports of 6,000 Miskitu Indians seeking refugee in the Atlantic province of Limón are exaggerated. Although there are some 8,400 Miskitus in Honduran camps, ACNUR workers estimate the number of Miskitus in Costa Rica at between 6 and 100.

"We recognize that refugees will continue to be with us," says Minister Gutiérrez. "This commission will analyze the future problems."

THE NICARAGUANS

When the Sandinista soldiers came after him, Adán Torres and his wife Corína Cernas gathered their nine children and eight horses and headed for the nearest border.

A year later, the close-knit farm family bides its time inside the Tilarán refugee camp, an overcrowded collection of concrete-block buildings huddled amid the low hills of northern Costa Rica.

The Torres family is among thousands of Nicaraguans leaving behind the violence and hard times of their homeland for neighboring Costa Rica, swelling refugee camps, spawning community protests, and alarming Costa Rica's leaders.

"It's a tremendous problem," said Luis Alberto Cordero, vice-minister of the Costa Rican presidency who oversees refugee affairs. About 30,580 refugees—nearly all Nicaraguans—are registered in Costa Rica. But Costa Rican president Oscar Arias says there may be as many as 250,000 Nicaraguans, a figure questioned by some refugee officials.

Costa Rica has invited the International Committee for Migrations, a United Nations–affiliated group, to attempt a count.

If Arias's estimate is true, it would mean that one of every ten people in Costa Rica is from Nicaragua.

Flow Has Slowed

Though refugee officials say the flow of Nicaraguans into Costa Rica has slowed considerably in recent months, practically none are headed in the opposite direction.

The United Nations is paying the bulk of the costs for feeding and housing those Nicaraguans who register as refugees but that does not solve the social and political problems posed by their presence in Costa Rica.

"When we want to install a refugee camp in one community or another, the first response is: 'No,' " said José María Mendiluce, head of the United Nations refugee office in the capital of San José. "For them it means disease, crime, that the Nicaraguans are going to take their jobs and bring a whole series of problems."

Nowhere to Go

To help Costa Rica absorb the influx, which began in 1982, the United Nations has opened six refugee compounds. Three are full. Two other camps originally intended as reception centers have become virtually permanent as refugees with nowhere to go extend their stay.

The sixth center, built with funds from Holland and the United Nations, opened last year on two hundred acres in the southern part of the country. Playa Blanca, as it is called, is a rural settlement whose residents help support themselves through fishing and agriculture. The center, being opened by phases, will eventually house five hundred people.

The oldest and largest of the camps is Tilarán, located in Guanacaste Province some fifty miles south of the Nicaraguan border. Built fifteen years ago as a center for workers building an electric plant, Tilarán was reopened in April 1983 as a refugee settlement.

It was originally intended for no more than 1,500 workers, but Tilarán now houses 2,537 refugees who crowd into long and narrow tin-roofed buildings, with several families sleeping together dormitory-style. Wooden bunk beds line the walls of each building.

Tilarán's residents receive housing, food, and medical attention. Adults as well as children have a chance to go to school. A few of the refugees hold jobs outside the camp, picking coffee or cutting sugarcane when the work is available.

Adán Torres and his family abandoned the family's small farm near Blue-fields on January 27, 1986, after the Sandinistas accused Torres of collaborating with U.S.-backed *contra* rebels.

"We cared for the *contras,*" said Torres, who says his motives were never political. "When they came to our house, we gave them food to eat," he said. "They are *campesinos,* just like us. A lot of them are our friends."

Fleeing Farmers

More than 7,000 registered refugees are living at the various camps; another 23,000 scattered throughout the country also receive U.N. assistance. Like forty-four-year-old Torres, many of the refugees are farmers fleeing Nicaragua's rural areas.

While many say they fled Nicaragua for political reasons, refugee officials believe economic conditions motivated large numbers to steal across the two-hundred-mile border.

Last year, the United Nations poured $7.5 million into refugee assistance programs in Costa Rica; this year it expects to spend $9 million. The Dutch and Canadian governments, as well as the European Economic Community, also have funded programs.

Costa Rica's leaders say the outside support does not subsidize all their expenses. Beyond that, government officials must also contend with resistance from Costa Ricans afraid of losing their jobs or their communities to the Nicaraguans.

"The Costa Ricans don't like us," said Torres, exhausted after earning $5 cutting sugarcane for a day. "Right in front of us they say we come to take their jobs. They say, 'What a mistake we made letting in these Nicaraguans.' "

Vice-Minister Cordero said that despite the problems brought on by the recent wave of Nicaraguans, there have been positive aspects. Farmers have come to rely on them as they harvest sugarcane, coffee, and cotton crops.

NOTES

1. Luis Burstin, "Costa Rica Teeters: Can 'Perpetual Neutrality' Survive?" *New Republic,* June 18, 1984; Samuel Stone, "Costa Rica's Political Turmoil: Can Production Support the Welfare State," *Caribbean Review* 10, no. 1 (1981): 42–46.

2. *New York Times,* 12 April 1981.

7.5 In Fearful Costa Rica, the Yanquis Are Welcome*

BY STEPHEN KINZER

Even though Costa Rica adopted a stance of neutrality in Central America, public opinion has been far from impartial. Anti-Nicaragua sentiment is pervasive. Yet as Stephen Kinzer indicates in this reading, Costa Ricans' anti-Sandinista or anti-Communist sentiment is at times hard to distinguish from their long-standing attitudes of cultural superiority, sometimes with racist overtones, toward Nicaragua. Encouraged by the conservative media, fear of Nicaragua and the Sandinistas intensified after diplomatic skirmishes, border clashes, and occasional incidents of domestic political violence. These concerns also provided the main impetus for the modernization of the Costa Rican security forces. But as Kinzer notes, suspicion of Nicaragua was so widespread that little opposition was voiced to upgrading the Civil and Rural Guard forces or to the presence in 1985 of U.S. military advisers.

Kinzer has been a correspondent for the New York Times *in Central America.*

AS the United States gradually increases its military aid to Costa Rica, one thing seems missing in this country without an army: popular protest.

To a remarkable degree, Costa Ricans are united by the belief that they face a threat from neighboring Nicaragua. They perceive the small but growing American military presence here as necessary to guard against that threat.

"We are not preparing an army," said President Luis Alberto Monge in May after the arrival of the first contingent of American Green Berets, who are training a new unit of the Costa Rican Civil Guard, but he added, in a clear reference to Nicaragua, that Costa Ricans should be prepared "to defend ourselves against terrorism, subversion, and the possibility of foreign invasion."

Since 1981, when American security assistance was renewed after a thirteen-

New York Times, 11 July 1985.

year lapse, the United States has provided $26 million to train and equip Costa Rican forces. Much of the money has been used to strengthen government forces operating along the border with Nicaragua.

A TRADITION OF TRANQUILITY

"In terms of dollars, Costa Rica is a bit player in what we are doing in Central America," said an official at the United States Embassy here. "But in political terms it is very important. We very much want to maintain Costa Rica as it is."

Costa Rica emerged from civil war in 1949, and the army was abolished. Two uniformed forces, the Civil Guard and the Rural Guard, which total about ten thousand soldiers, are charged with enforcing law and order and protecting national security.

Costa Rica is traditionally tranquil, and guard units have not sought sophisticated equipment or training until recently. A Western diplomat said this week that his residence was guarded by a civil guardsman who did not carry ammunition because "it would be too dangerous."

But a series of terrorist attacks over the last five years in Costa Rica, some of which were said to have been instigated by Nicaraguans, as well as continuing border incidents, have convinced many Costa Ricans that Nicaragua seeks to undermine their country and its pro-American government.

CHARGES OF MILITARIZATION

As the climate in Central America changed after the 1979 revolution in Nicaragua, many leading Costa Ricans supported efforts to modernize the guard. This has led to charges that the country, which jealously protects its image as a neutral democracy, is being militarized with United States help.

The American aid program here will arm civil guardsmen with "the same kind of equipment as a United States infantryman," according to one of the officials involved in drawing it up. This means each soldier would be equipped with an M-16 automatic rifle, and that units along the border would have grenade launchers, 80-millimeter mortars, M-60 machine guns, and other combat weapons. Delivery of these items and others, including communications equipment, has already begun.

American assistance has also paid for paving roads and other improvements in northern Costa Rica and for the purchase of several helicopters and patrol boats. Last week, four small planes were delivered to the Civil Guard.

Other countries have also provided security assistance to Costa Rica in recent years, though the United States remains by far the main source of such aid. According to diplomats here, Israel and West Germany have provided training to a small antiterrorist squad about which little has been disclosed publicly. They said Venezuela, Taiwan, and South Korea have provided small amounts of assistance.

SPAIN AGREES TO HELP

Minister of the Interior Enrique Obregón said last month that Spanish police officers "highly specialized and experienced on matters of terrorism and drugs" would "help train selected members of the Rural Guard."

Such steps have led Sandinista leaders to charge that Costa Rica has, in effect, created an army, in violation of a constitutional ban. Officials here deny the charge, noting that the standard accouterments of an army, such as a justice system, a corps of general officers, and a body of strategic doctrine do not exist in the Civil or Rural Guard.

Aside from a few small protests organized by university students and leftist politicians, there has been no important criticism of the campaign to strengthen the security forces.

Costa Rica's suspicion of Nicaragua, it is generally agreed here, has two strong motivations, anticommunism and a generalized feeling of contempt for Nicaraguans of all persuasions.

A LEGACY OF CIVIL WAR

Costa Rican anticommunism is largely a legacy of the 1948 civil war, in which Communists were defeated in a bid for power. The anti-Nicaraguan feeling is even older than that.

"We consider ourselves somewhat cultured here," said an engineering student who reflected widely held opinion. "The Nicaraguans are thick-headed Indians."

Public opinion surveys support the conclusion that Costa Ricans strongly oppose the Nicaraguan government and want more foreign military assistance. Carlos Denton, who heads a polling firm affiliated with the Gallup Organization, said anti-Sandinista sentiment had become "so overwhelming that we're even wondering whether to keep asking about it."

"More than 80 percent of the people favor the presence of the military advisers," Mr. Denton said. He said his polls had a 2.5 percent margin of error.

There is, however, one prominent Costa Rican who has refused to join the anti-Sandinista chorus. He is perhaps the most widely respected of all Costa Ricans, José Figueres, the two-time president who defeated the Communists in the late 1940s and then abolished the army.

"I would like the Sandinistas to change their attitudes and language," Mr. Figueres said in an interview. "I would also like the United States to stop telling Nicaragua what to do and to stop telling Costa Rica what to tell Nicaragua to do, which is what is happening."

7.6 Terrorism: Fallout from Area Violence Shook up Ticos*

BY THE *TICO TIMES*

Beginning in the early 1980s, a wave of violent incidents heightened concern that Costa Rica, no longer a peaceful oasis in a turbulent Central America, was becoming destabilized. Some journalists and political analysts raised the specter of "Lebanonization," with small bands from elsewhere in the region carrying out vendettas on Costa Rican soil. The Costa Rican Right and the U.S. Embassy pointed to the "terrorist threat" as the key reason for modernizing the country's security forces and for periodically cracking down on foreign exiles and refugees. This review of violence in 1982—the worst year for terrorist incidents—highlights the diverse political motives of those involved and suggests something of the fear produced in traditionally tranquil Costa Rica.

THE year had barely begun when Ticos had another bitter taste of terrorism, setting a frightening pattern for the rest of 1982.[1] Most of the violence involved Central American groups using Costa Rica for terrorist activities directed against their foes back home, but the new administration of President Luis Alberto Monge blamed local Communists, and their links with Nicaragua and Cuba, for attempting to destabilize Costa Rica's democracy.

No matter who was to blame, the violent fallout from Costa Rica's neighbors alarmed Ticos, and the new government responded by appealing for security assistance from friendly governments around the world, beefing up the nation's poorly trained, ill-equipped Civil and Rural Guard forces, training an elite antiterrorism force, and calling for a volunteer corps of citizens to help battle terrorism.

Costa Rica's determination to defend itself did nothing to improve relations with the Sandinista government in neighboring Nicaragua, which grew steadily chillier as the year progressed, finally hitting a new frosty low when the Nicaraguan [government] accused Costa Rica of "selling out" to the United States, and Costa Rica retorted by blaming Nicaragua for involvement in local terrorism.

The first incident to shake up Costa Ricans occurred in early January, when twenty-year-old Kaveh Yazdani, the son of a wealthy Iranian family living here, was kidnapped by three men in a parking lot outside a San José discotheque.

*Tico Times, 1982 Review, p. 5.

It was to become one of the year's unsolved mysteries, as reports of a feud with another Iranian family here, and the suspension of the former National Security Agency subdirector following discovery of weapons in the Yazdanis' Curridabat mansion, clouded the case. A week after the kidnapping, a Salvadoran being tailed by police investigating the case fled and then shot himself after shooting it out with police. He was found to be carrying false immigration documents, but his connection to the kidnapping was not clear.[2]

Only a week later, a foiled kidnapping attempt against Salvadoran businessman Roberto Palomo, head of the giant ADOC shoe company in El Salvador who was overseeing a local branch of the firm, resulted in three would-be terrorists dead and three injured in a shootout with rural guards in Tres Ríos.

Two Salvadorans captured in the melée confessed to being members of a group called the Central American Revolutionary Workers' Party (PRTC), founded in 1980 and receiving some of its training in Nicaragua. A Guatemalan and two Salvadorans killed in the shootout were traveling on false passports, and police said the group had intended to ask a $3 million ransom for Palomo. It was the first time Ticos had heard of the PRTC, but it was to resurface later in the year.

Raids on dozens of local homes uncovered a "safe house" in Curridabat holding a well-equipped "people's prison" beneath a trapdoor in a closet, apparently built to house Palomo. University of Costa Rica professor José Luis Rojas, who was renting the house with his wife, was arrested.

In late February, unidentified terrorists blew off the door of the Rohrmoser apartment of Nicaraguan counterrevolutionary leader Fernando Chamorro Rapaccioli with a high-powered bomb, and a lone gunman fired at Chamorro's twenty-one-year-old son, Fernando, Jr., wounding him seriously. Also wounded were Barbara Kelly Smith, the Canadian wife of U.S. economist and author Jerome Smith, when shrapnel from the bomb blast peppered the couple's apartment next door, and Marvin Araúz, a Nicaraguan friend of Chamorro's. Chamorro, Sr., said the attack was meant for him. The gunman was never caught.

Costa Ricans realized just how dangerous things had become when in mid-March, police staking out a suburban house on the trail of Yazdani's abductors stumbled on one of the biggest arms pipelines to the guerrillas in El Salvador.

Police seized $250,000 worth of arms and ammunition and arrested nine suspects, including Nicaraguans, Salvadorans, Costa Ricans, a Chilean, and the group's alleged ringleader, Argentine Carmelo Sbezzi, who was carrying Argentine, Swedish, and Costa Rican passports. They also raided a garage where fleets of cars were outfitted with special compartments and documents for the overland gun run to El Salvador.[3]

This find was followed two weeks later by the discovery of an arms cache in the home of veteran Communist leader Manuel Mora, who claimed the guns, ammunition, grenades, and TNT were for his "personal security" and had been stored at his home by his son, who had fought with the Sandinistas.

Violence erupted again in early July, when the San José offices of SAHSA, the Honduran national airline, were destroyed by a powerful bomb blast. No one was injured in the 1 A.M. explosion, which apparently was coordinated with similar blasts in Honduras, following a "declaration of war" by Honduran army officers against leftists. A week after the blast, a Colombian who said he had worked with the M-19 guerrillas in his country fingered three Nicaraguan diplomats here as the "intellectual authors" of the bombing. Costa Rica ordered the diplomats expelled, and Nicaragua promptly retaliated by expelling three Costa Rican Embassy officials.[4]

In August, rural guards in the northern area of Sarapiquí found an arms cache buried on a farm, and called it the "tip of the iceberg." In early September, a group calling itself the "Families of Political Prisoners in Costa Rica" made its first public accusations against Costa Rica, charging that jailed terrorist suspects had been tortured and their trials had been intentionally delayed. Government officials angrily denied the charges, and blamed the trial delays on the court system's unfamiliarity with terrorist crimes and the complexity of the cases.

In late September, a routine investigation into the murder of a money-changer resulted in the arrest of four Nicaraguans identified as members of the ultraright-wing Fifteenth of September Legion, an anti-Sandinista group composed of former Somoza national guardsmen. Police seized lists of weapons and ammunition, maps of the Peñas Blancas area near the northern border, and addresses of "safe houses" and local contacts. It was the first evidence that former *somocistas* were operating here.

In October, Ticos realized that in addition to acting as unwilling hosts for assorted terrorist groups, they were also providing the backdrop for spy-vs.-spy vendettas. Salvadoran Embassy civil attaché Eduardo Avila was declared persona non grata after another Salvadoran, Dagoberto Zambrano, testified before a Limón court that he had watched Avila plant a bomb in the car of Cuban Luis Medina in August.

The bombing, in which Medina was critically injured, originally was believed to be the result of a love triangle. But Zambrano confessed to being a Salvadoran secret agent, and said Avila—who later turned out to be implicated in the 1981 murder of three land reform officials in El Salvador—was running an espionage center in Costa Rica. Medina was later identified as a convicted murderer who had escaped from a Florida prison and was believed to be running guns to El Salvador. Both Medina and Avila had disappeared from Costa Rica before the revelations were made.

The same week, Argentine Héctor Francés was kidnapped in front of his Los Yoses home by four men who wrestled him into a car driven by a woman. The ex-Argentine army lieutenant was later identified by local police as a covert operative for the Argentine government, and in early December appeared on a videotape distributed to international news agencies denouncing CIA plans to destabilize Nicaragua. His wife charged he had been coerced into making the tape.

In November, five Salvadoran men and one woman brandishing automatic weapons tried to kidnap Japanese executive Tetsuji Kosuga from his Sabana home. The kidnap was foiled by police and neighbors, but Kosuga was critically injured in the ensuing shootout and died of complications from his wounds three weeks later in a Houston hospital.

One kidnapper also died and one was wounded in the shootout, which also left a neighbor, a passerby, and a policeman wounded. Three captured terrorist suspects were identified as low-echelon members of the PRTC, sent to Costa Rica to kidnap Kosuga and hold him in a "people's prison."

Reacting to the violence, Costa Rica moved to beef up its security on several fronts. Vice-President Armando Araúz announced that immigration rules would be tightened, and the department was moved from the Ministry of Public Security to the Ministry of the Interior. Costa Rica asked for—and received—$2 million in "nonlethal" security assistance and $150,000 in training from the United States, patrol cars from South Korea, riot gear from Taiwan, rifles from Venezuela, police training from Panama, and the promise of credit for the purchase of patrol cars and shotguns from Argentina.

In late November, an executive decree authorized the formation of the Organization for National Emergencies (OPEN), and fifteen hundred citizens of all ages and walks of life responded to the Ministry of Security's call for volunteers to undergo training in elementary police procedure every night at ministry headquarters.

Costa Ricans prepared for 1983 with a sad sense that the old days of peace would never come again—but with a fierce determination to combat the new threat together.[5]

NOTES

1. Prior to 1982, there were a number of significant incidents, including the December 1980 *contra* attack on *Radio Noticias del Continente* and a series of clashes in March–June 1981 that involved a leftist Costa Rican group variously known as the *Comando Carlos Agüero* (after a Costa Rican who had died fighting Somoza) or *La Familia.* The latter group's actions began with a bombing of the Honduran Embassy and an attack that wounded four U.S. Embassy marine guards. Subsequently, *La Familia* and the authorities engaged in two shootouts, one of which left three police, a taxi driver, and a guerrilla dead. Most of the band was later rounded up, tried, and convicted. Before being brought to trial, one member, Viviana Gallardo, was killed in her jail cell by a guard who claimed to be enraged by her involvement in the death of his fellow policemen. He was later convicted of her murder, but rumors and speculation about a possible conspiracy lingered.—EDS.

2. Yazdani was freed in January 1983 in Panama, where he had apparently spent much of his captivity. He implicated members of the Salvadoran guerrilla movement in his kidnapping. —EDS.

3. The members of this group were sentenced to between ten and twelve years and then pardoned on condition they leave the country. Every Latin American country refused to receive them and they eventually were admitted to Libya.—EDS.

4. The arrested Colombian was also a draft dodger, who may have been threatened with deportation. A former Costa Rican ambassador to Colombia, who was acquainted with the accused, described him in a telegram quoted in the press as having a "fantasizing and unreliable personality." Although he was subsequently acquitted of all charges, Reagan administration officials continued to cite this incident as demonstrating Nicaraguan complicity in "exporting terrorism." See *Semanario Universidad,* 10–16 September 1982; *Tico Times,* 22 April 1983.

5. Violence abated in 1983, although in June, a bomb, possibly intended for leaders of the Nicaraguan ARDE *contras,* exploded prematurely in a San José parking lot killing one Nicaraguan and wounding another, who were believed to be the bombers themselves. The following year, a time of increased feuding within the *contra* movement, saw the La Penca, Nicaragua, bombing directed at Edén Pastora (see Reading 7.10) and an attempt on the life of *contra* leader Alfonso Robelo.—EDS.

7.7 The Fragmentation and Disappearance of the Costa Rican Left*

BY MANUEL SOLÍS

The "threat" of leftist destabilization has been a recurring theme in the rhetoric of both the Costa Rican Right and the Reagan administration. Yet, as Manuel Solís indicates in this article, the Left in Costa Rica is small and divided, with few immediate prospects for improving its position. In spite of the severe economic crisis of the early 1980s, the Left parties have had little success in extending their political influence. Increasingly, they have been wracked by divisions over doctrinal and tactical issues. In terms of electoral strength, the Left parties have also lost strength. In 1982 they elected four deputies to the fifty-seven-member Legislative Assembly—the most since being permitted to return to electoral politics in 1970—and received 7.7 percent of the votes for deputies and 2.7 percent of the votes for president; in 1986 they elected only two deputies and received 5.1 percent and 1.3 percent of the vote for deputies and president respectively. Many Costa Rican political analysts believe that in 1990, the Left may be without any representatives in the Assembly.

Solís holds licenciatura *and master's degrees in sociology from the University of Costa Rica and is a doctoral candidate at the Free University of Berlin. The author of several books on Costa Rican politics and development, he has served on the faculty and as director of the University of Costa Rica's School of Anthropology and Sociology.*

WHAT is the meaning of the December 1983 split in the oldest, most consolidated party in the Costa Rican Left, the Popular Vanguard Party (PVP)?

*"Fragmentación, proliferación y desaparición en la izquierda," *Aportes* 18 (1984): 48–49. For a more detailed analysis of the issues discussed here, see Manuel Solís, *La crisis de la izquierda costarricense: consideraciones para una discusión,* Serie Tiempo Presente No. 1 (San José: CEPAS, 1985).

Is it just one more of a number of splits that Left parties have experienced, or does it have greater implications? We do not believe these questions, recently raised by many people, can be answered easily nor by a single person, so this discussion will be limited to indicating points that should be included in any debate on this topic.

One thing is immediately clear. The PVP split occurs at a time when the Costa Rican Left appears to be extremely weak and politically incapable of responding to the country's crisis. Obviously the worsening of the economic crisis has not been accompanied by a strengthening of this left political alternative. With few exceptions, popular discontent has not been channeled politically or taken an organized form. In this sense, the crisis has become a backdrop against which the Left's accumulated weaknesses appear in their true dimensions. The PVP split, the recent split in the Revolutionary People's Movement (MRP), divisions within the Socialist Party (PSC), and the very disappearance of the Popular Front (FP) all share something fundamental, which cannot be simply attributed to the failure of particular individuals or groups, or to organizational or disciplinary problems.[1] For a force as institutionalized as the PVP to disintegrate, a political reason must exist, one that even the protagonists themselves may have failed to discern in all of its dimensions.

Second, the split in the PVP, like earlier splits in other leftist organizations, is an indication of political crisis. But it is clear that the crisis was a reality before the split actually took place. The crisis of the Left expresses itself in such divisions precisely because once they occur, debate centers on their particular form, rather than on their underlying causes. The two Communist parties existing today consider themselves heirs of a political tradition that they never call into question.[2] Such traditions encompass these parties' relationship with the International Communist Movement, their basic definition of the nature of this country, and the tasks they set for themselves. I am not interested in discussing here whether the political line and tactics followed to date are "correct." While the parties are always debating the "correctness" of their political line, they never seriously debate Costa Rica's concrete historical reality. Discussing this would require the Left to engage in a self-critical review and reinterpretation of our country's history. This is the truly crucial issue. To agonize, as if this were the point, over finding quotes from Lenin to use against Martov, or giving more or less democratic interpretations to "democratic centralism," is simply a sterile exercise and only a repetition of what occurred in the Socialist Party split six years ago, an experience that should be recalled if only as a reminder of how not to get to the heart of the problem.

Third, a political crisis is a crisis in thinking, in conceptualization. The Left is not where it is today because it lacks people willing to work and sacrifice. It is where it is because it has been unable to come up with a political program responsive to Costa Rica's historical reality. Such a program would have to include adequate definitions of the problems a political strategy should solve if it is to have any hope of success. It would also have to consider Costa Rica's specific situation in the Central American and Latin American contexts without reducing it to general formulas.

Certain things are quite apparent. Some people on the Left believe that in this country political reflection consists of discussing subjects like the "paths to revolution," "the stages," the "labor-*campesino* alliance," or "armed or peaceful struggle." Yet these concepts have only peripheral relevance to our historical and social realities. More specifically: What statement of any substance has come from the leftist parties on the system of domination that has characterized Costa Rica? Have they clarified its basis, why and how it reproduces itself, what explains its degree of legitimacy? What effort has been made to understand the political role of the small and medium-sized agricultural producers of the Central Valley, a politically unknown quantity that is indisputably a part of any popular project? What about the middle sectors, their role in the maintenance of the political system or their overall importance in the life of this society? With what qualitatively superior improvements would the Left replace liberal Costa Rican democracy? Is it really enough to offer the formula of a popular government or the experience of the existing socialist states? One could raise many other similar questions, to which only rudimentary answers exist.

Comparing the theoretical political arsenal of the Costa Rican Left with that developed in his time by Rodrigo Facio [see Reading 2.1], the weakness of the former seems pathetic. In a country where theoretical and ideological debate should hold the same status as armed resistance does elsewhere, we find that the Left itself lacks the kind of systematic reflection that could serve as the basis for a convincing program, one that would be attractive to the people. It is curious that a volume of the collected speeches of Manuel Mora was published four years ago, yet even now nobody has critically evaluated it, despite the nature of the experience it documents.[3] What is the significance of a Left that fails to reflect upon its own experience? There are only two possibilities: either everything is so self-evident that there is no need for any reaction, which is totally untrue; or this kind of reflection is accorded low priority, which brings us back to the question we raised about the marginality of our theoretical groundwork.

Fourth, in discussions of the PVP split, the problems of defining a Leninist organization and, more specifically, of democratic centralism, have reemerged. As suggested above, these are not the pivotal questions. The 1978 split in the Socialist Party occurred over practically the same issues. Now, in the PVP, those who once defended democratic centralism in an "orthodox" way (that is, the defeated Mora faction) are opposed by leftists who base their argument on democratic centralism. Now, democratic centralism's erstwhile defenders join the ranks of those branded as factionalists working to undermine the party.

A political program relevant to the history of Costa Rica must begin, not necessarily by denying, but certainly by questioning the appropriateness of what is called Leninist organization. If we start off with an indisputable principle, such as democratic centralism, we not only prevent debate on forms of organization, but we also largely condition our ability to reflect upon reality itself. The Left parties' reading of Lenin gives us a vision of the world according to which subjects that should be discussed in concrete, specific terms are not seen as important objects of reflection because a readily available thesis pertaining to them exists. There are some very clear symptoms of this syndrome. The world tends to be proletarianized; we lose sight of the real popular classes. Social sectors tend to be grouped together in accordance with superficial, general formulas. The definition of the state is greatly simplified. The problem of democracy appears unworthy of much reflection, either in terms of criticizing liberal democracy or defining what will replace it. Even less attention is paid to what democracy ought to mean for the process of coalescing the popular sectors and for their struggles. A debased Marxism leads to formulas without content, to political movements that are incapable of carrying out a consistent criticism of society.

Fifth, the events of recent months indicate to us that there are two minds among the organizations of the Left. One is an orthodox mind, which applies elevated formulas concerning revolutionary theory. The other is a pragmatic mind, which—because of its other, orthodox side—ends up playing with a poorly understood and ineffective "realism." This is very clear with respect to the PVP split. Within the two groups, it is possible to identify a nationalist tone more "suited to the circumstances" in Manuel Mora and his sector, in contrast to that of his more orthodox and Leninist adversaries. In the PVP, this schism occurs in the form of an abrupt organizational split.

In cases like those of the PSC and, as far as we are aware, the MRP, similar processes have resulted in a displacement or softening of positions over the years. At first in these groups, and particularly in the MRP, there was a radical, orthodox stage. Today both the PSC and the MRP seem to have moved in a direction that is somewhat similar to the initial, more "national" positions of the Popular Front [see note 1] and, therefore, to those of Manuel Mora. In the cases of the MRP and the PSC, it seems to us that the reason for this displacement is their recognition of their weakness as political organizations. In fact, one of these groups (the PSC) is practically extinct.

Where will the MRP and PSC wind up in this process of becoming more flexible, given that they are no longer following the guidelines of orthodox language? This terminology reflected a type of political commitment. But in its absence, the realism-pragmatism now used as a political criterion may very well lead to these organizations being limited to supporting the proposals of various sectors within the traditional parties, with the consequent risk of being converted into mere left-wing pressure groups. If they fail to arrive at a fundamental redefinition of the Costa Rican situation, how will they maintain their autonomy? What political programs will nourish them? They may make simple tactical adjustments to momentary problems, but this is a long way from offering a different social alternative that could attract the majority of the people in this country.

In this connection, what occurred among the principal leaders of the Popular Front merits reflection. From a kind of nationalist innovation they moved to the Right, an occurrence not attributable only to the individual influence of their leader Rodolfo Cerdas. There were political elements, such as those outlined above, that permitted this shift to occur.

This is certainly an incomplete list of problems to be discussed, and the current situation in all of its ramifications remains to be explained. For the moment, it seems important to us to make clear that the question of fragmentation-proliferation-disappearance of leftist organizations has a wider impact. The problems raised also affect that large group of persons who, though unaffiliated with any particular organization, desire something better for this country and for its people.

NOTES

1. The Revolutionary People's Movement (MRP), which at times presented itself as the Workers Party *(Partido de los Trabajadores),* was a small organization to the left of the traditional Communist PVP. Its main support came from university sectors and peasants and agricultural workers in a few regions of the country. Originally self-defined as Marxist-Leninist, it changed its name in the early 1980s to Movement for a New Republic (MNR) and moved closer to the ruling social democratic National Liberation Party (PLN). The small Socialist Party (PSC) also defined itself as Marxist-Leninist, although it has modified this stance in recent years. The Popular Front (FP), which was led by political scientist Rodolfo Cerdas and existed for most of the 1970s, considered itself a multiclass Left organization and called for a "new democracy" based on national, Costa Rican traditions.—EDS.

2. Since the 1983 division in the PVP, Costa Rica has had two Communist parties. One, led by Arnoldo Ferreto, retained the PVP name. The other, led by former PVP secretary general Manuel Mora, calls itself the Costa Rican People's Party (PPC).—EDS.

3. Manuel Mora Valverde, *Discursos* (San José: Editorial Présbere, 1980). Manuel Mora was secretary general of the Communist Party (and its successor, the Popular Vanguard Party) from its founding in 1931 (see Reading 2.7) until the 1983 division in the PVP.—EDS.

7.8 Costa Rica's Right-Wing Paramilitary Groups*

BY JEAN HOPFENSPERGER

Not content with the pace at which the government was beefing up its security forces, growing numbers of right wing Costa Ricans have joined paramilitary organizations. These groups have a variety of goals that include evicting squatters from large landowners' properties, preparing for a Nicaraguan invasion of Costa Rica, aiding the contras, and repressing Costa Rican leftists. This analysis by journalist Jean Hopfensperger notes

*Originally published as "Costa Rica: Seeds of Terror," *The Progressive,* September 1986, pp. 24–27.

the ties of the armed right wing to the U.S. Embassy, the Costa Rican Security Ministry, and the nation's largest newspaper, La Nación.

Hopfensperger (also the author of Reading 7.3) covered Central America for several years for a variety of publications. Currently, she is a reporter for the Minneapolis Star Tribune.

VICTOR Wolf, a third-generation German cattleman, is a successful rancher in northern Costa Rica. Tall and tanned, he looks more like the Marlboro Man than a typical Costa Rican. That's because Victor Wolf is not a typical Costa Rican.

Wolf has worked for the CIA for years, says former minister of security Juan José Echeverría. Wolf describes himself as a leader of a "nationalist Costa Rican group that is dead set on not letting this country fall into the hands of the Reds." Members of the group, says Wolf, include "anyone who has something to lose"—ranchers, businessmen, skilled tradesmen. They receive paramilitary training, spy on leftists, infiltrate university discussion groups, break up squatter settlements, and wage their own private battle against drug traffickers.

"We've followed Communist agents who sneak into the country," Wolf says. "They come in with a black case with $1 million in it. The first thing they do is go to the Nicaraguan Embassy." These agents pay off hundreds of people, he contends. "I tell myself, what can you expect from someone who doesn't believe in God," says the rancher, who claims his crusade against communism is divinely inspired. "My commander isn't even on Earth."

Wolf's group is convinced that Costa Rica, with no standing army, is incapable of defending itself against the "internal and international Communist threat." Members are trying to inform and organize students, business people, ranchers, and religious workers across the country.

"I think the civilians know the problem, but they don't know what to do about it," says Wolf. "They're not trained. So when we see a problem, we take care of it."

Wolf is part of an armed right-wing movement gathering strength in Costa Rica. At least six paramilitary groups have taken shape during the last few years, and these groups are changing the face of Costa Rica, long considered democracy's showplace in Central America. Most of the groups operate with the knowledge and approval of the Costa Rican Ministry of Security, and four of the organizations have been integrated into Costa Rica's national reserve. Members of the paramilitary groups hold prominent positions in the Costa Rican government.

For the moment, these rightist forces have not resorted to the type of death-squad activity that marks their Salvadoran or Guatemalan counterparts. However, they are planting the seeds of internal repression that could ripen in the future.

"They do not pose a threat now," says former minister Echeverría. "But if there is a government that doesn't maintain their privileges, these groups could be converted into something more dangerous."

Most of these groups include members with ties to the United States, through military training, collaboration with the CIA, friendships with U.S. Embassy personnel, or work as security officers with U.S. multinational corporations.

Ronald Reagan is their patron saint. One of the groups sent Reagan a letter congratulating him on the invasion of Grenada. Several color photographs of Reagan and Vice-President George Bush adorn the walls of the San José headquarters of the Free Costa Rica Movement. Explains one Movement militant, "For us, having Reagan as U.S. president was great luck."

Directly or indirectly, the United States provides the paramilitary groups with arms, training, and political ammunition. The four groups that have been integrated into the national reserve receive military instruction with U.S. weapons donated to the Costa Rican Civil Guard. And the many members who belong to the Costa Rican national security forces also benefit from training by U.S. military officers based in the country.

"Officially the CIA has no links to the reserve," says Echeverría. "Unofficially, they do."

Adolfo Jiménez was a pilot in the Bay of Pigs invasion. Today, he lives in Costa Rica. A cattle exporter in the northern province of Guanacaste, Jiménez continues the fight against communism.

"We're dead anti-Communists" without U.S. support, Jiménez says. Wealthy cattle ranchers and sugarcane growers refer to the president of the United States as "Papa Reagan," Jiménez adds.

Ludwig "Viko" Starke also worked with the U.S. government on the Bay of Pigs operation. He allowed 1,500 Cuban exiles to receive military training on his ranch in northeast Costa Rica before the invasion. Like Jiménez, Starke carries on the ideological battle; he is one of the founders of Patriotic Union.

On two occasions, CIA officers visited a reserve command outside San José, says a trainer at that unit who prefers to remain unidentified. The trainer expresses concern about the ideological instruction that has come to characterize the reserve. "One of the shouts was 'Good Communist, Dead Communist,'" he recalls.

U.S.-financed weapons for the Nicaraguan *contras* wind up in the hands of the paramilitary groups. Some members say they have purchased arms from the *contras* or received them as gifts. John Hull, reportedly the CIA's liaison with the Nicaraguan Democratic Front (FDN) in Costa Rica, sold weapons on two occasions to members of the Free Costa Rica Movement, says Peter Glibbery, a British soldier of fortune who says he took orders from Hull. "The FDN sold weapons to anyone who'd buy," Glibbery says [see Readings 7.9 and 7.10].

The most visible and influential group is the Free Costa Rica Movement

(MCRL), a right-wing civic organization with an armed branch. This year marks the twenty-fifth anniversary of the organization, which was created in 1961 "to thwart Cuban expansionism," members say.

Some of the founding members had close ties to the U.S. Embassy, which donated boots, backpacks, canteens, and other equipment to the fledgling anti-Communist group. "They gave us a lot of equipment, especially for the boys in the mountains," says Gilbert Alfaro, a San José attorney and member of MCRL's board of directors. "But they didn't give weapons."

Currently the Movement does not receive material aid from the United States, he says. But U.S. agencies apparently do share intelligence. Before the Central American Peace March made its ill-fated trip through Costa Rica last December, the U.S. Embassy gave Movement members a document discrediting the march, says Rubén Vargas, head of the Costa Rican Taxi Drivers Union and Movement member. "They had documentation to show that the KGB was behind the march," says Vargas. "It showed the whole hierarchy of organizers."

The peace marchers were later jeered and stoned when they entered San José. Ironically, some of the reservists who were "protecting" the marchers against Movement protesters were also members of the paramilitary group.

Hundreds of drivers of the red taxis that dart through San José belong to the Movement as well, Vargas says. According to Vargas, MCRL provides instruction using Fal and Galil rifles, mortars, and antiaircraft weapons.

"There's a law that prevents the use of arms used in war," Vargas says. "But you can get around it."

One way to receive formal military instruction is to join the volunteer national reserve. Former vice-president Armando Araúz confirms the practice. "It's better to have them in the reserve than out there doing other things," he says.

The arrangement benefits the paramilitary groups as well. "It's more secure," explains one MCRL member. Many reserve instructors are private trainers in the Movement. As reservists, they use the Civil Guard's weapons and train at police academies and private ranches. Some of these ranches are also used for private paramilitary instruction, says former Rural Guard deputy director Pedro Arias. If a private training camp is uncovered, members can claim it's a ranch used by the reserve, says Arias, who uncovered a Movement training camp near San José last year.

Adolfo Louzao, a Costa Rican who fought with the U.S. Marines in Vietnam, says his paramilitary group also was integrated into the reserve. Louzao was the military trainer for the North Huétar Democratic Association in 1983, a group based in San Carlos, the heart of cattle and *contra* country.

"I trained the men in guerrilla warfare," he says. "I got some retired North American [military] specialists I knew from Vietnam to help. . . . Our group was called 'Special Forces' of OPEN" (the Organization for National Emergencies, which is now the national reserve).

Louzao, a former guard at the U.S. Embassy, says his group was training to defend Costa Rica from a potential Sandinista invasion. While waiting for the attack, they've kept themselves busy.

The group reportedly broke up squatter settlements on members' land, and it squelched a hospital-workers' strike in San Carlos.

"We told them [the strikers] that if they didn't leave San Carlos, we'd whip them," Louzao says. "We had all the truck drivers go to the hospital with chains, just waiting to go in. The strikers got scared and left."

Cattle rancher Wolf employs a similar technique for helping his friends remove squatters who set up shacks on their land. "We went in and told them they had five minutes to think about it," says Wolf. "Once they realized they'd get shot at if they didn't, they left."

Some actions by these groups are more explicitly political. Militants of the Free Costa Rica Movement led an attack last year against the Nicaraguan Embassy in San José, during which they ripped the national shield off the building and hurled stones and rocks at the embassy.

The photograph of the attack that appeared in the country's largest daily newspaper, *La Nación,* contained small black spots over part of the shirts of the men hurling the stones. The photographs had been altered to eliminate the insignia of the Free Costa Rica Movement, the University of Costa Rica newspaper later revealed.

Such favorable treatment of the Movement is hardly surprising, since the vice-director of *La Nación* happens to be vice-president of the Movement. (A sign in the reception area of the newspaper's suburban office reads, Private Enterprise Produces Liberty.) At least one other journalist is on the twenty-member board of directors. The Movement has a press club which "prepares articles for publication," said Carlos Federspiel, a San José businessman who is a member of the group's board of directors. Although the Movement places a full-page ad in the paper each week, "most of the news appears in other pages," he says.

Much of this so-called news comes from the Movement's files on leftists and subversives. All the groups have intelligence systems, ranging in sophistication from the North Huétar association's eavesdropping to a reported computerized information system used by a group called Patriotic Union.

The groups try to infiltrate the major universities, which are viewed as prime recruiting grounds for Communists. MCRL, for example, has a university branch that monitors professors and students. Wolf's group goes so far as to seek out and plant right-wing agitators in campus lectures. "We stress intelligence," says Wolf. "We want names, who they talk to, what they do."

The existence of these groups is a well-kept secret guarded by national-security officials and the influential members of the press. Few Costa Ricans, even in government, have ever heard of them.

The groups attract rural and civil guards, wealthy Costa Ricans trained at

U.S. military institutes, combatants in the 1948 civil war, powerful ranchers, and former pro-Nazi Germans and their children.

A GUIDE TO COSTA RICA'S RIGHT

At least six paramilitary groups operate in Costa Rica. Information on these groups is based on interviews with members and Costa Rican officials.

Free Costa Rica Movement (MCRL) is the oldest, most visible, and most influential of the groups. Its 1,000-strong armed branch is divided into the "Blue Berets" for younger men and "Tridents" for more experienced fighters. The members reportedly train on ranches near San José and near San Isidro General in the south. Some members hold important government-security positions, including jobs as trainers in the national-reserve forces. The MCRL maintains ties with the White Hand Death Squad in Guatemala, the Miami-based exile group Alpha 66, and the World Anti-Communist League.

Patriotic Union is a group of about 1,000 men who claim they are preparing to defend Costa Rica against a Nicaraguan invasion. Formed in 1983 by former combatants of the 1948 civil war, it has members throughout the country. They say their goal is to guard Costa Rica's infrastructure during an attack and to fight off an aggressor for at least twenty-four hours. Although not all members have weapons, the group claims it has a system in place to provide arms and ammunition to all members in the event of an emergency. The group maintains a sophisticated intelligence service which shares its information with the government.

The North Huétar Democratic Association, based in the northern city of San Carlos, began with about 200 members in 1983. The number has now dropped to about fifty. The group's first objective was to help the *contras.* But members have broken up squatter settlements and squelched a hospital strike in the zone. They have asked to patrol Costa Rica's northern border to prevent Sandinista incursions, but the Costa Rican government denied the request. The U.S. Embassy also refused to allow the group to participate in a committee selecting guards for the local Voice of America tower.

The Reserve is the name that one cattle rancher gives to a subgroup of national-reserve volunteers who have formed their own paramilitary group. The men, mainly from the city of Liberia, receive private military instruction on members' ranches in addition to their reserve training. Unlike regular reservists, who return their weapons after training, this group has purchased its own arms and uniforms. A top priority of this group is aiding the Nicaraguan *contras.* It provides logistical and economic support to the rebels and funnels aid from sympathetic Costa Ricans and Central Americans. Some members also allow the *contras* to train—and recuperate—on their ranches.

The North Chorotega Democratic Association, based near the town of Liberia, is a group of about thirty men that is loosely connected to the North Huétar Association.

Country and Liberty is a group based in the province of Guanacaste that took responsibility for the 1985 bombing of an electrical tower that supplied electricity to Nicaragua. According to a press communiqué issued at the time, its objectives included mining the grounds around the electrical tower to identify Costa Ricans who would risk their lives to defend the Sandinistas. The communiqué warned "immoral" Costa Ricans to change their ways or they would be subject to "similar actions." It also said Costa Ricans should "keep watch over their neighbors because at any time we will be visiting homes looking for information." The group includes supporters of former Nicaraguan dictator Anastasio Somoza and of the Independent Guanacaste Movement, an organization that wants the province of Guanacaste to secede from Costa Rica and become a U.S. state.

Most of the groups were formed in 1983 and 1984 with the backing of the local economic elite, the Ministry of Security, and the *contras* who use Costa Rica as a base of operations against Nicaragua. Some Costa Ricans believe they are part of a larger U.S. plan to facilitate an invasion of Nicaragua and the repression of Costa Rica's Left under the pretext that they are Sandinista sympathizers.

"Because of the *contras,*" warns former Costa Rican congressman Miguel Angel Guillen, "a military infrastructure is now in place that can be used in the future for whatever purpose these paramilitary groups want."

Several internal factors have also accelerated the formation of these groups. During the administration of Luis Alberto Monge, who was in power from 1982 to 1986, the groups enjoyed the government's support. The new minister of security was Benjamín Piza, a founding member of the Free Costa Rica Movement. As Patriotic Union founder "Viko" Starke put it: "Piza was a true democrat."

In the new administration of President Oscar Arias, which took power in May 1986, six MCRL members are in high positions, says Movement director Bernal Urbina. The vice-minister of national security, for example, acknowledges he is a former member of the Movement's board of directors. And the vice-minister of interior is a "sympathizer" of the group, said a Movement member who preferred to remain unidentified.

At the same time, the nation's judicial system apparently is unwilling to crack down on members of these groups. Two members of one group who confessed to bombing an electrical tower that provided electricity to Nicaragua spent only a few weeks in jail, says former Rural Guard deputy director Pedro Arias. And when Arias discovered a military training camp used by the Free Costa Rica Movement last year and filed suit, the judge dismissed the case, claiming the camp was used by the reserve.

"That's how things always end," says Arias.

Such a lax attitude may have its costs. "We're playing with fire," says Arnoldo Ferreto, a former legislator and leader of Costa Rica's Communist Party. "People talk about the Central Americanization of Costa Rica. How do they think the death squads began in El Salvador? Do they want that to happen here?"

7.9 Foreign Mercenaries and the Contras*

BY JACQUELINE SHARKEY

As the contra *war against the Sandinistas heated up, Costa Rica began to attract an increasing number of foreign adventurers, some linked to the CIA or the U.S. National Security Council's "private network" and others freelance fighters offering to train* contra *troops or supply them with weapons. This reading by Jacqueline Sharkey describes the role of foreign mercenaries in the* contra *war's southern front and that of the North American farmers in northern Costa Rica who provided them with support and bases.*

Sharkey is assistant professor of journalism at the University of Arizona.

"I came down here to raise hell," said Steven Carr, twenty-six, as he lit up a Marlboro in the visitors' area of La Reforma prison outside San José, the capital of Costa Rica.

Carr said he came to Costa Rica "to go to war. . . . My brother was in Vietnam, and I was really pissed that I didn't get to go. . . . I grew up with John Wayne movies. I was in ROTC, the Civil Air Patrol, and I was weaned on that stuff."

Carr got tired of waiting for his chance at combat, so last March he decided to become a real-life Rambo and traveled to Costa Rica to fight "the Communists."

He wanted to join the *contras*—the U.S.-backed rebels trying to overthrow the leftist Sandinista government of Nicaragua, which lies on Costa Rica's northern border.

For six weeks, Carr lived out his dreams. He was armed and transported

*Excerpted from "Disturbing the Peace," *Common Cause Magazine,* September/October 1985, pp. 21–32. Research for this article was supported by The Fund for Investigative Journalism. Kathleen E. McHugh and John S. Day also contributed to this article.

to the *contra* camps by anti-Communist groups he said were led by Cuban exiles and a farmer from Indiana who Carr and Glibbery said was a CIA liaison in Costa Rica.

The high point of Carr's short-lived career came around mid-April, when he claims to have participated in a raid on a Sandinista camp a day and a half's march inside Nicaragua. He thinks about thirty Sandinista troops may have been killed.

Carr believes bad publicity about that raid may have contributed to the narrow defeat of one of President Reagan's requests for aid to the *contras* last April.

He added he believes the defeat of the *contra* aid ultimately may have led the CIA to arrange for his arrest. Carr said that the day after the House vote, he and four other foreign-born adventurers were sent by an alleged CIA liaison to a *contra* camp in Costa Rica, where they were arrested hours later by Costa Rican public-security forces.

Some people dismiss Carr as nothing more than a crazy adventurer, but his story has serious implications. He is a link in a chain of private groups and individuals in the United States who stepped in to help the *contras* in Costa Rica and Honduras after Congress refused to extend funding for the rebel movement in mid-1984. These private groups have provided the *contras* with an estimated $25 million in arms, ammunition, and supplies since then. Some organizations also are sending men to train and fight with the rebels. Their leaders—who include retired military officers—also pass military intelligence and other information to top administration officials. . . .

When he left his Naples, Florida, home last March for Costa Rica, Steven Carr had no idea that the events that followed would have international repercussions. All he was looking for was a little excitement.

Carr talked about his experiences in late July during an interview at La Reforma prison, fifteen miles outside the Costa Rican capital of San José.

He had been there since late April, when he was arrested with four other men—another American, two Britons and a Frenchman—who allegedly were also working with the *contras.* The five were charged with possession of explosives. A trial date had not been set at the time of the interview.

Carr and one of the Britons, Peter Glibbery, met me in the visitors' area of the medium-security section of the prison. No guards accompanied the two men. They simply walked into the room—a large, cheery office—sat down at a wooden table and started to talk.

Carr immediately made several things clear. His checkered past includes military service, a short stint as a door-to-door magazine salesman in Bangor, Maine, and a criminal record. He was on probation for grand theft when he came to Costa Rica. Carr and Glibbery said they are not mercenaries. "We didn't expect pay," Glibbery said. "It would have been nice; I wouldn't have refused it," Carr added. He said he spent over $1,000 of his own money to come down to Costa Rica.

"We were just stupid ideological people" who wanted to fight communism.

Carr's and Glibbery's experience with the *contras* is a story of arms smuggling and alleged Central Intelligence Agency (CIA) covert activities. The men said these activities included discussions about having the *contras* carry out terrorist operations in Costa Rica and blaming it on the Sandinistas.

Carr's saga began in June 1984, when he visited Costa Rica for the first time.

His stepfather, a Naples businessman, had some friends who told him to contact Bruce Jones, an American who owns two farms and an interest in a citrus nursery in northern Costa Rica. Jones was later declared persona non grata and forced to leave the country because *Life* magazine published an article earlier this year identifying him as a "key" CIA liaison with the *contras*.

Carr said Jones told him he couldn't join the guerrillas until he had learned Spanish, so Carr returned to the United States.

Carr said he corresponded with Jones and that last January he met him in Miami, where Jones led Carr to members of Brigade 2506, a *contra* group led by Cuban exiles, including several survivors of the abortive 1961 Bay of Pigs invasion. Leaders of the group wanted to establish a base camp in southern Nicaragua, and Carr was to show them how to set up perimeter defenses and stage raids.

First, however, he helped them obtain weapons. U.S. law forbids American citizens who aren't licensed from exporting arms, but Carr was undeterred. He said that during the weeks he spent in Miami, he helped collect .50 caliber machine guns, M-16 rifles, and a 20mm cannon.

He said they also got lethal equipment from Tom Posey, the head of Civilian Military Assistance, an Alabama-based group that recruits people to fight with the *contras*. Peter Glibbery says it was Posey who helped him get to Costa Rica.

Posey has acknowledged to reporters that he provides the *contras* with fighting men, but denied that he deals in weapons.

Carr said he also got help obtaining weapons in Miami from another American—Robert Thompson, a former Florida law enforcement officer who was later arrested and jailed with Carr in Costa Rica.

Carr said Thompson told him he had been with the largest *contra* group, the Nicaraguan Democratic Force (FDN), in Honduras the previous year.

Carr said that while he and Thompson were in Miami, Thompson ran into some Dade County, Florida, police officers who were off duty. "They said, 'We'll bring some stuff that we've got in our closets at home,' so they brought us a case of shotgun shells, gas masks, flight jackets, flares."

Thompson denies this. He said in an interview that he came to Costa Rica to write freelance newspaper articles about the *contras* and was using his time in prison to write fiction. He has issued a statement calling Carr and Glibbery "crazy people" and disassociating himself from their statements.

Carr flew to Costa Rica in early March. He said he zipped through customs with the help of someone who had been associated with the country's public-security forces.

After spending several days in San José, Carr went to Muelle San Carlos, a settlement about two hours north of the capital. There he picked up his weapons and supplies, which he said had been shuttled from El Salvador by private plane to a remote dirt airstrip in Costa Rica.

Glibbery was already in Costa Rica when he met up with John Hull, a farmer and landowner who Glibbery said acted as a CIA liaison in Costa Rica.

Hull, originally an Indiana farmer, is said to be a naturalized Costa Rican citizen who has extensive holdings in northern Costa Rica, including a citrus nursery that he owns along with Bruce Jones.

The *Life* magazine reporter who wrote the story about Jones's alleged CIA involvement said in a recent interview that several sources in Costa Rica told him that Hull also was a CIA liaison. Several *contra* representatives in San José confirmed that Hull works with them.

Hull could not be reached for comment. He broke one appointment for an interview at his Costa Rican farm and did not respond to several phone calls. In the past, he has told reporters that he supports the *contras'* cause and allows wounded rebels to be evacuated from his airstrip. But he has denied working for the CIA and supplying the *contras* with weapons and equipment.

A spokesperson at CIA headquarters in Langley, Virginia, said, "As a matter of policy we don't confirm or deny allegations of agency employment. [Furthermore,] if you recall, Congress cut off CIA involvement with the *contras,* and we adhere to our legal obligations."

Glibbery said Hull told him that he finances *contra* operations in Costa Rica and southern Nicaragua with $10,000 a month sent by the National Security Council. Glibbery said Hull told him the money is deposited in a Miami, Florida, bank and that Hull once joked "God help me if the IRS finds out about it."

When advised of this allegation, a White House official laughed and said, "The NSC has not sent $10,000 or any other amount of money" to finance *contra* activities in Central America. "That's totally absurd," the official added. "We don't do those kinds of things."

Glibbery said that at one point Hull took him to a sawmill in northern Costa Rica and showed him a stash of M79 grenades and land mines. Glibbery thought the mines might be useful for the *contras,* but he said Hull told him, " 'We may need [them] to do an embassy later on.' . . . I'll never forget those words."

Glibbery and Carr added that Hull at one point discussed "blowing a few holes in Los Chiles," a town in northern Costa Rica, and making it look as if the Sandinistas had carried out the attack. The implications of such an action are especially disturbing in light of President Reagan's statements that he believes Nicaragua is a terrorist nation. The administration is considering retaliating against the Sandinistas for any terrorist incidents in Central America.

Carr said Hull became more cautious as the congressional vote concerning giving aid to the *contras* approached last April. The vote was expected to be very close, and Carr said Hull was concerned that negative publicity about *contra* activities might cause representatives who were undecided about the aid package to vote against it.

Carr said that for this reason Hull decided a *contra* raid on the Sandinista outpost of La Esperanza should not take place. But Carr said he went along when one of the Cubans decided to carry out the raid anyway. He said he and about twenty rebels marched to La Esperanza, fired rocket-propelled grenades at the Sandinistas while they were eating dinner, and may have killed about thirty Nicaraguans.

Carr said he believes the raid was the beginning of the end of his *contra* career. He said bad publicity about the raid may have contributed to the narrow defeat of the *contra* aid package in the House two weeks later. Carr and Glibbery said that the day after the House vote, Hull instructed all five of the foreigners who were with the *contras* to go to a *contra* camp inside Costa Rica. There they were arrested by the Costa Rican Rural Guard.

Carr said he believes Hull set them up because the CIA regarded them as loose cannons. "I feel John Hull had us set up because the CIA wanted us out of the way," Carr said.

He added that he and Glibbery kept silent after their arrest because they believed Hull would help get them a lawyer who would quickly obtain their release. When this did not happen, the two men began telling their story to Costa Rican reporters.

Carr and Glibbery may cast themselves as idealistic adventurers, but they represent a movement that has become a major force in the Central American conflict.[1] The two men are part of an informal network of private individuals and groups who have been arming, training, and fighting with the rebels since Congress refused to extend funding for the *contras* in mid-1984.

One of the key people in this network is citrus farmer Bruce Jones, the man who led Carr to Brigade 2506 in Miami.

Jones himself was identified as a "key" CIA liaison last spring by *Life* magazine, which also printed photographs of Jones training *contras* on his farm.

After seeing the magazine, Costa Rican officials declared Jones persona non grata and said Jones, who was in the United States at the time, could not return to Costa Rica.

Jones freely admitted in an interview that he provided logistical support for the rebels, but denied he worked for the CIA. Steve Robinson, the *Life* editor who worked on the story, said Jones's CIA connection was confirmed by a number of sources in Costa Rica. "Not one iota of information has passed across my desk that would refute a single thing in the story," Robinson added.

Since he couldn't return to Costa Rica, Jones settled in a middle-class subdivision carved out of the desert on the south side of Tucson, Arizona. Jones does not look like a man involved in international intrigue. When we met at his home for an interview recently, he was dressed in camouflage shorts and an open-necked shirt.

Jones said he spends his days managing a pistachio nursery, keeping in touch with Hull about the citrus business, and raising money to provide weapons, ammunition, and supplies to the *contras.*

He recently helped organize the Tucson chapter of the U.S. Council for World Freedom, the American arm of the World Anti-Communist League, whose leader is retired Army Major General John Singlaub, the most influential U.S. fundraiser for the *contras.*

Jones said the group is providing information about the Central American situation and is raising money for the rebels. Ironically, Jones said that the *Life* piece has helped rather than hurt his current efforts to aid the rebels. After the article appeared, people called him saying, "Here's $100," or "Here's $5,000."

Jones said his group also plans to provide food, clothing, and medicine to the *contras.* Jones pointed out that such nonmilitary assistance—whether provided by the U.S. government or private groups—helps the *contras* militarily because the money the rebels ordinarily would spend on these items can be used to purchase weapons.

Jones said he is now coordinating his activities with Singlaub. In fact, Jones met with Singlaub one day in July when the retired officer visited Tucson to speak to the "River Rats," a group of U.S. fighter pilots who fought in Vietnam and were meeting to dedicate a park at Davis-Monthan Air Force Base. Jones said he and Singlaub were going to discuss forming a national organization to coordinate private U.S. fundraising efforts so that arms, ammunition, and equipment could be channeled to the *contras* more effectively.

Singlaub—whose military career came to an abrupt end in 1977 after he publicly disagreed with President Carter over troop commitments in South Korea—agreed to be interviewed in Tucson following his speech to the River Rats. He is a short man who gazes intensely at people he is talking to.

Singlaub spoke proudly about his work with the rebels, whom he calls "freedom fighters." He said that in the last year he has raised "tens of millions of dollars" for arms and ammunition, and millions more for nonmilitary supplies.

Singlaub bristled at suggestions that he might be circumventing Congress with his activities. "It's our view that we are ahead of the view of the Congress," he said. "We believe that Congress was fooled by the massive disinformation program of the Sandinistas" when it refused to continue to fund the rebels in 1984.

Singlaub added that he believes the House and Senate's decision last summer to renew so-called nonmilitary aid to the *contras* "was a better representation of the will of Congress. But there are some hard-core left-wing [members of Congress] like [Reps.] Michael Barnes [D-Md.] and [Edward] Boland [D-Mass.] and Ron Dellums [D-Calif.] and quite a few others that have always supported the Communist organizations around the world. They tend to believe that socialism is the wave of the future and the best foreign policy of the United States is to cooperate with these socialist moods."

Singlaub said that he has assisted the *contras* by setting up an overseas bank account to handle weapons purchases. (U.S. law prohibits Americans who aren't licensed from sending weapons abroad.) He said that when U.S. contributors want to be assured their money will be spent on arms and ammunition, he gives them the foreign bank account number and tells them to send the money there. But he hastens to add that he makes it clear they can't claim the contributions as a tax credit.

Singlaub believes his activities have the approval of the White House and added that he understands that President Reagan "has been informed" of what he is doing. "Now occasionally I make telephone calls to friends [in the administration] and say, 'Look old buddy, this is what we're about to do and if you have any objections to this, if you think I'm doing the wrong thing, send me a signal. Otherwise this is what I'm going to do' . . . and I say, 'If at any time you think I'm doing something that's dumb, send me the word.' Well, until I get some word, I'm going to continue to do what the freedom fighters want me to do."

Singlaub told one reporter that he consults with Marine Lieutenant Colonel Oliver North, the National Security Council's liaison with the *contras.* North's role in providing military and fundraising advice to the *contras* and his visits to rebel camps in Central America have drawn heavy criticism from some members of Congress, who say the White House has improperly used the NSC because Congress barred government entities involved in intelligence activities from helping the *contras.*

Singlaub said he has tried to carry out some of the functions that Congress has prohibited the CIA from performing. And he added, "Now, I'll admit that the good many years that I've had serving in the CIA . . . gives me a feel probably [of] what they were doing, which probably makes me more efficient."

But he denied that this violates the law, and insists neither he nor his fundraising groups have direct CIA connections. "That's absolutely absurd," he said.

Currently Singlaub says he's invited about one hundred U.S. groups "with similar goals" but no "international connection" to become part of a Coalition for World Freedom. He says the coalition can help "democratic revolutions," such as the *contra* movement, raise funds, and counter "disinformation" programs. In addition, Singlaub said he supports the work of a number of organizations concerned with Central American issues including:

Civilian Military Assistance, Decatur, Alabama—Provides supplies to the rebels and recruits people to fight with them. This is the group that Peter Glibbery said helped him get to Costa Rica.

The Western Goals Foundation, Alexandria, Virginia—For the last several years the foundation has been sending "humanitarian relief supplies," such as clothing, to the *contras,* according to a spokesperson.

The Council for Inter-American Security, Washington, D.C.—Brings rebels to the United States to speak to different groups and arranges for journalists and others to visit with *contras* in Nicaragua. The council has also helped raise money for one of the *contra* groups according to a spokesperson.

The American Security Council, Boston, Virginia—Conducts educational and lobbying efforts regarding Central American issues, Singlaub said.

The Heritage Foundation, Washington, D.C.—A conservative think tank, the foundation denies that it is involved in the *contra* movement, although it does support the ideological goals of the *contras.*

The Conservative Caucus, Vienna, Virginia—The caucus has been lobbying hard to restore government funding for the *contras.*

Singlaub said he is also involved with several organizations working to help Nicaraguan refugees—people who have had to leave Nicaragua because of the conflict in that country. This type of assistance helps the *contras'* military effort in several ways. Many *contras* benefit directly because they operate out of refugee camps. An estimated 2,500 rebels live in refugee camps in Costa Rica alone, according to a source in San José.

Also, many *contras'* families reportedly are refugees, and the rebels have had to allocate money to support them. Fernando "El Negro" Chamorro, leader of a *contra* group called the Nicaraguan Revolutionary Armed Forces (FARN), echoed the feelings of many *contra* leaders when he said in a recent interview, "We have had to maintain the families of the combatants and also the refugees. That is a moral responsibility." But he said when the *contras* get "humanitarian" aid from the United States, the *contras* can then use their own money to buy weapons and bullets.

Singlaub says he also helped the Nicaraguan Freedom Fund, a refugee assistance group originally organized by the conservative daily *The Washington Times,* by putting fund officials in contact with the *contras.*

Singlaub is on the board of directors of yet another group—Refugee Relief International, Inc. This tax-exempt, nonprofit corporation, which provides medical services to refugees, was set up with the help of the Omega Group Ltd., which publishes *Soldier of Fortune* magazine. One of the top people involved with the magazine, Colonel Alexander McColl, served under Sing-laub in Vietnam.

In addition to Refugee Relief International, *Soldier of Fortune* is involved in several projects that provide direct assistance to the *contras.*

Most people dismiss *Soldier of Fortune* as a publication for mercenaries who love to tell war stories. But it is much more. A magazine with a slam-bang writing style that sells about 200,000 copies a month, *Soldier of Fortune* is also involved with the El Salvador/Nicaragua Defense Fund, which provides non-lethal equipment such as boots and uniforms to the *contras.*

And although *Soldier of Fortune* editors insisted in an interview that they do not recruit people to fight with the *contras,* the magazine has been sending "private-sector military professionals" to Central America to train and advise the rebels. These men, typically ex-military personnel and *Soldier of Fortune* staffers, spend time with different *contra* groups and then frequently write about their experiences for the magazine.

Sometimes, however, the magazine's instructor-journalists get involved in the fighting in various places. *SOF* founder and publisher Robert Brown once told an interviewer, "I've been shot at many times for this magazine. It's always been worth it."

SOF's most recent trip to Costa Rica took place last winter. The team traveled to San José to make contact with the *contra* group called FARN—the Nicaraguan Revolutionary Armed Forces.

Editors said the *SOF* team traveled with FARN leaders into southern Nicaragua and then spent several days instructing the *contras* in combat skills such as how to shoot down Russian-made helicopters. The June 1985 issue of *Soldier of Fortune,* whose cover is adorned by actor Sylvester Stallone attired in "Rambo, First Blood II" garb, carried a breathless, first-person account of the training team's activities.

Alexander McColl, director of special projects for the Omega Group, said that *SOF* is considering sending more training teams to Costa Rica.

The magazine is involved in other efforts as well. One goal, McColl said, is to increase public awareness about "the threat" of communism in Central America, and it does this not only through the magazine but through television appearances and other high-visibility operations. For example, *SOF* founder Robert Brown's recent offer to pay $1 million to any Sandinista who defected with a Soviet high-tech Mi-24 helicopter made the front page of *USA Today* and numerous other publications.

"The whole plan, you know, is you buy the helicopter for $1 million and then you turn around and sell it to U.S. or other free-world intelligence for about $2 million, and then you've got $1 million left over to buy beans and rice for the troops. That's how that works. You know, we may be dumb but we're not stupid," McColl said. "The more profit we make, the more fun and games we can play in Central America."

McColl said the staff maintains close relations with members of the Reagan administration and shares military data and other information that they acquire on their trips to Central America.

He said the editors "have access to various very senior people in Washington. We can go in and sit on the guy's doorstep and tell him what's going on and so on."

He denied, however, that the group has any connection with the CIA, as some Reagan administration critics have alleged.

McColl, who has a Harvard law degree, also denied that *SOF*'s activities circumvent congressional restrictions on U.S. government involvement in Central America.

"The president makes foreign policy and we are simply attempting to carry on as much of the president's foreign policy as our rather limited resources permit," McColl said.

"What we have been trying to do, both in Salvador and in Nicaragua, is to carry forward the objectives declared by the commander in chief and president, and which the Democrats in the House of Representatives were doing the best they could to sabotage."

Another American who is trying to carry out the president's foreign policy goals is John Cattle, a gunrunner who spends about six months a year in Central America.

Cattle, who mixes Christian dogma with anti-Sandinista rhetoric, is the head of the American Freedom Fighters Association of Camden, Tennessee, which supplies arms, ammunition, equipment, and fighting men to the *contras*. In an interview in July in San José, Cattle said he was in Central America to carry out God's will.

Cattle said he complies with U.S. law by purchasing weapons in places such as Jamaica and Canada. He has no doubt that the White House approves of his conduct.

He is contemptuous of the *Soldier of Fortune* types who have come to the region. He said they have come not to fight, but to seek "fame and glory." He said *SOF* magazine founder Colonel Robert Brown is "a viper playing on the lives of the people here for his own gain."

Cattle said the American Freedom Fighters include thousands of fund-raisers and about forty "hell raisers" who buy guns, munitions, and equipment for the rebels and fight alongside them.

Cattle, who described himself as a "profoundly religious" person with "a little bit of violence" in his background, said he spends much of his time inside Nicaragua with the Miskitu Indians and Creoles who are fighting the Sandinistas. He carries in his wallet pictures of himself with the rebel fighters, along with snapshots of his wife and two little girls.

Cattle said one of his priorities is to strengthen the *contras'* southern front, which runs along the Costa Rican–Nicaraguan border two hundred miles north of San José.

During his current trip, Cattle explained, he planned to try to lay the groundwork for setting communications and supply lines through Costa Rica to ensure an uninterrupted flow of guns and ammunition to the rebels. Cattle was upset that some Costa Rican officials were making this task difficult for him.

"How can they expect the freedom fighters to get a foothold in southern Nicaragua if they can't get supplies regularly? The Costa Rican government has no right to criticize [the *contras*] for hitting the Sandinistas and then running across the river" into northern Costa Rica, Cattle said.

Cattle hoped the "problem" with Costa Rica could be resolved by the time he returned in September.

He added, "Somebody from the U.S. government, maybe the ambassador . . . should sit down with these people and jerk them up and tell them what's going on."

Cattle agrees with the objectives of President Reagan's Central American policy, but he is concerned about the way the policy is being carried out. He is especially disgusted with the CIA. Cattle said he runs his own intelligence operation in the area, which he claims does a better job of keeping tabs on the Sandinistas than the CIA does. The government's agents "don't know how to get out in the dirt and get information," Cattle said.

"You want to know how to find a Company [CIA] man in Tegucigalpa?" he asks. Just go to the major hotel, "and there's a big round table. . . . They're all there playing with their girlfriends, waiting for someone to come in from the field and tell them what's going on," Cattle said scornfully.

Cattle has even less regard for members of Congress.

"Congress doesn't mean anything in regard to the law. God's word is the law. The Bible is the law and I believe every word in it," he said.

"President Reagan has let us know that he's pleased with us. He hasn't told us in so many words, but he's let us know," Cattle declared.

Cattle predicted that the *contras* would overthrow Nicaragua's Sandinista government before the conclusion of Reagan's second term, with or without the help of Congress.

He said he "wouldn't bet peanuts" that the new government of Nicaragua will be a democracy, but added that isn't his problem.

"I have one job: to overthrow communism. The new government may be a dictatorship. Hopefully it won't be as bad as Somoza's, but who knows? The big thing is, it won't be Communist," Cattle said.

"I am profoundly religious. As I see it, there are two armies—the Sandinistas' army and God's army. I'm in God's army. My job on this earth is to try to destroy the work of the devil."

NOTE

1. While still in prison, Carr told the *Tico Times* (October 18, 1985) that he feared his talking to reporters would lead to attempts on his life by elements of the Costa Rican government, the CIA, and right-wing Cuban exiles. "I'm pretty sure they're going to dust me off [kill me] when

I get back to the States," he remarked. He was released on May 16, 1986, and later claimed that he left Costa Rica for Panama with the assistance of U.S. Embassy officials. On December 13, 1986, he was found dead of a cocaine overdose near a friend's California apartment.—EDS.

7.10 The Carlos File*

BY MARTHA HONEY AND TONY AVIRGAN

*On May 30, 1984, a press conference called by ex-Sandinista-turned-*contra *Edén Pastora at the Nicaraguan border settlement of La Penca ended in mayhem when a powerful bomb exploded. The assassination attempt took place at a time when Pastora was under heavy pressure from the CIA to align his ARDE* contras *with the* somocista-*dominated FDN. In the aftermath of the blast, journalists Martha Honey and Tony Avirgan, who was injured at La Penca, uncovered what even their editors at* The Nation *referred to as a "bizarre" tale of an FDN* contra *hit squad linked to right-wing Cubans and Americans and to the Costa Rican security forces. It was part of a much broader plan, they argue, to establish a* contra *force financed by drug and arms smuggling enterprises. While many details of the story remain murky, some key aspects of their allegations have subsequently been confirmed by other investigators, and by the congressional Iran-*contra *probe. With the help of the Christic Institute, Honey and Avirgan later filed a lawsuit against key figures in the Iran-*contra *scandal.*

Honey is a freelance journalist who reports for the Times *and the* Sunday Times *of London, the BBC, and Pacifica Radio. Avirgan is a cameraman for ABC and reports for the BBC and National Public Radio.*

FOR the past eighteen months we have been investigating the explosion of a bomb at a May 30, 1984, press conference called by Edén Pastora Gómez, head of the Democratic Revolutionary Alliance (ARDE), which operates along the border between Costa Rica and Nicaragua. Three journalists and five *contras* died in the blast, which took place in the Nicaraguan border town of La Penca, and twenty-six others, including Tony Avirgan, were injured. Propelled by our personal link to the tragedy and by the growing realization that no government or police agency was seriously investigating the bombing, we sought to uncover the identity of the bomber—a man who, journalists at the press conference say, posed as a Danish photographer, planted a metal box containing the bomb and vanished, uninjured, shortly after the explosion. Our research was supported in part by the Newspaper Guild and the Committee to Protect Journalists.

A year's worth of interviews with more than one hundred people in Central and South America, the United States and Europe failed to uncover the bomber's name or many of the details of the plot. We did, however, gather

The Nation, 5 October 1985, pp. 311–15.

proof that U.S. officials and Costa Rican security officers planted stories in the press, pinning the blame on the Sandinistas and the Basque separatist organization, Euzkadi Ta Azkatasuna (ETA). A number of leads also pointed to Central Intelligence Agency participation in the bombing. Several current or former CIA agents and informants—including a high-ranking Uruguayan police officer and a Cuban from Miami—told us that the agency was behind it. And in the course of our investigation, several names recurred: John Hull, an American who owns and manages a ranch and other extensive properties in northern Costa Rica; a high-ranking official in the Costa Rican Ministry of Public Security; and an anti-Castro Cuban named Felipe Vidal Santiago. Many of our sources implicated these three men in the bombing and said that they all have ties to the CIA. (In an interview with us, Vidal denied he had a CIA connection, and Hull told other reporters that he was not involved with the agency.) Despite all our efforts, we were still no closer to discovering the identity of the bomber.

Then, in March, a young Nicaraguan walked into a San José bar and sat down next to a Costa Rican carpenter named Carlos, the neighbor of a North American woman who works in our office. The Nicaraguan, who called himself David, told Carlos about the existence of a dirty tricks squad working for the Nicaraguan Democratic Force (FDN), the leading *contra* group, and said he knew the identity of the La Penca bomber. Through his neighbor, Carlos contacted us, and in the months that followed we supplied him with questions to ask David as well as with approximately $50 for David's cab fare, to facilitate their meetings. David's story raises numerous questions, and some of it cannot be verified. But as long as there is a chance that he was telling the truth, his story must be published so that journalists and members of the U.S. Congress can investigate his charges.

David's story opens with a string of coincidences that strain North American credulity but are plausible in the overheated, factionalized atmosphere of Central America. On Friday, March 29, 1985, Carlos was sipping a beer in the Rendezvous Bar near the U.S. Embassy in downtown San José. Three men came in; from their accents Carlos judged them to be Nicaraguans. Two of them then left, telling the other to wait for them. This man, described as short, dark skinned, and young, with a smooth round face and straight black hair, immediately turned to Carlos. "You must help me," he whispered. "Hide me. I want to get away. I don't want to be involved any more in their things. They are going to dynamite the U.S. Embassy and many innocent people will die. I want to get out."

For the next ten minutes, David poured out his story. He claimed to be part of a right-wing group composed of anti-Castro Cubans, Nicaraguan *contras,* Costa Ricans, and North Americans with ties to the CIA. They operated from safe houses and *contra* camps in Honduras, Costa Rica, Panama, Nicaragua, and Miami, he said, moving "in and out of Costa Rica like a dog from its own house." He said the group was responsible for the La Penca bombing and was planning a series of terrorist attacks which would be blamed on the Sandinistas. These include bombing the U.S. Embassies in Costa Rica and in Honduras, attacking the offices of Costa Rican president Luis Alberto Monge Alvarez, and assassinating the U.S. ambassador to Costa Rica, Lewis Tambs, Miskitu leader Brooklyn Rivera, and Urbina Lara, a well-known *contra*.

David trembled as he spoke and seemed near tears. "I am an anti-Sandinista," he told Carlos. "But these people are much more evil than the Sandinistas." He also claimed they trafficked in cocaine, marijuana, and arms. "They are making money off the blood of my brothers and using our cause to get rich." When Carlos asked why he didn't tell his story to the Costa Rican authorities, David replied that a number of government and security officials were collaborating with his group. Out of desperation, he had chosen to confide in a sympathetic-looking stranger. Carlos explained that he could not hide David in his house. As the other two men entered the bar, David urged the carpenter to keep in touch.

Carlos mulled over David's story for several weeks. On three separate occasions he saw David's companions near the U.S. Embassy. Once they got into a gray limousine without license plates. But what overcame Carlos's reluctance to get involved was the announcement, on April 2 that Costa Rican rural guardsmen had arrested nine Nicaraguan *contras* and five foreign mercenaries at a FDN camp located on a farm managed by John Hull of the United States. David had told Carlos that part of his group used that camp. Now Carlos feared that the U.S. Embassy really might be bombed. He contacted his neighbor thinking that she might be able to alert U.S. officials. She notified us, and we spoke with the embassy's security officer, George Mitchell, who seemed unimpressed.

David's story represented a possible breakthrough for us. At last we might have a source who could confirm the rumors we had been hearing and fill in the gaps in our investigation. We urged Carlos to contact David again, and one Saturday not long after, he saw David and the two others near the U.S. Embassy. When David's companion left to make a telephone call, Carlos slipped him a note with our number. David refused to meet with us because of the danger of being seen talking to "gringos," but over the following weeks, he met with Carlos at a series of prearranged spots—a park near the university, a hotel, a bus. We supplied specific questions and Carlos tape-recorded their conversations whenever possible, took notes, or simply remembered what David had told him.

Carlos described David as being extremely nervous, repeatedly telling Carlos that the others in his group didn't trust him and had threatened to kill him and his brother who was with the FDN inside Nicaragua, if he was caught passing information. David was planning to flee but was awaiting his brother's arrival from Nicaragua with the rest of the hit team. In the meantime, he told Carlos, he wanted to expose the dirty tricks squad.

David told Carlos that the man who had planted the bomb at the press conference and who had identified himself as Per Anker Hansen, a Danish photographer, was a right-wing Libyan exile named Amac Galil. He was hired in Chile by two FDN officials and a CIA agent who poses as a journalist, David said. Galil was considered ideal for the job because if his identity became known, most people would assume that he was working for Colonel Mu'ammar al-Qaddafi. David said the bombing was planned at meetings in Honduras attended by FDN leader Adolfo Calero Portocarrero; two Miami Cubans, Felipe Vidal Santiago and René Corbo; John Hull; and a North American who was identified to David's group as being from the CIA.

This story meshed with other accounts we had heard. After analyzing a voice recording of the man later identified as the bomber, made by journalists on the scene, linguists concluded that he was not a native Spanish speaker, and several speculated that he was either Libyan or Israeli. Some of the people whom David and others had implicated in the plot circulated a story that the bomber was a Libyan working for Qaddafi.

In addition we knew something about several of the alleged conspirators. Calero's desire to get rid of Pastora so the FDN can open a second front in southern Nicaragua is well known in *contra* circles. We have a copy of the diary of a U.S. mercenary soldier who served with the FDN. In it he describes a meeting at Calero's house in Miami at which the murder of Pastora was discussed by Hull, some unnamed Cubans, and another man, who identified himself as being "from the company." Pastora's aides claim to have evidence linking the CIA to a plot to eliminate "Comandante Zero."

Hull is by his own admission a *contra* patron. Prior to the bombing he aided Pastora; since then, he has quietly supported the FDN. Pastora, Costa Rican security officials, and mercenaries we have spoken to all claim that Hull works for the CIA and coordinates FDN operations in Costa Rica.

Two soldiers of fortune, Peter Glibbery and Steven Carr, who say they worked under Hull, told us that he discussed with them several schemes to provoke direct U.S. military action against Nicaragua. These included staging an attack against the northern Costa Rican town of Los Chiles and "spreading around some Sandinista bodies" to make it appear as if Managua were responsible. Glibbery said that on one occasion Hull forbade him to take some Claymore mines because "we may need them for an embassy job later on."

Contra and Cuban sources say that Hull introduced Vidal and Corbo into ARDE as military trainers. The two, who have been connected with ultraright Cuban exile groups in Miami, arrived in Costa Rica in mid-1983, and Pastora aides told us they have long suspected that Vidal had a role in the bombing.

We already had reason to believe that several Costa Rican officials assisted in the plot, helped the bomber escape, and planted stories in the press. David named two of them: the man from the Ministry of Public Security and Colonel Rodrigo Paniagua, a former agent for the ministry who maintains close ties with it. Former and current ministry employees had told us that the high-level official was responsible for circulating the stories and phony documents blaming the ETA and the Sandinistas for the bombing. They also had said he works closely with the CIA. Both government and *contra* sources say that Colonel Paniagua serves as liaison between Hull and security officials. ARDE sources suspect that Paniagua knew of the bombing because he personally urged Pastora to hold the ill-fated press conference.

David also told Carlos that Galil sometimes stayed in Managua at the home of anti-Sandinista relatives of President Daniel Ortega Saavedra, who are involved in drug and arms smuggling.

On July 17, David told Carlos that Galil and his hit team would arrive in Costa Rica in a few days and carry out attacks on the embassy and other targets. Soon after, other strikes would be carried out in Honduras. On July 17, in a diplomatic note delivered to Managua, the U.S. government warned that Nicaragua would be held responsible for terrorist attacks against U.S. personnel anywhere in Central America. Horrified by this message, we contacted a Costa Rican government minister we knew to be a strong supporter of neutrality and an opponent of *contra* activities in the country and told him about the plot. He went straight to President Monge, who instructed him to work with several other officials in carrying out an investigation and snagging the hit team if it entered the country. We exchanged information with Major Harry Barrantes, an official of the Costa Rican Rural Guard, who had infiltrated the FDN.

Several days later, as David and Carlos were about to part after a long meeting, they were pushed at gunpoint into a jeep by three Costa Ricans, who cried, "We caught you, we've caught the informers." They were driven four hours until they reached what David recognized as one of the *contra* camps located near Hull's ranch house. By assaulting one of the guards, the two managed to escape. When Carlos reached San José, he called us. Tony found him, near tears from exhaustion and fright, and got him an out-of-town hiding place. Several days later Carlos insisted on returning to his house.

During the next few days, Carlos received anonymous telephone calls warning him not to talk to anyone. Known *contras* and Cubans cruised past his house, according to government security guards who had been stationed outside at our request. Then, one night, five shots rang out. Several days later, ARDE officials, who knew David because he had once fought with their group, said that they had learned that he had been murdered, and that the *contras* were after Carlos. Costa Rican officials told us the same thing.

Shortly thereafter, Major Barrantes suddenly left for the United States. His startled superiors later learned that the U.S. Embassy had issued a special invitation for him to attend a course at Fort Benning, Georgia. One of his superiors said he has "no doubt" that Barrantes was lured out of Costa Rica to cripple the government's investigation of the terrorist unit. Although we were able to confirm that Barrantes is at Fort Benning, we were unable to reach him for comment.

We made arrangements for Carlos and his family to leave Costa Rica for about a year, and on August 18 they boarded a plane for Western Europe. Several days later, the Costa Rican daily newspaper *La República* carried a distorted story that Rural Guard officials had obtained information from someone named Carlos that the La Penca bomber was a Libyan who fled to Managua after the incident. The paper implied that the bomber was working for Colonel Qaddafi and the Sandinistas.

How accurate is David's story? Does it solve the mystery of La Penca or deepen it? We have confirmed some portions of it; other sections are more difficult to verify. Some coincidences can be explained, others cannot. For example, we still don't know why David chose to confide in a stranger who happened to be the neighbor of one of our co-workers. Nor did Carlos and David ever discuss why David's companions left him in the Rendezvous Bar.

We can account for other strange assertions. It is difficult on the face of it to believe that a Libyan could pass for a Dane; and even harder to accept that a Libyan could convince the Swedish television reporter with whom he traveled for several weeks before the bombing that he was a Dane. But "Hansen" claimed that he had been raised in Latin America, which explained why he spoke Spanish but no Danish. He and Peter Torbiornsson, the Swedish journalist, conversed in English because Torbiornsson wanted his Bolivian assistant to learn the language. And Torbiornsson does not appear to have been particularly curious about his companion—not wondering, for instance, why Hansen's wallet was always stuffed with $100 U.S. bills although Torbiornsson said he claimed to be working for an obscure (in fact nonexistent) photographic agency; or, even more damning, why Hansen didn't know the most popular brands of Danish beer. Although Torbiornsson was a suspect in the bombing, David and our other sources denied that he was involved.

How could David, a relatively minor figure in the terrorist ring, know so many details of its operations? David said that his immediate supervisor was involved in the Pastora bombing and told him much about the operation.

Still, there are details we have not been able to verify. In many cases, David did not know names or positions—of a woman in the Nicaraguan Embassy, for example, who was supposed to be passing money to the *contras,* or of the Costa Rican security officials who were cooperating with the terrorist ring. And Nicaraguan officials have not been able to check out David's assertions about Galil's links with the relatives of President Ortega. Most important, we have not found independent confirmation of Galil's identity.

For all its ambiguities, however, David's tale strongly suggests that the CIA is involved in dirty tricks in Central America which are designed to provoke U.S. intervention. If that is true, Costa Rica may become the Tonkin Gulf of America's next war.

7.11 "The Government Can Be Neutral, but Not the Police." An Interview with Civil Guard Captain Víctor Julio Quirós*

BY MANUEL BERMÚDEZ

The U.S. and Costa Rican governments repeatedly argued that training the security forces—and specifically a Civil Guard counterinsurgency unit—would help guarantee Costa Rica's neutrality. Here, however, an officer of that unit—trained by U.S. instructors in Panama and Honduras, as well as at the Murciélago base in northern Costa Rica—speaks of the realities of Civil Guard activities along the Nicaraguan border. Víctor Julio Quirós sheds light not only on the Costa Rican security forces' collaboration with Nicaraguan contras, *but also on police corruption, the U.S.-directed construction of a secret* contra *airstrip and the bloody May 31, 1985, border incident at Las Crucitas, in which two Costa Rican civil guards were killed. His vigilance cost him his job.*

Manuel Bermúdez, the journalist who interviewed Quirós, writes for the University of Costa Rica's weekly Universidad *and other publications.*

HOW did you decide on a career in law enforcement and what path has your career taken?

I joined the Civil Guard in 1976. I was twenty-two years old at the time and I was attached as a private to the First Police Station [*Comisaría*], which was called the Third Company. Within a few months I was promoted to corporal on the orders of Colonel Rojas. From the very beginning I noticed how many organizational errors were being made, but I couldn't speak up about them since I had to respect the high command and obey orders. Later on I became a member of the Military Police both because of my qualifications and my height. I am more than 1.90 meters [6 feet, 3 inches] tall. I spent eight months there and then I left law enforcement work for personal reasons. Five months later I rejoined, right in the middle of the 1978 election. At that point I was chosen along with some of my colleagues to put on civilian clothing and attend the National Liberation Party's [PLN] election events as a "shock force." Supposedly this group's purpose was to provide transportation for voters. But our real function involved vandalism and violence, and although it is not permitted by the Election Board [*Tribunal Supremo de Elecciones*], the PLN has always done this.

*From *Semanario Universidad,* 15 May 1987, pp. 14–16, 20.

Later, during the Carazo administration [1978–82], I had already been promoted to instructor sergeant and was chosen to go to Venezuela to attend the Police School [*Escuela de Carabineros*]. But since I had been a PLN supporter, not only was I not allowed to go, but I was fired too.[1] I came back to my job three years later with Monge's PLN administration. When I was reinstated, I was not given the rank of instructor sergeant and they left me at corporal, but I took some tests which I passed with the highest marks in the class and they named me sergeant major.

In 1983 the Panamanians came and gave a course at the Santa Ana police school. They said it was a basic police course, but it was really a military course. In fact, it was the toughest course I can ever remember having taken. I graduated second in the class. As a result of my grades I was sent to Panama later that year.

Why did you and your colleagues receive military training if you were policemen?

What they told us was that the country was unprotected and in case there's any subversion they knew some military stuff and we had to be prepared. In Panama I spent twenty weeks in the Basic Infantry Course for Officers, which was completely military. Four of us Costa Ricans were there and we trained along with military men from Peru, Ecuador, and Honduras. In spite of the competition, we still passed with flying colors. I spent a year teaching after I came back from Panama.

In 1985 forty-five officers were selected to go to Honduras for another basic infantry course, this time for learning how to lead troops and develop leadership abilities. It was a three-month course at the Regional Military Training Center [CREM] under the auspices of the U.S. Special Forces, better known as the Green Berets. The Hondurans acted as a support force to be commanded by the officer trainees.

Only two of us came back with the rank of company commander: Captain Francisco Ramírez Pacheco, who is now also retired, and myself. Because we had received the highest marks they sent us to a new base that had opened at El Murciélago. There we continued to work with the Green Berets, preparing ourselves to be chiefs of the rapid response battalion that would be trained there. This course consisted of light infantry training, no airborne or armored stuff. . . .

How did you arrive at the northern border and what were your responsibilities there?

After the training at El Murciélago, we were sent to the border. They had already gathered a battalion of eight hundred men trained over six months' time. From May of 1985 until my retirement I stayed in that zone. I was commander of the border companies and my orders were to prevent the entry of foreign forces, that is, to enforce neutrality. But neutrality is a poor name for it, because the truth is that we have never been neutral. But that's a separate political discussion. Organizationally, the Public Security Ministry can be divided into two parts: the minister and vice-minister above and the director of the Civil Guard down below, which is what creates the problem. The High Command [*Estado Mayor*] doesn't exist, and the director puts himself in charge of making all the decisions. At that time it was Colonel Oscar Vidal. He and the subdirector didn't behave as they should have, because of their contacts with the counterrevolution. They coordinated their border operations with the *contras* instead of with the Costa Rican government. Orders were given verbally to avoid generating compromising documents.

First I spent time in Los Chiles. I was posted with Company B and we relieved the guard that was already there so they could train at El Murciélago. We were the first shipment of trained personnel to arrive in the zone, and the force was under my command. We realized that the previous force and their commanders worked directly or indirectly with counterrevolutionaries inside Costa Rican territory.

These guards were corrupt?

Definitely. Colonel Aponte, whom I relieved, worked with the *contras.* I say this because *contra* leaders themselves, such as Julio Bigotes [see Reading 7.12], came to tell me that their system was known and approved by the Security Ministry and that I could sell my services to them if I allowed them to operate freely in my zone.

When I learned of this, I informed my immediate superior, Colonel Oronte Salomón Luna, who told me to carry out my duties as originally ordered. From that moment on Colonel Luna was head to head with the director and the subdirector of the Civil Guard, although this was never revealed publicly.

What was your work like when you were on the border?

First I discovered that when a peasant tries to tell the authorities there are *contras* in the area, he does so out of fear. But the authorities are not afraid of the *contras,* but that people might find out about the corruption in the area. One time a problem came up in Las Chorreras. I told a journalist, José Rodolfo Ibarra, who had come up to our area from Telenoticias, to come along while I checked it out so he could see how the *contras* operated. But he declined and told me all he could give me was a minute on camera. That wasn't enough time to prove anything.

A short time later Company C relieved us, and we went back to the Police Academy. Then they sent me to relieve the commander of Company A, which was stationed in Upala. When I arrived, I discovered that my colleague Captain Ramírez had been accepting a lot of bribes. A *contra* offered me money and told me the commander before me had accepted it. I declined. Many others accepted bribes when they found out that their superiors worked with the counterrevolution.

What I found in Upala was that the civil guards, on orders from their superiors, functioned as logistical or rearguard support for the *contras.* That was their purpose for being there. We were just one more element of the counterrevolution. Of course, since there were only verbal orders and nothing was written down, one was kept in the zone or transferred according to how one worked. I was no use to them, because I had been prepared to clean the *contras* out of the area and that wasn't exactly what they wanted. I wasn't working for the *contras* or for the directors of the Civil Guard.

What happened when you had direct encounters with the contras?

The *contras* were mobilizing to the north of San Antonio, along the road to their training school. I had my first armed confrontation with them on that road. One day I ordered my unit to lay an ambush. Not a single shot was fired and we captured various counterrevolutionary leaders, a total of fifty-six people. Right then and there we came to an agreement that either they removed all those people from the area the next day or they surrender right there. They told me that my superiors were already aware of their presence and I replied that I didn't care and that my job was to clean out the zone. That was how the difficulties and conflicts leading to my dismissal began.

The next day at twelve noon, the *contras* removed all the trained personnel they had in the area, more than one hundred men and their equipment. It was election day and they left in two buses and a blue cargo truck with National Liberation Party flags. I don't know if they were headed toward Los Chiles or some other area, but I removed them from my zone and never heard anything about them again.

But was that the period when the contras *had a camp in Upala?*

No. The camp is four hundred meters from the border in Nicaraguan territory, but the equipment and weapons go through Upala. I found that out from some peasants who confided in me because I was an officer with principles. I counted on the peasants. My subordinates were not trustworthy, because they worked for the *contras* and the *contras* had an espionage network and "ears" [spies] in the area.

Who was the contras' *commander in this area?*

The commanders never approached us to talk themselves, they used intermediaries. In Upala there is a man who fought Somoza with the Sandinistas and who is now aiding the *contras*. These people have made the war and the people's suffering into a business, and some civil guards have found it convenient to help them do so.

What was this man's name?

Víctor González, of the González family of Upala. They have collaborated extensively with the *contras*. I don't know if they still do, but they did when I was there. Colonel Paniagua was also there, he's passed away now, and he was one of the people in charge of delivering arms and equipment to the *contras*. These supplies may have come from the Costa Rican Security Ministry.

Captain, what did you discover about the [May 31, 1985] border clash at Las Crucitas, which resulted in the death of two Costa Rican civil guards?

I was assigned to the area shortly after this incident. When I arrived at Los Chiles, I confirmed that the *contra* commanders had received insignias like the ones used by the Costa Rican guards to differentiate themselves from the *contras* and the Sandinistas. This measure was, I believe, the result of an agreement between the *contras* and the Civil Guard. A major whose name I cannot recall—he was second in command after Aponte—gave these badges and other Costa Rican insignias to the *contras*.

The *contras* put on the Costa Rican insignias and carried out an operation in Nicaragua. They caused a lot of Sandinista casualties and with good reason, because the Sandinistas didn't attack them thinking they were Costa Ricans. That's why I believe it was an error to send Costa Rican civil guards to Las Crucitas, knowing that only eight days before *contras* disguised as Costa Ricans had attacked the Sandinistas.

Logically, the Sandinistas immediately pursued the disguised *contras*. They were disoriented, and went for whatever action opened up for them, with or without distinguishing enemy insignias. The Sandinistas are people who have to defend themselves and their territory. We got ourselves in trouble with the Sandinista army when we sent our men to the zone. Possibly the orders had been to help the *contras* remove some of their wounded, which always happened after a battle. When the Costa Ricans arrived, the *contras* retreated to some hills on the banks of a little river that comes out there called the Infiernillo. At that point the Civil Guard was a perfect target for the Sandinistas, who had no means of distinguishing them from the *contras*.

And did you find out who gave this order?

Since orders are never written orders it's impossible to know. But the problems at the border are always the fault of the *contras* and of the support we have given them and continue to give them.

And neutrality?

We aren't neutral, because although the central government and its policies are neutral, the leaders of the Civil Guard are not, and the rest must obey their orders. The problem is that in police forces there is no chain of command. The minister believes what his commanders tell him. For a very long time there has been corruption in the middle levels of the Security Ministry and it is that corruption that leads us into serious conflicts, such as the trial at the Hague.[2] The Costa Rican government is in the right because it assumes the Guard obeys orders. But the Sandinistas are also right because they've seen what happens on the border. . . .

Your subordinates included those who were at Las Crucitas. How did they behave when they told you what happened there?

They were scared. Because they were taken somewhere and ordered to say what they said. This operation may have taken place to create an anti-Nica pretext for something. But they didn't take into account that the animals taken to the slaughter were human beings. I'm still not sure it was intentional on the part of the government, but it is possible.

It's a given that we don't share the Sandinistas' ideas and that they don't understand ours, but this doesn't mean we have to do things like that. Whether or not they're expansionists, it remains to be seen whether we ourselves are opening the doors to communism. I believe that corruption is the largest such door we could possibly open.

One other thing, what did you discover about the secret contra *airport?*

When I was an instructor, we spent some time at the El Murciélago base. We didn't go away for the weekend and we decided to get to know the area, to verify with our own eyes whether or not there were armed people there. We were a small group. There was one kid, Captain Wood Aguilar, who died in Liberia in a traffic accident during our training. We discovered that there were indeed armed people and knew that it wasn't the Civil Guard, because at that time no personnel had been assigned to the area. When we reached a certain distance from the base, we saw a helicopter drop cartons that were apparently filled with supplies. It was a CH-48, a military cargo helicopter. The person who certainly was aware of all this was Colonel Montero, who traveled with the patrols in this zone. Montero retired recently with a lot of money and property, as have some others.

You've recounted your experience during the Monge administration, but what happened after the government changed?

Almost nothing. They moved a few people around, but the system is still the same and the commanders are too. Maybe it's gotten worse, because trained people retired and Colonel Luna who supported my clean-up operation was forced to resign. That is what happened to me, too. When I was in Upala, I decided to initiate my own clean-up operation in the area. I knew I'd lose my job, but I had to do something because that was what the president had ordered.

During that period some observers came from the Organization of American States [OAS]. The Civil Guard leadership arranged for the *contras* to retreat fifteen kilometers inside Costa Rican territory, so that when the observers showed up there wouldn't be any problems. I found out about this when a Cuban *contra* arrived and told me what they were going to do. So I called the subdirector of the Civil Guard and told him what was going on and he told me to calm down and stay out of it.

But you had authority to arrest the Cuban who spoke to you?

Arresting one person is counterproductive, because it scares off the whole flock. You have to surround them so that all can be captured. So I looked at the map and developed a plan that consisted of dividing the area into six zones and covering the whole area bit by bit. In the first zone, because they only let me get that far, I captured fifteen *contra* rifles. My plan was to send all the supplies and people we might capture to San José's Plaza de la Cultura, so the Costa Rican people would find out what was going on at the border. Because to keep their war going, the *contras* use our territory, the image of Costa Rica, and us her citizens. I made a mistake in discussing my plan with a subordinate and the headquarters in San José was informed. They transferred me just when I had located the *contras* in a place called Cuatro Bocas, up river from the Río Niño.

I was assigned to the Crime Prevention Unit [UPD], where I had nothing to do, given that my training was in another field. I went on vacation, so I wouldn't have to do my job irresponsibly. They had also removed Colonel Luna and replaced him with Colonel Barrantes, who decided to dissolve the team [*Plana Mayor*] which the commander uses to coordinate operations. This way, he was the only one to give orders and nobody knew his motives. Barrantes had been commander in Los Chiles and had so little preparation that during the period he was in charge of Upala there was a confrontation between the Civil Guard and the Rural Guard. But he is a trusted colonel in the National Liberation Party.

And Barrantes was corrupt?

On this subject I can tell you that he had had legal problems when he was commander on the southern border, as a result of a clothing smuggling scheme. His appointment was so arbitrary that at one point Colonel Barrantes was commander of the southern border and the northern border at the same time. It's very difficult to determine if he received money from the *contras* or if others received it, because there are no documents, receipts, photographs, or anything else. But the facts speak for themselves. If vigilance is poor, it's not for lack of equipment or personnel, but rather because there is corruption. That's why they find it convenient to have poor vigilance, because if the *contras* left, they would no longer earn money by selling them their services.

How did you finally come to retire from law enforcement?

When the government changed [from Monge to Arias], [Public Security] Minister [Hernán] Garrón assigned Colonel Luna to the northern border again and he asked me to come back to the rapid reaction brigade. This was in June of 1986. But Barrantes and the *contras* pressured them to get rid of the honest officers once and for all. Colonel Luna had made me his S3 or trusted associate. But shortly thereafter, Colonel Luna was pressured to retire, in July or August, and they dismissed me on September 1 without a reason. So they got rid of me because of *contra* pressure and the agreements between themselves and Colonel Barrantes, and because I wouldn't tolerate corruption.

So you don't intend to return to law enforcement?

I think that's impossible. I'd like to be able to fight it from the inside, but one swallow doesn't make it summer time and under current conditions I wouldn't want to work there. I want people who go into the Civil Guard to know about the corruption that exists there.

NOTES

1. Traditionally most Civil and Rural Guard jobs are filled by the ruling party. Since 1948, the only instances of parties remaining in power for two consecutive terms have been the PLN victories of 1970 and 1974, and 1982 and 1986. Most civil and rural guards have thus been fired after serving four years, a practice that has contributed to limiting the strength of Costa Rica's already weak quasi-military institutions.—EDS.

2. In 1986 Nicaragua brought suit against Honduras and Costa Rica in the International Court of Justice (World Court) in the Hague, charging both countries with facilitating *contra* attacks. The suit against Costa Rica was later dropped when the Arias administration began to play an active role in the Central American peace process.—EDS.

7.12 Problems of the Southern Front*

A MEMO FROM ROBERT OWEN ("THE COURIER") TO LIEUTENANT COLONEL OLIVER NORTH ("THE HAMMER")

In this confidential 1985 memo, an emissary of the U.S. National Security Council outlines the difficulties encountered in setting up a southern front for the Nicaraguan contras. *Corruption, drunkenness, and drug trafficking are only some of the problems U.S. intelligence operatives faced in trying to turn the Costa Rica–based* contras *into an effective fighting force. As the memo indicates, the same individuals in or being considered for* contra *command positions were those suspected of "indiscretions." The document is also noteworthy for its description of efforts to woo Edén Pastora's field commanders to the* contra *faction under U.S. control and for its indications of direct collaboration between the NSC and the "private" U.S.* contra *aid network.*

Robert Owen was Lieutenant Colonel Oliver North's liaison to the contras *during the period in which Congress barred aid to the rebels. In 1985 Owen founded the Institute for Democracy, Education, and Assistance (IDEA), a* contra *lobby group that received a $50,000 grant from the State Department's Nicaraguan Humanitarian Assistance Office.*

TO: The Hammer [Oliver North] [April 1, 1985]

FROM: T.C. ["The Courier," Robert Owen]

SUBJECT: Southern Front

The following paper discusses a series of meetings the author has had over the last several weeks concerning the future of the Southern Front. These meetings

*Exhibit RWO-7 of the 1987 House-Senate Committee to Investigate the Iran-*Contra* Affair. Provided by the National Security Archive, Washington, D.C.

took place in the South and in Washington. The most recent ones were held on Friday and Saturday, March 29 and 30 in Washington.

Project for Reconstruction

The Project was conceived by seven people. They are:

- Leonel Poveda Sediles
- Carlos Coronel
- Guillermo Mendieta
- Luis Rivas Leal
- Alejandro Martínez Sáenz
- Harold Martínez Sáenz
- Juan Zavada [sic].[1]

Meeting with me in Washington were: Poveda, Mendieta, and Alejandro Martínez.

The meeting was originally proposed and set up by Arturo Cruz, Jr..

About four months ago some six of the seven came to Washington, at the urging of Nat Henry, to meet with Senator Helms. They gave the Senator the attached paper and discussed their idea but they never heard another thing from the Senator or his staff. Out of desperation they came one more time hoping to meet with the Hammer.

I had met Poveda during the summer of 1983 when I visited Costa Rica. He recognized me and was glad the meeting was with someone he knew. All three realized the reasons for the meeting with me instead of with the powers that be.

The concerns of these people and who they represent are valid. They include:

- Lack of leadership in the South
- An alternative to Pastora
- Lack of coordination between several small groups now operating
- The need for a new organization to mount operations

In essence, these people are offering their services to structure and organize a new southern front.

They say they represent El Negro Chamorro's camp, which now consists of some 43 men under the command of José Robelo (Chepón), and another camp which is under the command of the Cubans and Calero's people. This last camp is actually under the day to day command of a Nicaraguan named Jesús, but overall is under the wing of *Pape*.

Before coming to Washington, they said they had met with El Negro and had talked with the Cubans in Miami who are working the other camp. The former is true, but they did not come representing the Cubans or the other camp.

Poveda said he and Carlos Coronel had had breakfast with Calero on March 2 in Costa Rica and had discussed the possibility of building a new southern command structure. According to Poveda they have Calero's blessing.

The new organization would fall under the political leadership of UNIR and the new Nicaraguan Democratic Resistance. Militarily it would come under the command of Leonel Poveda, who along with the other seven would help structure and command the new force.

The crux of their plan is to develop small bases of no more that 100–150 men several hours away from each other on the Nicaraguan side of the border. . . . Initially they want to start with 150 men.

These groups would be resupplied by purchasing the food and other basic necessities from the small towns and villages along the Costa Rican and Nicaraguan border. They would not buy the food and other material in San José and truck it out like Pastora used to do.

Weapons and ammunition can be purchased on the black market to start. AK's go for about $300 a piece. An inventory of their equipment is attached. Once things get moving, they believe material can be either airdropped or flown into small fields. This was done and is still being done to bring supplies into Pastora and the other groups. There are strips big enough to land a DC-3 on.

To accomplish this effort, Poveda would like to start with some financial backing on a monthly basis. He is more than willing to account for all funds spent. Attached is an initial estimate of immediate needs for funds. On top of this, they would like to start with a minimum of between $150–200,000. This would cover the expenses of moving a couple [of] high level people back to CR, including Luis Rivas and Martínez or Mendieta.

They believe the time is right to begin establishing a new structure. There are many people who are financially on their last legs and if this does not come through they will have to abandon the fight, so they are in hopes something will work out.

Obviously, they hoped for an answer in the near future. I put them off and said I or someone will get back to them in the next two to three weeks.

They believe they are capable, have the leadership and the knowledge necessary to undertake this effort. Although they will operate in the south, they will stay away from Pastora and not infringe on his territory. They will work closer to the Pacific. It was stressed they would work in concert with the North [Honduras-based *contras*].

One last comment that they made and has been made by others: some of Pastora's field commanders are ready to join any side which will provide them with food and medicines. They have not been resupplied in at least 8 months.

In fact, several of his commanders want to leave and actually aren't controlled by Pastora, he just talks with them over the radio. These include according to Poveda: Lionel; Sam, Oscar, and Navegante.

Others who will leave include two Panamanians, ———— who between them have about 1000 men supposedly.

Update April 9, 1985

Sparkplug has decided to go with El Negro Chamorro as the military commander of the South. There will be a political/military council which will have supervisory capacity over Chamorro. This will be made up of:

- El Negro Chamorro
- Donald Lacayo
- Indalacio [sic] Pastora[2]
- Picasso (who is married to Calero's wife's sister)
- Poveda (possibly and others)

Pape has broken down the camp that was under him into 4 small camps and thus spread the men around. He is waiting for equipment to start coming in from El Salvador. Moral [sic] is good and the men will start working in small teams.

The concern about Chamorro is that he drinks a fair amount and may surround himself with people who are in the war not only to fight, but to make money. People who are questionable because of past indiscretions include:

- José Robelo (Chepón): potential involvement with drug running and the sales of goods provided by USG.
- Carlos Coronel: Talks with all sides, potentially too much with the Sandinistas and is making $ on the side.
- Leonel Poveda: Rumored to have been involved with the sale of goods and pocketing certain "commissions."
- Sebastián González (Wachán): Now involved in drug running out of Panama.[3]
- Alvaro Cermeno (Tadeo)
- Julio Bigotes
- Héctor Sánchez
- Sebastián González (Wachán)

These are just some of the people Sparkplug and others should be wary about.

Whatever structure is established for the South, tight control must be kept on the money and resources. In the past it has been too easy to sell goods and too many people have learned how to make a good living off of the war. Money and equipment must be accounted for and when there are differences, examples should be made.

CMA [Civilian Military Assistance[4]]

Posey has an individual willing to outright donate between 70,000 and 80,000 lbs. of medical supplies to the effort. It is a wide assortment of goods and someone will have to look at it to see what is good and what isn't. It is now located in South Carolina.

The material can be shipped as far as Alabama by the individual who is going to donate it, but it has got to get from Alabama to New Orleans.

Flako [*sic*] is back in business.[5] He has established himself in New Orleans and is working on some new scams. He is staying at the Providence Hotel. It is time someone paid him a visit and told him to go back to the hole he comes from.

NOTES

1. Leonel Poveda (a.k.a. "Comanche") was an aide to Edén Pastora during the Sandinista revolution who briefly served as vice-minister of internal commerce in Nicaragua and later followed Pastora to become a *contra*. Luis Rivas (a.k.a. "Wicho"), Alejandro Martínez (a.k.a. "Domingo"), and Carlos Coronel, son of María Kautz de Coronel (see Reading 6.5) and a former Nicaraguan fisheries minister, are also former Sandinistas-turned-*contras*. Juan Zavala is a lieutenant of *contra* leader Fernando Chamorro.—EDS.

2. Fernando "El Negro" Chamorro Rapaccioli briefly attained fame in 1960 when, with his brother Edmundo and a handful of followers sympathetic to the Conservative Party, he attacked Nicaraguan National Guard barracks in the towns of Diriamba and Jinotepe. In 1978 he was arrested for firing a bazooka at Somoza's bunker from a room in Managua's Inter-Continental Hotel. Freed from prison as a result of Edén Pastora's 1978 takeover of the National Palace, Chamorro fought briefly against Somoza on the southern front. He went into exile in 1980 and founded the UDN-FARN *contra* organization. The small UDN-FARN group first worked along the Costa Rican–Nicaraguan border. In 1983 it shifted its operations to Honduras and announced a merger with the FDN. The merger plan failed, and Chamorro and the UDN-FARN returned to the Costa Rican front and collaborated with ARDE. When ARDE split in 1984 over the question of unity with the FDN, Chamorro briefly became commander of ARDE, although his forces maintained their separate identity. With the collapse of Pastora's forces in 1985, Chamorro became the Reagan administration's preferred chief on the southern front. But following the 1987 signing of the Central American Peace Plan, "El Negro" was one of the first *contra* leaders to return to Managua, where he rejoined the Conservative Party.

Indalecio Pastora is a Nicaraguan landowner with large properties in northern Costa Rica (see Reading 6.2).—EDS.

3. José Robelo (a.k.a. "Chepón") is the son of *contra* leader Alfonso Robelo. Just months after Owen wrote this memo, he expressed concern in another document (see Reading 7.13) over Chepón's involvement in torture and execution.

Sebastián González (a.k.a. "Wachán") fought against Somoza with Edén Pastora on the southern front. Like Pastora, he left Nicaragua and became a *contra* in 1982. In November 1984, after being accused of cocaine trafficking in the northern Costa Rican town of Liberia, he fled to Panama. He was one of the principal suspects in the murder of Hugo Spadafora, a Panamanian physician who fought first with the Sandinistas and later with Pastora and the Miskitu Indian *contras,* and who was decapitated near the Costa Rica–Panama border in 1985. See *La Nación,* 26 November 1986.—EDS.

4. Civilian Military Assistance (which later became Civilian Materiel Assistance) is a private Alabama-based *contra* aid group founded by Tom Posey. In 1984 two American CMA members died in northern Nicaragua when a helicopter they were piloting in support of a *contra* unit was shot down.—EDS.

5. Flaco ("Slim") almost certainly refers to former CMA mercenary Jack Terrell, who worked as an FDN *contra* commander from late 1984 until March 1985. Terrell later accused *contra* leaders of placing *contra* aid funds in private bank accounts in the Cayman Islands. He also charged that a Costa Rica–based shrimp export company, *Frigoríficos de Puntarenas,* was being used to launder *contra* aid funds and as a cover for smuggling cocaine into the United States.—EDS.

7.13 Building a Contra *Air Base**

A MEMO FROM ROBERT OWEN TO LIEUTENANT COLONEL OLIVER NORTH

U.S. interference in Costa Rica's internal affairs was epitomized by the secret contra *air base constructed on an isolated farm just twelve miles from the Nicaraguan border. This memo from Robert Owen to Lieutenant Colonel Oliver North, the National Security Council's deputy director of political-military affairs, details the NSC's plans for building the hidden airstrip, as well as other aspects of U.S. efforts to strengthen the* contras' *southern front. Under cover of an agricultural company owned by " 'crazy' gringos," NSC operatives collaborated with Costa Rican Civil Guard officers in finding, guarding, and administering the farm. Mortar training in the nearby Murciélago base (see Reading 7.11) provided a convenient excuse for declaring the zone off limits to the public. Other questions discussed in this document include internal disagreements among* contra *leaders and* contra *human rights violations. Several words, phrases, and names were blacked out for "security" reasons before the memo was made public.*

Owen, also the author of Reading 7.12, worked as a courier to the contras *for the U.S. National Security Council's Lieutenant Colonel Oliver North.*

TO: **BG: FOR YOUR EYES ONLY**

FROM: TC[1]

SUBJECT: August 19, 1985 Trip

ITINERARY: August 19—Washington–Miami
20—Miami–San José
21—San José
22—San José–New Orleans
23—New Orleans–Washington

*Exhibit RWO-9 of the 1987 House-Senate Committee to Investigate the Iran-*Contra* Affair. Provided by the National Security Archive, Washington, D.C.

Meeting with ———— and ————

This took place in ———— office and in attendence [*sic*] were ———— and
———. Very cordial meeting with the emphasis on where's the best place to
locate the farm. Two sites were discussed, but the decision was made to use
just one, as there would be less chance of discovery.

The area decided on is on the west coast, bordered by a National Park on the
north, the ocean to the west, the Pan American Highway to the east, and
mountains and hills to the south. The property is owned by an American living
in New York. It is managed by a Colonel in the Civil Guard who will be glad
to turn it over to ———— who has been designated by ———— to be administrator for the project. Am presently waiting for the name of the American so
information on him can be found out and he can be approached by a company
wishing to rent the land for a year with the option to buy. A guess is the cost
will run between $10,000 and $20,000 for a year.

The cover for the operation is a company, owned by a few "crazy" gringos,
wanting to lease the land for agricultural experimentation and for running
cattle. A company is in the process of being formed. It might be a good idea
to have it be a Panamanian company with bearer shares, this way no names
appear as owners. The gringos will own two planes, registered to the company
and duly registered in the country in question. Cattle will be purchased as will
some farming equipment and some land plowed.

The main house, which sits next to the Pan American Highway, will be vacated
and used by the Gringos. It will be possible to use third country nationals,
although this was not extensively discussed. The Colonel will provide a cook,
the *peones* to work the farm, and security.

A number of improvements will need to be made to the property. They
include:

- Building an airstrip next to the main house
- Putting in gas storage tanks by the house and a hangar and maintenance
  shed
- Building a road usable by 4 wheel drive to the 2nd site, about 10,000
  meters
- Leveling and grading a second strip, about 800 meters
- Drilling a well by this site
- Building storage facilities
- Clearing a road to the beach

Once the new strip is completed it will be designated a military zone and will
be guarded by the Colonel's people. The cover is it will be being used [*sic*] for
mortar and rifle practice. There are no houses or farms near by and the strip

is right off the water and in a draw between two ridge lines, so it is well out of sight.

Initial costs for the project include:

- Construction costs
- Purchase of at least two vehicles, both 4 wheel drive, a truck and pickup
- Cost of land, cattle and farming equipment
- Establishing the company, lawyers and registration costs
- Colonel's costs; should not be too high
- Salaries for gringos
    —Air ops (Spanish speaking)
    —2 pilots
    —Mechanic
    —Loadmaster/packer/rigger
    —Civil engineer to oversee construction of the strips
- Registration of two planes in country
- Fuel

Requirements in the States for the project:

- Form company
- Off-shore bank account
- Contact and negotiate with present owner
- Budget project
- Contract personnel

Next trip to the country should be with a civil engineer and air ops officer to begin the project with site survey, follow-up meeting with the Colonel, transfer of the property, establish company, begin construction.

The timetable will depend on how quick the company is formed and personnel contracted.

The rest of the meeting was spent discussing the move of forces away from the border area. They want this done as soon as possible. They might be willing to help facilitate the move by providing trucks to take the people to a jumping off point. ———— was more in front then [*sic*] his boss. It was left that they would be kept informed.

They were concerned with a base reported to be some 10 to 15 klics [kilometers] inside [Costa Rica]. If it was still there this weekend it was to be raided.

It was a very positive meeting and they want to work with us, but there are obvious concerns. The biggest on both sides is how long the operation will remain covert.

Meeting with Robelo

On the evening of the 21st I met with [Alfonso] Robelo at the request of
————. This followed our previous meeting and ———— thought I could
reinforce the need for Negro [Fernando Chamorro] and his boys to move
quickly. A number of issues were covered and as we already discussed them
I will just briefly mention the significant points.

The Move: On Friday a decision was supposed to be rendered as to how best
to carry out moving the approximately 280 people and some 16,000 lbs. of
supplies. The only two viable options are either:

- Across the lake [Lake Nicaragua] after an airdrop to include rubber boats
  and motors.
- By truck at night without equipment to a location probably above Boca
  San Carlo [*sic*], the equipment would follow. The heavy stuff could even
  be cached, then picked up later and air-dropped in once they are settled.

Once a plan is finalized it will take a period of time to set up the logistics.
Earliest possible time for a jump off is probably at least 10 to 14 days. Even
then it is pushing it the way these people operate.

There is resistance against the move, especially by Negro and his staff. They
will drag their feet as long as possible. They complain they don't know the
area.

If they go by boat they will have to be supplied with the following:

- Between 8 and 10 18 ft. zodiacs
- The same number of motors plus an extra 3 in case of breakdowns. They
  should be probably around 50 hp.
- Fuel tanks to be used for the motors.

This could be done by air out of [El] Salvador.

They would move across the lake to between San Miguelito and Morrillo. The
trip would take about 6 hours each way and would require a number of trips
depending on the number of boats.

Meeting with [Edén] *Pastora and Negro* [Chamorro] *:* Pastora wants Negro to
join him and work with BOS [Opposition Bloc of the South].[2] Says the Gringos
are out to screw Negro, thus he should protect himself and his people and join
BOS. He reminded Negro if he goes inside he goes into his [Pastora's] territory.
    Negro believes Pastora is finished. His people in the field only talk to him
on the radio in hopes he will be able to supply them with ammo or whatever.

Human Rights Violation: The internal investigation shows Chepón [José Robelo, son of Alfonso Robelo] did order the torture and the ultimate execution. It was decided Negro should decide what punishment he deserves and was supposed to decide by Friday. He gave Robelo indications if Chepón is forced out of the movement he may choose to resign. If this is the case, the whole movement may be better off. If Negro decides on this course of action, it was suggested to Robelo he and [Arturo] Cruz go public immediately to get a jump on the press.

BOS: It is thought the organization may be receiving as much as $50,000 a month for expenses and travel; most probably from Pérez.

Robelo's Personal Feelings: To quote Robelo, "I'm tired of the lack of equivalency in the Triple A. Cruz and I were integrated into the FDN to clean their face."[3]

Major things he is concerned about include:

- He has not received his $30,000 for August.
- Calero gave Fred budgets for the FDN in the Miami meeting, including one for an FDN Red Cross, not a UNO Red Cross.
- ———— took Calero's side in the meetings in Tegu [Tegucigalpa, Honduras] on almost every issue.
- By the next meeting of the Triple A he wants an inventory of money funneled into the FDN and where it is going.
- Wants to be consulted on what is bought
- Made it very clear he will not accept any more money from Calero.
- Is finding it extremely difficult to work with Calero as he believes Calero looks on him and Cruz as appendages, not equals.

He made it clear he was not threatening to quit, yet. But he also wanted the message conveyed that things must change and he expects Calero to be more accommodating, or at least to make a pretense of it.

Meeting with Wycho[4]

I flew to New Orleans and spent about 6 hours with Wycho on Thursday night. I brought him as up to date as possible and answered his questions as best as possible.

His concerns were what was going to be the CR's [Costa Ricans'] stand, would his financial situation be taken care of, and deep down he was subtly asking if he had what it will take, or was he walking into a no-win situation. I think this is his biggest concern; that is why I promised he would have a gringo by his side to advise him and provide him with as much help as possible.

If he decides, he would like someone to call or visit his boss to explain the situation as he believes he owes him a great deal, including an explanation.

His decision is due on Monday, August 26.

NOTES

1. BG is an abbreviation for either "Blood and Guts" or "Bill Goode," both pseudonyms used by Lieutenant Colonel Oliver North. TC refers to Owen's nickname, "The Courier."—EDS.

2. BOS or the Opposition Bloc of the South was formed in 1985 when Alfonso Robelo left ARDE to join the U.S.-sponsored, FDN-dominated UNO coalition. BOS was an umbrella group of *contra* organizations, such as Edén Pastora's ARDE, that resisted unity with the *somocista*-dominated FDN *contras.*—EDS.

3. "Triple A" refers to the first names of the three members of the directorate of United Nicaraguan Opposition (UNO), a U.S.-sponsored, FDN-dominated *contra* umbrella group founded in 1985. The UNO directorate's members were Adolfo Calero, Arturo Cruz, and Alfonso Robelo.—EDS.

4. "Wycho" (or Wicho) is a nickname for Luis Rivas Leal, a *contra* commander on the southern front (see Reading 7.12). Owen's discussion here almost certainly concerns U.S. efforts to have Edén Pastora's field commanders, including "Wycho," switch allegiance to Fernando Chamorro, who was more closely controlled by the CIA and NSC.—EDS.

7.14 The Raid on the Airstrip*

A MEMO FROM RAFAEL "CHI CHI" QUINTERO TO GENERAL RICHARD SECORD

When Costa Rican security forces raided the secret airstrip described in Reading 7.13, they just missed catching Rafael "Chi Chi" Quintero, a Cuban-American who was helping coordinate air supply flights to the contras *from El Salvador. A veteran of the Bay of Pigs and numerous CIA covert operations, Quintero was employed at the time by the Virginia-based Stanford Technology Trading Group. Headed by retired Air Force Major General Richard Secord, Stanford Technology had Swiss bank accounts, which were later linked in congressional testimony to the diversion of Iran arms sales profits to the* contras. *In this document, Quintero, referring to President Oscar Arias as a "boy," suggests something of the contempt for Costa Rican sovereignty that was typical of the secret network's operatives. Several words and phrases were deleted for security reasons before the memo was made public.*

[Exhibit contains handwritten notation "To Goode," i.e., Lieutenant Colonel Oliver North.]

*Exhibit of the 1987 House-Senate Committee to Investigate the Iran-*Contra *Affair. Provided by the National Security Archive, Washington, D.C.

9/10/86 1730 HOURS.

Costa Rican security forces raided plantation yesterday and impounded 77 drums of gas. Rumors [words deleted] aprehension [*sic*] for questioning denied late last night. One raiding official who claims saw facilities for 400 men at site arrested [several lines deleted].

[Words deleted] he will break down and blame me and by consequence U.S. Embassy. [Word deleted] decided to have me spend night at his home and send me to airport to catch first flight out hoping my name was not yet on stop list. Obvious surveillance spotted last night at my hotel as [word deleted] and I left. Don't know if hotel security or government official. Possibility of news leak 50 percent, but situation too confusing to predict anything. I am in possession of 2 other DZ coords [air-drop zone map coordinates] and everything arranged between [word deleted] and me to continue drops without disruptions regardless of situation. [Word deleted] coming to Miami on Friday but still I will be able to relay messages to and from [words deleted] and Bob from Miami. Alert Ollie [North] Pres. Arias will attend Reagan's dinner in New York Sept. 22nd. Boy needs to be straightened out by heavy weights.

BT [begin transmission]

7.15 A CIA Station Chief's Testimony before the Joint Congressional Committee on the Iran-Contra Affair*

BY JOE FERNÁNDEZ (A.K.A. TOMÁS CASTILLO)

These excerpts from closed-session testimony given by the CIA's Costa Rica station chief shed light on a number of key aspects of the contra *war and U.S. policy toward Costa Rica. Fernández describes the difficulties of getting the* contras *out of their Costa Rican bases and into Nicaragua, the problems of coordinating airdrops, the allegations of* contra *drug trafficking, and the CIA's collaboration—despite congressional prohibitions—with NSC efforts to support the* contras. *He also suggests that he was not averse to lying to official investigators.*

Fernández, who used the pseudonym Tomás Castillo while in Central America, was CIA station chief in Costa Rica. He was recalled in January 1987 for allegedly overstepping his authority in aiding Lieutenant Colonel Oliver North and Major General Richard Secord's contra *support network.*

---

*Testimony given on May 29, 1987, before the House-Senate Committee to Investigate the Iran-*Contra* Affair.

MR. FERNÁNDEZ. While we were doing our best to keep faith with the legal constraints of the amendments and at the same time carry out our duties with respect to the Nicaraguan resistance, we were faced with political dimensions of a broad issue of support for the Nicaraguan resistance.

Those dimensions adversely affected our operations on several occasions. It was—it often seemed to us that the next upcoming vote in Congress on support for the resistance was the most important consideration governing the perceptions of what activities were permissible.

The press has speculated extravagantly concerning my possible involvement with director William Casey in connection with the Nicaraguan resistance. I met with director Casey on a few occasions during my tenure as chief of station [deleted]. I briefed him, as did my officers, on station operations, as it was our duty to do so. That is all.

During those briefings, Mr. Casey never suggested or implied, nor did he ever infer, that he expected me to undertake activities which would violate in any way the laws of the United States.

PAUL BARBADORO, a lawyer on the staff of Arthur L. Liman, chief counsel to the Senate committee. It posed a political problem for you to have these Nicaraguans in [deleted] didn't it?

A. Most definitely.

Q. And you tried to encourage them to get to Nicaragua and to fight to get them out of [deleted]?

A. Yes sir.

Q. And there was a reluctance on the part of Negro Chamorro to go into Nicaragua to fight?

A. Yes sir.

Q. In fact, you had to be constantly encouraging him to get in there and fight, right?

A. Yes sir. I know of only one occasion when Chamorro actually went into Nicaragua to fight.

Q. Could you describe that?

A. It occurred in '83 when he appeared in a joint attack with the FDN [deleted]—near the [deleted] Nicaraguan border—and he attacked a border post about thirty meters inside Nicaragua and when he came under heavy attack, he immediately retreated to [deleted].

Q. And he called you from a pay phone, didn't he?

A. And he telephoned me at CIA headquarters—

Q. In Washington—he called you from a pay phone in [deleted] and what did he ask you to do?

A. Send mortars.

Q. Did you do it?

A. Of course not.

Q. Exhibit 1 is a cable dated August '85. Could you tell me who wrote that?

A. I did.

Q. And who did you send it to?

A. Headquarters.

Q. What the cable says is that Ambassador Tambs obtained the permission [deleted] to F.A. airstrip built to resupply the southern front troops, isn't that right?

A. Yes sir.

Q. You got a response to this cable, didn't you?

A. It . . . advised the station that neither CIA nor DOD can become involved either directly or indirectly in assisting [deleted] in implementing this policy.

Q. How many successful flights in total were there from [deleted] to the southern front forces?

A. To the best of my recollection, sir, including this one, nine.

Q. The first one you have just described. When was the last one?

A. I believe it was September 23, 1986.

Q. And all but two of those nine drops occurred in September. Is that right?

A. All but three.

Q. All but three, excuse me, occurred in September. Is it fair to say that there were problems in getting the operation functioning properly?

A. Well, yes, sir, because the first one occurred in April. The next two occurred in June, May, June or July, in that space of time, and then there was the whole period of July–August in which there were no flights at all.

Q. Were there also attempts that were unsuccessful?

A. Many.

Q. What was the reason why these attempts were unsuccessful?

A. Mainly because of decrepit aircraft, unskilled pilots, no equipment for radar or navigational equipment.
   Several drops that were made, parts of the drops were never found. If there were eight bundles, maybe they recovered five, possibly six. The only way that the pilots could identify the drop zone was if the people on the ground lit bonfires. There was no—they had no ability to navigate right to the place where they were supposed to, so the way it would work is the comunications center in [deleted] would tell them the airdrop is due between 2 and 2:30 A.M., please light your bonfires fifteen minutes before and keep

them burning for fifteen minutes afterwards of the period when the drop is expected.

Then the plane, if it got to the area at all, would circle, an ever-widening circle, to try to spot the bonfires on the ground. Obviously, if it is raining, this is a jungle, a rain forest or tropical jungle, you don't always find wood that will burn, you don't have kerosene or gasoline because of where they are located, so it was simply by chance that they would keep the fires burning for an hour, and then they would have to be big enough.

So if they saw it, they made the drop. This resulted in the fact that later on in September, some of the drops were made in daytime because that was the only way they could spot where the drop zone was due to the fact that they didn't have navigational equipment, which eventually led to the C-123, on which Hasenfus was a crew member, to be shot down.[1]

We would never have run in CIA an airdrop operation in the middle of the day in enemy territory and using the same flight path six or seven times in a row.

SENATOR SAM NUNN. Let me move on to one other point. Let's just summarize this. You have been in the business a long time. Isn't this cable in effect a CYA [cover your ass] cable?

A. Yes sir.

Q. They were covering their rear end back in Washington, weren't they?

A. Yes sir.

Q. And they were putting it all on your head?

A. Well, they just weren't resolving my problem.

Q. Leaving it all on your head?

A. They were satisfying their situation, but not mine.

Q. They were leaving you hanging out there wherever you were before you raised the problem, you were still hanging out there by yourself, weren't you?

A. Well, that is perhaps one way of looking at it.

Q. Would you agree with this statement or disagree with it made October 14, 1986, and I quote, and I will read it carefully: The CIA is not involved directly or indirectly in arranging, directing, or facilitating resupply missions conducted by private individuals in support of the Nicaraguan democratic resistance.

A. I would have to disagree with that. My participation did facilitate because it provided the information. I couldn't interpret that to mean otherwise.

Q. This was a statement made on October 14, 1986, to the Intelligence Committee of the House of Representatives by the DDO [deputy director of operations], Mr. Claire George. I think I would read it the same way you read it.

REPRESENTATIVE PETER W. RODINO, JR. Did you ever have it called to your attention that some of these planes which were being used in the resupply operations were planes that had been used actually in drug trafficking?

A. I heard in the testimony of one of the witnesses—and I don't recall who it was, I think it was Rob Owen—that, in fact, one of the NHAO [Nicaraguan Humanitarian Assistance Office] planes that was used in a resupply or attempted resupply had, in fact, come under suspicion of the DEA or one of the countries that it had some connection with drugs.[2] But I did not know of that until that testimony was given.

Q. Knowing just that, was there any further concern on your part that this might be the case and that these same resupply planes would be trafficking in drugs and going back and forth to the United States with them?

A. I had no reason to believe that at all.

Q. Was there any evidence that you were aware of that any of the southern front commanders were involved with individuals who were engaged in narcotics trafficking?

A. We had received reports from time to time that that was so.

Q. Did you report this to the CIA lawyers?

A. To CIA lawyers and to the DEA. Each and every time, regardless of whether it was confirmed or unconfirmed, or whether it was a rumor, every hint of it was immediately transmitted to the appropriate agency, and the reasons for that is that I knew that any taint whatsoever of drug trafficking with the resistance would be the death knell for the resistance.

Q. Were you aware of what action was taken when you—when this was reported?

A. Yes.

Q. What action was taken?

A. Well, the DEA conducted a very active investigation into several people who were connected with Edén Pastora, several of his pilots, several of his lieutenants. I understand that several cases have been made against them or that they were in the process of, as of the fall, summer or fall of 1986, in the process of bringing to fruition several other cases.

REPRESENTATIVE DANTE FASCELL. Is that your lawyer on your right-hand side?

A. Yes sir.

Q. What is his name?

A. Thomas Wilson.

Q. To your knowledge is he a CIA asset?

A. Absolutely not.

Q. Is anybody in his law firm, to your knowledge?

A. I don't believe so, but I would like to defer to counsel to answer the question.

Q. If he cares to.

MR. WILSON. I would be happy to, Mr. Congressman. . . . I have no relationship whatsoever with the CIA, nor have I ever had since I left the service.

Q. Which service?

A. The Army, sir.

Q. I was curious, because I have never seen so many baby-sitters for a witness before any committee in the Congress. I don't mean to be derogatory about it at all, just curious. We have, as I understand it, a representative from the CIA who is a congressional liaison representative, is that correct, in the audience? We have a White House counsel in the audience. We have three or four CIA representatives here somewhere. One representative. Were there others here earlier, Mr. Chairman, that I didn't know about?

REPRESENTATIVE LEE H. HAMILTON. I am not aware of any others except the ones immediately behind the witness, Mr. Fascell.

REPRESENTATIVE LOUIS STOKES. During the twenty years you have been employed by the CIA, on how many occasions have you worked with the National Security Council?

MR. FERNÁNDEZ. This is the only occasion, sir.

Q. Being familiar with the term "chain of command," did you consider that a lieutenant colonel, such as Lieutenant Colonel North, being a staff member of the National Security Council, was inside or outside of your chain of command?

A. He was outside the chain of command, sir.

Q. If a case officer working under you were to be secretly in touch with the National Security Council staff, would he be inside or outside the chain of command?

A. He would be acting improperly.

Q. Now, you were interviewed by the OIG and also the Tower Commission, were you not?

A. Yes sir.

Q. And in the case of the OIG when you were first interviewed by them, were you entirely truthful with them?

A. No sir.

Q. The Tower Commission, when they interviewed you, were you entirely truthful with them?

A. No sir, I was not.

Q. OK.

A. However, I was acting within the guidelines that I understood both with the IG and the Tower Commission, concerning my participation in the resupply activity.

Q. You say you were acting within the guidelines that you understood. You mean you understood from whom?

A. That is correct, I understood it from the division chief, [deleted] and I believe I also discussed it with a staff officer of the Central American Task Force, and it was my understanding that the deputy director of operations had negotiated with the IG that I would be questioned only about my participation in the air supply activity. And when I was queried by both the IG and the Tower Commission, I responded in that, within those parameters.

Q. But no one ever told you, did they, that you were not to tell the truth?

A. Oh, no, not to—no.

Q. No one told you that you should be deceptive, did they?

A. That is correct, sir.

NOTES

1. On October 6, 1986, Nicaraguan air defense forces shot down a C-123 cargo plane that was making an air supply drop to the *contras*. Eugene Hasenfus, a cargo handler who was the only surviving member of the crew, claimed to be an employee of Corporate Air Services, a company that was subsequently linked to the NSC's *contra* support network.—EDS.

2. President Reagan created the State Department's Nicaraguan Humanitarian Assistance Office with an August 29, 1985, executive order. It was supposed to administer the $27 million in "humanitarian aid" Congress appropriated for the *contras*. Later evidence emerged that at least $4 million of its funds were missing and that other funds had been skimmed off by *contra* leaders. For a detailed discussion, see Peter Kornbluh, *Nicaragua: The Price of Intervention* (Washington, D.C.: Institute for Policy Studies, 1987), pp. 198–201.—EDS.

7.16 The Arias Peace Plan

BY PRESIDENT OSCAR ARIAS SÁNCHEZ

In early 1986, just after his victory in Costa Rica's presidential elections, Oscar Arias began speaking openly about his disagreements with the Reagan administration. Support for the contras, *he said, would not bring peace to Central America. By early 1987, Arias had drawn up a plan that he hoped would lead to peace. Where Washington had called for confrontation and pressure, Arias urged negotiations and reconciliation. The Arias plan, also known as Esquipulas II for the Guatemalan town where the five Central American presidents worked out a final version and where an earlier meeting of regional leaders in May 1986 had agreed to establish a Central American parliament, was finalized on August 7, 1987. It calls for cease-fires, free and fair elections, restoration of press freedom and civil liberties, amnesty for political prisoners, efforts to repatriate refugees, and the start of genuine dialogue between governments and "unarmed internal opposition." The plan does not address some of the United States' security concerns for the region, and President Reagan called it "fatally flawed." But for Arias, its principal author, it won the 1987 Nobel Peace Prize.*

Oscar Arias, elected to a four-year presidential term in 1986, is a longtime activist in the National Liberation Party (PLN) and its general secretary from 1979–86. He studied economics and law at the University of Costa Rica, and earned a doctorate in political science at the University of Essex in England. His books include Grupos de presión en Costa Rica [Pressure Groups in Costa Rica] *(1970),* ¿Quién gobierna en Costa Rica? [Who Governs in Costa Rica?] *(1976), and* Nuevos rumbos para el desarrollo costarricense [New Routes for Costa Rican Development] *(1980). Arias has held two cabinet posts in previous administrations, and has been a deputy in Costa Rica's Legislative Assembly and a university professor.*

THE governments of the republics of Costa Rica, El Salvador, Guatemala, Honduras, and Nicaragua, determined to achieve the objectives and to develop the principles established in the United Nations Charter and the Charter of the Organization of the American States, the Document of Objectives, the Caraballeda Message for Peace, Security and Democracy in Central America, the Guatemala Declaration, the Punta del Este Communiqué, the Declaration of Panama, the Esquipulas Declaration, and the Contadora Treaty Proposal for Peace and Cooperation in Central America of July 6, 1986, have agreed on the following procedure for establishing a firm and lasting peace in Central America:

NATIONAL RECONCILIATION

Dialogue

To urgently carry out, in those cases where deep divisions have resulted within society, steps for national reconciliation which would allow for popular participation with full guarantees in authentic political processes of a democratic nature based on justice, freedom, and democracy. Toward this end, to create those mechanisms which, in accordance with the law, would allow for dialogue with opposition groups. For this purpose, the corresponding governments will initiate a dialogue with all unarmed internal political opposition groups and with those who have availed themselves of the amnesty.

Amnesty

In each Central American country, except those where the International Commission of Verification and Follow-Up determines that such a measure is not necessary, an amnesty decree will be issued containing all the provisions for the guarantee of the inviolability of life; as well as freedom in all its forms, property, and the security of the persons to whom these decrees apply. Simultaneous with the issuing of the amnesty decree by the government, the irregular forces of the respective country will place in freedom all persons in their power.

National Reconciliation Commission

In order to verify the compliance with the commitments that the five Central American governments subscribed to by the signing of this document, concerning amnesty, cease-fire, democratization and free elections, a National Reconciliation Commission will be established whose duties will be to verify the actual carrying out in practice of the national reconciliation process, as well as the full exercise of all civil and political rights of Central American citizens guaranteed in this document. The National Reconciliation Commission will be comprised of a delegate and an alternate delegate from the executive branch; a bishop delegate and an alternate bishop delegate recommended by the Episcopal Conference, and chosen by the government from a list of three candidates which should be presented [by the conference] within a period of fifteen days upon receipt of a formal invitation. This invitation will be made by the governments within five working days from the signing of this document.

The same procedure will be used to select a delegate and alternate delegate from the legally registered political opposition parties. The said list of three [candidates] should be presented within the same above-mentioned period.

In addition, each Central American government will choose an outstanding citizen, outside of public office and not belonging to the party in power, and his respective alternate to be part of this commission.

The decree, which puts into effect the agreements for the nomination of the members of the respective national commissions, shall be communicated immediately to the other Central American governments.

Exhortation for the Cessation of Hostilities

The governments make a vehement appeal so that in the states of the area, currently suffering from the activity of irregular or insurgent groups, a cessation of hostilities be arranged. The governments of these states commit themselves to undertake all the necessary steps for achieving an effective cease-fire within the constitutional framework.

Democratization

The governments commit themselves to promote an authentic democratic, pluralist, and participatory process that includes the promotion of social justice; respect for human rights, [state] sovereignty, the territorial integrity of states, and the right of all nations to freely determine, without outside interference of any kind, its economic, political, and social model; and to carry out in a verifiable manner those measures leading to the establishment, or in their instances, the improvement of representative and pluralist democratic systems which would provide guarantees for the organization of political parties, effective popular participation in the decision-making process, and to ensure free access to different currents of opinion, to honest electoral processes, and newspapers based on the full exercise of citizens' rights.

For the purpose of verifying the good faith in the development of this democratization process, it will be understood that there shall exist complete freedom of press, television, and radio. This complete freedom will include the opening and maintaining in operation of communications media for all ideological groups, and the operation of this media without prior censorship.

Complete political pluralism should be manifest. In this regard, political groupings shall have broad access to communications media, full exercise of the right of association, and the right to manifest publicly the exercise of their right to free speech, be it oral, written, or televised, as well as freedom of movement by members of political parties in order to proselytize.

Likewise, those governments of Central America, which have in effect a state of exception, siege, or emergency [law], shall terminate that state and reestablish the full exercise of all constitutional guarantees.

Free Elections

Once the conditions inherent to every democracy are established, free, pluralist, and honest elections shall be held as a joint expression of the Central American states to seek reconciliation and lasting peace for its peoples. Elections will be held for a Central American parliament, whose founding was proposed in the Esquipulas Declaration of May 25, 1986. In pursuit of the above-mentioned objectives, the leaders expressed their will to progress in the formation of this parliament and agreed that the Preparatory Commission of the Central American Parliament shall conclude its deliberations and submit to the Central American presidents the respective treaty proposal within 150 days.

These elections will take place simultaneously in all the countries throughout Central America in the first half of 1988, on a date mutually agreed to by the presidents of the Central American states. These elections will be subject to vigilance by the appropriate electoral bodies. The respective governments commit themselves to extend an invitation to the Organization of American States and to the United Nations, as well as to governments of third states, to send observers who shall bear witness that the electoral processes have been held in accordance with the strictest norms of equality, of access of all political parties to the media, as well as full guarantees for public demonstrations and other kinds of proselytizing propaganda.

The appropriate founding treaty shall be submitted for approval or ratification in the five countries so that the elections for the Central American parliament can be held within the period indicated in this paragraph. After the elections for the Central American parliament have been held, equally free and democratic elections shall be held with international observers and the same guarantees in each country, to name popular representatives to municipalities, congresses, and legislative assemblies, and the presidencies of the republics. These elections will be held according to the proposed calendars and within the periods established in the current political constitutions.

Cessation of Assistance to Irregular Forces or Insurrectionist Movements

The governments of the five Central American states shall request the governments of the region, and the extraregional governments which openly or covertly provide military, logistical, financial, propagandistic aid in manpower, armaments, munitions, and equipment to irregular forces or insurrectionist movements to cease this aid, as an indispensable element for achieving a stable and lasting peace in the region.

The above does not include assistance for repatriation, or in lieu thereof, the reassigning of assistance necessary for those persons having belonged to these groups or forces to become reintegrated into normal life. Likewise, the irregular forces or insurgent groups who operate in Central America will be asked to abstain, in yearnings for a true Latin American spirit, from receiving such assistance.

These petitions will be made in accordance with the provisions of the Document of Objectives regarding the elimination of arms traffic, whether it be interregional or extraregional, intended for persons, organizations or groups attempting to destabilize the governments of the Central American countries.

The Non-Use of Territory to Invade Other States

The five countries which signed this document reaffirm their commitment to prevent the use of their own territory and to neither render nor permit military or logistical support to persons, organizations, or groups attempting to destabilize the governments of the Central American countries.

Negotiations on Matters Relating to Security, Verification, Control, and Limitation of Armaments

The governments of the five Central American states, with the participation of the Contadora group in exercise of its role as mediator, will continue negotiations on the points still pending in the Contadora Treaty Proposal for Peace and Cooperation in Central America concerning security, verification, and control.

In addition, these negotiations will entail measures for the disarmament of the irregular forces who are willing to accept the amnesty decrees.

Refugees and Displaced Persons

The governments of Central America commit themselves to give urgent attention to the groups of refugees and displaced persons brought about by the regional crisis, through protection and assistance, particularly in areas of education, health, work, and security, and whenever voluntary and individually expressed, to facilitate in the repatriation, resettlement and relocation [of these persons]. They also commit themselves to request assistance for Central American refugees and displaced persons from the international community, both directly through bilateral or multilateral agreements, as well as through the United Nations High Commissioner for Refugees and other organizations and agencies.

Cooperation, Democracy, and Freedom for Peace and Development

In the climate of freedom guaranteed by democracy, the Central American countries will adopt agreements permitting for the intensification of development in order to achieve more egalitarian and poverty-free societies. Consolidation of democracy presupposes the creation of a system of economic and social justice and well-being. To achieve these objectives the governments will jointly seek special economic support from the international community.

INTERNATIONAL VERIFICATION AND FOLLOW-UP

International Verification and Follow-Up Commission

An international verification and follow-up commission will be established, comprised of the secretary generals of the Organization of American States and the United Nations or their representatives, as well as the foreign ministers of Central America, of the Contadora Group and the Support Group. This commission will have the duties of verifying and following up the compliance with the commitments undertaken in this document, as well as the support and facilities given to the mechanisms for reconciliation and verification and follow-up. In order to strengthen the efforts of the International Commission of Verification and Follow-Up, the governments of the five Central American states shall issue declarations of support for [the commission's] work. All nations interested in promoting the cause of freedom, democracy, and peace in Central America can adhere to these declarations.

The five governments shall offer all the necessary facilities for full compliance with the duties of verification and follow-up of the National Reconciliation Commission of each country and of the International Commission of Verification and Follow-Up.

Calendar for the Implementation of Agreements

Within a period of fifteen days from the signing of this document, the foreign ministers of Central America will meet as the Executive Committee to regulate, promote, and make feasible compliance with the agreements contained herein, and to organize the working commissions so that, henceforth, the processes leading to compliance with the contracted commitments may be initiated within the stipulated periods by means of consultations, undertakings, and other mechanisms deemed necessary. Ninety days from the signing of this document, the commitments pertaining to amnesty, cease-fire, democratization, cessation of assistance to irregular forces or insurrectionist movements, and the non-use of territory to invade other states, will enter into force simultaneously and publicly as defined herein.

One hundred and twenty days from the signing of this document, the International Commission for Verification and Follow-Up will analyze the progress [made] in the compliance with the agreements provided for herein.

After 150 days, the five Central American presidents will meet and receive a report from the International Commission of Verification and Follow-Up and they will make the pertinent decisions.

Final Provisions

The points included in this document form part of a harmonious and indivisible whole. The signing of [the document] incurs an obligation, accepted in good faith, to simultaneously comply with the agreement in the established periods.

We, the presidents of the five states of Central America, with the political will to respond to the longings for peace of our peoples, sign [this document] in the city of Guatemala, on the seventh day of August of 1987.

OSCAR ARIAS SÁNCHEZ
JOSÉ NAPOLEÓN DUARTE
VINICIO CEREZO ARÉVALO
JOSÉ AZCONA HOYO
DANIEL ORTEGA SAAVEDRA

7.17 Let's Give Peace a Chance*

BY PRESIDENT OSCAR ARIAS SÁNCHEZ

Less than two months after the five Central American presidents signed the peace accord (see Reading 7.16), the plan's author came to Washington to address the U.S. Congress. An adept politician, Arias heaped praise on the United States and expressed gratitude for its economic aid and friendship. There were also subtle elements of discord in his speech, however. Promising to "tell you what we think even if it is not what you want to hear," he called for a "dialogue unmarked by submission," promised that Costa Rica would not "dehumanize its economy" to meet foreign creditors' demands and, in what may have been an oblique reference to the acclaim accorded Oliver North, declared that neither the United States nor Costa Rica would "honor as heroes men who lie or cheat." In announcing that schoolchildren would compete to design a new uniform for Costa Rica's Civil and Rural Guards, Arias also signaled that the police would no longer wear U.S.-donated surplus camouflage fatigues. This speech, delivered on September 22, 1987, is an important—if limited and extremely diplomatic—assertion of a small nation's right to autonomy.

Oscar Arias Sánchez became president of Costa Rica in 1986 (see Reading 7.16 for additional biographical information). In 1987, two weeks after this speech to the U.S. Congress, Arias received the Nobel Peace Prize for his efforts to resolve the conflicts in Central America.

PRIDE OF A FREE PEOPLE

On behalf of a fellow democracy, I thank you for the invitation to speak here. I should like to say a special word of appreciation to the speaker of the House of Representatives, the Honorable James Wright, for his constructive interest in peace and development, and to all those who are here today. Many of you are known to me personally. Some I have met during visits here, while others have talked with me in Costa Rica.

What a splendid opportunity it is to address Congress, where you sit as the freely elected representatives of your constituents. Surely parliament is the finest hall of freedom in a democracy, for it represents both the power of justice and the soul of a free people.

There is only one offense that can be committed here, and that is not to speak freely, sincerely, and truthfully. So I have come to speak as a free man, with the same pride that you feel and with the freedom that makes all persons and nations equal. In 1921, the Costa Rican educator Joaquín García Monge said:

*Speech to the United States Congress, September 22, 1987.

"Even small nations, if they are worthy, if they are not servile, if they are enlightened and hard working have the same right to freedom as any great nation. People, who rise up as one to defend their most cherished freedoms, are possessed by the only true sacred passion."[1]

DIFFERENCES THAT DO NOT SEPARATE US

There are any number of differences between this powerful nation and Costa Rica. Differences of size: mine is one of the smallest countries and yours is one of the largest. Differences of population: my homeland has two and one-half million people; the United States, two hundred and fifty million. Differences of wealth: fifteen hundred dollars per capita in my country; fifteen thousand in yours. Differences of armament: my country maintains no military establishment whatsoever; your nation has found it necessary to maintain a powerful military force.

Yet none of these differences separates us. Not one alters our status as brothers in freedom. For the great nation you represent and Costa Rica share the most noble values won by mankind since the dawn of history: democracy, freedom, respect for human rights, and the struggle for justice and for peace. We both believe in the wisdom of pluralism, and in the rule of law.

Our countries stand as equals, united by the values we hold dear and our efforts to put them into practice. I know that you want to share with us your finest achievements, just as we want to share with you our joy in liberty and the affection and hospitality of our people.

THE DIALOGUE OF FRIENDSHIP

The relationship between our two countries has been a model friendship. Whenever our century-old democracy has been threatened by an attempted coup or foreign invasion, the United States has always supported our cause. Whenever you have embarked on a crusade to defend the free world from totalitarianism, small Costa Rica has never hesitated to join you. There is not a single economic crisis in our history in which you have failed to extend to us a helping hand. Costa Rica is proud of its friendship with the United States of America, and proud to proclaim it to the entire world. We feel free to tell you exactly what we think, even though it might not be what you want to hear. You do much the same with us. This is the dialogue of sincere friendship, a dialogue unmarked by submission. A dialogue in which we honestly seek a convergence of views.

THE ESSENCE OF MY COUNTRY

When President Ronald Reagan visited Costa Rica in December 1982, he cited in his speech these words of a distinguished Costa Rican president of the past century, José Joaquín Rodríguez: "I am not impressed by hearing proclamations of great principles. What I admire is the men who know how to put them into practice."[2] President Reagan added: "Costa Rica is a proud example of a free people practicing the principles of democracy. And you have done so in good times and in bad, when it was easier and when it required great courage."

Costa Ricans appreciate these words. They express the essence of my country. For us, the real meaning of politics is the day-by-day struggle to translate vision into reality. I know you feel the same way. Indeed, this is perhaps the greatest treasure and the greatest privilege our two countries share.

Neither you nor we can rest knowing that freedom is threatened. Neither you nor we can rest knowing that the promises of democracy are not completely fulfilled, that there is still poverty and hunger. Neither you nor we will choose war when we can make peace. Neither you nor we will honor as heroes men who lie or cheat. Neither you nor we will refuse to look to a future that holds out a promise of more free men, more democracies, more justice, and more peace. Neither you nor we can ever reject the hope that things will change for the better, that changes can occur wherever injustices exist or peace is threatened.

MY SMALL COUNTRY

I belong to a small country that was not afraid to abolish its army in order to increase its strength. In my homeland you will not find a single tank, a single artillery piece, a single warship, or a single military helicopter. In Costa Rica we are not afraid of freedom. We love democracy and respect the law. Our democracy has been in place for one hundred years; it is the oldest in Latin America and one of the oldest in the world. Development and peace with our neighbors are our highest goals.

We have made considerable progress in education, health, and nutrition. In all of these areas our levels are comparable to the best in Latin America. Although we are poor, we have so far been able to reach satisfactory social goals. This is largely because we have no arms expenditures and because the imbedded practice of democracy drives us to meet the needs of the people. Almost forty years ago we abolished our army. Today we threaten no one, neither our own people nor our neighbors. Such threats are absent not because we lack tanks, but because there are few of us who are hungry, illiterate, or unemployed.

THE MODERN ECONOMY

During these years of persistent economic crisis, we Costa Ricans have realized that we need a modern economy. The basis for any lasting change, however, must be a guaranteed peace in Central America. In six years, regional trade has declined from $1 billion to $400 million. Only peace can restore that market. Equally serious have been the negative effects of the decline in investments and the increase in capital flight.

We are engaged in bringing about far-reaching changes in our productive structure, linked to a modern concept of economic and social development. Our political democracy will remain invulnerable only if we can create a more democratic economy. We seek to build a society of many proprietors rather than one vast proletariat. For as Daniel Webster said: "Power naturally and inevitably follows property."

As we restructure the productive system, we must not lose sight of the social sensitivity. This has been a hallmark of our history. We are a country of delicate balances deeply rooted in mutual respect. Some have been surprised that during difficult economic times we have been unwilling to abandon social programs. Make them more efficient and improve them, certainly. But dehumanize our economy, never. That is why we are currently launching a special program of low-cost housing, and have extended free medical coverage to the entire population. If we were to lose the solidarity we have been able to maintain despite our relative poverty, we would destroy the basis of our democratic coexistence.

To structure the new economy without endangering stability, we are negotiating economic stabilization programs with the International Monetary Fund and structural adjustment plans with the World Bank. Domestically we are concerned with modernizing the financial system. We have significantly reduced our fiscal deficit to 1.5 percent of gross domestic product, and are now engaged in a large-scale effort to diversify and expand our exports.

We want to attain a modern economy with more private ownership in which productivity and individual effort will determine worker income. We cannot accept the false premise of "economic efficiency or justice." Instead, we intend to pursue both goals simultaneously.

My government is taking firm action to obtain the full potential of private initiative. We are determined to extend the profit motive by enabling workers to participate in profit sharing. We are involved in transferring state enterprises to cooperatives. Last week we transferred the largest agroindustrial company in my country, the Central Azucarera Tempisque [a sugar refinery], to two thousand cooperative members.

The new economic organization must be based on equity and security. No economy based on greed and intimidation can ever be established in Costa Rica in the name of efficiency.

UNITED STATES COLLABORATION

We have received generous collaboration from the United States in our efforts to build our new economy. This collaboration has taken the form of loans and grants, as well as new facilities for our products in the U.S. market. The

Caribbean Basin Initiative, the product of President Reagan's concern for the region and the bipartisan support of the Congress, recognizes the vital link between international trade and economic development. This is gradually becoming a mainstay for our new exports.

However, there are problems that remain to be solved. We are a small nation and none of our products represents a threat to industries in this country. We are negotiating now to include other products in the agreement. We are also confident that the administrative sanctions will be eliminated for Costa Rica and that the quotas for some of our exports will be raised. Our imminent acceptance to the General Agreement on Tariffs and Trade may help to solve some of these problems.

Our aim in establishing a modern economy is to replace gradually external aid for opportunities to create a more autonomous development. Unfortunately, we must contend with heavy external indebtedness, unstable access to new markets, and persistent deterioration in our terms of trade.

We are following with interest the progress of several legislative proposals: the efforts of Congressmen Gibbons and Pickle to expand the Caribbean Basin Initiative; Senator Bradley's proposal to deal with external debt relief; and Senator Sanford's commission on Central American development, which focuses on regional economic recovery.

THE GREATEST CHALLENGE

I said that our greatest challenge is to bring peace to Central America, a desire that I know you share. In August, the five Central American countries signed a peace accord in Guatemala City. Behind the problems besetting the region today, there is a history of two hundred years of injustice. Millions of human beings still live in grinding poverty, the fundamental cause of the present tragedy we face. We are convinced that the risks we run in the struggle for peace will always be less than the irreparable cost of war.

THE PEACE PLAN

The peace plan encourages national reconciliation in countries where brothers are set against brothers. "To bind up the wounds," in Lincoln's phrase, we ask for dialogue and amnesty, a cease-fire as soon as possible, and democratization without delay. We call for free elections reflecting the true will of the majority of the people. We call for the suspension of military aid to insurgencies. We want guarantees that no territories will be used to attack other states. We seek a reduction in armaments. We request national and international supervision by the Contadora Group and the Support Group and by the secretaries general of the United Nations and the Organization of American States. In an atmosphere of democracy and freedom, we can return to the path of development that will enable a lasting peace. These points reflect years of efforts by the

Contadora Group. For Costa Rica they reflect the power of a century of democracy and freedom.

The countries of Central America are now talking with each other. Their presidents, their ministers, and their experts are talking. So are their writers and journalists, and their church people as well. We ask for assistance in this Central American dialogue. We know better than anyone how hard it is to open up paths in the tropics, but we are determined. Reconciliation commissions have been formed. During the last few days Costa Rica has again exerted all of its moral authority to encourage dialogue in El Salvador and Nicaragua leading to prompt negotiation of a cease-fire. Costa Rica also served as an intermediary in the agreement to reopen *La Prensa* in Managua. If the guns fall silent, and if brother no longer kills brother, this dialogue will have proved its worth.

The peace accord is a means, a procedure whereby we have all committed ourselves to work for peace. We have set deadlines. Above all, we strive for common goals. Some steps may be taken before those deadlines expire, others may require a longer period. We will not fall into a trap set by someone who shows us a calendar every day, anxious to bury the last hope. We have opened the door to the rule of reason in Central America and to reconciliation and dialogue. As long as there is a will to succeed, hope should never be lost.

THE RIGHT CHOICE

As we stand at the crossroads of peace and development, or war and poverty, we must not make the wrong choice. For neither you nor we can undertake this struggle separately. The struggle for peace in Central America is the historic struggle of democracies. Now, as never before, a time has come in history for the people of the United States and of Costa Rica to bring to bear the full power of the principles and values they share.

The history of Central America is a heartrending one. In the past few years over one million persons have been made homeless. More than one hundred thousand have died. If we were to engrave their names on a wall, as the names of those who died in Vietnam are engraved here in Washington, we would have to build a wall twice as long to inscribe all of the Central Americans who have fallen victim to violence in those years.

You are as dedicated to the search for peace as we are. Plans such as the proposal of President Reagan and the Speaker of the House, Mr. Wright, suggest significant openings to facilitate peace and guarantee democracy, disarmament, and regional security.

RESTORING FAITH

It is time to focus on the positive. War signifies the failure of politics. Let us restore faith in dialogue and give peace a chance. Let us not allow fear to prevail. If we work together, we will achieve peace. It will be difficult. But has progress ever been easy? Here in the United States it was a hard-won struggle to wrest a living from the land, to win equality for all people, to preserve freedom, and to conquer space itself! Yet the more difficult the obstacle, the greater the satisfaction in overcoming it.

Dear friends, we are most grateful for your friendship. With your help we hope to secure new and better development opportunities. With the help of the United States we hope to exchange threats of war for opportunities of peace.

Let us reaffirm our faith in our long and sincere friendship. Costa Rica wants to retain its cherished traditional values. When President John F. Kennedy visited us twenty-four years ago, he said: "And today the principles of nonintervention and the peaceful resolution of disputes have been so firmly imbedded in our tradition that the heroic democracy in which we meet today can pursue its national goals without an armed force to guard its frontiers. In few other spots in the world would this be true."

At this difficult hour we are more than ever convinced of the truth of President Kennedy's words. This year we have decreed a yearly celebration of the "Day of Army Abolition" in Costa Rica. We have eliminated all military ranks for our police forces, and scheduled a contest among local schools to design the new civilian dress to be worn by guard members. We are as proud of our traditions as you are of yours.

That is why I would like to say how moved I am to be present as you are celebrating the 200th anniversary of your magnificent constitution—one that has inspired free men and women everywhere in the search for peace and freedom.

Let us then combat war with peace. Let us combat totalitarianism with the power of democracy. United in ideals and principles, joined by dialogue and democracy, we can and will bring hostilities to an end. We must give peace a chance.

Thank you very much.

NOTES

1. Joaquín García Monge (1881–1958) was a Costa Rican essayist, novelist, and journalist who for some four decades edited the influential literary magazine *Repertorio Americano*. Politically, he was influenced by the anarchism of Tolstoy and the anti-imperialism of Peru's Víctor Raúl Haya de la Torre, supported the losing side in the 1948 civil war, and was active in opposing dictatorships in Central America and the Caribbean.—Eds.

2. José Joaquín Rodríguez, president from 1890 to 1894, closed the Congress and suspended constitutional rights during his first year in office. He then ruled by decree until late 1893, when he reinstated the constitution in hopes of influencing the 1894 presidential election.—Eds.

Selected Bibliography

This bibliography is limited to works in English and does not include articles and books that are excerpted or reprinted in this volume. Works on Central or Latin America as a whole are included only when they contain significant material on Costa Rica. Readers of Spanish who wish to do further reading may consult the Costa Rican social science journals listed below, as well as the articles and books cited in the different readings in this book.

PRINCIPAL COSTA RICAN JOURNALS

Anuario de Estudios Centroamericanos (Universidad de Costa Rica)
Aportes (Centro Nacional de Acción Pastoral)
Ciencias Económicas (Universidad de Costa Rica)
Costa Rica: Balance de la Situación (Centro de Estudios para la Acción Social)
Cuadernos Centroamericanos de Ciencias Sociales (Confederación Superior Universitaria Centroamericana)
Cuadernos de Ciencias Sociales (Facultad Latinoamericana de Ciencias Sociales)
Estudios Sociales Centroamericanos (Confederación Superior Universitaria Centroamericana)
Polémica (Facultad Latinoamericana de Ciencias Sociales)
Relaciones Internacionales (Universidad Nacional)
Revista de Ciencias Sociales (Universidad de Costa Rica)
Revista de Historia (Universidad Nacional)

SELECTED BIBLIOGRAPHY OF ENGLISH-LANGUAGE SOURCES

Books

Ameringer, Charles D. *Democracy in Costa Rica.* New York: Praeger, 1982.
———. *Don Pepe: A Political Biography of José Figueres.* Albuquerque: University of New Mexico Press, 1978.
Avirgan, Tony, and Martha Honey. *La Penca: On Trial in Costa Rica. The CIA vs. the Press.* San José: Editorial Porvenir, 1987.

Barlett, Peggy. *Agricultural Choice and Change: Decision Making in a Costa Rican Community.* New Brunswick, N.J.: Rutgers University Press, 1982.

Bell, John Patrick. *Crisis in Costa Rica: The 1948 Revolution.* Austin: University of Texas Press, 1971.

Biesanz, John and Mavis. *Costa Rican Life.* New York: Columbia University Press, 1946.

Bird, Leonard. *Costa Rica: The Unarmed Democracy.* London: Sheppard Press, 1984.

Blutstein, Howard, et al. *Area Handbook for Costa Rica.* Washington, D.C.: U.S. Government Printing Office, 1970.

Bulmer-Thomas, Victor. *The Political Economy of Central America Since 1920.* Cambridge: Cambridge University Press, 1987.

Creedman, Theodore S. *Historical Dictionary of Costa Rica.* Metuchen, N.J.: The Scarecrow Press, Inc., 1977.

Denton, Charles F. *Patterns of Costa Rican Politics.* Boston: Allyn and Bacon, 1971.

DeWitt, R. Peter. *The Inter-American Development Bank and Political Influence with Special Reference to Costa Rica.* New York: Praeger, 1977.

English, Burt. *Liberación Nacional of Costa Rica: The Development of a Political Party in a Transitional Society.* Latin American Monographs, Series Two. Gainesville: University of Florida, 1971.

Gudmundson, Lowell. *Costa Rica before Coffee: Society and Economy on the Eve of the Export Boom.* Baton Rouge: Louisiana State University Press, 1986.

Hall, Carolyn. *Costa Rica: A Geographical Interpretation in Historical Perspective.* Boulder, Colo.: Westview, 1985.

Helms, Mary W., and Franklin O. Loveland, eds. *Frontier Adaptations in Lower Central America.* Philadelphia: Institute for the Study of Human Issues, 1976.

Herrick, Bruce, and Barclay Hudson. *Urban Poverty and Economic Development: A Case Study of Costa Rica.* New York: St. Martin's Press, 1981.

Karnes, Thomas L. *The Failure of Union: Central America, 1824–1960.* Chapel Hill: University of North Carolina Press, 1961.

Krehm, William. *Democracies and Tyrannies of the Caribbean.* Westport, Conn.: Lawrence Hill, 1984.

LaFeber, Walter. *Inevitable Revolutions: The United States in Central America.* New York: W. W. Norton, 1983.

Leonard, Thomas M. *United States and Central America, 1944–1949: Perceptions of Political Dynamics.* University, Ala.: University of Alabama Press, 1984.

Low, Setha M. *Culture, Politics and Medicine in Costa Rica.* South Salem, Mass.: Redgrave Publishing, 1985.

MacLeod, Murdo. *Spanish Central America: A Socioeconomic History 1520–1720.* Berkeley: University of California Press, 1973.

Nelson, Harold D., ed. *Costa Rica: A Country Study.* Washington, D.C.: U.S. Government Printing Office, 1983.

Palmer, Paula. *"What Happen." A Folk History of Costa Rica's Talamanca Coast.* San José: Ecodesarrollos, 1977.

Peeler, John A. *Latin American Democracies: Colombia, Costa Rica, Venezuela.* Chapel Hill: University of North Carolina Press, 1985.

Rosengarten, Frederic, Jr. *Freebooters Must Die! The Life and Death of William Walker.* Wayne, Penna.: Haverford House, 1976.

Rowles, James P. *Law and Agrarian Reform in Costa Rica.* Boulder, Colo.: Westview, 1985.

Sanders, Sol W. *The Costa Rican Laboratory.* New York: Priority Press Publications, 1986.

Seligson, Mitchell A. *Peasants of Costa Rica and the Development of Agrarian Capitalism.* Madison: University of Wisconsin Press, 1980.

Shaw, Paul R. *Land Tenure and the Rural Exodus in Chile, Colombia, Costa Rica, and Peru.* Gainesville: University of Florida Press, 1976.

Stewart, Watt. *Keith and Costa Rica: A Biographical Study of Minor Cooper Keith.* Albuquerque: University of New Mexico Press, 1964.

Williams, Robert G. *Export Agriculture and the Crisis in Central America.* Chapel Hill: University of North Carolina Press, 1986.

Woodward, Ralph Lee. *Central America: A Nation Divided.* 2d ed. New York: Oxford University Press, 1985.

Wortman, Miles L. *Government and Society in Central America: 1680–1840.* New York: Columbia University Press, 1982.

Articles and Published Working Papers

Blachman, Morris J., and Ronald G. Hellman. "Costa Rica." In *Confronting Revolution: Security through Diplomacy in Central America,* edited by Morris J. Blachman, William M. LeoGrande, and Kenneth E. Sharpe. New York: Pantheon Books, 1986.

Booth, John A. "Representative Constitutional Democracy in Costa Rica: Adaptation to Crisis in the Turbulent 1980s." In *Central America: Crisis and Adaptation,* edited by Steve C. Ropp and James A. Morris. Albuquerque: University of New Mexico Press, 1984.

———. "Are Latin Americans Politically Rational? Citizen Participation and Democracy in Costa Rica." In *Political Participation in Latin America,* vol. 1, edited by John A. Booth and Mitchell A. Seligson. New York: Holmes & Meier, 1978.

Cardoso, Ciro F. S. "The Formation of the Coffee Estate in Nineteenth-Century Costa Rica." In *Land and Labour in Latin America,* edited by Kenneth Duncan and Ian Rutledge. Cambridge: Cambridge University Press, 1977.

Carvajal, Manuel J., and David T. Geithman. "An Economic Analysis of Migration in Costa Rica." *Economic Development and Cultural Change* 23 (1974): 105–22.

Del Aguila, Juan M. "The Limits of Reform Development in Contemporary Costa Rica." *Journal of Inter-American Studies and World Affairs* 24, no. 3 (1982): 355–74.

Early, Stephen. "Arms and Politics in Costa Rica and Nicaragua, 1948–1981." Research Paper Series, no. 9. Albuquerque: University of New Mexico, 1982.

Edelman, Marc. "Recent Literature on Costa Rica's Economic Crisis." *Latin American Research Review* 18, no. 2 (1983): 166–80.

Edmunds, John C., and William Renforth. "The Costa Rican Solution: An Innovative Approach to Export Promotion." *Caribbean Review* 14, no. 2 (Spring 1985): 27–29, 45.

Feinberg, Richard E. "Costa Rica: The End of the Fiesta." In *From Gunboats to Diplomacy: New U.S. Policies for Latin America,* edited by Richard Newfarmer. Baltimore: Johns Hopkins University Press, 1984.

González-Vega, Claudio. "Fear of Adjusting: The Social Costs of Economic Policies in Costa Rica in the 1970s." In *Revolution and Counterrevolution in Central America and the Caribbean,* edited by Donald E. Schulz and Douglas H. Graham. Boulder, Colo.: Westview, 1984.

Grynspan, Devora. "Technology Transfer Patterns and Industrialization in LDCs: A

Study of Licensing in Costa Rica." *International Organization* 36, no. 4 (1982): 795–806.

Gudmundson, Lowell. "Costa Rica and the 1948 Revolution: Rethinking the Social Democratic Paradigm." *Latin American Research Review* 19, no. 1 (1984): 235–42.

———. "The Expropriation of Pious and Corporate Properties in Costa Rica, 1805–1860." *The Americas* 39, no. 3 (1983): 281–302.

Guess, George. "Narrowing the Base of Costa Rican Democracy." *Development and Change* 9, no. 4 (1978): 599–609.

Heath, Dwight B. "Costa Rica and Her Neighbors." *Current History* 58, no. 342 (1970): 95–101, 113.

Lines, Jorge A. *Anthropological Bibliography of Aboriginal Costa Rica.* Occasional Paper, no. 7. San José: Tropical Science Center, 1967.

Maloney, Thomas. "Continuities and Discontinuities in Modes of Production and Exploitation in the Cane Sugar Processing Industries of Costa Rica." *Dialectical Anthropology*, no. 8 (1984): 293–302.

———. "Appropriate Technology and Costa Rican Sugar." *Dialectical Anthropology*, no. 4 (1979): 127–33.

Peek, Peter, and Carlos Raabe. *Rural Equity in Costa Rica: Myth or Reality?* World Employment Programme Research Working Papers, WEP 10-6/WP67. Geneva: International Labour Office, 1984.

Reding, Andrew. "Costa Rica: Democratic Model in Jeopardy" and "Voices from Costa Rica" [Interviews with José Figueres, Daniel Oduber, Rodrigo Carazo and Javier Solís]. *World Policy Journal* 3, no. 2 (1986): 301–45.

Rosenberg, Mark B. "Social Security Policymaking in Costa Rica: A Research Report." *Latin American Research Review* 14, no. 1 (1979): 116–33.

Seligson, Mitchell A. "Public Policies in Conflict: Land Reform and Family Planning in Costa Rica." *Comparative Politics* 12, no. 1 (1979): 49–62.

Seligson, Mitchell A., and John A. Booth. "Structure and Levels of Political Participation in Costa Rica: Comparing Peasants and City Dwellers." In *Political Participation in Latin America,* vol. 2, edited by Mitchell A. Seligson and John A. Booth. New York: Holmes & Meier, 1979.

Seligson, Mitchell A., and Edward N. Muller. "Democratic Stability and Economic Crisis: Costa Rica, 1978–1983." *International Studies Quarterly* 31 (1987): 1–26.

Stycos, J. Mayone. "The Decline of Fertility in Costa Rica: Literacy, Modernization, and Family Planning." *Population Studies* 36, no. 1 (1982): 15–30.

Taylor, J. Edward. "Migration: A Study of Population Movements in Costa Rica." *Latin American Perspectives* 7, nos. 2–3 (1980): 75–90.

Tomasek, Robert D. *The Deterioration of Relations between Costa Rica and the Sandinistas.* Center for Hemispheric Studies, Occasional Paper Series, no. 9. Washington D.C.: American Enterprise Institute, 1984.

Trejos, Juan Diego. *Costa Rica: Economic Crisis and Public Policy, 1978–1984.* Latin American and Caribbean Center, Occasional Papers Series, no. 11. Miami: Florida International University, 1985.

List of Abbreviations

AECA Arms Export Control Act
AID U.S. Agency for International Development
ANCR *Archivos Nacionales de Costa Rica* (National Archives of Costa Rica)
ANDE *Asociación Nacional de Educadores* (National Educators Association)
ANEP *Asociación Nacional de Empleados Públicos* (National Public Employees Association)
ANFE *Asociación Nacional de Fomento Económico* (National Economic Development Association)
ARDE *Alianza Revolucionaria Democrática* (Democratic Revolutionary Alliance)
BCR *Banco de Costa Rica* (Bank of Costa Rica)
BNCR *Banco Nacional de Costa Rica* (National Bank of Costa Rica)
BOS *Bloque Opositor del Sur* (Opposition Bloc of the South)
CACM Central American Common Market
CATD *Confederación Auténtica de Trabajadores Democráticos* (Authentic Confederation of Democratic Workers)
CBI Caribbean Basin Initiative
CCSS *Caja Costarricense de Seguro Social* (Costa Rican Social Security System)
CCTD *Confederación Costarricense de Trabajadores Democráticos* (Costa Rican Democratic Workers Confederation)
CCTRN *Confederación Costarricense de Trabajadores Rerum Novarum* (Rerum Novarum Costa Rican Workers Confederation)
CENAP *Centro Nacional de Acción Pastoral* (National Center for Pastoral Action)
CENPRO *Centro de Promoción de las Exportaciones* (Export Promotion Center)
CEPAS *Centro de Estudios para la Acción Social* (Center for Studies for Social Action)
CGCT *Confederación General de Trabajadores Costarricenses* (General Confederation of Costa Rican Workers)
CIA U.S. Central Intelligence Agency
CINDE *Centro de Iniciativas para el Desarrollo* (Center for Development Initiatives)
CMA Civilian Military Assistance (later Civilian Materiel Assistance)
CNP *Consejo Nacional de Producción* (National Production Council)
CNT *Confederación Nacional de Trabajadores* (National Workers Confederation)
CODESA *Corporación Costarricense de Desarrollo Sociedad Anónima* (Costa Rican Development Corporation [Inc.])

CONACOOP   *Consejo Nacional Cooperativo* (National Cooperative Council)

CSUCA   *Confederación Superior Universitaria Centroamericana* (Higher Central American University Confederation)

CTC   *Central de Trabajadores Costarricenses* (Costa Rican Workers Central)

CTCR   *Confederación de Trabajadores de Costa Rica* (Costa Rican Workers Confederation)

CUS   *Comité Unitario Sindical* (Union Unity Committee)

CUT   *Confederación Unitaria de Trabajadores* (Unified Workers Confederation)

DEI   *Departamento Ecuménico de Investigaciones* (Ecumenical Research Department)

DGEC   *Dirección General de Estadística y Censos* (General Statistics and Census Directorate)

DINADECO   *Dirección Nacional de Desarollo de la Comunidad* (National Directorate of Community Development)

ECLA   United Nations Economic Commission for Latin America

EDUCA   *Editorial Universitaria Centroamericana* (Central American University Publishers)

ESF   Emergency Support Funds (from USAID)

FARN   see UDN

FDN   *Fuerza Democrática Nicaragüense* (Nicaraguan Democratic Force)

FDT   *Frente Democrático de Trabajadores* (Democratic Workers Front)

FENATRAP   *Federación Nacional de Empleados Públicos* (National Public Employees Federation)

FSLN   *Frente Sandinista de Liberación Nacional* (Sandinista National Liberation Front)

ICAP   *Instituto Centroamericano de Administración Pública* (Central American Institute of Public Administration)

ICE   *Instituto Costarricense de Electricidad* (Costa Rican Electrical Institute)

IDA   *Instituto de Desarrollo Agrario* (Agrarian Development Institute)

IMAS   *Instituto Mixto de Ayuda Social* ([Mixed] Social Aid Institute)

IMF   International Monetary Fund

INFOCOOP   *Instituto de Fomento Cooperativo* (Cooperative Development Institute)

INVU   *Instituto Nacional de Vivienda y Urbanismo* (National Housing and Planning Institute)

ISA   U.S. Army Intelligence Support Activity

ITCO   *Instituto de Tierras y Colonización* (Lands and Colonization Institute)

ITCR   *Instituto Tecnológico de Costa Rica* (Costa Rican Technological Institute)

JAPDEVA   *Junta de Administración Portuaria y Desarrollo Económico de la Vertiente Atlántico* (Atlantic Port Administration and Economic Development Board)

MCRL   *Movimiento Costa Rica Libre* (Free Costa Rica Movement)

MIDEPLAN   *Ministerio de Planificación* (Ministry of Planning)

MNR   *Movimiento de la Nueva República* (New Republic Movement [formerly MRP])

MRP   *Movimiento Revolucionario del Pueblo* (Revolutionary People's Movement)

NSC   U.S. National Security Council

OFIPLAN   *Oficina de Planificación Nacional y Política Económica* (National Planning and Economic Policy Office)

OPEN   *Organización para Emergencias Nacionales* (Organization for National Emergencies)

PLN *Partido Liberación Nacional* (National Liberation Party)
PPC *Partido del Pueblo Costarricense* (Costa Rican People's Party)
PSC *Partido Socialista Costarricense* (Costa Rican Socialist Party)
PUSC *Partido Unidad Social Cristiana* (Social Christian Unity Party)
PVP *Partido Vanguardia Popular* (Popular Vanguard Party)
RECOPE *Refinería Costarricense de Petróleo* (Costa Rican Petroleum Refinery)
SOF Soldier of Fortune (magazine)
UACA *Universidad Autónoma Centroamericana* (Autonomous Central American University)
UCR *Universidad de Costa Rica* (University of Costa Rica)
UDN-FARN *Unión Democrática Nicaragüense-Fuerzas Armadas Revolucionarias Nicaragüenses* (Nicaraguan Democratic Union-Nicaraguan Revolutionary Armed Forces)
UFCO United Fruit Company
UNA *Universidad Nacional* (National University)
UNACOOP *Unión Nacional Cooperativo* (National Cooperative Union)
UNAM *Universidad Nacional Autónoma de México* (Autonomous University of Mexico)
UNED *Universidad Estatal a Distancia* (State University at a Distance)
UNIA Universal Negro Improvement Association
UNDP United Nations Development Programme
UNICEF United Nations Children's Fund
UNO *Unidad Nicaragüense Opositora* (United Nicaraguan Opposition)
UPEB *Unión de Países Exportadores de Banano* (Union of Banana Exporting Countries)
USAID U.S. Agency for International Development

Index

Many Spanish-speaking people use both their father's and mother's family names, although the second (mother's) last name is frequently dropped after first mention or not used at all. Thus, for example, Oscar Arias Sánchez is referred to most succinctly as Señor or President Arias, since Arias is his father's last name. Some married women add the suffix *de* (of) and their husband's first (father's) last name after their own last name(s). For example, Margarita Penon de Arias is the wife of Oscar Arias Sánchez.

Selected Titles from Grove Weidenfeld
Food First and Latin American Studies

___ EVITA	0-8021-5124-8	Barnes, John EVITA—FIRST LADY: A Biography of Eva Peron	$5.95
___ CENTR	0-8021-1185-8	Barry, Tom THE CENTRAL AMERICA FACT BOOK (Revised)	$19.95 (cl)
___ CENTRP	0-8021-3038-0	Barry, Tom (ed.) THE CENTRAL AMERICA FACT BOOK	$14.95
___ OTHSID	0-8021-5125-6	Barry, Tom OTHER SIDE OF PARADISE: Foreign Control in the Caribbean	$11.95
___ CUBA	0-8021-3043-7	Brenner, Philip THE CUBA READER	$14.00
___ CUBAC	0-8021-1010-X	Brenner, Philip THE CUBA READER	$24.95 (cl)
___ OUTLAC	0-8021-5094-2	Cockcroft, James D. OUTLAWS IN THE PROMISED LAND	$14.95
___ OUTLA	0-8021-1206-4	Cockcroft, James D. OUTLAWS IN THE PROMISED LAND	$19.95 (cl)
___ NICAR	0-8021-3067-4	Collins, Joseph NICARAGUA: What Difference Could a Revolution Make?	$11.95
___ NICARC	0-8021-1207-2	Collins, Joseph NICARAGUA: What Difference Could a Revolution Make?	$22.50 (cl)
___ COSTA	0-8021-3124-7	Edelman, Mark THE COSTA RICA READER	$14.95
___ COSTAC	0-8021-0181-9	Edelman, Mark THE COSTA RICA READER	$24.95 (cl)
___ FREED	0-8021-5156-6	FREEDOM FIGHTER'S MANUAL	$2.00
___ GUATE	0-394-62455-6	Fried, Jonathan (ed.) GUATEMALA IN REBELLION	$12.50
___ FATE	0-8021-3121-2	George, Susan A FATE WORSE THAN DEBT	$8.95
___ FATEC	0-8021-1015-0	George, Susan A FATE WORSE THAN DEBT	$17.95 (cl)
___ ELSAL	0-394-62345-2	Gettleman, Marvin E. EL SALVADOR	$12.95
___ BETR	0-8021-3027-5	Lappe, Frances Moore BETRAYING THE NATIONAL INTEREST	$8.95
___ BETRC	0-8021-0012-0	Lappe, Frances Moore BETRAYING THE NATIONAL INTEREST	$18.95 (cl)
___ HUNGER	0-8021-5041-1	Lappe, Frances Moore WORLD HUNGER: Twelve Myths	$9.95
___ NICUN	0-8021-3106-9	Rosset, Peter NICARAGUA: Unfinished Revolution	$15.95
___ PEDRO	0-8021-3119-0	Rulfo, Juan PEDRO PARAMO	$4.95